*Cacti—"green and thorny torpedoes
that continue to lend an aggressive harshness
to the earth."*

PHOTO BY VLADIMIR SLADON

*Popo from Cholula.*

*An Indian farmer, near Taxco.*

PHOTO BY BERNARD G. SILBERSTEIN, RAPHO GUILLUMETTE

*Church in Puebla.*

*In Guanajuato.*

PHOTO BY BERNARD G. SILBERSTEIN, RAPHO GUILLUMETTE

*Children of Taxco.*   PHOTO BY VLADIMIR SLADON

*A street in Taxco.*

PHOTO BY VLADIMIR SLADON

*Taxco.*
*"My love affair with Taxco was born the day I saw*
*the first photograph of this old city."*
PHOTO BY VLADIMIR SLADON

*At prayer.*

PHOTO BY VLADIMIR SLADON

*Man and dog, Mexico City.*  PHOTO BY VLADIMIR SLADON

*View of the Palacio de Bellas Artes, Mexico City.*

PHOTO BY VLADIMIR SLADON

*Mexico City at night.*
PHOTO BY VLADIMIR SLADON

*The Library, University City.*
PHOTO BY VLADIMIR SLADON

*Newsboys, San Luis Potosi.*

PHOTO BY VLADIMIR SLADON

*Mexican Indian at tribal ceremony.*

PHOTO BY VLADIMIR SLADON

# MEXICO

# MEXICO

ERICO VERISSIMO

TRANSLATED FROM THE PORTUGUESE BY LINTON BARRETT

THE ORION PRESS

NEW YORK

First published in the Portuguese language as *Mexico
História duma Viagem* by Editôra Globo, Brazil, 1957.
First Printing. All rights reserved.
Library of Congress Catalog Card Number: 60-13621
© Macdonald & Co., (Publishers) Ltd., 1960
Designed by Wladislaw Finne
Manufactured in the United States of America

# Contents

# List of Illustrations

# MEXICO

# Prologue

"Shall we go to Mexico?"

I launched the question when I reached home that April evening. It was in Washington, and the cherry trees were in bloom on the banks of the Potomac. My wife, who was reading the *Evening Star*, raised her head and fixed her blue eyes on me.

"Mexico?" she repeated vaguely. And she bent her head again, her eyes and her attention on the newspaper.

I took off my jacket and dropped the whole weight of accumulated weariness, together with my body, into an easy chair. Gradually the family sounds wrapped about me. On the floor above, my daughter was reciting a passage from *Macbeth*, preparing her lesson for the following day at the dramatic school of the university. On the ground floor my boy was nursing the mouthpiece of a saxophone, sucking from it the thick warm milk of a blues tune. From the kitchen the thin crepitation of a lamb roast on the stove came to my ears. I closed my eyes.

Strange world, Master Shakespeare! The slow fire of the Washington Gas Company is gilding the ribs of a lamb possibly born in the meadows of Montana. Through the labour and the art of the blues composer, and thanks to the skill and the lips of the young saxophonist, at this moment, in this room, I listen to the moan of the lament that many years ago tore at the heart of a slave on a Mississippi plantation. Upstairs yonder Lady Macbeth is trailing her remorse around the room, imagining she sees blood on her white, sinner's hands. A singular world, my old poet, in which madame is reading the latest speech of John Foster Dulles, while here am I, eaten up with yearning for a holiday. Yes, a holiday, William Shakespeare, a vacation. Have you ever seen a tired man? Well, here's one. Tired in body and mind. I don't want to play tragedy. I am no candidate for Hamlet or King Lear, and I'm too old for Romeo. I am only on office worker tired of bureaucracy and the world around him. But wait! I want you to understand me. I love this country, I like Washington. It is an enchanting city, a placid garden of tourists, diplomats and office workers—*correcte, charmante et ridicule.* A model of organization, a perfection of city planning. Everything here functions accurately, "On time and the hour," as Dona Maurícia, my late grandmother, used to say. Listen, my bard, listen. Yesterday I gave a talk at the weekly luncheon of the Happy Bears' Club. Were there such organizations in your day? No? Great times, those! Well, my Bears roared, told stories, put grotesque paper hats on their heads, applauded my speech with handclapping and whistling. Extremely cordial, not a doubt of that, highly entertained! And when the question-and-answer period came, what do you think they inquired about? I'd hoped they would ask how Brazilians live, how they love, dance, sing, dream and die. But not at all! They wanted me to give them statistics on the exportation of coffee, the per capita income of the population, the figures on rainfall. The gentleman beside me, his lips touched with vanilla ice-cream, wanted to know what our government is doing to combat soil erosion. I replied that Villa-Lobos had written a symphony with the title of *Erosion,* and that we all hoped that would solve the problem definitely. You don't suppose the man took my answer seriously and wanted technical details? Well, he did, poet. I am constantly surrounded by old ladies. Clean, gay, neat, respectable, elegant, thirsty for information and animated by the purest civic sentiments. They belong to a thousand clubs, a thousand committees, a thousand fraternal societies. They get things done, they organize things, they want to know things. I collaborate with them, I give them lectures on all subjects, even—and principally—on those I am not acquainted with. I answer their questions with filial patience. But they are smothering me, Bill, ah, they are driving me mad! Hurrah for our Brazilian old women! Hail to Dona Maurícia with her checked shawl, her embroidered slippers, her tapioca cakes, her crocheted

2

napkins, her asthma and her silences! She never belonged to any club. She never went to a lecture, God bless her!

The saxophone's nasal lament stopped. But Lady Macbeth kept on with her tragic soliloquy. Madame murmured something about the lamb or about John Foster Dulles—I didn't hear clearly. I half-opened my eyes, enough to gather that it was not a question that required an answer and that the reader was unfolding the paper, passing from the political to the comic page. I returned to my reverie.

There's still more, my old friend. Night before last I went to a diplomatic dinner. Black tie. The South American military attaché on my right spent the whole time, from salad to dessert, trying to prove that Bach is a fool. Why should "that German" enjoy so much fame? His compositions are nothing but a tiresome, monotonous whine, with neither beauty nor novelty about them. He said awful things about Johann Sebastian during the whole dinner, without giving me leave or opening to speak a word. I limited myself to nodding at intervals, agreeing automatically with *el señor general.* Somewhere about the time for the toast of honour the fellow seemed to take note of my existence and asked which was my favourite composer. Timidly I murmured, "Bach." The general sat pensive for an instant, stirred up some bubbles in his glass of champagne, and then, sententiously, muttered between his teeth, "Of course, a great composer, one of the rare geniuses of Humanity." I felt that the man was putting an enormous *H* on "Humanity". I nodded again. Well, friend Bill, that's the kind you usually encounter at diplomatic dinners. To be sure, there are exceptions. But I'm going to confide a secret to you: I am a man persecuted by the usual kind. A misfortune. It's just as I tell you. This symmetrical city, which works like an electronic machine selecting cards, is beginning to weary me and bore me. Since I came here I have not written a line. I don't feel like it. I have the impression that I am living on a coloured postcard, lustrous, charming, yes, but lacking a third dimension. And perhaps that missing dimension is the simple fact that I was not born here, I possess no past in this country, no sentimental roots in this land. It is possible that everything is going too well for me. Or that I miss the Brazilian frictions and difficulties. Hasn't it been said (it must have been Shakespeare or Goethe, for there isn't anything you boys hadn't said before anybody else did)—hasn't it been said that the pearl is the product of a disease of the oyster? A Japanese discovered that by provoking an irritation in a certain part of the oyster's anatomy the repellent creature can be made to produce a secretion that in time will blossom forth in a pearl. Well, I believe that the novel is the product of an irritation of the novelist. But it has to be a certain special kind of irritation. This one that has taken me over is of no use, it is sterile, it only leads to yawns. And we know that life, old man, merits no yawns. It is too rich, too serious, too interesting and, particularly, too short for us to take an attitude of boredom toward it. In short, I'm tired of this logical world, I yearn to go back, even if for only a few days, to a magic world. I feel a longing for Latin American disorder, for the images, sounds and smells of our little world in which the clock is merely a decorative element and time a subject for poetry. Give me Mexico, magical Mexico, absurd Mexico! A little over a year ago I visited that country, my poet, and I returned to Washington disturbed by the little I saw and the much that I divined. The taste of Mexico has not yet left my memory. Sweet? No. Bitter? Not that either. Rare, strange, different, a mixture of *tortilla,* straw cigarettes, chili and blood. A dry taste, sometimes with a certain harshness of desert land, not infrequently with unexpected and perishable sweetnesses of tropical fruit. If I were to assign it a colour, I should say it is a grey taste. If I were asked to qualify it, I should venture: the taste of rustic tragedy. Heavens! Can I be turning metaphysical? Positively, William Shakespeare, I urgently need a vacation.

I get up abruptly. Madame is startled.

"What's the matter? Nightmare?"

"Who said I was asleep?"

My daughter was now slowly descending the stairs. Obviously, she was not at home but on a stage, in the fifth act of *Macbeth.* Rubbing her hands incessantly, she was staring at them with demented eyes, muttering: "Here's the smell of the blood still: all the perfumes of Arabia will not sweeten this little hand. Oh, oh, oh!"

Madame intervened: "Lady Macbeth, go set the table."

"But wash those hands!" the saxophonist recommended. And immediately he applied himself to playing scales furiously.

Putting more conviction in my voice, I repeated my invitation: "Shall we go to Mexico?"


There, in a rather schematic and stylized fashion, is the narrative of the origin of my second visit to Mexico.

That night the Family discussed the matter and argued long at the dinner table. As madame has a horror of air travel, we decided to face the probable discomforts and annoyances of a train journey. The children would stay in Washington following their normal routine, while the parents would follow the trail of adventure. (At this point sister and brother naturally exchanged a mischievous glance.) The tourists would take little baggage and an Argus camera, which neither of us knew how to handle very well. My wife had learned to change the rolls of film, and I admired her for her prowess. As for me, I had a vague notion of how to focus on the subject. And when the youth asked whether in such ignorance we expected to get good coloured slides of the trip, I answered yes, for we were certain we could count on the technical aid of God our Lord, according to our old Brazilian habit.

And so, in the first days of May, when the cherry blossoms were already withered but the Spring was reaching its prime, I installed myself with my companion in a clean and comfortable train bound for Los Angeles. And if I say that I had been invited to make the inaugural address of a round table at the University of California five days thence, I shall have explained the reason for taking the long way round to the capital of Mexico.

Between trains we visited old friends in the Art Institute of Chicago: Van Gogh, Cézanne, Gauguin, Renoir. In San Francisco we ate *abalone* in a restaurant on Fisherman's Wharf. And in the same city, as later in Los Angeles—where I made my speech—we revisited places and persons important in our sentimental geography.

And one beautiful morning we found ourselves with arms and baggage on the platform of the station in El Paso, Texas, waiting for the little train that was to take us to Ciudad Juárez, on the other side of the river on Mexican territory.

# 1. The Journey

The legendary Río Grande, that part of it where we crossed and at that season of the year, was no more than a slender thread of water running melancholy along its bed of burnished copper.

"The dry season," the ticket-collector, a short man with a sharp Aztec profile, explains laconically.

Our train—two cars with extremely few passengers—was being hauled by an elderly locomotive, slow and wheezy.

"You see," I murmured to my companion, "nobody in his right mind makes this trip by train."

"The crazy ones go by air," she smiled. "So far I have no reason for complaining."

The examination of passports was rapid. The American inspector was blond, lean and jovial. The Mexican, fat, hairy and taciturn. We had no trouble with Customs: at sight of my *laissez-passer* with the seal of the Organization of American States they desisted from inspecting our bags. We slowly entered the territory of Mexico. Under the light that falls from a faded sky, a metallic tone, this part of Juárez next to the railway station reminds us of a city of the Brazilian Northeast, with its low houses, some painted yellow, blue or pink, the sandy ground and the dry air of a glittering transparency. Barefoot Indian men and women, standing in the streets, raise their enigmatic, earth-coloured faces toward the train. They are stumpy, ugly, dirty and sorry-looking. I see men dressed in white sitting asleep in the shade of trees, folded over themselves in a fetal position, their straw hats tilted over their eyes, just as in the most conventional pictures that claim to represent Mexico. Boys in blue jeans of visibly Texan influence are playing baseball in a field. The towers of an old church loom above a clump of trees, sharp against the May horizon. I am gradually being invaded by that sensation which, in certain places we visit for the first time or in certain situations, leads us to think: "I've been here before. This has already happened to me."

I see and hear the bursting of a rocket in the air. When we step down on the platform of the Juárez station, a lottery ticket vendor assails me. "Your fortune, *patroncito!*" I tell him I hate money, and try to slip away. Flies swarm about our heads. Ammoniac emanations penetrate our nostrils, mingled with the acrid smell of coal smoke. A blind man approaches, led by a boy. "Alms, for the love of God! A little charity for the blind, *señor!*" the lad begs in his clear, tinkling voice. The blind man's eyes, wide open, seem to reflect the zinc light of the Chihuahua sky. I give him a peso.

Blind beggars, fireworks, lottery tickets, flies—I am at home! There comes to me suddenly, in a flood, the urge to write. The novelist who had hibernated for two years on the banks of the Potomac is re-emerging at the first contact with this dramatic world, so close to the land and to the roots of life.

Porters with the faces of gallows birds effect in thick silence the transfer of our luggage. We take our first snapshots. The methodical, the cautious, and—why not say it?—the sensible people use exposure meters to measure the intensity of the light, in order to see how long an exposure is needed or what opening to give the shutter. We, however, confine ourselves to reading swiftly the little sheet of instructions accompanying the film, and to trusting to our eyes, which leads me to a psycho-sociological reflection that I crystallize in a sentence: "The Latin always uses his body in situations where the Anglo-Saxon prefers to use one of his many gadgets. Result: they do things better, but we enjoy ourselves more."


The train that is to take us to Mexico City is standing beside the platform. On the side of the restaurant-car I read a name: *Juventino Rosas.* He must be a general, I imagine to myself, a deputy or an ex-governor of this province. Later someone informs me that it is the name of a popular composer, author of the famous waltz "Over the Waves." "Mexico, I love you!" I exclaim. And in this frame of mind

I get into the train. Our Pullman looks like all the Pullmans of the United States. A little less well preserved—what of it? The air-conditioning system perhaps doesn't work perfectly, but it exists, and that is quite a lot. We do not have one of those stout, polished, smiling American Negroes with bass voice for a Pullman porter. Ours is a lean, bald fellow with a cadaverous face and a two-day beard. He speaks little and never smiles.

Through the window my wife is watching the *peones* who are carrying ice to the dining-car. One of the blocks of ice falls in the dust, where islets of manure glisten greenly. The men put it back on their shoulders and go off, haloed by flies.

Squalid women lift their arms to the car windows offering *tamales* and *tortillas*. One of them is carrying, on a tray, several deep dishes with a yellowish, greasy liquid, on the surface of which float slices of carrot and leaves of parsley.

I sense that my companion is a little restless. I catch sight of the car attendant. I try to establish an atmosphere of camaraderie with him.

"Well, when do we arrive, my friend?" I ask, smiling.

The little man shrugs his shoulders and responds, *"Pues, quién sabe?"*

And he goes off. We hear muted voices in the next compartment. A baby starts crying in the corridor. Someone hawks, rasping an invisible throat, a convulsive cough rips the air, in a threat of bronchitic neighbours.

"It's hot," murmurs my wife.

I go to ask the attendant whether the air-conditioning machinery is working. He answers that there seems to be "an imperfection in the apparatus." I find the word *desperfecto* delightful, although it presages something terrible. Cross the Chihuahua desert in a steel car without air conditioning? It isn't good even to think about. To my companion I bear the gloomy result of my investigations. And she, recalling a famous page of school anthology, remarks, *"Aqui começa o sertão chamado bruto—*Here begins the wasteland called savage."

And indeed it was beginning.


The train starts up. Little by little we leave the city of Juárez behind in quest of the interior of the State of Chihuahua, whose surface is in great part a plateau that descends in gentle slopes to the ravines of the Río Grande. This means that henceforth we shall be climbing all the way to the Meseta Central, where the Federal Capital of Mexico lies. What we have before us for the next twenty-four hours or more—*quién sabe?*—is a sandy, arid savanna that some travellers compare with the deserts of North Africa.

The State of Chihuahua has a scant million of population for an area of some 95,000 square miles. Agriculture has made very little progress in this region on account of the lack of water and the near impossibility of artificial irrigation. Toward the west, among the tremendous spurs of the Sierra Madre, there are high valleys of volcanic soil of great fertility, and deep gorges of a beauty to rival that of the Grand Canyon. It is in the districts of this mountainous zone that the important cattle-raising of the State is to be found. But the principal wealth of Chihuahua is mineral. In their majority the cities through which we shall pass on this journey—Villa Ahumada, Ojo Caliente, Moctezuma, Chihuahua—were born around mines of lead, zinc, copper, mercury, coal, gold and silver.

In vain do I attempt to concentrate on reading a Simenon novel: my eyes cannot resist the lure of the landscape. It is an almost morbid fascination. I have never seen such desolation. The savanna the train is crossing is of a coppery grey, bristling here and there with cacti and magueys. The only note of freshness and colour in this desert is furnished by the tenuous bluish profile of the mountains, very far off, something like an uncertain kind of mirage. From just looking at that picture my lips grow dry, thirst grips me by the throat. Happily, we have fresh water in our compartment and the air-conditioning is working reasonably well.

The train makes mysterious stops in the middle of open country where I can see no post nor station, and then resumes its indolent way. A silent functionary comes to ask for our tickets. I try without success to start a conversation. The man, who is phlegmatically chewing a toothpick, confines himself to glancing at us out of the corner of his eyes of yellowed whites, and then departs muttering to himself, "Thirty-five, thirty-five . . ." My wife and I look at each other, mute.

I read half a page of the novel and again look out.

We are now passing along an old wall blotched with dark stains. Blood of men shot in past revolutions, I think. From time to time the wind lifts a wave of dust, and it is as though I feel on my lips and teeth the harshness of the sand. The dust falls back, and there once more lies the desert in its monotonous immobility. The sun is like a chronic ulcer in the pallid texture of the sky. And over that pitiless pupil of fire not even the eyelid of a cloud comes down to afford a moment of relief to the scorched land.

Something is beginning to bother me. I have not yet seen in this countryside any river, lagoon, waterfall or even a creek. Two things seem to be absent from this inhospitable world: water and smiles. I make this observation to a taciturn man with whom I strike up a conversation on the platform of the coach, and he demolishes me with these words: "Do you think these poor Indians have any cause for smiling?"


Like the landscape, the Indian of the region is sad, dry and solitary. I have never in all my life found greater identification between man and earth. The ground here is a coppery grey like the skin of its inhabitants and the adobe of their houses. Land, faces, houses—everything of the same colour, as though made of the same substance. I am beginning to have the feeling that the Mexican Indian is not born like other mortals: he grows out of the soil like a plant. There is much of the vegetable, or even of the mineral, about him. It occurs to me now to compare him to the maguey or agave, that variety of aloe, a strange plant of dark green that looks like a bundle of dark swords, with its fleshy leaves adorned with thorns and terminating in a sharp point. From the pulpy heart of the maguey the Indian extracts a sap, the *aguamiel* or "honey-water," which, fermented, produces pulque, a whitish drink of nutritive properties. From another kind of maguey tequila is obtained, a strong distilled beverage, the rum of the Indian. The maguey also yields a fibre from which is woven a cloth of great durability. Like the maguey, the Indian is short and thorny, in a permanent attitude of defence. Like the plant, he derives his scanty sustenance from the arid soil.

There exists in Chihuahua a type of Indian, the Tarahumara, who, to catch the wild ducks that go every November to hibernate on the lakes of the high tablelands, sometimes remains motionless for a whole day, as if he were a tree or a stone, and he does it with as much perfection and even with as much *conviction* of his vegetal or mineral nature that the very birds are deceived and come to alight fearlessly in the vicinity of the hunter. It is only then that he moves, using his bow, and then it is no longer a matter of hunting but of massacre. The Tarahumaras always go in couples, the husband a few steps ahead of his wife.

About this curious aboriginal type Alfonso Reyes wrote:

*Desnudos y curtidos,*
*duros en la lustrosa piel manchada,*
*denegridos de viento y sol, animan*
*las calles de Chihuahua,*
*lentos y recelosos,*
*con todos resortes del miedo contraídos*
*como panteras mansas.*

(Naked and sunburned,
hard of lustrous, spotted skin,
blackened by wind and sun, they move about
the streets of Chihuahua,
slow and suspicious,
with all the springs of fear coiled tight
like tame panthers.)

I saw a Tarahumara couple in the outskirts of Juárez, the man with his red cap and his tunic falling to the middle of his bare thighs. The woman, following him at a respectful distance, clothed in her multiple full skirts, looked like a coloured tub on legs.

The train stops again at a little rustic station, on the platform of which I see a half-dozen Indians and hundreds of flies, the latter concentrated in a stand where juicy rounds of pineapple and mangoes of orange yellow are displayed. I stand contemplating the old woman in charge of the stall, and I conclude that, with a little imagination, we can see in the bodies of these natives tokens of the mineral products of their province. In the general look of the Indian there will be the heaviness and the sombre colour of lead. In his wary attitude, the slippery, distrustful quality of mercury. In his skin, the copper. The coal, in his eyes.

Well, all this is nothing but literature. Let the train proceed!

There are some who maintain that the Indians of this part of the world are autochthonous. Here we have science confirming my poetic intuition, I tell my travelling companion. According to the converted Indian Ixtlilxochtl, who wrote his *History* after the Conquest, the cosmogony of the Aztecs recognizes the existence of four Epochs or Suns since the creation of the world. During the second Epoch, called the "Sun of Earth," the world was peopled with giants, the Quinametzins. Then, however, came tremendous seismic tremors that destroyed this race, a bare few of its representatives escaping. "Sun of the Wind" was the name of the third Epoch, in which the human races of the Olmecas and the Xicalancas, having killed the last giants, took possession of the earth and founded the city of Cholula, going as far as Tabasco. It was in this age that the great Quetzalcoatl—the Feathered Serpent, or God of Civilization and Learning—had his kingdom and made his preachments. This Sun ended with the transformation of men into monkeys and with a series of cataclysms that destroyed the earth.

"What Epoch are we now in?" asks my wife.

"In the fourth, the 'Sun of Fire,' which will end with the burning up of the world."

She looks out of the window and murmurs, "I don't doubt it."

And we start out, hallucinated, towards the *Juventino Rosas* in search of cold drinks.

At night I dream that I am wandering in agony through a desolate, opaque region peopled with silent forms in which I do not see but sense the faces of dead friends. They are trying to tell me something, but from their mouths emerge no words, only sand falls. Among the shades walks my father, I see he is lost, I have the duty to help him but cannot, because I do not know the way, I am dumb, and even if I managed to speak, I should not know the language of the dead. I make an effort to see better, to comprehend, to explain the confused situation. I say to myself: you must be calm, because all this may well be only a dream, wait till day breaks: the phantoms will vanish. But in the very moment I tell myself these things I feel the anguish of losing my father all over again, of leaving him abandoned in this desert, alone, without water or grave. Afterwards—I don't know what happens or how much time goes by—I am on the bottom of a river, water is coming in my mouth and nostrils, strangling me. I struggle in futile efforts to reach the surface, my heart swells in my chest—more and more, I am going to burst . . . I wake bathed in sweat, I take several seconds to realize where I am. I see the purplish square of the window, I hear the rhythmic sound of the train wheels. The anguish persists, nevertheless, aggravated now by the airlessness and the heat of the compartment. The air-conditioning apparatus must be working badly. I jump out of bed and try to open the window. Useless. I stand with my head pressed against the glass, staring stupidly out, observing the moonless night, the mysterious dead world through which the train is going and which so much resembles the one in my nightmare. Now in my mind is the image of my father, we resume old dialogues I should prefer to forget. Sweat is running down my face, my neck, my sides. I turn on the light and look at my watch. Hardly two in the morning. So early! I desire the morning and the sun, which will free me from these incubi. I thrust my head into the basin and turn on the tap. The water, tepid, gives me only momentary relief. I try to convince myself that if I go back to bed I shall sleep peacefully. The sensation of ill-being, however, continues. Why do I so repeatedly have these dreams in which I am dying of asphyxiation at the bottom of a river or buried alive?

A grown man! Go back to bed. You're in a train, on the way to Mexico City, on a pleasure trip, and everything up to now has been going well. Come! I humbly obey my own order and stretch out on the bed. But the desire to break the window glass continues, and all my anguish—now a little attenuated, it is true—is concentrated in my breast in a kind of strain. In the next compartment someone bursts out coughing convulsively. The speed of the train gradually diminishes, until with a grinding of iron the train comes to a halt. The lights of a station come in through the window. I hear voices: *"Tamales calientes! Enchiladas! Taquitos!"* I want none of them. I want the day. I want the sun. I want fresh air. I want to get out of this steel tomb!

The train stands there for an eternity. I hear steps in the corridor. I close my eyes, I think of Pancho Villa, of Emiliano Zapata's white horse and, by association, of a *gaúcho*[1] leader in the Revolution of '23. But what a difference between the arid plains of Chihuahua and the green fields of Rio Grande do Sul.

Now the Lincoln Memorial glimmers white in my mind, and then disappears to give way to some American faces. How is it possible— I ask myself—for two countries as different as the United States

[1]This is not the Argentine gaucho, but the native of Rio Grande do Sul, of Brazil.

and Mexico to exist so near each other? I wonder how far American influence can be modifying the Mexican character and customs. It is what I hope to find out on this trip. I begin mentally composing a letter: "I am writing you from the queerest train, one that seems to be travelling not in temporal space but in Eternity . . ." And the word "Eternity" was the permit that sleep was awaiting to capture me and project me once again into dreams.

When I wake up the sun is already high.

A new day is beginning. I get off at some station, I stroll among Indians, suitcases, sacks, stands and stalls crowned with flies. I try to start a conversation with some of the people I encounter on the grimy platforms. Useless. Some merely stare at me with cold eyes, as if they had not heard or understood me. Others don't even look at me. A barefoot urchin covered with rags begs me for *una propina*, a tip. His eyes are black, adult. I leave a copper in his coal-blackened hand.

The train whistles. I climb into the car and the journey continues. We have a good appetite, but it is without the slightest pleasure that we pay our visits to the *Juventino Rosas*. We feel a nostalgia for the whiteness of the tablecloths of the American dining-cars, for the silvery gleam of their knives and forks, for the clean rigidity of the chilled curls of butter. Here the cloths are of poor quality and are full of spots of wine, grease and coffee. The butter is yellow as margarine and comes to the table half-melted, in the consistency of pomade. The "silver" is of inferior quality and usually the handles are greasy. The sugar is coarse and dubiously white. And as we know that in every drop of water they serve us a whole population of protozoa may be nestling cosily, we drink only Tehuacán mineral water. I complain of all this to my wife, who remarks, "Your magic world."

I react: "Ah, but we shall have compensations! Just wait."

"It's that hope that keeps me going."

On the second night of the journey, after dinner, we sit chatting with two middle-aged Mexican ladies, natives of Juárez, both fat and swarthy, evidently of mixed bloods, one of them in deep mourning. They are more communicative than any of the people we have met up to now.

The lady in black holds a rosary in her hands, and her lips move inaudibly. The other explains that her companion is praying alternately for the soul of her husband (murdered with five bullets in his chest, *señor*) and for the safety of all who are travelling on this train.

"She is praying to Our Lady of Guadalupe to protect us from disasters."

She adds that derailments are common on this line of the *Ferrocarriles Nacionales Mexicanos*. Just last month a train ran off a cliff. Bridges? *Virgen Purísima!* Always in bad condition. Rails? Weak, rotten. To travel in Mexico is to risk your life.

My wife and I look at each other. The remainder of the conversation takes less sinister turns. The ladies want to know where we are from and why we have come. I tell them. They know nothing about Brazil. They ask whether we intend to visit Puebla. Of course it is on our itinerary. One of the ladies, the one with the wart on her chin, says:

"A lovely city, lordly and noble. It's too bad the people there are so stingy. If you go to visit a friend and you arrive at lunch or dinner time, he will hide the meal in a drawer of the table made expressly for that purpose. The *Poblanos* are not at all hospitable. Very stingy!"

The one in black looks at me and nods in confirmation of this. Then she interrupts her prayer to recommend to my wife: "In Puebla, *señora*, don't fail to buy some *camotes*."

*Camote* is yam, a sweet potato. Puebla specializes in *camote* sweets, little round cakes of mashed sweet potato made with condensed milk and flavoured with vanilla, strawberry, lime or pineapple.

When the conversation begins to languish we catch sight of the lights of Chihuahua, capital of the State, lying in a valley between two spurs of the Sierra Madre. The city was founded early in the eighteenth century around a silver mine. It has about 200,000 inhabitants today. They say that many of its modern shops are the property of Frenchmen. The Syrian-Lebanese business element is very strong, and the people of Chihuahua—the lady with the wart informs me—apply to the members of that colony the general name of "Turks."

When the train stops in the spacious station I get out and stand gazing long at the perspective of an illuminated avenue along which automobiles and omnibuses are running. Then I return to my compartment, lie down with a novel on my chest, and so I doze off. The two Chihuahua ladies appear in my dream, their images merge with those of dim aunts I have in Rio Grande do Sul. And the wart on one of them pursues me throughout the night, as in fevered dreams, and is alternately a stone mountain, a sand dune, the bead of a rosary, a rose, an anemone, a cancer. A cancer that afflicts me on one cheek. I realize I must wake up to go to see a doctor, but I cannot because my slumber is stronger than my fear. My apprehension, nevertheless, continues and I cannot understand how it is that the lady's cancer is hurting me. Finally I waken, put my hand to my face and feel a bump on one cheek. I turn on the light and, like the detective in the novel on my chest, I hunt down the black, agile, tiny criminal that has assaulted me.

Morning of the third day of the journey. The wild desert has been left behind. We see some green spots, a few waters. The mountains, which before seemed so fleeting in the distance, are coming nearer. When the train halts at stations, I jump out onto the platform. I feel the air is thinner. How is it that the air is getting cooler and cooler as we approach the Equator? The reason is that our progress is not just horizontal but vertical. We must be at six thousand feet or more, and that explains the Spring that envelops us.

Now one of our diversions is to sit at the window looking for church cupolas. Someone has said that Mexico is the land of cupolas. With their yellow, blue or red tiles and their ingenuous baroque grace, they pop out to our view in the most unexpected places, at times in the midst of those great cacti—green and thorny torpedoes that continue to lend an aggressive harshness to the earth.

We are also entertained when along the dusty roads that not infrequently run, or rather, drag, parallel to the rails we see little burros at a reluctant trot, with pack-baskets loaded, shaking their ears, kicking up dust, giving a Biblical touch to the landscape. I think of the *Platero* of Juan Ramón Jiménez, and of the patient little donkeys of Francis Jammes. The survival of these hairy "little brothers" of ours as beasts of burden in the era of the jet plane touches me, giving me a secret hope in something or other, I don't quite know what.

We glimpse in the distance a mountain with snowy peak. My wife asks for information about the famous Mexican volcanoes.

Yes, the volcanoes . . . I took a quick course in the subject from a *simpático* American geologist while we were absorbing a cordial lunch at the Cosmos Club, shortly before our departure for Mexico.

The Mexican volcanic axis is a belt about 560 miles long and between forty and sixty wide, stretching from the Gulf of Mexico to the Pacific Ocean. But already on the United States border begins the chain of volcanoes that extends practically uninterrupted down to the southern tip of the Continent.

The volcano that dominates the State of Sonora has a tranquil, pineappley name—Piñacate. The Nevado, in Toluca, frightfully active in bygone times, seems to be quite retired today. There is one that boasts the disturbing name of Fuego—fire. Two colossi rise before us at one of the entrances to Mexico City, Ixtaccíhuatl and Popocatépetl, both of them acquaintances of mine from my primary school days. The most beautiful, the tallest and most imposing of all the Mexican volcanoes is Orizaba, which rises with its snow-covered crest to 18,541 feet. For my taste, however, the most representative volcano of this wild land and this untamed people is Paricutín. Its history is one of today.

Some two miles from the town of San Juan Parangaricutiro, in the south of Mexico, surrounded by volcanic hills crowned with clumps of pines, there used to be a little valley almost wholly covered with fields of maize. It was not unusual to see a cultivated patch inside the crater of an extinct volcano. On the property of one Dionisio Pulido there was a hole some sixteen feet in diameter and five feet deep that attracted the attention and the superstitious mistrust of the inhabitants of the valley. Doña Severina Murillo, a long-time resident, used to tell how, when a child, she used to play in that hole in spite of her father's having forbidden it, not only because he suspected the opening of being the entrance to an ancient Spanish mine but also because frequently subterranean noises that sounded like the rolling of great stones could be heard there. More than one farmer declared that on rainy days he would see a kind of thick fog rising from the hole. Early in February of 1943, the farmers at their ploughing felt the earth shudder under their feet. The tremors were repeated, stronger and stronger, and after a couple of weeks the earth suddenly split open and began vomiting smoke, lava and stones. And gradually from the womb of the earth, in thunderous birth, emerged a black cone.

The man who related the story to me, with a wealth of technical details, was my excellent geologist, between mouthfuls of fish and tartar sauce. He described the geological phenomenon from his cold, scientific angle; I saw the drama with the warm eye of the novelist. I asked him how long the new volcano took to become what it is today.

"Paricutín," he answered, "took two and a half years to reach a definite standard of activity and for its volcanic structure to be considered mature and well established."

Mature and well established!

There today is Paricutín (I made its acquaintance on an earlier trip to this country) with its dark, menacing cone thrusting up to a height of 1,200 feet, dominating the valley whose look and history its appearance changed.

"The Mexican soul," I say sententiously, "may be compared to a maize field of tranquil appearance. But watch out, stranger! At any moment the field may explode in a volcano without previous warning. And all the pent-up burning lava of the subsoil will burst forth in fury, completely changing, in a few minutes, the countryside round about."

My wife remarks that this is cheap philosophy. A commonplace? But may not the commonplace have one day been an explosive and unexpected volcano to which time and use have ended by giving— as my geologist friend would say—"a mature and well-established structure," even though nowadays it lacks any unexpectedness, force or novelty?


The last day of the journey! We shall arrive this morning in Mexico City. The train is five hours behind time, which does not seem to me exaggerated. Expectation of the arrival and the biting chill of the air contribute to lessen our depression. I step down at the Dañu station and take what I hope may be my photographic masterpiece. In the foreground, an enormous grey-green cactus, the kind with fat leaves that look like the sole of a human foot, not lacking the simulacrum of the toes in the shape of little, thorny fruits. In the middle distance, a Mexican in an indigo-blue waistcoat, cigar-coloured trousers and white straw *sombrero*, pulling along a little burro whose back is weighted with two panniers full of mangoes yellow as egg yolks. In the background, the green plain— all this under a morning sun of new gold. There! The moment and the images are stamped on the celluloid. I place myself under the protection of Our Lady of Guadalupe and trust that all comes out well and pretty. And now it's time to return to the train, which has already given the signal for departure.


One of the hundred most delightful things in life for us is to sit at the window of a train or automobile watching the landscape, letting our minds run with the vehicle carrying us—but running free of the tyranny of the rails, without set itinerary, at the whim of spontaneous associations of images and ideas. If it were possible to search our thoughts in such moments, who could understand afterwards that saraband danced outside time and space? Many novelists have tried to reproduce the "stream of consciousness." I don't know whether any one has succeeded really well. The word is too slow and heavy a pachyderm for so difficult a choreography. I shall not even attempt to give an idea of all that passed through my mind (a demented cinema, an aimless film, a photograph of now two, now three and even four dimensions with abrupt cuts and continual fusions of images) in those delicious moments of reverie at the window of the railway car.

I remember only one bit of that surrealist film. A cactus shaped like a candelabrum turned itself into a synagogue, an image that melted into that of a rabbi and then into that of an old Jewish friend who spoke a phrase to me that the Pullman's wheels kept repeating only to end by chanting in my mind a passage from Villa-Lobos' "Quartet in E." Has anyone ever imagined the *explosion* of a quartet? Well, that is what is happening now. The train suddenly stops, and my wife and I are almost hurled against the compartment wall. I hear a noise of colliding iron, followed by other thuds and bangs. The first idea that occurs to me is that the earth has opened and swallowed the locomotive. I see the telegraph wires violently shaking, some of them on the point of snapping, as if a post had been knocked down. I dash into the corridor, where I find the attendant. "What's happened?" He shrugs. We both go outside.

A golden light is spilling on the plain. It is ten o'clock in the morning. But why the devil am I consulting my watch at this time? Cursed habit! A passenger who has also alighted explains, laconic and cold: "Derailment."

Full of hope I venture: "A small matter, is it?" The man makes a gesture of doubt. My wife is at my side, camera in hand. She does not seem much alarmed by the disaster, but gazes at the ground around her, fearing she might step on a rattlesnake.

We walk toward the locomotive. Our Pullman and two other cars are standing on the rails, intact. The *Juventino Rosas* has also survived. From the dining-car forward all the rest are off the rails, some completely down, others tilted; two of them are propped against each other like wild colts in combat. There are more than a hundred yards of tracks torn from their bed. But what impresses most is the position of the locomotive, which is quite upside down, like an enormous black beetle almost with its feet in the air. We see emerge from it, impassive and apparently unhurt, the driver and the fireman. The injured are beginning to come out of the other cars. Most are Indians, travelling second class. Some are bleeding freely. A baby with empurpled face is bellowing loudly. I catch sight of a man stretched out on the ground. The others pass by him without looking. Each one is trying to get out of the cars with his bundle of clothes, his cages, his family. They all do so with deliberate movements, in absolute silence. They are behaving in this dramatic situation with Britannic phlegm.

Like worms abandoning the carcass of an animal, the passengers continue to emerge and move away from the train. The chief of the crew contemplates the scene in silence, hands at his belt. Passengers talk in muted tones: "Lucky the train wasn't going very fast," remarks one. "Might have been worse." The other nods agreement. And the victims of the disaster? Of an Indian who resembles Pedro Armendáriz I ask whether the injured are not going to be aided. He replies, "I'm no authority, *señor.*" And off he goes, tucking his tin trunk, painted with flowers, under his arm. A blond man comes up and says, "How shameful for us Mexicans. In your country, in North America, these things don't happen." I retort, "But when they do happen, my friend, they are much worse. More people die." I make no attempt to explain that we are not Americans. It would be futile, since my wife has blue eyes and is desperately taking photographs.

I look about. The ground, gnawed away in many places by erosion, is of an ashy grey. Of greyish-green and pale wheat colour is the low-growing vegetation that, like the cacti, accentuates the desolateness of the landscape. Far off, at the foot of a hill, the houses of a village make a white patch. About half a mile from where we are glistens the blue, glassy surface of a lagoon. Silhouetted sharply against the pallid horizon, at once lyrical and terrible, the Sierra Madre seems to be spying on the scene.

We contribute the medicines we have with us—hydrogen peroxide, iodine and aspirin—for the first-aid. A mestizo of some twenty-odd years seems to be seriously injured. He has ecchymoses on face and hands, and gives the impression of having suffered some very serious internal injury.

It hurts me to see a young white girl, about fifteen, lying on the ground with her head in the lap of a lady who must be her mother. Her face is swollen and purple, and from the corners of her mouth glide two threads of blood that gradually soak her blouse. Time passes. I try in vain to catch the eye of some one of these Indians to say a word of comfort to him. But none will look straight at me. They are evasive as eels. Everyone looks after himself. By order of the train chief they pass on to the cars that have stayed upright. Their faces remain impassive. I note that the injured do not moan, they suffer in a stoic dumbness.

Writing about his trip to Central America, Aldous Huxley said that the fiestas in these regions of indigenous population have a sinister, aquarium-like quality. Only the fiestas? I have the feeling that these Indians live in a world apart from ours, like fish in an aquarium watching us furtively out of their motionless eyes in a liquid, oblique silence. Hostility? No. Perhaps indifference. I don't think we can ever break the glass that separates us from that aquatic world. And all the tragedy of the mestizo lies in his dubious, amphibious status.

Now, observing the ground more closely, I discover in it a wealth of shadings I had not noticed before: copper, pink, gold, grey, violet.

The sun mounts toward the zenith. Within less than an hour the curious begin to arrive, coming from the neighbouring town—men, women, girls in their Sunday best, in a wealth of *rebozos* of vivid colours that cumulatively bedeck the landscape. Also a sergeant arrives with soldiers armed with rifles. They seem, in their features, colour of skin, stature and type of helmet they wear, like soldiers of South Korea. Little by little a small and festive crowd gathers around the train, and the whole affair takes on the air of a fiesta. No one appears to be in a hurry. And the worst is that nobody knows what to do. Sitting on their trunks in the shade of the overturned cars, several Indians are eating *tortillas* stuffed with chopped meat and chili pepper.

After five hours help arrives. A locomotive from Dañu will pull the cars that are still upright. "But where?" I ask the train chief.

"Back," he informs me.

"How many kilometres are we from Mexico City?"

"Less than two hundred."

"Can't we go on?"

"No."

"Have we a long way to go back?"

"Certainly."

"And how many hours will it take to get there?"

"*Quién sabe?*"

I expel a sigh of impatience. The train chief stares at me for an instant and says then, "We are alive, *señor*. That's the important thing."

Fundamentally the man is right. We return to the car. The air-conditioning apparatus is not working. The heat is like a furnace. I succeed in opening the window.

Then begins the strangest trip of my life.

It is not only the air-conditioning system that is not functioning. In a few hours my own geography becomes upset and I feel lost, without map, without compass and without being able to count on the slightest help from the train crew. I know vaguely that we are going to pass through Querétaro, a place famous for the fact that here it was that the Emperor Maximilian was shot. Aside from this, silence and mystery. At first it doesn't bother us, for as it grows later the countryside grows more beautiful, the light shifts, changing the colour of the mountains, old churches appear more frequently, and ripe wheat fields—a thing that until then I knew only in sonnets—show off their gold in contrast with the dark earth, but in a beautiful chromatic relationship with the grey of the adobe houses. Before long, however, we fall to imagining the difficulties and annoyances that await us. Now that the windows are open, the dust enters freely into the cars together with the flies. The train's supply of cold drinks has been exhausted. The *Juventino Rosas* has ceased to be the oasis where we refreshed ourselves during the crossing of the desert. From time to time I go to the other cars to visit the injured. What most impresses me is the baby, now completely purple, in a coma. The parents contemplate it in silence with their faces of stone. Emotion does not move a single facial muscle, but I can see sorrow in their black, warm eyes. For that matter, sadness never leaves the Indian's gaze.

The stench in these cars is unbearable—today's sweat added to that of many days or weeks or months past, mingled with the odour of onion and chili, for the natives seem to be always eating. Suspect liquids trickle on the floor. An evil smell rises from the bundles piled between the benches or in the aisle. A blonde, skinny passenger has turned herself into a nurse and is directing the first-aid. She seems to be the only active and articulate person in the whole train. Her thin, bloodless hands, smelling of eau-de-cologne, flutter like birds, frightening away the flies that insist on alighting on the patients' faces.

We stop for more than an hour in a station, waiting for the ambulance that is coming for those of the injured whose condition is most critical. The others are going to continue the trip. The medical aid arrives. Before removing the girl and the young man to the ambulance, the medical attendants give them blood transfusions. All this keeps us more than an hour in the station.

At last the locomotive pulls out. Night falls. The Pullman attendant passes like a shadow by our door and I stop him.

"Well, my friend, when do we arrive?"

He hesitates for a second: "I think around ten p.m."

Well, that's something.

It is nearly seven. We head for the *Juventino Rosas* with the intention of dining. The waiter hands us the spotted menu. Down the aisle of the dining-car pass the Indians one by one. It is a parade of smells. The corners of their ponchos touch our plates. They are men, they are our brothers, I tell myself with the best Franciscan intention. I want to love them. I want at least to tolerate them. I stealthily slip a peso to a boy who in passing gives us a long look. He takes the banknote indifferently, under the yet more indifferent eye of his mother. Why did I do that? A sense of guilt? Can it be that with that peso I am seeking to do penance for being a "sentimental *petit bourgeois*," as Jorge Amado would say, for having what I have, for not having been born an Indian in an adobe hut in the Chihuahua desert?

My wife and I look at each other. Where are the jovial, fresh tourists who, in a Rotarian gaiety, took a silvery train in Washington? What are we going to eat? Neither of us seems to have the slightest appetite. I find it vaguely sacrilegious to eat in this car when in the other there are injured people suffering, their skins and clothes still stained with blood.

The train lurches. I have already observed that when the traveller is sad or tired he lets himself be shaken up without reacting. He abandons himself to the sway of the train. It is a sort of suicide. It no longer matters to him to preserve an erect posture, to maintain appearances. What he wants is to reach his destination. Or to die.

"Have you chosen?" I ask, indicating the menu card.

My wife shakes her head in negation.

"I'm not going to eat anything. What about you?"

"Not a thing."

We order mineral water and begin to sip it unenthusiastically. Its tepidity turns it thick and even somewhat viscous. I look out. A crimson sash tinges the horizon beyond a mountain of deep purple. I wonder where we can be going. How many derailments are ahead of us? When shall we get there?

To these mute questions the train replies with the rhythmic click-clack of its wheels: never, never, never. . . . And the Indians continue passing by. Each seems deep in his private aquarium of roiled water. And in the face of that contained suffering, that resigned misery, I feel a certain shame at being a tourist.


Night has fallen completely. I am at the window of the car in order to breathe better. I feel we ought not to lie down, since we are to arrive at ten. It is a moonless night, cool and starry. The train is crossing a mysterious plain where lights glimmer here and there. Where are we? I ask the train chief, who without stopping shrugs and mutters, *"Pues, quién sabe?"*

Here is the response I hear most frequently through this interminable night in which I stubbornly refuse to go to bed, for we may reach Mexico City at any moment. My eyes are heavy with sleep. I whistle, I hum, I summon optimistic thoughts, I imagine myself in the hotel under a cold shower or clad in fresh clothes, stretched out on a clean bed. Useless. The reality is here. It stares me in the face. Gradually I am learning that there is no country more substantial than Mexico, where all things *are* intensely, with no half-terms.

My wife, more realistic than I, makes herself comfortable on the bed, convinced that we shall not arrive before tomorrow morning. The mulish fellow stays sitting by the window, catching in his eyes the dust from the roadbed mixed with the sand of sleep. Now and then I throw myself on the bed, lie uncomfortably, diagonally.

Suddenly I wake with a start and return to the window in hopes of glimpsing in the distance the lights of the capital. Again I lie down, determined not to surrender, clinging with nails and teeth to the hope of arriving soon. And there are moments when I cannot say for certain whether I am asleep, dozing torpidly, or awake.

Now, when I try to recall that journey, I remember vaguely mysterious stops at which, in torpor, I heard voices. *"Café negro— quién toma café?—*Black coffee—who'll have coffee?"* In my mind that black coffee made the night blacker and more indecipherable. More than once I leaned elbows stupidly on the window ledge and saw the red or green light of a lantern bobbing along in the darkness. Other trains passed ours, puffing locomotives exhaled their hot breath in my face. Most times, though, it was only the savanna, the same slate colour of the sky, in which my gaze was lost, hypnotized. There was one moment at a stop when the headlamp of an automobile, bursting out of the darkness, revealed a whole world: a station in the shape of a castle, some mud houses, trees—all in a swift second. The light was extinguished and the world disappeared. The dark was left, and some lost voices that I remember now more as images than as sounds. Sometimes I would slip into one of those superficial drowses in which we can still hear voices and noises. Waking from one of these heavy dozes, I turned on the light and looked at my watch. Two o'clock. The train was moving slowly. At the next station someone was singing to the accompaniment of a guitar. It was a man's voice, warm and languid, moaning a sad song. How romantic the serenade would be if together with the singer's voice the fragrance of jasmines should come in the window, and not the fetid emanations from a railway outhouse!

I stand up, run water over my face, step out of the compartment to stroll like a sleepwalker along the corridor. I ask the attendant, "What station is this?"

And the man, methodically peeling an orange, responds without looking at me, *"Pues, quién sabe?"* I feel like a Kafka character in a phantom train wandering aimlessly outside time and space. And— oddly—this notion in a way amuses, consoles and calms me.

# 2. Tenochtitlán

According to Legend—which in the magic world holds more authority than does History—in the year 1325 of the Christian era an Aztec tribe, the Méxica, was wandering over the tableland in search of a site on which to settle, when one day Huitzilopochtli, the God of War, appeared to the High Priest and ordered him to keep on marching with his people until they found an eagle perched on a cactus, holding a serpent in his claws and beak, for in that spot they were to build a city. The Méxicas continued their peregrinations, and in a long valley at the entrance to which rise the volcanoes Popocatépetl and Ixtaccíhuatl they found the cactus, the eagle and the serpent, just as the severe divinity had predicted. On an island in the middle of Lake Texcoco, which covered the central part of the valley (this is now commencing History), the Aztecs erected their first mud-and-rush cabins, giving the settlement the name of Tenochtitlán. Only at the end of the fourteenth century did they construct the first houses of stone and the pyramids, or *teocallis,* for sacrifices. Between the founding of Tenochtitlán and the coming of Hernán Cortés two hundred years passed, during which the Méxica tribe increased in number, power and glory. The problem of living space was solved by the construction of vast rafts— *chinampas*—which were anchored around the principal island. On these rafts, covered with earth, trees and grasses were planted. Time did the rest. Sediments accumulated beneath the *chinampas*, and the roots of the trees on top of them, penetrating deep into the lake bed, ended by transforming the rafts into little islets.


Thanks to Bernal Díaz del Castillo, who wrote a chronicle of the Conquest, to the letters of Hernán Cortés and to the mural Diego Rivera painted on the walls of the National Palace four centuries later, it is possible for us today to have a view of the fabulous Tenochtitlán as it was in the year 1519, just before its total destruction.

Yonder lies the metropolis of the Aztecs in the vale of Anáhuac, under the clear Mexican sun, gracious as Venice and imposing as Babylon. It has fifty thousand houses, as many as Seville at the same date, and its population is no less than three hundred thousand.

Its centre is an island, oval in shape, bordered by green floating gardens in vivid contrast to the blue water of the lake. Upon platforms that look like truncated pyramids the temples of the clans rear in solid majesty above the cluster of houses whose façades are covered with white stucco or spattered with pulverized pumice stone of a more intense red. What great pyramid is that in the main square? It is the *teocalli* of Huitzilopochtli, the fierce God of War, whose altars from time to time are bathed in human blood. The other, smaller temple is dedicated to Quetzalcoatl, the "plumed serpent," a deity more kindly and friendly to a man, to whom, in his passing through this world, he taught the art of cultivating the soil and of working gold and silver.

Three great avenues, interrupted at intervals by drawbridges, link the largest island to the mainland, all the roads converging on the centre of the city.


The streets properly so-called are few, but straight and broad. Uncountable canals criss-cross among the small islands, cut by movable bridges, clotted with vessels transporting passengers or carrying to the city markets the produce of the orchards and farms of the outskirts. In the streets no cart is to be seen, for this civilization knows neither the wheel nor animal traction. Slaves walk along bowed under the weight of bundles, under the hard eye of their masters and their stone gods.

Yonder is the great market of Tlaltelolco, where warriors, members of the nobility, clan chieftains, priests and merchants rub elbows, each with his showy garments, arms and insignia. The women, more simply dressed than the men, wear flowers in their black hair. Plebeians are going hither and thither and, with the slaves and the beggars, comprise the colourless note in the lively scene.

In the shade of arcades merchants offer products of the three kingdoms of nature and of the thousand kingdoms of fantasy, of the skill of gold and silversmiths, of the weavers, the basket-makers and other artisans. Each kind of merchandise has its special place in this fair. Here we see the fruits of the earth—sapodillas, *capulí* cherries, avocado pears, mangoes, pineapples, tomatoes, all heaped in colourful pyramids. Yonder are the birds and the fish. In another area, aromatic and medicinal herbs, roots with magical properties. Flies swarm about the bulging jars of honey, beside which are piled bars of wax. The women seem to take more interest in the gold, silver and jade jewellery. But both they and the men examine with enthusiasm the rich assortments of bird feathers in the form of tiaras, cloaks, rugs and adornments in the most varied designs and patterns. As money does not exist in the Aztec empire, the customary form of transaction is barter. A noble buys a basket of red chili peppers from a gardener, whom he pays from a purse full of cacao beans. A lady hands over duck feathers dusted with gold in exchange for a large, tri-coloured rug. A priest offers T-shaped bits of tin for a cotton cloak.

Thousands of persons are milling about in this great square. But there are other markets and business streets. For example, this is the street of game—palpitant with wings, squawking and warbling—where we can buy, dead or alive, wild ducks, partridges and other edible birds. In their reed cages little multi-coloured birds catch the attention of children. In these streets, houses and arcades, doves are neighbours to eagles, falcons and deer. Rabbits and hares with timid eyes shrink back in alarm when one of the birds of prey stretches and beats his strong wings. Owls from their dark corners gaze, apparently in envy, at the rich plumage of the talkative parrots. And what strange animals are those over there, fastened by collars, that seem products of the crossing of a pig with a dog? They are hairless dogs that the Aztecs raise for eating, after castrating them.

Here, too, is the street of the herbalists, odoriferous of wild perfumes, where one can find leaves, grasses and roots for the diseases of the body and of the mind. And also species of drug stores with their unguents and mysterious potions.

What we are looking at now, can it be a barber shop? Not the least doubt of it. The barbers here wash and shave heads.

This one, now, is the street of pottery, where crockery of the most varied shapes and colours is sold—pitchers, water tumblers, cooking pots, domestic utensils. It is worth while to inspect the beautiful cotton textiles in that other street, with their bright colours and patterns. Afterwards it will be interesting to visit the place where they sell colours for painters and potters. . . . But enough of trade!

Now let's follow this canal opening off the principal avenue. Where will it take us? We come to a lesser square in the centre of which we see a pyramid. In a nearby patio youths are receiving military training, learning to handle weapons. Sweat is running down their olive bodies, while under the eyes of their instructors they devote themselves to their duels, brandishing their short maces with shouts and parrying their opponents' blows with their shields. In a group apart other adolescents are practising the hurling of the *atl-atl,* a kind of elongated dart, a throwing stick.

Let us leave the future warriors (we know they will never fight in earnest, for the strange army of white men that is to destroy the Aztec empire has already disembarked on the beaches of the lowlands) to return to the principal square, to the Imperial Palace, to that solid edifice before whose portico of porphyry and jasper soldiers are mounting guard. We come at a good moment, since the banquet that brings together the nobles, the notables of Tenochtitlán, as well as potentates from other provinces of the empire, is drawing to a close. More than three hundred guests are eating and drinking in the great hall of the palace. The floor is strewn with flowers and aromatic herbs that the servants trample and crush as they pass here and there with salvers of silver, drinking cups, pitchers and baskets. Before the banquet began, they brought basins of water and towels, for it would be inconceivable that a guest should start eating without first washing his hands. But where is Montezuma? Served not by slaves but by nobles, the Emperor is dining behind a screen, so that the vassals may not watch him under these less than sublime conditions. The principal dish is a roast of turkey, prepared with a special sauce and served up with vegetables. In the gold and silver cups there is a great variety of drinks, three of them extracted from the maguey and all of them unknown to the European palate, as is the vanilla-perfumed chocolate the Emperor seems to prize so highly.

Upon a large gold tray with incrustations of jade and turquoise can be seen the remains of a great delicacy also unknown to European tables. If he were called in to explain, Montezuma's cook would say quite candidly, "Roast meat from a brave enemy warrior sacrificed this morning to the God of War."

The dinner is over. The servants bring pipes with various mixtures of tobacco and odorous herbs to the guests. At a sign from the Emperor the show commences. Into the hall dash mountebanks, jugglers, dancers and a whole regiment of dwarfs and other human aberrations from the private collection of the Emperor, who in this particular is not different from other sovereigns, European and Oriental. And misshapen humans, clowns and acrobats leap, pirouette, dance, exhibit their skills, while musicians garlanded with flowers blow sadly into their flutes and conch shells to the rhythmic beat of a cylindrical drum.

It is a sad, monotonous tune. The remains of the warrior on the table are to us nauseating. The spectacle of the dwarfs is not at all inspiring. Let us pass on to another room, of less festive decoration. It is here that on certain days Montezuma's vassals wait for the Emperor to grant them audience. The room is deserted and dark now. In that other salon, less severe and bureaucratic, rich carpets with designs made of the most gorgeous feathers of birds cover the floor. In the apartments where Montezuma lives with his two wives the carpets are incrusted with gold, silver and precious gems. No less luxurious are the bedrooms of the Emperor's many concubines. There they are now, busy at their domestic tasks: weaving, embroidering, decorating rugs, and talking. Ugly? Pretty? Why, that is a question of taste, and, after all, one of more direct interest to Montezuma.

Now let's go into the hall where the tribal treasures are kept, presents that conquered peoples have sent to the Emperor of the Aztecs, and also the products of the sackings in hundreds of wars. It is as though we had entered the cave of Ali Baba's thieves. Precious stones, shields, panoplies, jewels of the most exquisite workmanship, tiaras and breastplates, wristlets and épaulières are gathered here as in a coruscating congress of colour and splendour, together with cloaks, plumes, rugs, covers. . . . It is possible that some of these ear-rings, bracelets and necklaces still retain vestiges of blood from the necks, ears, breasts and heads from which they were torn. But no! It is well known that the Aztecs have an obsession for cleanliness. The Imperial Palace possesses innumerable bath-rooms, and everyone knows Montezuma takes daily baths and changes clothes at least three times a day.

After visiting the treasure room, it is natural that we should pass over the silos where the grain harvests are housed. But it is worth an instant's pause to contemplate the zoological garden of the palace. In this aviary are found birds of all the climes of the empire, from the macaws of vivid, hot plumage brought from the torrid jungles of the lowlands near the sea, to the vultures and eagles of less brilliant plumage, captured among the frozen mountain peaks. They say that the condor there, staring at us with his cold, gelatinous eyes, came from the Andes, from the region inhabited by the Incas. A short distance from the aviary jaguars and ocelots prowl restlessly in their cages, and their eyes glitter like those of the images of certain gods. In the serpentarium snakes sleep, coiled.

We are now in the garden, in the shade of pines and cypresses. We look toward the hill of Chapultepec, where the summer palace of the Emperor stands. It is from there, on that great clay aqueduct, that the potable water for the people of Tenochtitlán comes, for the water of the lake is slightly salt.


Before leaving the metropolis of Anáhuac, why not follow that procession going yonder toward one of the temples? The men in black must be priests. I don't know why among them marches, so solemn, a man in scarlet garments. In the centre of the cortège, as a principal figure, walks a handsome youth of impeccable form, wearing on his head a plume of multi-coloured feathers, in one hand a mirror and in the other a handful of flutes. Who is he? Where are they taking him?

One year before this ceremony the youth was chosen to incarnate Tezcatlipoca, the most powerful, beautiful God of Eternal Youth, who holds in his hand a smoking mirror in which the world and its creatures are reflected. The priests prepare the chosen one for this tremendous moment. They have made him presents of incense and perfumed flowers. They have given him as wives four of the loveliest virgins of the empire. And not long ago they have snatched him from the arms of the women and brought him to the boat that has conducted him to this place through the canals, among the acclamations of hundreds of persons waving at him from the banks.

Women loved him when they watched him pass standing in the prow of the vessel. Other youths envied him. Because in that moment he represented the beauty that is never extinguished, the youth that never ends. He was Tezcatlipoca himself, Soul of the World, greatest of the gods after the Supreme Being.

The cortège now approaches the highest part of the temple. The adolescent rips the plume from his head, divests himself of his rich garments, and starts up the steps, flanked by the men in black. As he climbs, he breaks one by one the flutes he has played on his nights of love. Five of the priests lift the adolescent in the air and set him on the sacrificial stone, next to the image of Tezcatlipoca all of black stone, its breast of massive gold. The youth is still smiling because he knows that only now is his life going to begin. The priest in scarlet raises his obsidian knife in the air. The multitude suddenly hushes, and a great silence that seems to descend from the mountains covers the entire valley. In a swift gesture the sacrificer tears open the breast of the Aztec youth with an incision running from the breastbone to the base of the stomach. Then, thrusting his hand through the cut, from which the blood is spurting, he grasps the heart of the victim and tears it, still palpitating, from the chest. Tezcatlipoca seems to contemplate with his eyes of black stone the scene of the sacrifice, which is all reflected in his dark mirror.

The executioner raises the adolescent's heart in offering to the Sun, and then casts it at the feet of the idol.

The multitude, in mystic delirium, bursts into song and shouting.


And the life of the metropolis goes on. A caravan of merchants, protected by soldiers, is going out at this moment bound for the provinces of the North. The slaves are marching and singing, sad under the weight of their burdens. Popocatépetl blows high his plume of smoke. Boats sail along the canals, breaking the reflections of the palaces and the temples. In the centre of the great square several members of the Council of Ancients are conversing around the Calendar, a marvel of Aztec genius, as if they wished to read on that circular stone, in that mirror of time, the future of the empire.

# 3. The Federal Capital

We reach Mexico City on a luminous Sunday morning four hundred and thirty-five years after Hernán Cortés. We take a room at the Hotel Génève, where we find only American tourists with their wholesome picnicky gaiety, their slacks and loud ties, their cameras slung from their shoulders, and their animated, gaily dressed elderly women—hail! hail!

Here in the very lobby of the hotel I mentally voice an invocation. Oh Tezcatlipoca, God of Eternal Youth, I offer to you in sacrifice these old women of adolescent souls, these unbreakable plastic hearts. Take them, oh Soul of the World! But first make them happy in Taxco and Guadalajara, let them visit all the picturesque and historic places of this and other cities. Permit them to dance in Acapulco with the bold, bronzed divers. And let them buy in the market-places *sarapes* and *rebozos* with all the colours of the rainbow. Feed them *tortillas, quesadillas, enchiladas, tamales, taquitos, chicharrones*—all this without the slightest worry, oh Tezcatlipoca, for these ladies, besides having stomachs and livers of pure steel, always keep their handbags stuffed with little discs of Alka-Seltzer. And afterwards, yes, afterwards lead them all to the stone of sacrifice.

But at the hall-porter's desk they assure me that the Aztec gods are dead, that the present government no longer allows that type of human sacrifice. There must be others, for where and when are there none?

They give us a room at the back, overlooking the terrace of an apartment house from which the sounds of a radio reach us, and the crying of a baby and the gabble of a parrot.

In a prolonged shower bath we find compensation for the days of heat and absence of water in the countryside of Chihuahua.

We go out to the street with the caution and deliberateness appropriate to persons unaccustomed to great altitudes, for this city is 7,800 feet above sea level. I am conscious of my short breath, a slight pain at the back of my neck and a certain weakness in my legs.

In the early years of this century the capital of Mexico had not more than a half-million inhabitants. The hotel manager swears that today it has four millions. I think there is a little patriotic exaggeration in this, even if we count the suburbs and adjacent towns that the metropolis, in expanding, has incorporated into its area. But that at the very least three million human beings live here, there is apparently not the slightest doubt.

I wonder why this city has so strong a personality. What is it that makes it so different from all others? Whence comes the aura of drama that envelops it? I believe the factors are various: many the tints that, combined, produce—despite all the sunshine—that dark, ominous tone that gives us the sensation that something tragic is always about to occur—a murder, an earthquake, a revolution. . . . In the first place we must not forget that this city was erected upon the corpse of the Tenochtitlán murdered by Cortés and his soldiers. I am inclined to accept, with some imaginativeness, the idea that a city may be shadowed by a sense of guilt. Take into account also the permanent, formidable presence of those two volcanoes mounting guard over the valley. Earth shocks make themselves felt here with some frequency, if not with excessive violence. Add to all this the singular enchantment of mountain cities, where the rarefied air, combined with details of topography, seems to determine a type of psychology that makes its inhabitants distrustful and taciturn. Another element of drama, and that visible to the naked eye, is the fact that, the waters of Lake Texcoco having been drained little by little over the centuries, this metropolis constructed upon a bed of sand, lava and porous rock is sinking. Yes; it is calculated that it sinks thirty centimetres—nearly a foot—per year, and not uniformly because of the uneven distribution of weight on the soil caused by skyscrapers. It is not unusual to see buildings out of plumb, houses half-tilted, flights of steps out of the vertical, walls split, towers leaning. And as if all this were not enough to make the capital of Mexico a unique city, she offers us the further peculiarity of bearing the stamp of five different cultures.

It will be interesting to seek signs of these during our wanderings.

We are in the Zócalo. In this plaza of monumental dimensions that was in times past the heart of Tenochtitlán and later of the Spanish colonial city, is found the great cathedral the Conquistadores built with the very stones of the Great Temple of the Aztecs. In its façade are combined varied architectural elements, and even a layman like me can see in it vestiges of the Corinthian, the Ionic and the Doric. The result of this mixture is something that could be called neo-classic. This great cathedral has a sombre, imposing quality, as if it had retained in its stones not only the mark of age and weather but also the accumulated memory and matured patina of all the suffering and violence it has witnessed. At its side rises the Metropolitan Sagrario, a beautiful example of the Churrigueresque, which an earth tremor shook out of plumb, adding to its aspect, already severe in itself, one more element of drama. Constructed in the form of a Greek cross, it consists of two naves crossing each other, with a cupola in the centre.

Other historic piles surround the great square, such as the Palacio Nacional, erected on the site where originally stood the residence of Montezuma and later the house of Cortés, which a fire destroyed; the Ayuntamiento or Palace of the City Hall on the south side of the Zócalo, and the Palacio de Justicia, of much more recent construction, on the south-east corner.

All these buildings have a massive look, a broad, low solidity, but they cannot be denied a certain respectable grandiosity. Many of them were made of *tezontle,* a pink stone of volcanic origin, taken also from the demolished Aztec monuments.

We stroll under the arcaded galleries covering the sidewalk on the west side of the Zócalo. As was the case in the days of Cortés, these *portales* shelter a series of tiny shops, or stalls.

It is strange to think that under our feet, a few yards beneath the asphalt, the Aztec metropolis lies buried. If I am not mistaken it was in this vicinity that they dug up the great Calendar Stone, which is now in the National Museum of Anthropology. It is said that early in this century the workers who were demolishing a business building on the corner of Guatemala and Seminario streets uncovered the foundations of an edifice believed to have been part of the Great Pyramid of the God of War.

We have, then, in this square—which continues to be the historic centre, at least, if no longer the social and commercial, of Mexico— vestiges of two civilizations, the Aztec and the Spanish colonial. But to what extent is the colonial purely Spanish? I have the impression —and so think many who know the subject better—that at the very moment the Conquistadores were putting up their houses and palaces in the image and likeness of those they had left in their father- land across the sea, they were already beginning to undergo the influence of the people they had subjugated. It was not merely the fact that they were using the material and to some extent the con- struction technique of the natives. It was more than that, mys- teriously and imponderably more than that.

We see also in the Zócalo something that is neither Indian nor Spanish. It is the automobiles circulating or standing parked here. And the billboards and posters advertising commercial products "made in U.S.A." One who contemplates part of the ruins of the Great Temple, visible only a few steps from the cathedral, then looks at the Catholic temple and then at the advertisements of Pepsi-Cola, may actually feel dizzy. The leaps in time are too vertiginous. And when I say "time" I am not thinking just of the chronological but also of the psychological.

If a great earthquake should some day knock down this church and these palaces, turning up the ground, possibly we should see emerging from the womb of the earth the corpse of Tenochtitlán, with which would be mingled the remains of colonial Mexico and those of the twentieth-century metropolis with its skyscrapers, cine- mas, night clubs and soda fountains. And our eyes would witness frightful scenes, as for example the head of an Aztec idol—Tezcatli- poca or Quetzalcoatl—crowned with one of those red Coca-Cola discs we can see sacrilegiously nailed to the faces of these old arcades.

When she listened to the description of this hypothetical catas- trophe, my wife thinks that my fancy is running with an over-loose rein, and attributes it to the altitude. We photograph the cathedral, the Sagrario, the famous Liberty Bell that Hidalgo caused to be rung in 1810 and that now, in retirement, sleeps yonder in silence over the central door of the Palacio—and then, gay and half-ethereal, we pass on to other streets and considerations.

My first night in Mexico's capital was nearly as anguished as the one I spent in the train after the derailment. I woke several times gasping for lack of air, always with the sensation of smothering. It seems to me I passed the whole night contending with obsessive dreams all based on a sort of leitmotiv that, this time, was the identity of the Emperor Maximilian and the Brazilian writer Vianna Moog, both blond and very big men. There were moments when their images melted together and my whole tribulation arose from inability to separate them, for I knew that if I did not separate them Vianna Moog would end by being shot, not in Querétaro but in São Leopoldo, on the banks of the Rhine. The devil of it is that somewhere along the line another element came on the scene— Benito Juárez, a kind of stone figure, motionless and silent, an ominous backdrop. And as though all these complications were not enough, there was an instant when Juárez was I myself. In my statue-like immobility I was listening to the whisperings of the monarch and the writer: "You can't trust an Indian," they were saying. I wanted to prove to them I had nothing to do with the shooting of the Emperor, it was all a historic fatality, something that had already happened. Useless. I could not manage to move a finger, and the water was pouring into my nostrils, my mouth, my eyes, asphyxiating me.

Next day, on waking, I straighten out my thoughts. Vianna Moog wrote a book called *A River Imitates the Rhine*. The man executed before a firing squad was Maximilian. I may have an Indian face, but I am not Benito Juárez. If anyone doubts it, let him look at my passport.

From the bathroom, shaving before the mirror and looking in annoyance at the accentuated, purplish bags under my eyes, I shout, "Do you know who's going to be here in a few days?"

"Who?"

"Vianna Moog."

I lose myself once more in thought, and then speak again: "Shall we visit the palace today where he lived?"

"Vianna Moog?"

"No. Maximilian."

At the breakfast table in a room of the Génève that smells of fried bacon, and where tourists are talking garrulously (I have never before used that word in my whole life), getting ready for the day's excursions, I ruminate the night's dreams. There is nothing more absurd, improbable and fascinating than the history of Mexico. This American country, conquered and colonized by Spaniards, with a high percentage of Indian blood, has already had an Austrian emperor and a French court.

The Castle of Chapultepec stands atop a hill of the same name at the end of the Paseo de la Reforma, surrounded by a large, beautiful park of gigantic cypresses, one of the oldest in the continent. Its stone structure, from the architectural point of view, is not impressive. To me, at least, it says nothing. But if we stop an instant to think of the hisory of this huge old building it will bulk large in our eyes with an aura of drama and romance.

The viceroy Gálvez—a citizen of whom I have but scant information—built it in 1783 on the very site where formerly stood the summer palace of the Emperor Montezuma. The castle, which became the residence of other viceroys, was finished only in 1840, when they fortified it and brought the Military College here.

With the exercise of a little imagination we shall be able to hear the voices of command that were sounding here just over a century ago, and the martial paces of the young Indian and mestizo cadets, probably short and swarthy, as they marched—One-two! One-two!— over these stones. How profoundly absorbed they are, these boys of seventeen to twenty, future officers of the Mexican Army! But before we feel inclined to call them, half-paternally, half-ironically, "little tin soldiers," it will be advisable to open a history book and read what happened here in the tragic year of 1847. Mexico and the United States were at war over Texas. The American troops invading Mexican territory enter the capital and besiege the Military School, where the young cadets fight on alone like men. It is a lost battle, they know, but they prefer dying to surrendering.

Yes, that monument down there at the foot of the hill, with its six columns and its white marble figures, was erected to honour the "boy heroes."

In 1866 Maximilian turned the castle into an imperial residence. Doña Carlotta herself, his wife, designed the gardens, where we find the delightful fountain of Don Quixote, around which the story of Cervantes' hero is summarized pictorially on the tiles covering the surface of the benches.

Tourists photograph the monument to the cadets without—I presume—having any idea of what it stands for. Others gather excitedly around the famous "Montezuma tree," which, a guide loudly informs them, is an *ahuehuete* nearly 230 feet high, with a trunk fifty feet in circumference.

We enter the castle, which nowadays is a museum of history. On the glass of the window over the entrance stairway we see the arms of the eighteen rulers Mexico had from the time of the Aztecs to Maximilian. We start wandering through the rooms—halls with very high ceilings, full of glass cases where uniforms, weapons, flags, documents, decorations, cameos, bric-à-brac, jewels and costumes worn by the ladies of Maximilian's court, personal articles belonging to the sovereigns, the table silver, the china of the imperial household, are all to be seen. On the walls hang pictures with heavy gilt frames, containing oil portraits of statesmen, generals, ministers of state, all of severe cast of countenance, many with a tiny beard in the style of Napoleon III, some in civilian dress, frock coat and false shirt-front, others in military uniform with golden epaulettes and buttons—all with an intense gaze that seems to follow us. It cannot fail to be disquieting for one to feel oneself the focus of those searching, half-hostile eyes coming out of the back of time. I have an impulse to stop, raise my head to the bigwigs, turn out my pockets and say haughtily, "You can search me. I haven't stolen anything!"

And here we are walking among relics with that cretinous haste of the professional tourist who doesn't visit places because he really wants to see them, but because he wants to have the right to say later to others and to himself that he has seen them.

We are now in the part of the castle where the monarchs lived. The furniture of the bedroom and the receiving room was presented to them by Napoleon III, the man responsible for this phantom empire. The upholstery of the chairs and sofas is woven with copies of the Gobelins in the Louvre. We pause at the door of the receiving room and look inside. We are back in 1866. Carlotta is playing a Haydn sonata on the piano.

No matter what effort I make, I cannot imagine her with the features I have seen just now in her oil portrait in one of these rooms. I see her with the face of Bette Davis. (The evil that poor, indifferent films have done!) The emperor is also there, seated, legs crossed, placidly reading a book. The *Essays* of Montaigne? The *Werther* of Goethe?

We continue our wanderings. This was the couple's bedroom. I abstain respectfully from any imagining. But on reaching the door of the bathroom, seeing the little marble tub in which Carlotta must have taken her perfumed baths but in which I am unable to imagine the emperor with his long legs, I cannot resist a remark: "I wonder what the Empress was like—plastically?"

"Probably squat and pudgy."

"I only wondered whether the Hapsburgs took as many baths as Montezuma."

"At this stage of history that detail no longer seems of much importance."

I nod agreement. And slowly we approach the balustrade of the broad terrace from which one can get a panoramic view of the city and the valley with its volcanoes, hills and mountains. For lack of a precise adjective for the colour of this May sky, I shall say that it was a Mexican blue.

Yonder is the perspective of the Paseo de la Reforma, a beautiful, broad, tranquil avenue edged with trees and interrupted at intervals by circles that are here called *glorietas*. It is owed to Maximilian, who perhaps wanted to give the capital of his troublesome empire a boulevard that would be reminiscent of the Champs Elysées. It is said that when the emperor went out riding in the mornings along the Paseo, Doña Carlotta would stay on this terrace to follow him with a jealous eye.

Wait. There comes the emperor now in person, with slow, full paces, hands clasped behind his back, head bent, his air pensive. I see him as in the portraits: hair as blond as his forked beard, grey eyes, dark dolman, white breeches tight on his legs, medals on his broad chest.

He approaches the balustrade and stands contemplating the city he loves so much. I think of a phrase from D'Annunzio that I have read somewhere, I don't know where or when: "Beautiful Hapsburg flower dropped on barbaric soil."

Does he know that his destiny is already laid out for him? The Civil War is over in the United States and now the powerful neighbour threatens to intervene in Mexico to restore the republic. An obstinate, Messianic Indian is gathering his men in the north, is receiving arms, munitions and money from the other side of the border.

Napoleon III, alarmed at the menace of Prussia, is going to abandon the Austrian prince to his fate. He has already ordered the withdrawal of French forces from Mexican territory. And in less than a year Maximilian will stand with two of his loyal companions in front of a firing squad, on the summit of the Hill of the Bells in Querétaro. I wonder whether he knows that all this is going to happen. If he does, why doesn't he take Napoleon III's advice and abdicate? If he doesn't, I feel that I, from my privileged position in time and space, ought to warn him of the danger. It is enough to take a couple of steps, touch his arm respectfully and murmur, *"Monsieur . . ."* Perhaps it will be advisable to tell him who I am and where I come from. I can even venture a little white lie: "Our Emperor, Dom Pedro II, sends you an embrace . . ."

"Wonderful!" bellows a loud voice in my ear. An American in a yellow shirt moves between me and my vision and, Kodak to his eye—click!—he snaps a picture of the view.

Many other traces of French influence besides the Paseo de la Reforma are to be found in this tentacular city. They nearly all come from the nineteenth century. Despite the proximity of an Anglo-Saxon nation and an Indian racial substratum, it is usually said that Mexico has, from the time of the Conquest, been a Latin nation. According to Samuel Ramos, this country was Latinized "under the two-fold influence of the Catholic Church and Roman legislation."

After the ill-fated experiment with a Creole emperor, Agustín I, Mexico became a republic and took France as her model in spite of having adopted a presidential system of the North American type. Catholicism has also contributed to bringing this nation closer to France, whose art and literature have always, especially in the past century, found the most enthusiastic partisans among the lettered classes. It was natural that during this period the French model should be followed in literature, in art and in politics. To General Porfirio Díaz, who remained in power for more than thirty years as one of the most solid dictators the country has ever known, is attributed the famous phrase: "Poor Mexico! So far from God and so close to the United States!" But it was, paradoxically, during that government so imbued with the doctrines of Auguste Comte and so enamoured of the spiritual conquests of France that the petroleum fields and other mineral riches of Mexico gradually passed into the hands of English and American enterprises.

In many of these old residential districts where we are strolling, architectural relics of the Porfirian era turn up before us—great mansions of French style, with porticoes, portecocheres, dormers, tall windows, statues, fountains, groves of cypresses and other civilized trees.

In the centre of the city we find many examples of the detestable *art nouveau,* with its cupolas, ornamented façades, marble stairways and sculptures. Beside the Alameda and facing Avenida Juárez appears the profile of the Palacio de Bellas Artes, begun in 1905, in the government of Don Porfirio, and inaugurated in 1935. I am afraid its style is an attempt to combine Mayan and Mixtec motifs with the classic architecture of French taste. The result is this mastodon crowned with a fat cupola topped by a bronze eagle with wings outstretched. Its white marble structure is so heavy that it has already sunk about six feet into the spongy soil. The palace contains the national theatre, several auditoriums and galleries of art. On the walls of its staircases Orozco, Rivera, Siqueiros and Tamayo have painted frescoes.

In the theatre one night we attended the performance—quite good—of *Jeanne d'Arc au Bûcher,* the poem by Claudel with music by Honegger. I thought the Indian faces of the chorus were delicious.

The inside of the theatre is all decorated in purple. A student confesses to me that when he comes in here he has the feeling that he is getting into the intestines of a cow.


In the Tenochtitlán of the Aztecs the practitioners of the same trade and merchants of the same kinds were grouped in the same streets. Apparently up to a short time ago that tendency predominated here. In Francisco Madero street, which was formerly called Plateros, there are still many silversmiths, but principally shops that sell articles from Paris. Tacuba street is full of footwear shops, and Donceles specializes in furniture.

Along all these streets we stroll in holiday mood, with no fixed schedule or programme, in free disposition of body and mind that alone is worth the trip.

What to say about this Federal District? Will it benefit anyone to say that the majority of its avenues run from east to west and its streets from north to south? Of course not. It will not be with statistics or mere data about population, topography, climate or economic progress that we are going to present the real physiognomy of a city.

I have spoken of the state of mind the capital of Mexico produces in the visitor: the feeling of imminent disaster or at least of something abnormal about to happen any minute. Parallel to that sense of ill-being—not at all disagreeable, I confess—I feel a sort of cordial irritation at this intractable city that will not let itself be classified, that repels all the adjectives I offer it, appearing before our eyes now modern, now ancient; now enchanting, then immediately sinister; here beautiful and farther on ugly. And in the end what do we decide? We don't. The best thing to do is walk, drink in, absorb Mexico through the eyes, through the pores, in the air we breathe, in the voices we hear, in the smells that penetrate our nostrils— burned gasoline, asphalt dust, *tortillas,* fried foods, fragrance of flowers and herbs. Onward! Perhaps later we shall be able to find the exact word. Meantime, let us be content with jotting down with pencil, in rapid sketches, the images and scenes before us, in order one day, boldly and lovingly, to paint the great mural of Mexico. One day or never.

This bit where Avenida Juárez joins Francisco Madero street resembles Los Angeles or San Francisco. But if we give full heed to details, we shall see immediately that we cannot be in the United States, despite the skyscrapers, the American automobiles running smoothly along the asphalt, the marquees of the cinemas with advertisements of Hollywood films, the *gringo* tourists and a few shops that might well be on Fifth Avenue in New York or State Street, Chicago. The fact is that the stamp of Mexico looms large on everything, unmistakable. It is this type of atmosphere, this tone of sun, a certain family air that establishes kinship between most of these faces, façades, sidewalks, trees. Suddenly, between two buildings of modern lines, like a Franciscan friar flanked by playboys, an imposing colonial house emerges before us, with its rows of windows covered by *rejas* and an old door of carved wood on which with a little imagination we can read the history of a hundred lives and a hundred dramas.

Our desire for simplification will lead us of necessity to say that the ancient city, of colonial flavour, is of a dark tone and with narrow streets; and that the modern is light and has broad streets and avenues. Between the very old and the very modern exists another, typically of the nineteenth century. But it is natural that in many places the three mingle and become confused with each other.

Yonder is the Alameda, a beautiful central park, with its poplars and its ash trees, its benches and its electric light globes bunched on silvery posts. Here in old days burned the bonfires of the Inquisition in which Indians, mestizos and Creoles experienced, before confronting the Creator, a kind of *avant-première* of Hell. At the beginning of this century the Alameda was so dark that its winding paths, shadows and bushes encouraged attacks and crimes. Now, profusely illuminated, during the day it is a tourist attraction and at night a rendezvous for shopgirls and soldiers.

A sign on the front of a restaurant-café catches my eye: *Lonchería.* Here is one of the many neologisms of English origin. It comes from "lunch," which these people, through their inability to pronounce the English "u" sound, alter to "lonch." *Lonchería* is a place that sells quick lunches, so much to the taste of American visitors. I can see inside a fountain with the employees all in white, double-peaked caps on their heads. I have already read and heard other neologisms, like *dona,* the Mexican version of "doughnut."

In the street the barefoot urchins, who beg us for money or want to sell us things, try to say phrases in English that they have learned like parrots to pronounce in their own way. I confess I am disappointed to find that these boys take me for an American. *"Pero con esta cara!"* I say to one. "With this face? Don't you know I'm a Mexican like you?" He smiles, incredulous, and with hand still out he repeats, "Please, *un pesito,* mister."

We cross the street to see the famous House of Tiles. It is a colonial gem. They say it was constructed at the end of the sixteenth century, and for a long time was considered one of the most beautiful residences of the city. The façade is completely covered with blue and white tiles made in Puebla. We enter, expecting to find the noble vestibule of a museum or the freshness of a Spanish patio, but we fall into the warm, perfumed, coruscating confusion of a typically American department store—Sanborn's. May all be for the love of God and the greater glory of Mexico!


I shall not say that Mexico is a city of contrasts because up to now I have never read any description of a city that did not repeat that cliché. Here, as for that matter in nearly all the capitals of Latin America, the most sordid misery rubs elbows with the most ostentatious wealth. It is the millionaire in his Cadillac and the Indian barefoot and walking. I see churches two steps away from brothels. An extremely modern, functional house opposite an eighteenth-century convent.

Near the Alameda one night I pass by the sinister Market of Wreaths. It is a long, zinc-covered shed in front of which are displayed huge wreaths close to six feet tall, for the dead. Close to this sombre market stands the building where prostitutes receive treatment for venereal diseases and where they are regularly inspected. A short distance from this out-patient clinic the severe façade of an old church looms dark.

A few yards from the temple, at the door of a big house of dubious aspect, I catch sight of a woman with imposing bust and thin bare legs, her huge head set on a taurine neck, her hair of an obviously artificial blondeness. The creature is leaning against the doorframe, smoking. I pause on the edge of the sidewalk, pretending to gaze toward the Alameda on the other side of the street, and stand observing the woman. Yes, this is not a prostitute. She is *the* prostitute: a symbol. She must be more than fifty. Her face is of a sickly white that the violet light from the clinic's sign turns livid. Her exaggeratedly darkened eyes seem to speak of nights of insomnia, marijuana and tequila. The carmine roses on her cheeks give her the grotesque air of an aged doll. Her teeth look tiny and dark, as though rotten. Obviously this woman is waiting for a man. And the most incredible thing is that that man will turn up, accost her, and then both will climb the dingy stair that will lead them to a poor room in which possibly there will be an iron bedstead, a kerosene lamp, *a china poblana*, blouse and skirt of heavy cloth, a sailor's photograph (dedicatory date: September, 1920) stuck to the mirror, and the indescribable smell of rooms of that kind—a mixture of musty cellar, perfume of cheap rice powder, stale odour of cigarettes from immemorial males. . . .

I know I ought to resume my stroll because the creature has certainly begun to feel a mistrust of me. A strange fascination, however, holds me to the sidewalk. Women like this I have known only in literature. The prostitutes of my adolescence were likeable beings, usually young or, if old, respectable. They had a sense of dignity, scruples, and an almost rigid ethic. But this one—by the ashes of Cuauhtémoc!—this one merits a poem, a frame, a museum. She inspires in me at once pity and revulsion. I feel I ought to eliminate the revulsion and concentrate on human sympathy. I do not see her as a woman, I cannot even imagine her as a sexual symbol, an object of pleasure. Her traffic must be cold, melancholy and scant. And the proximity of the funeral wreaths gives me the sensation that the poor creature has something to do with death, cemetery and decomposition. All these reflections are distasteful to me, for they seem to be a judgment, a condemnation. I have to attempt some gesture of sympathy. And suppose I addressed a word to her? Suppose I led her to the back part of one of these cafés and got her to talk? I should like to know what she is like, what she thinks, how she lives. A remote preacher of my childhood now outlines himself in my memory and I hear (or do I see?) his voice: "Vessels of iniquity!" Yes, here is an old, broken vessel of iniquity. Perhaps her speciality is to initiate adolescents into love. A sordid function? No. A social service. A meritorious woman! Just now, to avoid the pharisaical attitude, I thought of making an apostolic gesture. And now, fearful of falling into excessive sentimentality, I become cynical. What to do? Where to turn?

The best thing is to go away. I resume my walk. I bear in my mind all the elements of this ensemble: the venereal disease clinic, the wreath market, the brothel, the prostitute and the church.

Almost everything is there: sex, death, trade, stomach, religion. Marx, Freud, Ford and naturally God—God everywhere, clear or implicit. God enveloping all, like a possibility, a certainty, a doubt, a threat or a hope.

Mexico is a country that shakes us and stirs our thought and our emotions deeply. It is a land that does not permit indifference or neutrality. But be that as it may, I hold to my initial decision. I shall not repeat the trite commonplace that this is a city of contrasts. But that it is.


As the Aztec civilization did not know the wheel, its remote descendants who drive automobiles today here in Mexico apparently seek compensation for the many centuries in which their elders did not enjoy the benefits of that prodigious invention. And that is why they drive like desperate men now. I still don't know which is the madder traffic, here or that of Rio de Janeiro.

Here the term *libres* is commonly given to taxicabs, for obvious reasons. But not always are the *libres* free. We have used many of them since we came, and I find it amusing and instructive to talk to their drivers. Mexicans do not talk very much, but I have succeeded in getting some chauffeurs to respond to my questions. The ones I have known up to now are bronzed, hairy, short and taciturn. On one occasion I lack change to complete payment for a ride. With my Brazilian experience I expect an explosion on the part of the *hombre,* but to my surprise I hear him say gently, "It's all right, *señor,* next time you'll pay me the difference. *Hasta la vista!*" And off he goes. And that incident has been repeated many times, so many I am tempted to conclude that profit-taking is not a sin of that class of men here in Mexico.

On another occasion, referring to the confusion of the local traffic, to the dizzy circlings around these *glorietas*, I say to the driver of the car in which I am riding, "To drive a car in Mexico you have to have good nerves."

Without turning his head the man adds, "And character, *señor*."

Not in a *libre*, but in a friend's car, we are traversing residential and suburban zones. In the Polanco quarter (middle class), in houses blistered with reliefs and twisted columns, we find a false colonial ridiculousness. We roll along the Avenida de los Insurgentes, which the Mexicans say proudly is the longest in the world, for it cuts the city from north to south and passes through the University City, twenty-two kilometres from the centre, before it debouches into the highway leading to Cuernavaca.

We get out at the gardens of El Pedregal to see something extraordinary. Things like this can happen only in Mexico, the consequence of a strange combination of cataclysm and inventive talent. Several millennia ago the volcano Ajusco erupted, covering a good part of the capital's environs with lava. For several centuries that volcanic terrain, of a reddish black, was left in the most utter abandonment. Now then: A few years ago a group of Mexican city planners and architects dreamed up an audacious project that ended by transforming the Pedregal into one of the most beautiful and original residential sections I have seen. We find here houses of the most strictly functional style—cubes of cement in pink, green, violet, blue, grey, yellow and red—resting upon a terrain of tragic colour and irregular, distorted shapes. I do not know how they managed to make flowers spring from this rocky soil, but here they are in the most exquisite and capricious gardens, amid artificial fountains and lakes of unexpected designs. There was in this district, as far as I know, no considerable demolition of rock except that strictly necessary to open streets. With courage and imagination they took advantage of all the accidents of the terrain, and certain residences seem to maintain a precarious equilibrium on these miniature mountains, hills and ravines in which the age-old lava has pertrified. The walls of some of the houses were constructed in accord with the technique of the Aztecs. And the streets of the district bear telluric names like Agua, Viento, Sol, Luna, Cráter, Lluvia, Rocío, Fuego—Water, Wind, Sun, Moon, Crater, Rain, Dew and Fire.

This monumental university, also symbolically constructed upon the same plain of volcanic lava, is a proof of how much the tenacity and boldness, the genius and art of the Mexican can do. Some national engineers, nearly all of them young and, I believe, in their majority mestizos, are responsible for it.

Walking now through its streets, gardens, corridors and patios, looking at its impressive buildings, I cannot help feeling the spiritual presence of Francisco Madero, Emiliano Zapata (it matters little that the latter was illiterate), and other heroes of the Agrarian Revolution of 1910, a presence remotely, but in my opinion certainly, responsible for this University City and for other expressions of modern Mexico.

Erected during the government of Miguel Alemán, a man of many qualities and immense defects, it cost three hundred million pesos, or some twenty-five million dollars, and it occupies an area of rather more than 550 acres. An army of workmen laboured on its construction for four years under the direction of 156 architects and engineers.

Nearly thirty thousand Mexicans of both sexes are studying here today, among them young men and women from almost all the other republics of the continent. In the summer months more than two thousand students from the United States take special courses in this university.

The ensemble is of a colour and beauty that leave the observer in a state of poesy. Aztec and Mayan influences are mingled with modern architectural lines in the boldest manner of Le Corbusier, Niemeyer and Wright. I see a *jai-alai* court whose builder found inspiration in the Aztec pyramids. The Olympic Stadium—capacity 110,000—is of a form that recalls nothing else because it is absolutely and disconcertingly original.

The sidewalks, patios and corridors are paved with stones or mosaics in pink and grey. The School of Humanities is in a pavilion nearly a thousand feet long, considered the longest reinforced concrete structure in the world. The administration is housed in a blue building fifteen storeys high. At a short distance from that imposing block of steel and glass, upon a pedestal of volcanic stone, is set the statue of Don Miguel Alemán. "Why that's Stalin!" exclaims my wife on seeing it. She is right. I'll bet the similarity is no coincidence. Possibly the sculptor, a man of Communist sympathies or even a militant member of the Party, has had recourse to this stratagem to set up with impunity a statue of the Soviet leader on the soil of this official university. All he had to do was add more corpulence to Alemán's figure, alter the shape of the head, make the hair and moustache a little heavier, change the carefree countenance of the President of Mexico into the heavy, sombre features of Stalin, for the transformation to be consummated. (Or can it be nothing but the imagination of this writer?)

There is another handsome structure with a mosaic mural by José Chávez. A student courteously informs us that the picture's title is "Spring Revolution." We pass by the large Olympic pool, in the blue water of which young men and women are swimming. It is divided into four parts: one for the Olympic games, the second for water polo and fancy diving, and the other two for beginners.

And that white building with the concave roof? It is the laboratory where cosmic rays are studied. And the elongated one, with pink walls, set on piles? The Veterinary School.

I particularly like the library, with room for more than two million volumes. In its almost windowless thirteen stories it presents to the observer four faces that are parts of a grandiose mural in multi-colored mosaics, with Aztec and Mayan symbols and motifs, and scenes that reflect the good and the bad aspects of the Conquest. It is the work of Juan O'Gorman, and has been the motive for heated arguments, as happened many years ago with our Ministry of Education building in Rio de Janeiro. I stand there for some time gazing at the reflection of its façade on the surface of the artificial lake in front of the library, feeling sharply the contrast between this image of beauty and the violence of this land and this people.

At every moment other pictures on these walls leap to our eyes. Yonder is a painting in relief, by Siqueiros: a long arm, fist clenched. Threat? Promise? Protection?

Only now, with this University City—fabulous combination of forms and colours—only now have the Mexicans erected in this valley a city worthy of the Tenochtitlán which the Conquistadores destroyed.

Anyone who—starting from the Zócalo, from the ruins of the Great Temple and, passing the palaces representative of the colonial period, past the edifices in the French taste of the Porfirian era, and by the skyscrapers imitative of the United States—reaches this university, will have not only gone through four hundred years of the history of Mexico, but also will be rewarded with the privilege of having a luminous glimpse into its future.

Luis Guillermo Piazza is a young Argentine lawyer who fulfills functions here related to my department in Washington. About the functionary I shall say no more, for that is not pertinent to the story. Henceforth I shall designate that *simpático* gentleman from Córdoba by his nickname, Tito. I shall say further that he is a poet and prose artist of sensibility and that his wife, Yoly, is a pretty young lady with honey-coloured eyes and voice. (If anyone thinks a voice has no colour it is because he has never paid real attention to certain voices.)

Yoly and Tito are excellent companions and guides for us in this city they know so well. One night, in the winter garden of the Génève, Tito talks to me about the gigolos of Acapulco, the famous beach we shall not visit because I do not consider it representative of the Mexico that interests us.

Tito tells me that many of the spinster, widowed or divorced women tourists who come to Mexico in quest of adventures find their ideal in Acapulco, in those bronzed mestizo Apollos with whom they dance, drive along the roads in fast, bright-coloured convertibles, and overwhelm with presents.

He recounts the dialogue he once had with one of those gigolos, a slender youth with lifeless eyes and a rich mane of shining black, with fleeting blue lights in it. Let's call our hero Pancho.

Tito and Pancho are sitting at a table on the terrace of a hotel in Acapulco, watching the blue sea. The gigolo is clad in black trousers, his torso snugly covered by a red-and-white striped singlet, a Neapolitan fisherman's cap on his head. From one ear dangles a gold ring. Pancho allows himself the luxury of being bored. He sucks indifferently at his lemonade through the straw, pleating his fleshy red lips. His hands, with long fingers, have well-manicured nails. When the breeze stirs, Tito inhales the perfume coming from his companion. Chanel Number Five.

The Argentine asks, "Is it true, *hombre*, your American lady friend gave you a launch that cost thirty thousand pesos?"

"Sure."

Pancho's patroness is a fifty-year-old Californian, blonde, highly painted, who wears garish clothes. She owns stock in an oil company and is a childless widow.

Tito wants to satisfy a curiosity: "But do you like those *gringo* women?"

The Adonis shrugs, showing his handsome pearly teeth in a smile: "Well, it's a momentary thrill . . ."

"That ring you wear in your ear, is that to impress the tourists?" Pancho turns serious, as though offended.

"No, *señor*. It's a promise I made to the Virgin of Guadalupe. A lot of men make fun of me, think it's trifling nonsense. They don't realize I'm a *muchacho muy religioso*."

His face suddenly lights up. He raises his arm, waving his open hand, palm out. He has caught sight of his *gringa* signalling to to him with red kerchief.

"I'll be with you in a minute, honey!" he shouts in English.

And off goes Pancho, hips rolling, gold trinket glittering in the Acapulco sun.

Some of the Mexican journals, at least on first sight, strike me as rather provincial. Perhaps a more leisurely examination would make me change my mind. I read a daily of the federal capital and am amused by the tone of some items, principally those announcing baptismal or anniversary or wedding feasts. The language of such columns, as well as that of the legends under the photographs, has an innocence that reminds me of the papers of my native city in my childhood. But the innocence stops in the society column, because the rest is not silence but violence. Here, for example, is the summary of a quite expressive item:

"In the town of Xoxocotlán, uncle and nephew had an argument over the ownership of an old image of Christ crucified. The altercation became so bitter that the uncle ended by insulting his nephew's mother, not perceiving in his anger that he was thus insulting his own sister. The young man, blind with rage, seized the wooden crucifix and applied it violently to the older man's skull, so that he fell senseless to the ground, bleeding abundantly."

Now, I find that the bleeding from a head wound is never really abundant. But for the Mexican violence and sense of drama, when one bleeds it can only be in torrents.

Further on I see the news of a woman who set fire to her own clothes and ran out uttering piercing shrieks of pain. In another paper I read that an eight-year-old boy blew out his brains with a revolver bullet while playing "Russian roulette."

In *Ultimas Noticias*, a special edition of *Excelsior*, I find a picturesque page of police news. Under the photograph of a mestizo with the air of a suburban gallant I read these verses:

*Antonio Vázquez García*
*convertido en asaltante,*
*robó ayer a un policía,*
*a un señor, y a un estudiante.*

*Y puesto en ese camino*
*a nadie ya respetó:*
*cuando iba a asaltar a un cura*
*un gendarme lo atrapó.*

Which, paraphrased to English doggerel, might read something like this:

Antonio Vázquez García,
Turning to robbery with intent,
Yesterday victimized a cop,
A student, and then a gent.

Once launched on this carreer,
Indiscriminately he attacked:
When he went to rob a padre,
A bobby caught him in the act.

I go on to another column and see an Indian-like face with broad jaw, snub nose, thick lips fringed with dark down. The legend runs thus:

*Don José Jesús Ramírez*
*es un borracho irredento*
*que de pulque o de cerveza*
*siempre se encuentra sediento.*

*Ayer, con estos calores,*
*la sed le acrecentó;*
*para tener para el trago*
*un fino reloj robó.*

52

Or, unpretentiously as above, it might run in English:
Don José Jesús Ramírez
Is an irredeemable sot,
Ever avid for tequila,
Or pulque, beer—no matter what.

In yesterday's hot weather
His thirst he *had* to scotch;
To get for that the needful
He stole a jewelled watch.

Nearly all the newspapers today carry sensational headlines about the feud between two families in the Isthmus of Tehuantepec. That interests me in a very particular way, for we shall set out for that region in a week.

In Brazil we have many cases like this, in which the rivalry between two clans has degenerated into real war. That is what is happening in the vicinity of Oaxaca, one of the "starred" points on our itinerary, where, according to the papers, "terror rules." Ever since I came I have been following the fighting via the headlines. Today's are horror-fraught:

> *"Number of Hanged Reaches Fifty. Death Reigns in the Isthmus. More Hangings Expected in the Next Twenty-Four Hours. 'An Eye for an Eye, a Tooth for a Tooth' is the Law of Tehuantepec."*

It is said that a Mexican newspaper (but I think this is just anecdote, for I have already seen the story attributed to a Cuban daily) one day published this caption: *"Unnatural Son Murders Mother Without Justified Motive."*

And a model of macabre humour is the line heading the news that a young Mexican had murdered his own grandmother by throwing her into a cauldron of boiling water. *"Superlative Old Woman Soup."*

We are dining with the Piazzas, whose apartment, decorated with excellent taste, is loaded with specimens of Mexican popular art.

We sit down at table for a light meal, since one must eat lightly at dinner in this altitude, if we do not want to feel, all night long, as though we had swallowed a brick.

The maid comes in with the teapot and the cups on a tray. She is a little, bent old woman with skin of old ivory, her face pleated into tiny wrinkles but enlivened by quick, little, rodent's eyes. She greets us, casting inscrutable glances at us. Curiosity? Disdain? Distrust?

When she goes out, Tito tells us about her.

Her name is Macaria. She came from Oaxaca, she is an Indian, and her age no one knows with certainty: she is somewhere between seventy and ninety, probably. She is strong, intelligent, spry and picaresque. At first she served the meal in the country style: she put all the dishes on the table at the same time. When the mistress of the house told her that she preferred them to come one by one in a certain order, "Doña" Macaria listened in half-disdainful silence, hands on hips. When her mistress finished speaking, the Indian woman shrugged and said, "All right, but I didn't know you were all that superstitious."

Another type I have come to know, thanks to Tito, is Ermelindo, a messenger of the office the Organization of American States maintains here.

Short, slender, with humble air, Ermelindo is nearing forty despite a certain youthful look about him, which he will probably still have in his sixties.

The brief story I am going to relate might well bear the title "Ermelindo Against Technology." Late one afternoon at the office Tito shouts to the employee, "Telephone that number you know about to see what time it is."

He was referring to the number that the Mexicans, like the Americans, call for the correct time, which is given by a recording. Now Ermelindo, who never had any liking for this unhuman method, thought it better to telephone to a friend who works in an office in the vicinity of a church.

"Listen, buddy," he said, when he heard the other's voice, "look out the window there and see what time it is on the tower clock." He waited a moment and then, turning to his employer, informed him very seriously, "It's seven fifty-one, señor."

A recording is a dead thing—so Ermelindo must have thought— but his "buddy" Paco is a living creature. And could there be in the universe a more trustworthy clock than the one on the house of Our Lord Jesus Christ?

54

Since we are talking about human figures, I am going to tell one more story here, for I don't know whether I shall have another opportunity to do so.

When I was in Mexico the first time, I stayed at Vianna Moog's home. On the first day, after lunch, my host said, "Since you are a miserable plains-dweller, you must take a siesta after lunch. Here at this altitude it is advisable, at least at first."

I obeyed, for who would refuse to take a nap with so good an excuse in such a good home? The Moogs went out, leaving me to slumber and to dreams, which were many and confused.

How long did I sleep? Twenty minutes, or an hour? I don't know for sure. I only remember that at one juncture a knocking woke me. I leaped out of bed half-dazed and went to open the door. It was the maid:

"*Señor,* a gentleman is looking for you."

"What is his name?"

"I didn't ask."

"Where is he?"

"In the bathroom."

"Eh?"

I did not understand but I asked no further questions, for I knew that in Mexico it is not a good idea always to try to understand people and things. I slipped on a raincoat in lieu of a bathrobe over my convict-striped pyjamas and went to wait for the visitor in the living-room. Five minutes passed, ten, fifteen, and the mysterious character did not appear. The house was plunged in a pre-Columbian silence. (I don't know why I say "pre-Columbian," but it occurs to me as the best way to give some idea of that silence.) I saw on a table a book by a Mexican author and began leafing through it. In it there was an inscription to me. I began to comprehend. The author, a respectable, septuagenarian citizen, had had the courtesy to deliver the book personally. On entering, he had felt suddenly sick and gone into the bathroom. All was explained. Yes, but the explanation, far from calming me, left me more disturbed. Suppose the man had a heart attack? What to do? Call the First Aid? What number? Telephone to the victim's home? But how? What to say?

Well, the thing to do was to wait a little before sending out an alarm. I waited five, ten minutes. Finally, concluding that I, too, was behaving with the phlegm of the Mexican Indian that so intrigued me, I went to the bathroom door. I knocked, at first lightly, with all the respect due to a famous author, aged and ill. No response. I knocked harder. No answer. I turned the knob and imagined the scene in a fraction of a second as I was pushing open the door: the old man lying on his back on the brick floor, eyes glassy, mouth open, body still warm but heart stopped. I could read the headlines in the papers: "Famous Mexican Author Found Dead." Yes, and beside him in the photograph a Brazilian in striped pyjamas under a raincoat.

However, I saw no corpse. What I saw was a living man, sitting on the edge of the bathtub, torso bent forward, elbows on thighs, a necktie hanging from one hand. He was dressed in brown, a gentleman of perhaps forty, with black hair, the look of a mestizo, heavy beard, eyes striated with blood.

I stared at him in silence for some seconds. Who could the fellow be? What did he want? He seemed unaware of my presence. He was breathing with difficulty, fixing on the tiles the stare of a dead fish.

"Well, friend," I asked, "what's happened?"

Not a movement did the stranger make, not a word did he speak. I thought the situation called for a little action. I approached him with that rather paternal attitude of doctors, patted him a couple of times on the shoulder and then, stealthily, slipped my hand down that fat, sweaty back toward his waist, which I carefully felt to see whether he was armed. He was not, and that reassured me. I repeated my questions. Who was he? What did he want? Why was he there? The stranger did not even look at me. The most he would do now was shake his head slowly and growl unintelligible words. At that moment the maid emerged and, more realistic than I, remarked:

"*El hombre está tomado.*"

Yes, must be drunkenness. But it was not from pulque or tequila or mescal, for the gentleman did not smell of alcohol. It could only be marijuana. Whatever it might be, we had to get him out of there. I asked the maid to bring a cup of black, very hot, unsweetened coffee. And while she was in the kitchen preparing it, I kept on trying to start a dialogue. I tried everything. I was fraternal, persuasive, Machiavellian, casual. Then I resolved to speak loudly and harshly, deepening my voice and casting about, out of the corner of my eye, for a bottle of bath salts that might be turned into a bludgeon in case of need.

At last the coffee arrived. I took the cup and, once more with the air of a good Samaritan, approached the stranger. "Come on, take a swallow." I put the cup to his cracked lips. With an abrupt slap the man knocked cup and saucer against the wall, causing a noise that the good acoustics of the bathroom amplified. I lost my calmness. Mysterious voices out of my childhood whispered phrases to me, stories, examples. *One time Zé Bombachudo, in a bar in São Sepé, offered another gaúcho a glass of rum: "Let's have a drink, pal." But the other slapped at the glass and spattered the drink in the face of Zé Bombachudo, who didn't hesitate: he pulled out his dagger and stuck a hole in the ungrateful fellow's craw.*

I gripped the man under the arms and cried, "Let's put an end to this foolishness. Get up!" He got up and leaned on me. We went out of the bathroom and along the hall dancing a convulsive conga. In the middle of the living-room we halted, stepped apart—all this under the bewildered eye of the maid— and faced each other.

"Once and for all, what do you want?" I asked.

And the man spoke for the first time: "My wife," he babbled, beating his chest.

"Your wife is not here. You've mistaken the apartment. This is 868."

Apparently he did not believe me. He still stared at me with lack-lustre, distrustful eyes. He was a muscular type, of dark aspect. And while we stood there in that duel of silence, I thought about the stupidity of the story. Let's suppose that the man, suspecting his wife is deceiving him, comes home unexpectedly, drugged, dashes into the bedroom, and whom does he find there? A strange man in striped pyjamas. He pulls his revolver and puts five bullets into the body. There lie the remains of a Brazilian! And never would the widow and orphans succeed in explaining to friends that it was all just a tragic mistake.

Calmer, I took the man's arm and, enunciating the syllables carefully, emphatically, said, "This is not your apartment, understand? Your wife is not here. Now please get out!"

"You're not Pepe Mejía?"

"No, thank God."

I pushed him with gentle energy—if such a gesture is possible— toward the door. I opened it and invited him, "Come."

And the fellow, in a sudden and unexpected burst of politeness, retorted, "You first."

"After you."

"No. You go first."

It was too much. I gave him a shove that projected him into the hall, and that solved the problem. After closing the door, I saw I had kept the stranger's tie in my hand.

And when Vianna Moog returned later and heard the story, his reaction was precisely what I was expecting:

"Everything happens to you novelists! Subjects and characters offer themselves. We essayists have to sweat hunting for a subject. Now, go be lucky in hell!"

And he let off one of his wholesome guffaws.


To me the word "people" has always been a sort of figure of rhetoric. I have heard demagogues pronounce it in public gatherings thousands of times; as many more thousands I have read it in articles, poems and novels. But never have I *seen* the People. What was it like? Where was it?

I find the answer to these questions here in the capital of Mexico, where the word "people" takes on body, flesh, blood—in short, human expression. I see the People in these streets, I rub elbows with it, I am conscious of its smell, I hear its voice. And it enchants me, awes me, irritates me, fascinates me. It has thousands of faces and is capable of all miseries, all cowardices, all greatnesses, all courage. But here am I almost making a speech, and that was not my intention. What I wanted to do was to say how I saw People in Mexico.

In all the other cities I have visited, what is found in the streets is a middle class or a copy of it, to which are sporadically added a few specimens of the upper classes, the rich, when they deign to step out of their automobiles to walk on the sidewalks with other mortals. In the United States, a country almost wholly a massive middle class—and in this lies its great strength—one never sees People but individuals who by chance pass each other or meet in disciplined groups around tables as members of the same club for the purpose of eating, listening to and making speeches, launching campaigns; in lecture halls to hear the lecturer and then ask him questions; in the stadiums to cheer on the members of their team, as a rule directed by cheer leaders. And there are also the parades, the conventions, the congresses, which operate within disciplined bounds according to rules and with maximum efficiency. And because they are always gatherings of generally well-dressed and well-bred individuals, with more numerous conditioned reflexes than the Latins have, those North American crowds have never deserved, at least in my private dictionary, the collective name of People. People is Mexican.

The American of the north uses his streets only for walking or riding when he goes shopping or is headed for the place where he works, or is returning home from it. The Mexican, like the majority of Latin Americans for that matter, *enjoys* his streets. I would say that the parlour, the room for receiving visitors, of the people of this city is the street. Only parlour? No. Refectory, too. Here they spend the greater part of their time, here they meet, talk, visit and eat. These Indians seem never to sit down at table, at set hours, to eat. They eat in the street, at the pleasure of appetite, at the most unexpected times, and in general standing, alongside the numerous shops in the vicinity.

On these sidewalks, true, we find many tourists—an easily identifiable race. We also see well-dressed men and women going in and out of hotels, cinemas, cafés, restaurants and shops. In this particular Mexico City does not differ from any other capital in the world. American and European automobiles roll along, cause traffic jams in and ornament these streets, and I am almost inclined to say there are more Cadillacs here than in Rio de Janeiro, and may God forgive me for the heresy. I shall venture, too, to affirm that the commerce of this city is as rich and varied as that in São Paulo. I have seen here more and better bookshops than in Washington, Baltimore, Philadelphia or Chicago. I do not remember having found in New York more French books for sale than in the Mexican capital. I have been in restaurants and tea shops decorated with a tastefulness and grace such as I have never encountered in the other capitals of Latin America I have visited. Earlier I have described the University City and recounted the miracle of El Pedregal. The city is full of skyscrapers that defy, on one hand, the taste of a conservative bourgeoisie and, on the other, the perils of this yielding, movable soil.

If I enumerate all these manifestations of progress, economic wealth and good taste, it is not to run away from the People theme but to be able to come back to it with greater tranquillity of mind, for I do not want to leave the impression that the City of Mexico is a redoubt of miserable Indians.

Last Sunday I watched this People enjoying itself in Chapultepec Park. The multitude moving about in the shade of the old cedars and *ahuehuetes* was not made up of Sunday-dressed bourgeois but of people from the humblest class. There was a profusion of infants running and shouting, playing on the slides, on the swings, on the see-saws, hanging on the rings and the trapezes, riding on Shetland ponies, or swarming about the handcarts from which popcorn, roast peanuts, ice-cream, fruit ices on sticks, or spun sugar were being sold. Among them passed Indians with impassive faces, selling multi-coloured balloons. Boats navigated the canal that winds through the park, among the rosebushes and the bougainvilleas on the banks, passing under bridges and through tunnels of greenery. They carried numerous families whose adults bore serious coppery faces as though carved in *tezontle*. But the children were laughing, yelling, jumping and throwing their hands in the air or trailing fingers in the moss-green water. My wife, as I do, feels great tenderness for these little ones. Mexican infants generally have great black eyes of a liquid, velvety lustre, touched by a kind of cloud that is at once tenderness and sadness.

The park of green lawn and bluish shadow was all dotted with colours—the *rebozos*, blouses and dresses of the women and the shirts and waistcoats of the men. Through the number of figures, the movement, the polychromy and the rich expression of life and humanity the scene reminded me of a Brueghel picture, "The Battle Between Carnival and Lent."

I do not remember ever having known a people more human than the Mexican. I must, however, explain that I do not regard "human" as a synonym of "humanitarian." When I say "human" I am referring not only to the good qualities but also—and perhaps principally—to the defects inherent in the nature of men. And that humanity here appears almost entirely naked. The man of the people satisfies nearly all his needs in public, in the streets and parks, without the slightest attempt at concealment, in a sort of brutish innocence. I have seen many an Indian leaning against a tree in hydraulically suspect attitudes. And yonder now is a dark youth of some twenty-plus years hugging and kissing with a fat forty-year-old woman dressed in green. I exorcise the shade of Dr. Sigmund Freud and pass on.

I can see sensuality besmirch the eyes of some of these men who utter *piropos*—gallantries—at the *muchachas* who pass undulating their haunches, in an abundance of hair, breasts and hips. I have the impression that this male sensuality, so ready, quick, revealed in the way one looks at the female as though undressing her, and not rare in words and pornographic gestures, is rather an attribute of the mestizo. I have observed that in this particular the Indian is discreet, perhaps of a less exacerbated sensuality. In the aquarium in which he lives, his sexual activity must be rather cold, like that of the fishes.

And here we are, my companion and I, delightedly crossing this Brueghel picture. But why Brueghel, I ask myself, when this country has a Rivera?

One of Mexico's most curious spectacles is the Sunday market at Lagunilla, in the old part of the city. I visit it with Tito one warm sunny morning and we, full of curiosity, lose ourselves in these streets where on sidewalk and gutter vendors are exhibiting their wares, which run from the most plebeian junk with the rusty look of cast-off, worthless old iron up to procelains, crystal pieces, silver objects and jewels that, at least from a distance and at first sight, wear a certain air of nobility.

There is a little of everything here. It is said that one can fit out, furnish a whole house without needing to go outside Lagunilla. The customers are most varied and, as was to be expected, include everyone from the man of the people, interested in junk, through members of the middle class in search of dishes, silverware, a bathtub, a fruit salver or a lamp, to the member of "café society" in quest of antique silver articles, furniture and pictures, or the artist and the collector on the lookout for "retables," "ex-votos," or crucifixes.

I recall the Maxwell Street market, in the Jewish section of Chicago, which I visited one freezing winter morning in 1941. What a contrast between that fair and this! There, white skins and fair hair predominated. Here, dark faces and black hair. There, fog; here, sun. In Maxwell Street what was most on display was mechanical apparatus, things of practical utility, clothes. Here, decorative objects and images of saints predominate. Obviously the fact that the American market was in a Jewish district explains the almost total absence of saints and angels. What was of better quality in Maxwell Street was showmanship. The vendors were more aggressive, more theatrical, and some of them would bellow speeches even though they were proclaiming uninteresting items. Here everything goes on in silence or in a low voice, in the best Indian manner. The only seller who is talking in this square where we now are is a mestizo in the midst of porcelain pitchers—"Genuine Sèvres, *señores!*"—and oil-paintings and a set of drawing-room furniture in the style of Louis XV. The man has a thin beard, a hat like Cantinflas', a vivid print *gringo* shirt outside his trousers. Tito argues with him over the price of a retable that looks very old. They finally reach an agreement and my companion comes away happy with his find under his arm. I gaze in fascination at an object impossible to transport to Washington or to Porto Alegre: the huge crucifix leaning yonder against the blue wall of a house, with a yellow, long, thin, life-size Christ, the body damaged and a purple-and-gold cloth about the loins.

If I buy that crucifix, I think, where in my house could I set it up? I can imagine the faces of my friends when they see me arrive with the image: the perplexity of the heretics, the suspicion of the religious. . . . And at Customs, what would the inspectors say? How would they classify the queer baggage? For private use? Exempt from duty? Well, useless to waste time in cogitations of this nature, for I am not going to buy the crucifix. I walk away from it as from sinful temptation. I take about ten steps, and turn my head. A beautiful piece. It would look well in an inner patio. I see other, smaller, crucifixes. And a bewildering quantity of images I cannot identify. Peter? Paul? Anthony? Francis? They stand in profile in the gutters, they are of various sizes, of stone, clay, bronze, wood. And around the saints the ground is strewn with pots, frying-pans, cracked and broken sanitary apparatus, lead pipe, books with erotic stories, wrenches, hammers, nails and clocks of ancient aspect. Everywhere bargaining is going on. On all sides, are Indians eating *tortillas, guacamoles* and *tacos.* And in the stalls that sell food are tripes and bits of bacon frying in the hot grease of the pans.

I stop before an attractive collection of ex-votos and read one of them: "My husband Pepito and I were coming from Cholula to Mexico when a scoundrelly bandit attacked Pepito and threw him on the ground poor fellow and was killing him with his dirty knife and I knelt down and prayed for the urgent aid of the Virgin of Guadalupe and in that moment the soldiers came and killed the bandit and saved us from certain and ugly death. Cholula, October 3. Marcolina Gutiérrez." The painting is priceless: the bandit on top of Marcolina's husband with knife at the poor wretch's throat, the woman kneeling, hands in supplication; in the sky, in a luminous oval, the Dark Virgin smiling on the supplicant, while in the distance cavalry soldiers are approaching the scene of the drama at a gallop. All this in bright colours and in drawing extremely appealing for its innocence and its pseudo-realism.

I pick up another ex-voto and with difficulty read the story of still another miracle: "The woman that I loved did not love me and I was dying of love and could not eat and was getting drunk I wanted nothing and was thinking of killing myself with a dagger in my heart which is a great mortal sin and it occurred to me to invoke the aid of the Heart of Jesus and one day without any other explanation Amparito looked at me and smiled at me and we got married in the church and I was saved from the eternal flames of hell. Texcoco. 20 September. Antonio María Picón."

In the picture, in which red predominates, angels with Totonac faces are practically fishing Antonio María out of the flames of hell. In one corner Jesus is smiling as He points out to His heart, also in flames. In the distance a volcano—possibly Popocatépetl—is vomiting smoke and fire up to a greenish sky where a woman's image, Amparito, without the slightest doubt, appears, contemplating the scene with eyes so hard and so evil an expression that the observer gets the net impression that she preferred her suitor to kill himself and be burned up in the bonfire of the Devil.


A north-eastern Brazilian voice has been filling a certain classroom in University City this last year. It is the voice of Aurélio Buarque de Holanda, who is giving a course on "Brazilian Culture" under the auspices of the Brazilian government. I can imagine him on the dais, with his great head that might have been painted by Franz Hals, delivering a dissertation upon our literature, waving his arms and shaking his blond mane, not only *telling* his class but acting, assisting the word with gesture and onomatopoeia, achieving the miracle of making his students not only know what Machado de Assis was like, and what Carlos Drummond de Andrade is like, but how the former looked and the latter still does. This man from Paraíba, to whom Rio Grande do Sul owes a critical edition of its greatest teller of tales, Simões Lopes Neto, made with affectionate care; this philologist who has succeeded in removing the staleness and giving colour to Philology—this man is one of the most upright intellectuals I know.

To find him here with his wife, under this Mexican sky, is one more agreeable surprise that this trip is affording me.

Professor Aurélio is nearly always escorted by Marina, a kind of guardian angel, but a realistic angel with her feet on the ground, a modern angel who knows how to be, despite her feminine grace and charm, at once secretary, accountant and memory of the Professor. With the Buarque de Holandas and the Piazzas—a group communicating within itself in a sort of lingua franca, a mixture of Spanish and Portuguese that might well be called "Portunish"—we visit the Plaza Garibaldi one night. It is in the ancient part of the city. Without either trees or benches, it looks to me like merely a poorly lighted street. Like almost everything in this old zone of the city, it has an air of the market-place. I would say that it is a market of songs. Here are found traditionally the professional musicians, groups of three to six with one or more singers, known as *mariachis*, which must be a corruption of the French word *mariage*, since in the time of Maximilian whenever there was a wedding it was customary to hire such groups to gladden the occasion. They are generally dressed in *charro* costume: dark bolero jacket, embroidered, a red neckerchief of butterfly type, dark trousers tight on the legs, like riding breeches; on the head the famous conical high-crowned *sombrero* with broad, fancifully bedecked and embroidered brim. The *charro* is, in the final analysis, the show-off. We have seen many of them about the city at the most unexpected hours of the day, and always with guitars under their arms.

We find several automobiles with tourists here, parked along the narrow sidewalks. Beside each car a group of *mariachis* is playing and singing. The narrow, short street is full of the sounds of instruments, string and wind. Yes, and of human voices—those warm, beautiful Mexican voices that seem made of *tortilla*, avocado pear and sun. Men and women are strolling among the cars and the singers, they stop here and there, give money to the *mariachis* and go on to listen to other groups. We enter for a moment one of the many cabarets of the zone. Its name is "Guadalajara por la Noche," or "Guadalajara at Night." A glance around suffices to see that the place is not genuine, but prepared especially for the *gringo* tourist with all he expects to find here, after a thousand Hollywood films on Mexico. These *charros* in black and red, well-combed and shaved, are false. On their songs is an artificial varnish. The genuine ones are outside yonder with their frayed clothes, their rough Indian-like faces, their old instruments, their pure songs and their *dignity*. We go back to them. Tito leads us into El Tenampa, the most famous and authentic of the Garibaldi Square cafés. The room is not very large nor is the ceiling very high. The tables, between two wooden screens and the wall, are nearly all occupied. At great cost we obtain one of them, and after much struggle we reach it and sit down. In El Tenampa pandemonium reigns. Imagine this impossible thing: four, five or six groups of *mariachis* playing with all their might at the same time in this enclosed space, airless and overflowing with people. I see some tourists here, but the majority of the habitués of El Tenampa—indeed, it is obvious—are people of the country. Yonder is a thick-moustached Mexican with his black, rich, shining hair, already casting tender, viscous glances at the women of our group. In reprisal—but with all due caution—we stare at the Mexicans' women, brunettes with much-painted eyes, with mouths that look like open wounds. They are wearing rayon dresses in vivid colours—flag green, canary yellow, electric blue. They are females with imposing heads and generous bosoms—the kind of females one imagines the Amazons must have been, but when they get up to go to the ladies' room (Heavens, what must the ladies' room in El Tenampa be like?) they betray their real stature: short little women with normal bust, yes, but with short legs.

The north-easterner is a man who, wherever his physical presence may be, is psychologically always in his native land. He carries with him his landscape, his soil, his memories. Mestre Aurélio relates to us the history of the guitarists of the north-east. Tito orders tequilas. If I wanted to stir up trouble and get lynched, to order a Coca-Cola here would be enough. I order pulque and cast a proud glance at the figure of Emiliano Zapata painted over there on the wall, mounted on his white horse, in a field of cacti and maguey.

The pandemonium continues. A *mariachi* ensemble approaches us: three guitars, a cornet, a violin and a kind of giant guitar. We ask them to sing for us the songs most in vogue. The group practically forms a wall of glistening faces, *sombreros* and torsos in the attempt to isolate our table from the rest of El Tenampa.

One of them announces that they are going to sing "Cucurrucucu, paloma." The guitars, standard and over-size, burst into the rhythm of the *huapango* song, while the violin sketches the melody and the cornet embroiders on it. The soloist, eyes veiled in melancholy, in the grieving voice of a man deceived, sings the lyric, relating how there was a certain dove at whose voice heaven itself trembled. And then comes the refrain:

*Ay-ay-ay-ay-ay!* cantaba,
*Ja-ja-ja-ja-ja!* reía,
*Ay-ay-ay-ay-ay!* lloraba,
*De pasión mortal moría.*

*Ay-ay-ay-ay-ay!* it sang
*Ha-ha-ha-ha-ha!* it laughed,
*Ay-ay-ay-ay-ay!* it wept,
Of fatal love it was dying.

In the intervals between one verse and another, while the guitars strummed muted, the singers launched into the air their false lament, in prolonged cries: *Ay . . . ay . . . ay . . .*—in a falsetto tremolo: *huy . . . huy . . . huy . . .*—in a syncopated plaint that was like the howl of the coyote at night on the northern prairies. How they suffer! What sadness in these songs, in these voices, these glances! In the end it is revealed that *esa paloma no es otra cosa que su alma*—that dove is nothing other than his soul. And the refrain, the laments, the cries and convulsive tearfulness return, until the final chord from the guitars. We applaud and slip six pesos into the leader's hand.

"Another!" begs Aurélio.

" 'Prisoner Number 9,' " says the singer.

Mentally I rub my hands in anticipatory glee. I recall a dramatic Argentine song—"Convict Number 14"—that in times gone by my close friend Ernani Fornari used to sing to the guitar in half-serious, half-ironic style, in his beautiful tenor voice.

"Prisoner Number 9" is also a *huapango.* The melody has a tragic beauty that matches the lyrics well. The priest is going to hear the confession of the condemned man because *antes del amanecer la vida le han de quitar*—before dawn his life they are to take; for the man *mató a su mujer y a un amigo desleal*—has killed his wife and a faithless friend—and is going to be shot. In my imagination the *charro* costume of the soloist is transformed into the zebra-striped uniform of a prisoner, with Number 9 on his chest. I see him kneeling beside the priest, saying in his crushed voice: *"Los maté, sí, señor*—I killed them, yes, indeed, and if I were to be born again I should kill them all over again. Father, I do not repent, nor does eternity scare me, I know the Supreme Father in Heaven will judge us." It seems everything is going to depend on God's decision, but no! Prisoner Number 9 moans: "I am going to follow them up, I'm going to hunt them down in the beyond!" This being so, the pursuit of the lovers is going to continue in Eternity, which bothers and saddens me so that the only remedy is to drink my pulque, which tastes like sour milk. I look at Mestre Aurélio and imagine him in the leather hat of a north-eastern Brazilian bandit. Stories of Lampião, the famous outlaw of a quarter-century ago, visit my mind. Parallels sketch themselves. I drink some more pulque. Zapata says goodbye to a woman in El Tenampa's mural. Guitars whine. The cornet traces arabesques in the heavy atmosphere of smoke and emanations from glasses and bodies. Among the tables a lean old man wanders, offering something or other for sale, a box of polished wood in his hands. I beckon to him, he comes over, and, when I ask what he is offering, I discover the man is "selling electric shocks." The unexpectedness of the revelation and the innocence of the idea touch me. I take a shock, what else can I do? It costs fifty *centavos*. The little box resembles one in the consulting room of my grandfather, who was a doctor. I take another as a tribute to the Old Man and to my childhood. And yet another in honour of Zapata. I give six more pesos to the singers and ask them for another tragedy. " 'Three Days,' " announces the leader of the *mariachis*. The singer begins:

*Tres días sin verte, mujer,*
*tres días llorando tu amor!*

Three days without sight of you, dove
Three days of weeping for your love.

Six serious faces, as if all they were singing were God's own truth. Six broad, dark sad faces. A peso for each one.

*Hace tres días que no sé de ti—*
*Dónde, dónde estás, con quién me engañas?*
*Dónde, dónde estás, qué estás haciendo?*

Three days I've had no word of you—
Where are you now, who's now your lover?
Where are you now, what can you be doing?

Stimulated, I wish to step out in defence of the Mexican woman. Now that fellow, just because he has not seen his loved one for three days, imagines she is deceiving him with another man. What lack of confidence in his "malehood," if there is such a word. The poor thing is probably at home embroidering, cooking, making *tortillas* or lace. I discuss with Tito the lyrics of the Argentine tango, in which lovers or deceived husbands are always weeping over their sorrows, drowning their hurt in drink, promising to kill or die. Can it be the Spanish heritage that Mexicans and Argentines have in common? The whole thing smells to me of the Middle Ages and of the Arab world. At heart what those jealous, suspicious men want is to keep their women at home, locked up with seven keys and faces covered.

And I—who have often been irritated listening to the words of Brazilian songs in which the singer brags of his amorous conquests; I, who have never regarded sympathetically the philosophy of our sambas—"Work? Not I, not I!"—now, confronted with these Hispano-American jeremiads, with this eternal whimpering of deceived lovers, am inclined to view our songs with more sympathy.

The *mariachis* leave.

Two "artists" come up and sketch the caricatures of the members of our group. They succeed in getting us to pay them for their work, but they do not succeed in convincing us of the likeness of the portraits. Another such artist asks for the names of the ladies with us, and with their names designs figures: women with parasols, flowers, herons. The pesos keep passing from our pockets to those of El Tenampa's artists. In a corner sleeps an old man who sells miniature *charro* hats. We buy several, for tonight we must do a bit of everything. A new group of *mariachis* approaches. Now the grey-haired, big-bellied, fifty-year-old singer says life is worth nothing, since life begins in tears and in tears it comes to an end. Maybe so, but I refuse to agree with him. Between one bout of tears and the other many a good thing comes about. Mexico, for example. These friends. . . . Your health! I raise my glass to Zapata. The cornet traces in the air the golden notes of a *ranchera*. Suspect faces gaze at us from their tables. A drunken man falls to the floor. The waiters carry him outside with a certain tenderness and in silence. Zapata is going to depart for the mountains. He will not return from that trip—I know, I read it in history. They are preparing an ambush for him. I don't trust General Carranza. That face doesn't fool me.

The coyotes of El Tenampa lift their bronze snouts into the air and howl *huy . . . huy . . . huy . . . huy . . . huy*—they sob *ay . . . ay . . . ay . . . ay . . . ay*—they whinny and I pray to God, in a very personal talk, never to let Mexico change. Yes, let her progress, become rich, solve the problem of misery, of hunger, of the distribution of land, but never let her lose her style, her colour, her character. Now you can go, Emiliano Zapata. As in the best of the *huapangos,* one day we shall meet on the steppes of Eternity. *Adiós!*


We go out into the night, which is still full of songs and the sobs of guitars. We pay a quick visit to the Salón México, which inspired Aaron Copland, and then look into several dark little night spots. Once more in the street, I look at my watch: eleven forty-five. Tito suggests we end the evening in a variety theatre. Mestra Aurélio hesitates an instant, but the women, voting en masse in favour of the idea, decide our fate.

In Mexico City, as in almost all the principal cities of the Americas, there is nowadays a sort of reawakening of interest in good theatre. In every nook and cranny "little theatres" are to be seen, where groups of professionals, amateurs or semi-professionals stage modern or classic pieces. Priestley and Shakespeare, Alarcón and Tennessee Williams, Molière and Giraudoux are performed. Two days ago we saw a delightful play by a Mexican author—*Hoy invita la guerra,* or *War Extends an Invitation Today*—the plot of which is based on facts and characters in the history of Mexico. We are eager, my companion and I, to see the popular theatre.

We find good seats in a playhouse whose name I do not catch and, when the curtain rises, to the sound of a tiny orchestra that reminds me of the ones in the Recreio Theatre in Rio de Janeiro in the old days, we ask ourselves—with no one able to answer—what play are we going to see? Tito whispers that it is a revue. The title? He doesn't know.

A Mexican revue does not differ much from ours. There is always the *compère,* the man who accompanies the *compère,* the soloists, the chorus, the curtain-raiser. The type of humour is the same, about the level of a burlesque show, with the pepper of eroticism seasoning the sly allusion. What we are seeing today has a disjointed feel of something improvised. The chorus girls are ugly, unshapely, they dance badly and show on their legs the traditional red spots that may equally well be the results of casual beatings or the marks of mercury. In some dance numbers one immediately notes the inevitable American influence brought here by way of the cinema. In the sketches one gets the impression that either the artists have not learned their rôles or they are improvising along the general line of the story. A *muchacho* imitates to perfection singers like Agustín Lara, Pedro Vargas and others. Clavillazo, a comedian of the Cantinflas type, offers a few moments of humour. In the sketches there are satiric sallies and the target of the criticism is generally the police, the incompetence and venality of its representatives. In the sequence of the tableaux a certain unevenness can be noted: the passable, the bad and the worst rotate. The orchestra is metallic, rather nasal and not infrequently goes one way while the singers and dancers go another. As was to be expected, the show does not lack a baritone who sings seriously and in a throbbing, half-operatic voice of the "Granada" or the "Carib Prayer." And the best number of the evening so far is offered us by a group of *mariachis*.

The spectacle of the audience, however, entertains me still more than the one on the proscenium. Babies in arms are wailing, matrons bare their breasts in the dim light and feed their infants. From time to time a little two- or three-year-old starts running down the aisle among the groups of chairs. Not a protest is heard. The thing seems to be a part of the show, or a tradition. Some bring food to the theatre and at any time unwrap their *tortillas* odorous of onion and begin eating. To be sure, this will never happen in the beautiful modern theatre in Insurgente on the marquee of which is a mural by Diego Rivera. But in this common theatre and in others we later visited, they do. Rough jests spout from the floor, asides, *piropos*—flirtatious, spicy compliments—to the woman who sings popular songs. The applause is longer and more generous than I expected of these ordinary laconic, introverted folk.

In another theatre, on another night, we see Agustín Lara, with his damaged, quail-like face, a deep scar running the length of one cheek from top to bottom, all this contrasting with the elegance of his dress. He directs his orchestra, he sings with twisted mouth and rasping voice several of his own compositions. Like his compeer Pedro Vargas, Agustín Lara is one of the idols of the Mexican people. Then La Negra comes on, an enormous mulatto woman with volcanic breasts, clear strong voice, enlivening a scene from the Caribbean. As the fashion now is the *cha-cha-cha*, it is natural that we get it in massive doses in these variety shows, danced by the chorus girls and a group of *muchachos* with rather dubious gestures. One of the great tableaux in this other show has for its star a *gringa*, a blonde American with blue eyes, a Nordic goddess mislaid in this Aztec world.

And all this—revues, actors, audience—all this entertains us because it is one expression of Mexico we are seeking to know, always fleeing the spots prepared for tourists, full of a fake picturesqueness, a counterfeit local colour.

That these people love music particularly is immediately perceived. The most applauded numbers are those of the *mariachis*. And performances can never have a fixed schedule because their duration varies according to the requests for encores.

But who bothers with schedules in Mexico? I keep thinking that the best symbol for the Latin-American concept of time is Salvador Dalí's melted watches in his picture called "The Persistence of Memory."

Vianna Moog, who has just arrived, is now standing before me in the lobby of the Génève. After more than a year's stay in this stimulating metropolis he is pregnant with theories about Mexico. We even discuss the possibility of writing four-handed a book on the country. He would take over the ideas and I the images. To me would fall the job of describing persons, animals and things. To him, the task of interpreting them. We pause to imagine the result of that marriage.

"Probably a monstrosity," says the essayist.

"*Quién sabe?*"

We go out. Moog is going to take me for a leisurely drive about the city in his car. We roll along the Paseo de la Reforma, which has six *glorietas*, or circles, each with its monument.

"Have you noticed that no statue to Cortés exists in Mexico?" asks my friend.

"Nor to Maximilian."

Just as for this untamed people the North American is the *gringo*, so the Spaniard is the *gachupín*.

They say that fifteen years after the death of Hernán Cortés his ashes were brought from Spain and buried in Mexico. On the occasion of a revolt in 1823 Indians attempted to destroy the tomb of the Conquistador, on account of which his remains were taken to the church of Jesus the Nazarene.

We are now rounding the *glorieta* in the centre of which is the statue to Cuauhtémoc, last of the Aztec emperors. It is said that Cortés tortured him in the vain effort to extract the revelation of the hiding place of the imperial treasure. Every year on August 21, anniversary of that shameful deed, the Indians come to dance around the statue.

After a long ride which took us out Insurgentes and brought us back to the centre, we passed the monument to Carlos IV, known in the city as "El Caballito" or "the little horse." It is in the Paseo de la Reforma, in a circle where the Avenida Juárez begins. It is an equestrian statue, and thousands of tourists have jotted down in their notebooks the guides' words about the monument made from a single block of bronze; weight, thirty tons.

I recall that a taxi driver told me, a few days ago, pointing to the image of Carlos IV: "We got nothing to do with that one. He's a foreigner."

I have noticed in this rarefied air of the valley of Anáhuac a touch of xenophobia, which at bottom may be an aggressive form of patriotism.

"Then why don't you folks take the statue out of there?" I ask.

"But what about El Caballito, then?"

El Caballito? Only much later do I comprehend the meaning of the question. Carlos IV means nothing, but the horse is a part of the folklore of the city. And really a handsome sculpture (I am referring to the horse, not the monarch). The Mexicans speak of it with a certain fondness. The statue has come to be, among other more subtle things, a landmark. *"Mira, hermanito, te espero hoy a las cuatro al pie del Caballito"*—"Look, old fellow, I'll expect you today at four o'clock at the foot of El Caballito." Or, *"Mi casa queda a media cuadra del Caballito"*—"My house is just half a block from El Caballito."

Then we pass the horrifying monument to Juárez, a masterpiece of bad taste. That Indian, so serious, silent and Spartan, deserved a simpler homage. There he is in the Alameda, sitting in his chair, in a kind of parody of the monument to Lincoln, the *gringo* he so much admired. Behind Don Benito rises a figure I cannot discern clearly, and an angel with wings spread, in the act of crowning the hero.

The chair rests upon a tall pedestal of white marble, much ornamented, and in the centre of a gallery of Doric columns. Mounting guard on the pedestal are two lions, seated but with heads lifted in the alert look of beasts on the point of leaping at any moment to the defence of the statue. The whole seems a rather pompous mausoleum; an idea, this, accentuated by the gilded wreaths and garlands in relief on the marble.

Moog now delivers a dissertation on the great Mexican dichotomy: Indianism and Hispanism. And, absent-minded, he turns the wrong way into a one-way street.


At the time when Hernán Cortés and his soldiers disembarked in Mexico the tribes that formed the Aztec empire were living under the sign of magic. It is true that already some technical skills were cropping out among them, and something that might be called beginnings of an indigenous science, but in truth magic thinking dominated everything. Thus anthropophagy is explained, which among the Aztecs was purely ritual. They believed that in devouring the flesh of the individuals sacrificed to their ferocious gods they acquired all the qualities the victims possessed, and that were considered inseparable from the bodies of the same. There was another ceremony that wonderfully illustrates the attitude of the Méxicas toward the mystery of the universe. On the last night of each period of fifty-two years all fires were extinguished, and the crowds of people moved in solemn processions to a sacred place where—in order to prevent the fountain of life, the fire that lies in the womb of the earth, from being forever extinguished, and to give new light and vigour to the sun, the moon and the stars—the priests, with tremulous hands and hearts throbbing irregularly with apprehension, sought to produce fire by means of friction. But woe to them! woe to the people! woe to the world!—if they failed to strike the sacred spark. That would constitute a terrible presage, the sign of the death of the sun, of the extinction of the Great Fire, of the end of all life.

The Aztec religion was lacking in moral objectives, for ethical behaviour and spiritual perfecting belonged to the realm of social customs. It was a religion without Heaven or Hell to reward or punish the individual in the life beyond the grave in accord with his comportment on earth. One of the priests' functions consisted in attracting by means of prayers, sacrifices, offerings and other symbolic acts, the beneficent forces of Nature toward human existence and exorcising the maleficent ones. It was logical then, or rather magical, that the Aztecs should personalize the elements of Nature.

Before, however, speaking more extensively about the theology and the cosmogony of the tribes of the Valley of Mexico, it will be interesting to examine, even though as briefly as from an airplane in flight, or—less anachronistically—as glimpsed by an eagle in flight, the political, social and economic organization of the empire that Cortés conquered. I am convinced that, to understand the Mexican of today, it is indispensable to have an idea not only of his pre-Cortésian past but also of what the tremendous, bloody drama of the Conquest was.

# 4. Aspects of the Aztec World

Anthropologists do not agree about the age and the origins of the primitive peoples of the American continent. There are some who declare that the tribes populated America from 15,000 to 4,000 years before Christ, having come—and on this detail there are fewer divergences of opinion—from the Asiatic breeding-place across what is now called the Bering Strait. They settled first in the territory today belonging to the United States and from there moved on to Mexico and Central America.

The first peoples of the Valley of Mexico of which we have information lived there a few centuries before and a few centuries after the birth of Christ, and on a level that the anthropologists term Middle Culture, representing a mid-point between the tribes of hunters and the ritualistic civilizations endowed with more developed social and technical systems. Those peoples had their towns or cities, they lived principally on agriculture, they knew how to make artifacts from stone, bone, wood and clay, and it seems indubitable that they also knew the use of fire. They were ignorant, however, of the wheel, glass, wheat, barley, rye and—except in a very restricted area of Central America, where a special system of hieroglyphics was employed—they did not possess a system of writing. The American Indians were acquainted with the pig and the ox only after these animals were brought over to America by the Europeans.

In pre-colonial Mexico there were, not one, but many indigenous civilizations, among which the most important were the Maya, in Yucatan, the Tarasca, in Michoacán, the Mixtec-Zapotec, in Oaxaca and Vera Cruz, the Aztec, in the region of Mexico City, and the Toltec, earlier than the Aztec, which left impressive vestiges in Teotihuacán.

The Aztecs were the last of the Nahua tribes to reach the Valley of Anáhuac, where they established themselves, dominating almost all Central America until the arrival of the Spanish Conquistadores. At first they lived in a state of barbarism, but gradually became civilized under the influence of remnants of the Chichimecs and of the Toltecs, who had preceded them in the possession of that land.

Theoretically the Aztec State was a democracy. Each tribe forming the nation looked after its own affairs and interests and had a representative on the Supreme Council, to which was granted the power to elect a chief. To the latter fell the final word in secular and religious matters. In case of war the council named a chief especially for the purpose.

The individual was a member of a family, and the latter in its turn fitted into a *capulli*, or clan. A certain number of clans—usually twenty—formed a tribe.

Education and social life in the Aztec State were taken very seriously and rigorously planned, as in the totalitarian states of our times.

The child at birth was washed and swaddled by the midwife. At the moment of birth the sacred fire was lighted to propitiate one of the oldest of the Aztec gods. The first problem was to discover whether the day on which the baby was born was favourable or unfavourable, of good or ill omen. The father would run to the home of the priest, who, after consulting the *Tonalamatl*, the Book of Destiny, would give him the good or the bad news. Only four days later was the birth of the infant celebrated and the child given a name. The ceremony consisted in scattering foods and pulque on the sacred flames in an offering to the God of Fire. Then came the relatives and friends with gifts for the newborn. Was it a boy? They gave him toy weapons and instruments, and the father had to place them in his son's tiny hands and guide his movements in the simulacrum of work or combat. Was it a girl? They would bring her miniature domestic instruments, and there the baby would lie, aided by her parents, pretending she was weaving or spinning.

It was the custom to give male children the name of the day when they were born, in accord with the calendar. They were also given the name of some famous warrior or of an animal. Girl babies were generally given names composed with the ending—*xochtl*, which means "flower."

Since in our day we try so insistently (though full of doubts) to discover, in the light of psychoanalysis or of folklore, the best way to bring up our children, it will be interesting to take a quick look at the Aztecs' ideas about child psychology. They believed that with infants under nine the only recommendable method was that of pure admonition. After that age corporal punishment was necessary to discipline the disorderly, the idlers or the recalcitrant. These chastisements were richly varied. The most common was to prick the child's hand with a maguey thorn. If the fault committed called for more severe castigation, the child was tethered completely stripped in a mudhole. And if the little wretch did not mend his ways, he was sent out at night to endure, naked and alone, the intense cold of the mountains. It is generally believed, however, that the Indians treated their children with benevolence, rarely having recourse to these punishments.

At the age of fifteen or sixteen, boys before assuming posts of responsibility in the community life, were sent to the *telpuchcalli*, the House of Youth, a school supported by the clan, and there received civic and religious instruction and learned a trade, as well as how to handle weapons and work the land. If the lad should be destined for the priesthood, they sent him to the *calmecac*. Girls were usually trained in domestic tasks.

At twenty, men were ready for marriage. Women reached marriageable age at sixteen. The marriage was arranged by the parents of the bride and groom, after prior consultation with those directly interested in the matter. And just as today a prenuptial examination is made to test the rhesus factor, in the time of the Aztecs the priest tried to ascertain whether the fates of the couple harmonized or not. This problem resolved, the matter was again discussed at great length by the parents and, as was natural, relatives and close connections of the families took part. First of all, it was proved that the degree of relationship between the boy and the girl was not in conflict with the Aztec law, which, as ours does, condemned incest. The groom's father then sent two old members of the clan to carry presents to the bride's father, who, according to tradition, had to reject the proposal of marriage. The *comadres*[1] entered on the scene and leisurely consultations with both parties followed. What dowry would the bride bring? More or less than the groom?

The wedding night arrived. One of the marriage-makers had to load the bride on his back and carry her over the threshold of her future husband's house. The party began with speech-making. Nearly all the guests had their say. (That curse of numerous speeches, long and flowery, was to weigh heavily upon Latin America through the coming centuries.) At last came the hour for the nuptial ceremony proper. The tips of the bride's and groom's cloaks were tied together in a simple and beautiful symbolism. *Comadres* and *compadres* once more took the floor and strung out their long homilies, congratulations, advice and auguries. The pulque started on its rounds. They all knew that drunkenness was tolerated only on ceremonial occasions, and that even on those occasions it was not a good idea to overdo the intoxicating beverage. According to tradition, there are various degrees of intoxication in relation to the gods of the maguey or to the animal connected with it, the rabbit. When one says that a drunkenness is of fifteen or twenty rabbits, it is understood that the person got sufficiently merry to become good company. When it reaches four hundred rabbits it is considered a complete intoxication.

Let's imagine the scene. Amid the tangle of excited conversations and pulque fumes the newlyweds steal glances at each other. They know they can consummate the physical union only after a retreat of four days in which they will be obliged to fast and do penance. It is possible that, in this moment of anxiety or irritation, encouraging ideas may be passing through the bridegroom's head. He knows that his people's law accepts divorce and permits polygamy, although it guarantees priority to the first wife, and to her children the exclusive right to the paternal inheritance. He also knows that, if on one hand custom demands that the damsel be chaste and the wife faithful to her husband, on the other it tolerates the latter's having love affairs with other women, provided he

---

[1]Godmothers and godfathers of the infant are *comadres* and *compadres* to each other and to the parents, who are also *comadre* and *compadre* to the others. Sometimes the term is applied as between intimate friends, cronies.

respects married ones, without his breaking any social law. What other thoughts can be passing through the groom's head at the hour of marriage, reminding him of his privileges as a man? Perhaps he is thinking of the possibility of one day having many concubines, like certain powerful chieftains. Or of the right he enjoys of abandoning his wife, with the approbation of the law, in case she fails to give him children.

Now he is going to cultivate his family's lands. He will have his slaves and, through services to his tribe, he may some day be clan chieftain. It is not only the brave warrior, the bold hunter and the skilled artisan who enjoys prestige in the community. The tillers of the soil, like him, also are held in popular esteem.

Yes, it is very good to be a man! And thinking thus, the bridegroom takes another goblet of pulque and, with good reason, passes the thirty-rabbit mark.


The Aztec religion—it is well to repeat—was not concerned with matters of moral order and never invaded the field of ethics. The great sin, the grave crime, was the one committed against the social order. The punishment in such cases was determined by custom, so that among the Méxicas human behaviour was regulated by tradition.

An anti-social act might bring death or loss of civil rights to the one who perpetrated it. In many cases the transgressor was expelled from the community that gave him protection and means of subsistence, and that separation generally meant not only an insupportable loneliness but very possibly his physical liquidation at the hands of enemies or in the claws of wild beasts. The social order, then, existed for the benefit of the tribe and the duty of every man was to maintain it at all costs.

In our capitalist and highly competitive modern society, in which what someone has called "market nature" holds sway, the struggle takes place principally over the gaining of profit and the accumulation of material goods. In the Aztec society disputes arose more in the domain of public service, in the winning of hierarchic positions. It was natural that this competition should generate bloody struggles among members of the same clan, thirsty for political and social prestige. In such cases a special tribunal was appointed to settle the conflicts.

Rarely or never was a crime punished with prison. Crimes of

sacrilege were scarce, for who would dare rob a temple or blaspheme, knowing that with it he would call down infallibly the ire of the gods upon himself and the community?

Homicide was punished with the death penalty, even if the victim were a slave. And here a parenthesis is indicated, to explain that the prisoners of war were slaves (those who had some skill in the arts of peacetime, the rest were sacrificed), as were the members of the tribe itself who had been sold by their parents or who were fulfilling some penalty. Whole families of slaves existed, whose representatives were easily identified in the streets by their wearing a bar of wood fastened to the neck, like a yoke. Traitors and rebels also were executed, and the thief was forced to work as a slave until he made restitution for what he had stolen; not infrequently they made him pay by other means double the value of the theft, in which case one part went to the victim and the other to the clan treasury.

How did they punish the alcoholics? Tolerance for drunkenness in general depended on the social position and the age of the consumer of pulque. But often, when after having reached the four-hundred-rabbit mark in his libations a tribal member appeared in some public place, he risked being stoned or beaten to death by his fellow citizens, a circumstance, this, foreseen and tolerated by the law. Lynched also was the man caught stealing things in the public market. To steal maize was an ugly crime, principally when the theft was committed in the field itself, in which case the criminal was executed.

Defamers and slanderers had their lips cut off, and sometimes their ears, too. Adultery was punished with a severity that might lead the adulterers to the death penalty. Those who committed incest were hanged, and the most bestial of castigations was meted out to sodomites. Another serious crime that cost the guilty man his life was that of impersonating a high authority. And—a curious thing in a society so dominated by magic thinking—any person who practised acts of witchcraft or black magic was implacably condemned to death.


The Aztec economy was as simple as its social structure. Whence came the produce that supported the people? From the earth. Then the earth ought to belong to the tribe and not to the individual. The tribal council distributed tracts of land among the clans, whose chiefs in their turn divided them among the families according to the needs of each.

The basis of the Aztec economy was agriculture, and maize was its principal product. Several varieties of cotton, maguey, beans and squash were also cultivated, as well as sage, green and red chili peppers, and the sweet potato. And many of the fruits most popular among the Aztecs—like the avocado and the tomato—became known to the rest of world only after the Conquest. The maguey was especially useful because from its sap pulque was made, an alcoholic beverage of nutritive properties, and with its fibres ropes and cloths of great durability were woven.

From the hot zone where Vera Cruz is today they carried up to the highlands pineapples, vanilla beans and cacao beans with which the Aztecs made chocolate, which they esteemed highly. From those lowlands bathed by the waters of the Gulf came also rubber resins to Tenochtitlán to be burned as incense in religious ceremonies, and bitumen, used as adhesive and as an ingredient in the ink with which the Indians painted their bodies.

The Aztecs were rather poor in domestic animals. They raised several kinds of dogs, among them one edible variety. But among the farmyard animals there was none more important than the turkey. Another source of food for the Aztecs was game. In the apogee of Tenochtitlán the deer formerly abundant in the Valley of Mexico were already growing scarce, but there is no reason to believe that migratory birds had ceased appearing periodically; so it is almost certain that the Tenochcas' table fare was enriched from time to time with a roast goose, duck or partridge.

In an earlier chapter of this book it has been shown how the Aztecs utilized *chinampas,* floating islands or gardens, to expand the urban area when the population of its metropolis increased. Later, whenever they needed more land, they had recourse to a less picturesque and poetic solution: they threw themselves into wars of conquest, subjugated to their dominion the territory of other tribes and rewarded the captains who carried out the conquests with donations of lands that came to be cultivated by the very peoples conquered and reduced to slavery.

Another means of subsistence of the Aztecs was tribute. In the valley or in adjacent lands stores of raw materials, foods and products of domestic skills, cloaks, priestly vestments, etc., were heaped up. There were neighbouring friendly (or intimidated) tribes that paid these tributes voluntarily.

The time came when the domestic production of Tenochtitlán began to feel the stimulus of a flourishing commerce that, for lack of a means of exchange of fixed value like money, was carried on through exchange of goods. Manual trades were developed, but never to the point of clan members coming to neglect their principal task, that of cultivating the land and producing foodstuffs. The exchange of merchandise was practised not merely among members of the same community but also between different towns and cities.

Ordinarily the members of a family would manufacture clothing, utensils and implements in sufficient quantity for domestic consumption. This, however, did not eliminate or diminish the possibility of exchange. Each city or town specialized in one or more kinds of products, and this often was the consequence not just of a skill peculiar to the clan or tribe but of ecological factors. One community would produce a more beautiful ceramic, or of better quality, than that of its neighbours because its soil supplied a clay of inherently greater plastic qualities. Now, this same community might lack instruments of obsidian, a material abundant in another town situated on volcanic terrain. It was, then, natural that the exchange of clay instruments and utensils for blocks of obsidian should take place. The chili of a certain region was tastier than that of another, which in its turn produced better squashes. Here was another natural opportunity for barter; and so on.

The place where the swapping of merchandise was carried on was the fair, the market. On that public place converged, on set days of the week, local artisans and those from surrounding communities, bringing their goods. The transactions, nevertheless, were far from being simple. How compare pineapples with turkeys? Or tomatoes with pottery jugs? Which was worth more, a live ocelot or a mantle of feathers? Something, then, was needed that would have the function of what today we call "small change." The solution was found in an article that possessed the double virtue of being portable and highly prized: cacao beans. Thus cacao came to fulfill the functions of change to settle certain minor transactions. All that commerce, in short, was determined principally by the needs of consumption and never by the desire to accumulate riches. The absence of money facilitated the maintenance of that society of collectivist economy.

The Aztecs had a higher appreciation of jade—a stone to which they attributed medicinal properties—than of gold or silver.

Here a question arises. Was there in the Aztec empire an absolute economic and social equality? The answer, in my opinion, is No.


The preliminary objections is that one cannot speak of equality in a nation where slaves and beggars existed.

Some of the first Spanish chroniclers who wrote about the social organization of the Aztecs referred to the existence of classes. George C. Vaillant—one of the greatest authorities on the subject, and the author of *The Aztecs of Mexico*, which has furnished the greater part of the elements for this chapter—thinks that the Aztec society had no classes in the hereditary sense. What existed was a hierarchy. A member of the tribe, through services rendered to the community, could attain a position of great eminence. His son, however, did not inherit that position: he had to gain it through services of like value.

The land, as has already been stated, belonged to the community, but if the division was initially just, with the passage of time, owing to different factors of human or geological nature—a farmer less skilful or less hard-working than another, or with a tract of land less fertile than his neighbour's—the system weakened little by little and inequalities emerged. Generally the clan chiefs and the priests, whose lands tended to increase for various reasons, were in a much better situation than the average farmer. There have been some who classified the Aztec government as a theocracy. The designation seems to me incomplete, for not only the clergy but the military caste enjoyed special privileges. Among those privileges—without counting the honorary—was that of greater rights in the use of land and work instruments. This, Vaillant recognizes, created a "social and economic stratification." But the same author concludes: "In theory and practice the Aztec society was democratic, and communal ownership of the means of production constituted its economic basis." I should add: "More or less."


The divisions of Aztec society into castes or hierarchies was so clear-cut that it was visible to the naked eye. In a country of high living standards, like the United States of our days, it is very difficult to determine the social position or the economic level of a citizen by the way he is dressed. This, however, is less difficult in the countries of Latin America, where there is practically no racial discrimination, but where social discrimination persists under several guises, some crude, others subtle.

The ones who dressed with greatest pomp and exquisite care among the Méxicas were the warriors and the priests. In view of the fact that the supreme glory of warfare was not only the conquest of more lands but also the capture of enemy soldiers to swell the number of slaves or of victims for sacrifice, the greater the number of prisoners taken by a warrior, the more right he had to add insignia and adornments to his already fanciful habiliments. If the hero belonged to the order of the Ocelot or of the Eagle, his garments had to indicate one of the two. Everything points to the fact that the warriors showed a great predilection for cloaks and head-dresses of coloured feathers. Some proudly wore a wicker framework fastened on the shoulders and covered with mosaics of feathers.

On special occasions the priests wore clothing that varied in colour, cut and insignia according to the ritual.

The man of the people went bareheaded, with his hair usually long; he wore fastened on one shoulder a sort of apron that also covered the upper part of his body. When it was cold, he went shod in sandals of leather or of rope made of maguey fibre. Women protected their bodies from the waist down with a cloth held by a belt, and wore a kind of sleeveless house dress. They braided their hair and tied ribbons round their heads.

The clothing of the rich was of the same style, but of better texture and richer in adornments. The administrative chiefs in general displayed a gold, turquoise or diamond emblem indicating their functions.


One of the things that have most delighted me in Mexico is the survival of the artisan. In this technological era of ours in which we are little by little transferring to machines not only the job of doing things but also that of thinking, it cannot fail to be pleasant to find people who can still, with taste and imagination, use the oldest instruments of work known to man—the hands.

Everything indicates that the Aztecs of Tenochtitlán, as well as their ancestors the Toltecs and the majority of the tribes of Central America, used extremely few and very rudimentary implements other than the fingers. It is surprising that tribes of Indians unprovided with metal instruments, ignorant of the wheel and of animal traction, could have attained so high a degree of culture, constructing so many grandiose temples and producing so many works of art in the fields of architecture, sculpture, ceramics and precious metals. If we compare the history of these American tribes with those of Sumeria and Egypt, we shall find that in the two latter nations the first metropolitan centres rose during the period of transition between the end of the Stone Age and the dawn of the Bronze Age, when great changes took place in the methods of production and exchange, while the technology—if we may use the word here—of the ancient civilizations of Central America never went beyond a "neolithic" period.

George C. Vaillant states that the old art of ceramics was the most important in the New World, and that in no other continent did it offer so great and complex a variety of design and form. He attributes this in part to the good quality of the clay in the Mexican soil.

Pottery with geometric designs in black and white on a red band was very popular. During the time of Tenochtitlán's greatest splendour the Aztec potters followed the paths of naturalism, using on their clay pitchers, vases, cups, jugs and cooking pots designs representing birds, fish and flowers, executed with considerable care and with a delicacy that recalls certain Japanese paintings.

It was the need of producing articles for daily use—utensils to serve or to keep food in—that stimulated manual trades. Moreover, religion also stimulated craftsmanship, for every temple needed vases, urns, lamps and other objects of worshipful use. The privilege of furnishing this equipment to the temples fell to the most skilled potters.

Could the use of mirrors have been common among the Aztecs? All evidence points to the negative. Those that existed, of polished obsidian, perhaps were employed only in ritualistic magic. It is not difficult to imagine how mysterious, strange and deforming a mirror of black glass would be. Mirrors were also made with scales of burnished iron pyrites, arranged in the form of mosaic and glued to a backing of wood or shell.

Another ancient occupation much esteemed among the Indians

of Mexico was the trade of making mosaics of feathers. The shields, insignia and cloaks of the warriors and the nobles were ornamented with them. The most skilled artisans with the arrangement of coloured bird feathers succeeded in making designs that gave the impression of paintings.

The art of the mosaic was one of the richest and most delicate of Mexican craftsmanship. Stones and shells of the most varied forms and colours were utilized. Later the Catholic temples that the Spanish missionaries were to erect in the lands of Mexico would benefit greatly from that skill of the natives.

Aztec furniture was poor and scanty. The high functionaries and the important persons of the community sat on something like thrones of wood, but the common man slept and sat on *petates,* or rush mats.

Metallurgy, even in the last years of Tenochtitlán, was little developed. Copper was used beaten cold, and the workers in precious metals of the epoch, although they were ignorant of the formula for making bronze, knew how to mix copper with gold to make crotals, small spherical bells, and ornaments.

The Mexico of today is rich in textiles, carpets, cloths, in the most ingenious designs and the most agreeable colours. Few specimens, however, of the art of weaving among the Aztecs have come down to us. What has not rotted away under the action of weather and humidity, man has taken it upon himself to destroy or carry off. The same thing happened with baskets. But to judge by the other domestic arts, the Aztecs must have been excellent also at weaving cloth and making baskets.

And to end these remarks about craftsmanship, I shall mention a type of work in which elements of scrupulous taste are brought together to produce an instrument used in the barbarous ritual of sacrifice. I refer to the fantastic knives made of that volcanic rock that looks like black, opaque glass: obsidian. I do not know by what process the Indians succeeded in chipping fine laminas from that extremely hard rock crystal, but many of those daggers were exquisitely long and narrow. Some poniards had hilts that reproduced figures of warriors or animals, worked in the form of mosaics, with incrustations of jade and turquoise, in a combination of greens that frequently were tinged with the dark red of the victims' blood.

No one who today sees the admirable murals of Orozco, Rivera and Siqueiros on the walls of so many public buildings of Mexico's capital can fail to be amazed that these extraordinary painters have emerged in a country whose aborigines were so little notable in the domain of drawing and painting. Because the Aztecs' forte was sculpture and architecture.

Now, it can be said that the artisan is the father of the artist. It was quite certainly in the practice of domestic manual trades that the Mexican Indians prepared themselves for the higher flights of artistic achievements.

Just as the object of the Aztec economy was not the enrichment of the individual, and their religion did not aim at moral objectives, the art of the tribes of the Valley of Mexico had no aesthetic ends. In this particular the Aztec empire resembled Soviet Russia, where they seek to make art socially useful. Of course, the parallel ends there, because if in the Communist world art seeks to serve the interests of the proletariat and has a social end, in the Aztec empire it had an almost purely religious meaning.


As the skyscraper nowadays is the most typical architectural expression of the capitalist world, the temple was the most imposing symbol of the ritualistic civilization of the Méxicas, in that they attained a grandeur comparable to the ancient civilizations of Egypt and Mesopotamia. Their *teocallis* reared majestically above other edifices, and it was in them that the genius and the art of the Aztecs were revealed: they had an admirable sense of proportion and knew how to manipulate mass. The structure generally consisted of a platform whose sides in declivity were broken by three terraces. A vertical stairway led from the ground to the top of the temple, where the altar stood. Along the sides of the platforms ran bands of stones on which could be seen sculptured heads of serpents, ocelots, eagles, human skulls and other symbolic figures, these depending, naturally, on which god it was to whom the temple was dedicated.

The pyramids of the Aztecs are customarily compared to those of the Egyptians, but the similarity exists solely in the name and not the form or the function. Those of the Aztecs were not burial places. In the residential houses there was less concern with the beauty of proportions or ornamentation, the builders concentrating on the aim of providing shelter to the dwellers. And the public buildings, like the houses of the authorities or clan chiefs, were no more than amplifications of the private dwellings.

There are indications that Aztec sculpture had reached its maturity in the last fifty years preceding the destruction of Tenochtitlán. In the temples sculpture and architecture complemented each other in a harmonic partnership that, by way of contrast, brings to mind certain edifices of the Porfirian era whose figures in relief have nothing to do with the façade they ornament, or rather, disturb, and whose structure in its turn calls for anything but the gravid, verdigrised cupola that crowns it and at the same time crushes it.

The specimens of the sculpture of the Méxicas come down to us make me think of the many works of art the Conquistadores lost and destroyed, voluntarily or involuntarily, and of the many others that are still buried somewhere there awaiting an archæologist who will bring them anew up to this clear Mexican light, excavating with them—*quién sabe?*—some new theory that will overthrow many of those we accept today about that fascinating civilization.

The Aztec sculptors—who had not the custom of signing their works, another token of the collectivist spirit of that society—had a certain predilection for sculpturing stone in full relief and almost always in monumental proportions. They also used clay, a material that, like the ancient Chinese, they considered noble.

I paid a visit to the National Museum of Anthropology of Mexico City and came to know personally some of the gods who overshadowed the temples and the spirits of the inhabitants of Tenochtitlán.

There is something sombre and ferociously hard in those squat, short-legged deities of menacing aspect, usually seated or crouched, staring at us with their dark pupils of obsidian or with their empty orbits. Not one of these images is smiling. They seem to dislike me. The only smiling sculptures of Mexican Indians I know of are some masks made by Totonac Indians, the gayest people of the hot lands at sea level.

Whose is this imposing statue, all of basalt? I look at the distich: *Coatlicue.* It looks like a nightmare of Salvador Dalí combined with a delirium of Picasso. It is the terrible Goddess of Death, "Our Lady of the Serpent Skirt." It is a monument and at the same time an enigma, a jigsaw puzzle. Human hearts and hands cover her bosom, from the vertex of which a cranium, also human, comes out. Her skirt is all a nest of interlaced vipers. Where is her head? A man born and reared in the shadow or the light of an anthropomorphic religion, I demand that Coatlicue have a human head. But how can I, poor mortal, change the anatomy of a divinity? Two serpents rise erect from each shoulder of the image and join their heads, tongues and fangs displayed, to form a kind of frightful muzzle. I take a cautious turn around the statue, I fall back, I contemplate it with eyes half-closed and stand for some time as though hypnotized by its maleficent sortilege, by its repellent charm.

Coatlicue—explains another visitor to the museum who got into conversation with me—is the mother of the gods. "And you see that head over there? It is more than a metre in height and is the head of Coyolxauhqui, Goddess of the Moon, sister of the God of War." He informs me that, despite the monumental proportions of the image, it is a minor divinity, of the planetary group. Little by little—I conclude to myself with pallid pride—I am getting to know this vast family of gods, disentangling their relationships, learning by heart the face of each image. It is even possible that some day I may become a specialist in Aztec theology. A good pastime for old age.

But what is this? I stop short now in front of another image of Coatlicue. Not the least doubt of it: it is what I read on the explanatory card. There I see the powerful talons, the serpent skirt. But this image possesses arms and hands, yes, and for a head it has a skull. After all, which is the true version: this or the other one?

I wander off disappointed among the gods of stone and clay. Goodbye specialization!

Two themes seem to predominate in these sculptures: the image of the serpent and the idea of death. I have the feeling that in the majority of cases the most important thing for these Indian artists was not realism but dramatic force and rhythmic proportion. Exception to the rule is the head of a Knight of the Aztec Eagle, before which I stop. It has a beauty that makes us think of classic Greek and Roman sculptures. It is a secular work in which the warrior's features recall those of an Athenian noble.

I amuse myself discovering other analogies. I pass by figures that remind me of Chinese Buddhas, Sumerian sculptures, Hindu deities;

and suddenly there comes to mind the image I saw in photographic reproduction of a little clay figure discovered in Jalisco, representing a warrior or ball player with caricatured expression that not only in its features but in its dress is reminiscent of Grumpy, one of the seven dwarfs in the story of Snow White in Walt Disney's version.

I come finally to one of the most precious pieces of this most interesting museum: the Stone of the Sun, the calendar of Tenoch-titlán, an attempt, by combining Aztec science, art and magic, to catch in a circular stone about fifteen feet in diameter the infinity of time and the universe. The sculpture in relief, of a beautiful and fanciful lacy effect—possibly worked with obsidian instruments, with an incredible precision and skill—represents the history of the world in its different eras, and shows, surrounded by glyphs of jade and turquoise, evocative of the colours of the sky, the names of the twenty days. In another circular band appear rays of the sun and stellar symbols. The border of the calendar consists of two great serpents of fire representing the year and time. Right in the middle of the stone, the hideous face of Tonatiuh, the God of the Sun, flanked by four cartouches marking the four ages through which the world has already passed and which, together, represent the era in which we are living.

Important specimens of Aztec sculpture are found today in the British Museum in London and in the Museum of Natural History in New York, not to mention other museums and private collections. But what is seen here, principally in the realm of sculpture, ceramics, articles of gold and silver work, is sufficient to give to the most exigent and sceptical observer an idea of the importance of the art of the ancient civilizations of Mexico.


The painting and drawing of the Méxicas were poor compared with their architecture and sculpture. Many Aztec codices have come down to our day, revealing scenes of the social and religious life of the cities in the Valley of Mexico in primitive drawings and almost always in a caricatural tone. These codices have a great documentary value, and, as for their drawings properly so-called, I confess they amuse me with all their errors of perspective, their anatomical heresies, their grotesque, short-legged little men with clothes and insignia also disfigured by the caricature. I have the impression that these are the only humorous expressions of Aztec society. Those Indian artists must have been great satirists at heart, and in a certain way their drawings were real escape valves by means of which they relieved the pressure in which they lived in that violent world, where the individual never knew when he was going to have his heart cut out of his breast in honour of some god, or when he was going to fall in combat, downed by the enemy. The truth is that in the codices referred to, the scenes of human sacrifices are depicted in a humorous vein.


When we speak of working in gold and silver, naturally one name immediately comes to mind: Benvenuto Cellini: A century before the birth of that famous artist Mexican Indians were already working in gold, silver, copper, precious and semi-precious stones, making jewels and other adornments that, by their perfection of finish and tasteful design, might rival those of the Italian master.

It is supposed that the art of working in precious metals in the American continent originated in South America, possibly in Peru, Ecuador or Colombia, having been carried from there to Central America, where it was cultivated by the Mayas who, in their turn, passed it on to the Mixtecs in the south of Mexico, and the latter taught it to the Toltecs and the Chichimecs of the central plateau, where later the Aztecs became the highest masters of that delicate trade. Superlative lapidaries, the Méxicas succeeded, by what means I know not, in making minute sculptures in stones like jade, amethyst and rock crystal, giving them the form of human figures and of animals, flowers, fruits and miniatures of domestic utensils.

No less beautiful are their masks of solid gold, used by the priests in certain religious ceremonies. There were also death masks with which the faces of kings, warriors and nobles were covered when they were buried. In the Ethnographic Museum of Rome is one of the most notable Aztec masks known, all incrusted with pieces of jade and turquoise in the technique of mosaic. I saw some years ago in the Museum of Natural History in New York another marvellous Aztec mask of porphyry, secular in nature, and of an extraordinary realistic vigour. Another wonderful item, more or less in the same genre, is the human cranium found today in the collection of the British Museum, with incrustations of turquoise and obsidian and eyes of pyrites, the skull supposed to be the head of the god Tezcatlipoca. In the same museum is a strange skull carved out of rock crystal, of an admirable anatomical precision; it succeeds, much better than the original article, in conveying to the observer everything macabre about a human skull. Because that skull, product of an unknown artist, possesses a truly phantasmal luminous quality.

What can one say of the music of the Méxicas if all the melodies produced in the vale of Anáhuac have been carried off to the mountains by the wind, dissolving them forever in the silence of space and time? Of it nothing has remained written down in any scale. It was a pity that when they reached Mexico the missionaries did not try to gather up the aboriginal music, afterwards commencing their musical catechism, displacing those barbaric, pantheistic tunes by Christian music.

However, instruments of that epoch have survived, from whose tonal possibilities one can get an idea of what music among the Aztecs might have been.

A great number of flutes existed, some strident, others low, made of wood, rush, reed, clay or conchs. In a musical ensemble the flute —within its limitations, of course—was the only instrument that played the melody. The rest were drums, crotals and scraping instruments that marked the rhythm. Among the cylindrical, vertical and horizontal drums was one that consisted of an inverted gourd set in a container full of water and, when beaten, would produce a great resonance.

If the Aztecs were as gloomy as their direct descendants I find here today, I'll wager five pesos their music was no better than a monotonous tune with slow rhythm.

The important thing, though, is that the meeting of these Indians with Spaniards has produced, in the passing of time, that beautiful Mexican popular music, so rich in melodies, that fills these towns, cities, streets and skies, turning modern Mexico into one of the most musical countries of the American continent.

One gets the impression that among the Aztecs the dance was more important than the music. Of the original choreography nothing has come down intact to our times, since the Catholic padres naturally tried to make the Indians forget the gestures, steps and rhythms evocative of barbaric and bloody ceremonies like human sacrifices, acts of cannibalism, gladiatorial combats and invocations to the gods.

It is known, however, that the Aztec dances employed great masses and were accompanied not only by music but by song. The Méxicas danced at the annual fiestas or in honour of the God of Rain, when they prayed for water for their crops, and they danced likewise for the God of War when they were preparing for battle. In the sowing season they paid homage with dances to the God of Spring. There was a famous dance that symbolized the conflict between Night and Day. And another—the Dance of the Stag—that propitiated the God of Hunting. The use of masks representing human or animal personages was common in these dances. On such occasions the dance could not fail to be theatre, too, for its movements, its pantomime, recounted the history of the life of the gods or depicted a mythological or historical event.

It seems beyond doubt that the Indians of Mexico had a drama. In Teotihuacán, a short distance from Mexico City, exist the ruins of an amphitheatre not very different from those of ancient Greece.

And is it not logical that a people with so much talent for sculpture and architecture should be rich also in dances and other theatrical spectacles?


In the opinion of some investigators the Mayas were the first to use writing in the Americas, perhaps some three or four thousand years before the birth of Christ. Possibly they employed figures and hieroglyphic symbols, as the peoples of Egypt and Sumeria were doing in the same epoch. Before the fifteenth century the Méxicas were already using pictograms to illustrate their oral messages. When the Conquistadores arrived, the Aztecs' writing was a combination of several methods: ideographs, hieroglyphs, simple and symbolic figures. It was not possible to represent, with those pictograms, general concepts or to express abstract ideas, so that Aztec literature remained unwritten. It was probably limited to oral expression. Like music, it was carried off by the winds to the glacial silence of the mountains.

No great imagination is necessary to conclude that this people, so overshadowed by so many gods and superstitions, eternally perplexed before a Nature so violent, must have produced a literature of symbolic type, with its poetic colours, many mythological allusions and sonorous onomatopoeias—hymns, in short, of fearful praise to the gods, of ill-articulated fright at the volcanoes, at the snorts of the earth in its seismic convulsions; hymns of ferocious joy at sight of a hot, bleeding heart just torn from a human breast, or of a beautiful crop of maize; or, again, hymns full of prowess in war. And it is quite possible that all that literature was almost entirely at the service of the religious and social interests of the community, with little or no concern with aesthetics.

The Méxicas believed that the world had gone through four or five epoch or "Suns." Many versions of the Aztec cosmogony exist. I have already taken the opportunity to summarize one of them, the one by the Indian historian, Ixtlilxochtl, earlier in this book. The other version, which seems to be the official one, since it is symbolized on the Stone of the Sun, is the following:

The first era, *Ocelotl* (Jaguar), had as its patron Tezcatlipoca, the God with the Smoking Mirror, who ended by turning into the Sun itself, while jaguars devoured the men and the giants who in that epoch were peopling the earth. In the second age, *Ehecatl* (Wind), governed by Quetzalcoatl, the world was destroyed by hurricanes and men turned into monkeys. (I love that evolution in reverse.) Thanks to Tlaloc, God of Rain, the world once more had light in the third epoch, called *Quiahuitl* (Fire-rain), but was destroyed anew by a rain of fire. The fourth Sun, *Atl* (Water), was presided over by the Goddess of Water, Chalchihuitlicue, "Our Lady of the Turquoise Skirt." That time a flood came about that transformed men into fishes. We find ourselves now in the *Olin* (Earthquake) age, under the rule of Tonatiuh, the God of the Sun, and under the threat of seeing the world destroyed by an earthquake.

The Aztec conception of the universe had also a religious and magic sense. There was the horizontal universe—perhaps the most ancient concept—and the vertical one. In the first there are five directions: the four cardinal points plus the centre, where the God of Fire, a fundamental divinity in the Mexican theology, held sway. The East, a region of great fertility, was governed by the God of Rain and the God of Clouds. This concept of abundance must have a geographic explanation. It was from the fertile region which today is the State of Vera Cruz, to the east of Tenochtitlán, that the periodic rains came, caused by the condensation of warm air when the Gulf of Mexico was exposed to the cold winds that blew from the central plateau. But why did they attribute maleficent influences to the South? Perhaps because of the arid zones extending to the south from the territories now forming the states of Morelos and Puebla. Despite the idea of aridity linked to that cardinal point, in it ruled gods associated with the springtime and flowers, Xipe and Macuilxochitl. The North, dark zone of horror, was presided over by Mictlantecuhtli, the Lord of the Dead, a deity frequently related to the soul. The West, where shone the evening star, was a more favourable sector thanks to the protection of Quetzalcoatl, the God of Learning, often identified with the planet Venus.

The vertical world was divided, suitably for the social purposes of the Aztecs, into small heavens and hells lacking all moral meaning. To use a modern simile, it was like an apartment house in which the gods lived according to their hierarchic importance. The original creator occupied the top floor. One of the apartments, or rather, heavens, belonged to Tlaloc, who sheltered all who died by drowning, or were killed by lightning or any other cause connected with water. The remaining dead went to the cellar of the house, to an underworld they named Mictlan. To get there, however, they had to overcome a series of tremendous obstacles. From that idea came the habit of burying the dead with equipment and talismans (including a dog) that might facilitate their toilsome journey. The journey of the dead well reflects the influence of the Mexican landscape on the Indian mind. The traveller had to wander between two mountains that threatened to crush him; had to avoid the encounter, first, with a snake and then with a crocodile; to cross eight deserts; to scale eight mountains; to endure a freezing wind that hurled stones and obsidian knives at him; until he reached a broad river, which the deceased must cross mounted on a red dog. At his destination at last, he presented his offerings to the God of the Dead, who in his turn assigned the dead man to one of nine different regions.

In sum, the horizontal division of the universe was subordinated to geographic phenomena, while the vertical had more to do with hierarchy.

There were gods that lived on more intimate terms with mortals, intervening often in their everyday domestic affairs. One of them was the terrible Tezcatlipoca; the other, his rival Quetzalcoatl, a kind of Protean deity. These two gods sometimes changed name according to the different regions of Mexico. As for Quetzalcoatl, I shall not even try, I don't say to clarify, but to describe the confusion existing about that multiform deity, who was the God of Civilization, the Plumed Serpent, the god of the planet Venus and not infrequently a bearded god wearing an out-thrust mask, known as Ehecatl, Lord of the Wind.

One can understand very well the reason why, in a region as dry as the central plateau of Mexico, so much importance should be given to Tlaloc, the God of Rain, who in Tenochtitlán merited a place in the very temple of Huitzilopochtli, the "Humming-bird Wizard," God of War.

We must not forget a collection of goddesses of maize, young and beautiful maidens with attractive names like "The Young Mother of Maize," "Bird Flower," "Four Flower." Another attractive one is the goddess of the maguey, with her four hundred children who apparently lived in a permanent state of intoxication.

Tlaloc ruled over vegetation. "Our Lady of the Turquoise Skirt" governed rivers, lakes and seas. Xipe, the "Flayed One," symbolized spring time, and her vestment was a human skin representing the new vegetation with which the earth clothes itself every year. In the ceremonies in honour of this vernal god the priests wore the skin of recently flayed slaves.

The duality expressed in the struggle between Good and Evil in the Christian world was symbolized in the Aztec religion in the rivalry between Light and Darkness, North and South, Cold and Heat, East and West. The gods took part in these symbolic wars and even the stars lined up in armies—armies of the East against those of the West—and fought veritable pitched battles.

Combats like those of the gladiators of ancient Rome were popular in Tenochtitlán, and expressed that duality as a part of the religious ritual. The warriors of Huitzilopochtli and the Knights of the Jaguar participated in them.


Among the Aztec legends woven about the personality of Quetzalcoatl was one according to which that Protean god, before departing this earth, disappearing in the West, had promised his faithful to return to the world some day, coming from the East. (And could there not be in this legend a certain analogy with the daily miracle of the death and resurrection of the sun?) Thus, when the Spanish Conquistadores disembarked in 1519 in the place to which they gave the name of Vera Cruz, Montezuma was prepared to see in Hernán Cortés a new incarnation of Quetzalcoatl. Up to a certain point that explains the rapidity of the Spanish triumph. The Aztecs gave a magic interpretation to the Conquest. When they discovered the error it was too late: the destruction of their empire had already begun. According to Oswald Spengler, that is the only case known of a culture terminating by violent death—murdered, destroyed like "a sunflower decapitated by a passerby."

I do not know of an act of more violent audacity, of a more novelesque, sanguinary adventure than the Conquest of Mexico. Cortés deserves a niche in high relief in the gallery of the great adventurers of history, which does not mean that the cruelties and violent deeds he committed seem justifiable to me.

# 5. The Conquest

Hernán Cortés was born in 1485 in the town of Medellín in the Spanish province of Extremadura, the son of Don Martín Cortés, a professional soldier, who, being weary and disillusioned with so many, so hard and unrewarded military wanderings or because he did not think his son was cut out to be a warrier, tried to dissuade him from the career of arms by sending him to study law at Salamanca. The young Hernán learned his Latin and some veneer of law, but, concluding that he had no vocation for studies, he returned to the paternal home at seventeen and tried to find another course. In that time few were the roads that a young Spaniard could follow: "Learning, sea or royal palace." The first was already out of the question. Why, then, not serve his King in the lands beyond the sea? Hernán enlisted as a soldier in an expedition that, under the command of Ovando, was ready to sail for the Indies. Proudly he gets into a soldier's armour, buckles sword to belt, and one night goes out on amorous conquest. To reach the room of the lady he plans to win, he has to scale a wall, but an infernal weak spot in a mud wall yields to his weight and the hero falls with a crash that awakens the beauty's husband, who makes the most of having his rival on the ground and incapable of getting up, and gives him a Homeric beating that puts the poor boy in bed. And while friends are rubbing balm on his bodily wounds, without finding a remedy for those of his self-esteem, Hernán receives news that Ovando's ships are setting their sails for the open sea.

At nineteen he takes part in the expedition sent to the island of Hispaniola for the purpose of putting down a revolt headed by the lovely Haitian Anacaona, "Flower of Gold." The rebellious Indians, poorest of fighters, who in the words of a chronicler of the time, "used their bellies as shields," offered no resistance.

After that sorry "feat" of Spanish arms, Hernán wins as his prize an encomienda of Indians and the post as secretary to the *ayuntamiento,* or town council, of Azua, a position he fulfilled competently and, possibly, with boredom.

A new opportunity turns up for him in 1511 when the Spanish government decides to establish a colony in Cuba and charges Don Diego Velázquez with carrying out the conquest. Three hundred men participate in the expedition and Hernán Cortés is one of them. He does not go, however, as a combatant but as assistant to the treasurer who is to represent the Royal Treasury on the adventure.

The conquest of Cuba was as easy as a parade. The Indians offered little resistance, which did not prevent Velázquez from taking advantage of the opportunity to decimate them. The following year, the city of Baracoa having been founded, Cortés fulfils there the functions of secretary and at the same time those of a landowner. He devotes himself to the cultivation of vineyards, the raising of cattle, mares and sheep, and to the exploitation of gold mines without prejudice to other business and activities.

Don Diego Velázquez, the widowed, avaricious governor of Cuba, becomes infatuated with one of the four lovely Suárez sisters who had come from Spain to the island accompanied by their brother Juan. The evil tongues of the time hinted that the relations between the governor and the beautiful Andalusian were far from platonic. Cortés signed a marriage contract with one of the *niñas,* Catalina, but shortly afterward broke his promise. *Nombre de Dios!* The honour of the Suárez family is stained. The brother, standing *in loco parentis,* is infuriated. The governor of the island takes the Suárez side. On the other the friends of Cortés let their tongues wag in endless intrigues. Velázquez loses patience and orders the secretary arrested. One night, however, taking advantage of his jailer's dozing off, Cortés steals his shield and sword and runs to the church, where he takes refuge. Why doesn't the lord governor deport the insolent fellow? the courtiers ask. It is a matter of an act of rebellion that justifies a criminal prosecution. Velázquez hesitates. His hands, which love the touch of gold, are not at all clean. The public posts in the island are most of them filled by relatives and protégés of his. He is not ignorant of the fact that Cortés possesses documents that compromise him gravely.

Soldiers surround the church where the diabolic scrivener remains in sanctuary. After a while, tired of his prison, Cortés comes to take the air and sun close to the church door. Juan Suárez, the new governor of the fortress, falls upon him with his soldiers and overmasters him. They put him aboard a ship going to Hispaniola. Hernán manages to free himself from the irons they have put on his foot, exchanges clothes with the servant accompanying him and, as in the cloak-and-sword novels, protected by the shadows of the Antillean night, crawls across the deck between the mainmast and the foremast, leaps into a canoe and, so that they may not be able to pursue him, cuts the ropes of another tied to a near-by vessel. He then begins the struggle against the river current, and when he sees that he cannot handle the boat, dives into the water, after fastening to his head some papers compromising to the governor, and swims to shore.

What did the secretary do on gaining land? He lost no time; he took sanctuary in the church and his first act was to send friends to Suárez with proposals of peace and friendship, which were accepted. Immediately thereafter he marries Catalina. And now that the Suárez honour is washed clean, Cortés's first movement is to regain the governor's friendship, which he succeeds in doing thanks to the great political astuteness he is beginning to reveal.

Time passes. The name of Hernán Cortés is spoken of for the command of the third fleet being organized in Cuba destined for Mexico.

His friends exult. His enemies and those indifferent to him object that the young secretary may be able in the handling of the pen but not in arms.

Cortés ardently desires the post. Juan Grijalva had returned from the newly discovered lands bearing gold and precious stones and relating fabulous stories. In spite of his many enterprises in cattle and mining, Cortés is not rich. He leads an ostentatious life, he loads his wife with jewels and costly dresses, and is constantly persecuted by creditors.

There are several other candidates for the command of the expedition, and among them relatives and protégés of the governor. Finally, contrived by his sercetary, Andrés Duero, partner of Cortés in many business deals, Velázquez resolves to appoint the scrivener from Medellín as "captain of the third fleet."

The first thing Cortés does is deck himself out in a manner fitting to the post. The scribe has turned warrior. The goose quill becomes a gay-coloured plume and leaps from the hand to the *sombrero*. And there goes the young Cortés covered with insignia and gold lace, sword at belt, fire in his eye. Meantime, the expedition is beginning to get organized.

Early in March, 1519, Cortés reaches the coast of what is now the province of Tabasco with his fleet of eleven ships. He has under his command five hundred and eight soldiers, not counting the crews. He also has at his disposal sixteen horses, thirteen musketeers, thirty-two pack soldiers each with beast of burden, ten bronze cannon and eleven falconets.

The ships are anchored close to the delta of the Grijalva river, too shallow to permit the fleet to enter. Cortés takes his men in small boats to a point half a league from the town of Tabasco. He learns with surprise that the Indians, who had received Grijalva's soldiers in such friendly fashion, now show hostile intentions. The river is clotted with pirogues bearing armed warriors; among the rushes and canebrakes of the banks other combatants conceal themselves, lying in wait.

Hernán Cortés orders one of his men to tell the crew of a nearby pirogue that his intentions are friendly. The interpreter does the best he can, in bellows, but the Indians in reply brandish their weapons. The ex-secretary of Baracoa still tries peaceful methods. What he wants is for them to allow his men to jump to land, take on water and speak to the Indians of God and of His Majesty. Useless: the Indians refuse to be persuaded.

Cortés orders the attack on Tabasco. The Spaniards fight in water up to the waist. One chronicler tells that in the middle of the affray Cortés lost one of his sandals in the mud of the river bed, continuing to fight with one foot bare.

Gaining the shore, the Conquistadores reorganize and drive the Indians back with blows of lance and sword. A hand-to-hand fight ensues in the streets of Tabasco, ending in the victory of the invaders. The first battle is won. Hernán gathers his soldiers in the patio of one of the houses of the conquered town and, facing those exhausted, sweaty men—their faces, hands, beards, hair, uniforms filthy with mire and blood—he carries out a theatrical ceremony. He strikes thrice with his sword on the trunk of a coral tree, declares that he takes possession of that land in the name of his sovereign, Carlos V, and adds that, if anyone dares contradict it, he will defend with that very sword the rights of his king.

The Spaniards remain five days in Tabasco, vaguely frightened by that region of stifling heat, fearsome forests, swamps, rivers, lakes —water everywhere—as if there the world were still convalescing from the flood that in the Fourth Sun, the age of *Alt*, burst from the womb of "Our Lady of the Turquoise Skirt."

One thing spurs Cortés's curiosity. Where does all the gold come from, and the rich quantities of jewels brought to him by the vanquished chiefs with their homage and protestations of friendship amid clouds of incense and many obeisances? And when, through his interpreter, he asks the Indian chiefs that question, they point toward the west, saying that it is from a country called Colúa or México.

The Spanish priests have already begun teaching the doctrine. The first Mass is said in Tabasco, and on that occasion are baptized the twenty Indian female slaves the caciques had brought as a gift to the Conquistadores. One of them, who in the indigenous tongue was called Malinali, receives the Christian name of Marina. According to Bernal Díaz del Castillo, one of the most interesting chroniclers of the Conquest, she was "of good appearance, inquisitive and unabashed." It was not only the writer who noticed the "good appearance" of the Indian woman. Cortés did, too. He took so much interest in her that he ended by making her his mistress. And when she entered the Conquistador's quarters, Marina insinuated herself also into history. As a heroine? That depends on the observer's position. If a Hispanist, he will praise the girl's loyalty to the white chief, her desire to see her brothers converted to Christianity. But if an Indianist, he will proclaim La Malinche a traitor. The truth is that, angel or demon, thenceforth the clever Indian girl, who had a strong personality, conspired and worked against her people and her land, becoming the indispensable collaborator of Cortés, a personage of the first rank in the drama of the Conquest.

Náhuatl, or Aztec, was her mother tongue, and she had learned Maya in Tabasco. As Aguilar, Cortés's interpreter, spoke the latter, a very practical system of translations was set up that facilitated communication between the Conquistadores and the natives.

It was Marina who contributed most to strengthen in the Aztecs' minds the belief that Hernán Cortés was a new incarnation of the god Quetzalcoatl.

What to do now? If his officers have any doubt, he, Hernán Cortés, has absolutely none. It is imperative to conquer the empire of the highland about which the Tabasco Indians relate such wonders. La Malinche, too, must have filled her lord's ears and imagination with fantastic stories about the wealth of Tenochtitlán.

Cortés again puts out to sea with his whole fleet and, on Maundy Thursday, reaches a spot on the Mexican coast previously touched by Grijalva. Indian chiefs come aboard to receive them and to ask them, in the name of Montezuma, who they are and what they come for. Cortés replies that his intentions are brotherly and that the Mexicans must regard his coming as a good thing.

On Good Friday he orders the horses disembarked, the artillery installed and the tents set up. On Easter Sunday the chaplain of the fleet says the first Mass on land. The Indian chief Tenalitl, accompanied by a cacique, comes to parley with Cortés, who asks them for audience with Montezuma. The Indian chieftains are astonished at such intrepidity. This white man has only just arrived and already wants to see the emperor? Presents are exchanged. The Aztecs bring to Cortés pieces of gold, cotton cloaks, birds and fruits of the land. But Hernán stubbornly insists on seeing the emperor personally.

Tenalitl sends an emissary to Tenochtitlán. Before that, however, so that his emperor may get a clear idea of the strange white folk and their weapons and mounts, he summons one of his artists and has him draw portraits of Cortés, his warriors, the ships, the horses—those "monstrous stags"—and the cannon—"weapons that hurl the lightning bolt afar."

The emissary returns within a few days bringing, together with many presents, a message from the emperor for Cortés. The message is open and plain. The Lord of Tenochtitlán refuses to receive the white man and requests him to retire from Mexican lands with his soldiers. The gifts, however, are far from being simple. That was the greatest mistake in Montezuma's life. From the packs of the porters presents begin to stream forth: birds of solid gold, capable of moving head and wings; fishes with alternate scales of gold and silver; other animals of the valley, also modelled in gold, are set in rows between flowers and nuggets of gold upon the mats laid on the ground. The treasures of the Indies! The soldiers are wrought-up. Cortés can ill contain his excitement. And the chieftain, Tenalitl, continues proudly directing the show. He orders shields all covered with gold plate, with incrustations of jade and turquoise, laid at the Conquistador's feet; pictures made of coloured feathers; cloaks and garments richly embroidered. . . .

At that hour Cortés may have been thinking of the corpulent Diego Velázquez, whose custom it was to steal a good part of the gold and precious stones "ransomed" in the West Indies. To send all this to the governor of Cuba would be the same as casting pearls before swine. But here the height of the spectacle is reached. At a sign from Tenalitl, Aztec slaves come up slowly bearing an enormous wheel that many of the chroniclers later said was "like a cartwheel." The ex-secretary's eyes grow round in amazement. The wheel, all of gold, symbolizes the Sun. The royal treasurer calculates its value at twenty thousand gold pesos.

But that is not all. Other slaves approach, carrying another wheel as large as that of the Sun, but all in solid silver symbolizing the Moon. Cries of admiration and amazement can be heard. One feels that the soldiers are going to hurl themselves upon the treasures.

But Cortés masters his own enthusiasm. Recovering his calm, his cold reason, he insists on being received by the emperor. He wishes to deliver to him personally a message from Carlos V. Tenalitl hesitates, turns the subject, excuses himself. The Spaniard alleges that he has crossed the seas only to see Montezuma. The Indian chief points helplessly to the treasures, to the Sun of gold and the Moon of silver, which are scintillating in the warm, humid light of Villa Rica de la Vera Cruz.


Yes. Hernán Cortés had founded the town in the name of the "very powerful and very Catholic monarchs and lords Doña Juana and the Emperor Don Carlos V, her son." That act pleased the majority of his men, who were eager to carry on the Conquest. But some partisans of Diego Velázquez wanted to return; they alleged that they had orders only to "ransom" and not to colonize. Besides, they needed more soldiers, arms and munitions to continue so difficult and so perilous an enterprise.

Cortés, however, had his plans secretly made. Since the *ayuntamiento,* the town council, of Vera Cruz had been set up, he as the delegate of Velázquez had lost his authority. A new comedy was staged. He gathered together the town officials and, head bare, clad in his dress uniform, he solemnly announced that the Velázquez authority having terminated he, Hernán Cortés, came to offer his resignation from the post of captain-general to which the governor of Cuba had appointed him. Now, all this was part of a skilfully traced plan. The junta asked for time to deliberate, and shortly thereafter declared that after great reflection it had reached the conclusion that the former powers were annulled and that Hernán Cortés thenceforth would bear the titles of *justicia mayor* and captain-general.

But discontent is still gnawing at some officers of the expedition who want at all costs to go back to Cuba.

Cortés then makes a gesture of extraordinary audacity, the first in a series that would end by giving him the final victory. To prevent the defection of his men, he orders his ships dismasted, driving them aground.

The ex-scrivener had the habit of writing regularly to his king long and detailed letters, giving him information about his acts and the progress of the Conquest. When we compare the actions, deeds and wanderings of this prodigious adventurer with the descriptions that he himself makes of those things in his correspondence, we can really perceive the essence of early sixteenth-century style. What in real life has flesh, sinew, blood, life, in passing to paper hardens to marble. The asymmetrical takes on symmetry. Passions become as it were dehydrated, as they are put into words. The warm grows cold or tepid. The most horrible or the most heroic scenes end, through the miracle of a sober style, divested of all horror or heroism.

This is how Hernán Cortés relates to his sovereign the incident of the destruction of the ships:

"Besides those who acted thus because they were servants and friends of Diego Velázquez, there were others who wanted to leave on seeing how large and populous the country was, while the Spaniards were so few. Believing that, if I left the ships there, they would revolt with them, and, all those of like mind deserting, I would be left almost alone, by which the great service which I had rendered to God and Your Highness in this country would be undone, I determined, on the pretext that they were unseaworthy, to have the said ships beached. Thus, everybody lost hope of ever leaving the country, and I set out on my march securely, without fear that, when I turned my back, the people whom I had left in the town would fail me."

The whole immense gesture is described in the words: "I determined to have the said ships beached."

Hernán Cortés was not long in discovering the vulnerable spot in Montezuma's empire. The city-states between the Gulf of Mexico and the central meseta were independent communities whose peoples hated the Aztecs, who had required of them the payment of heavy tribute in consequence of wars of conquest in which the armies of Tenochtitlán had killed or enslaved their warriors and violated their women. Could not those peoples—reflected Cortés—become allies of the Spaniards in a war against the empire of Montezuma?

The dice were cast. In destroying his fleet Hernán Cortés had made the Conquest a dire necessity. In mid-August of 1519 he left Vera Cruz with four hundred soldiers, fifteen horses and seven bombards, determined to master an empire that must have had more than two millions of inhabitants.

He marches first upon Cempoala, where he is received as an ally. He continues to advance, now toward the mountains, with his troops reinforced by several thousand Totonac warriors. The next objective is the independent republic of Tlaxcala, mortal enemy of the Aztecs. How they will be received by the Tlaxcaltecs is still an unknown quantity.

It was, however, necessary to conquer the mountains first. Tenochtitlán was situated at more than 7,500 feet altitude and certainly more than 250 miles from where the army of the Conquistadores found itself.

It commenced the climb. Little by little it left behind the belt of hot lands with its tropical forests, its plantations of cacao and tobacco. And as the Spaniards climbed on and on, something like a retable of wonders unfolded itself to their eyes. Nature became more amiable, but no less beautiful and rich in colour for all that. The air, which near the Gulf was thick, heavy and humid, becomes now thin, dry and transparent, although its rarefaction leaves the soldiers short of breath, making the climb difficult for them. Mosquitoes and other harmful insects have disappeared. On all sides rise mountains, some with peaks white with snow. And, dominating them all, yonder the colossal bulk of Orizaba! Cortés was surprised to find there pines and other trees of cold climates filling the thin air with their fragrance. Birds that these white warriors had never seen alighted on trees also unknown to them, trees that later on European botanists were to declare valuable for their woods, fruits or medicinal properties. The soldiers ate, gingerly at first and then with gusto, the fruits they encounter, such as the giant sapodilla plums, mangoes and tomatoes.

The cold begins to worsen and the nights are especially hard for the members of the expedition. Nightly bivouacs are set up under the cold stars, and the volcanoes seem to keep watch far into the night over the sleep of the Conquistadores.

When morning dawned the climb continued. Hours and surprises succeeded one another. And at last, one day, three months after they had left Vera Cruz, the Spaniards arrived at the gates of Tlaxcala.


They launched their attack. The Tlaxcaltecs resist, but one gets the impression that they fight hopelessly, stunned by the idea that they may be confronting supernatural beings. The "monstrous stags" charge down upon them. The armour and helmets of the white men shine brilliant, and some of these whites have beards as yellow as the sun. The strange "dogs that spit fire" do not cease barking. Not only that: each harquebusier seems to hold in his hands the force of the lightning.

The Spaniards' victory is not long in coming. And little time does Cortés need to turn the enemies into allies. His troops are augmented by several thousand more Tlaxcaltec warriors. One day, after peace is made, Cortés is informed by men of Cempoala that the Tlaxcaltecs are laying an ambush for him. And when fifty of them appear with gifts of food at the cabins where the Spanish captains are billeted, Hernán takes one of them aside and, by frightening him, extracts his confession that warriors in great number are concealed behind the hills waiting for night to come to fall upon the invaders. And the ex-secretary, in a letter to his sovereign, serenely narrates the outcome of the story: "And seeing this I had all the fifty taken, and cut off their hands, and returned them to their chief, ordering them to say to him, that, by day or night or at any or all times he might come, he would see who we were."

And now here are the Conquistadores in the outskirts of Cholula, the Sacred City of the Aztecs. With their gala clothes, amid the smoke of copal, Cholula nobles and warriors come to meet the invaders with gestures of peace and friendship. Through the intermediary of interpreters Cortés and the local Indian chiefs hold parley. A difficulty arises. The elders of Cholula do not want the Tlaxcaltecs, their traditional enemies, to enter armed into the city. Hernán orders his allies to camp in the vicinity.

But in spite of the friendly reception the situation is tense. Something indefinable is in the air. The Cholultecs seem to be conspiring. Marina moves about, here and there, the bearer or the promoter of intrigues. She fills her master's ear with the stories she has heard, divined or invented. Does the lord captain know what is being said over yonder? The Cholultecs have sacrificed five babies to Huitzilopochtli, God of War, this morning; that means they intend to give battle to the invaders. More: the Tlaxcaltecs swear they have seen enormous caldrons being brought together by the people of the city to cook the flesh of the Spaniards with tomatoes. The Cempoala warriors, eager to carry out old projects of vengeance, also spread rumours of like nature.

Cortés needs no more to be convinced that they really are setting a trap for him. He decides he must take a forceful attitude, for it is inadvisable to reveal indecision or weakness before Montezuma, who, in Tenochtitlán, is undoubtedly being informed of all his movements, words and acts.

He causes them to send him an embassy composed of nobles and warrior chiefs, and orders them into a courtyard at the gates of which he stations armed guards with orders to let no one out. He alerts his own soldiers, arming them with harquebuses, lances, swords and shields, and tells them that as soon as they hear a musket shot they are to fall hard upon the Cholultecs. This done, he mounts his horse and makes a speech to the leaders of Cholula and to a crowd of three thousand standing in the enclosure or in its vicinity. Why do they want to kill him—asks the Spanish captain—when he comes

on a mission of peace, as a friend? He becomes more and more excited. He enumerates the things he knows, the signs that they are
planning treachery. And when his wrath reaches its peak, he shouts
that the law customarily punishes treachery and that today the
Cholultecs will perish and their city will be razed. The shot is heard
and the Spaniards fall upon the multitude, taking them by surprise
with slashes and thrusts of sword and lance. Mortars and harquebuses
go into action. It is a veritable massacre. The ground where corpses
pile up becomes soaked with blood, and amid an infernal yelling the
slaughter continues. In a letter to his king Cortés says that ". . . we
attacked them with such force that in two hours more than three
thousand died." And then in justification he explains: "In order that
Your Majesty may see how well prepared they were, before I went
out of our quarters they had occupied all the streets and placed all
their men." He adds further that it had been easy for them to rout
the Cholultecs because he had taken care to seize the military leaders
first.

Needless to say, the Tlaxcaltecs waited no long time to go into
action, and that day they had their great festival of blood. Years
later, commenting on the massacre, Fray Toribio Motolinia declared
that, since it had been impossible to avoid the slaughter, it had been
a good thing for the Indians of New Spain "to see and recognize
that those idols and all others are false and lying."


It was on a clear November midday, after the heavy rains, that
Cortés and his army reached the highest part of the saddle that joins
the volcanoes Popocatépetl and Ixtaccíhuatl. And it was from that
monumental portico that the Conquistador had his first view of
Tenochtitlán. Down there in the valley, half veiled in the fog, the
metropolis of the Aztecs gave the impression of being asleep at
the bottom of a lake. But when the mist cleared away, it shone in the
sun of Anáhuac with its towers, palaces and pyramids like a fantastic
city of silver.

Bernal Díaz del Castillo was to write afterwards: ". . . And when
we saw so many cities and villages built on the water . . . we were
amazed and said it was like the enchantments they tell of in the
legend of Amadís, on account of the great towers and cúes and
buildings rising from the water and all built of masonry. And some

of our soldiers even asked whether the things we saw were not a dream."

Hernán Cortés, however, was not a man to waste much time on contemplation. The following morning he marched with his forces toward Tenochtitlán along one of the great causeways.

The Spaniards could see no sign of armed resistance. The Méxicas who were plying the canals in their canoes drew near the causeway in curiosity to see at closer range those strange white warriors in glittering armour.

Montezuma comes to meet Hernán Cortés under a canopy decorated with *quetzal* feathers, embroidered with gold and precious stones. Cortés dismounts. The Aztec emperor approaches, guarded by two of his men. Before him nobles sweep the ground and spread rich mantles for the monarch to walk upon. By means of interpreters they exchange phrases of welcome and compliments. Cortés hands to Montezuma a necklace of pearls strung on a gold cord perfumed with musk.

Montezuma leads Cortés by the hand to the apartments he has ordered prepared for him. He takes leave of his guest and returns with his retinue to the city. The Spanish soldiers now advance with more confidence. From windows and rooftops hundreds of men and women gaze at them in silence. And the white warriors do not tire of admiring and remarking upon the tall temples, the palaces, the flowering islands, the strange people.

The first dialogue between the Conquistador and Montezuma is described in a very sober, restrained fashion in one of Hernán's letters to his king. The decoration of the room is sumptuous. The emperor is richly dressed. But the dialogue has something grotesque about it. The interlocutors are seated each on a dais. After giving rich presents to the visitor, Montezuma says that they, the Aztecs, are not native to this land but foreigners "come from very strange parts." Then: "And according to the part from which you say you come, which is that where the Sun rises, and the things you say of that great lord or king who sent you here, we believe and take as certain that he is our natural lord."

And he protests complete obedience, he and his vassals, to the white king of the far country.

Montezuma continues:

"Now that you are in your own house, take your ease, rest from the hardships of the journey and the wars you have had. I know well that the men of Cempoala and Tlaxcala have told you much evil of me. Give no credit but to what your own eyes see."

Finally, lifting his garments, he shows his body:

"Here you see me, I am of flesh and blood like you, and like every one of you I am mortal and tangible. See how they have lied to you. It is true that I have a few things of gold that my ancestors left to me. Everything I have you will have whenever you wish it. I am going to the other houses where I live. Here you will be provided with all necessary things, you and your men; and do not worry at all, for you are in your own house."

From the whole conversation it is evident that Montezuma sees in Hernán Cortés a new incarnation of Quetzalcoatl and in Carlos V the Supreme God.


The Conquistador seems to take all this as a natural thing.

Time passes. It has been six days since the Spaniards entered Tenochtitlán and the situation has not yet been clearly defined. Cortés and his officers have been paid homage with a great banquet and new presents. But the status of guest is far from satisfying the man who has come to take over the house and its occupants. Cortés is restless and eager to affirm his authority by means of a new act of violence and force.

The news reaches him that Montezuma's warriors have killed Spanish soldiers of the Vera Cruz garrison. After a night spent in prayer, Hernán with his interpreters crosses the main square of Tenochtitlán, enters Montezuma's palace, accuses him loudly of treachery and orders him to go with him to his apartments, to which the Aztec sovereign accedes. Supreme stroke of audacity: Cortés now holds the Aztec emperor as his prisoner in the very capital of the Aztec empire! And as if that were not enough, he demands of the obedient Montezuma the surrender of those responsible for the massacre at Vera Cruz, and orders them burnt alive in front of the imperial palace. Immediately thereafter he seizes the lord of Texcoco and several other notables, has a ship built, and orders Montezuma to gather together and deliver to him the greatest possible quantity of gold, silver and precious stones.

Soon a movement of rebellion begins to make itself felt in the city against the invaders. The movement is restricted, however, to the capital, for the neighbouring cities remain apathetic.

How is the revolt expressed? In a kind of passive resistance. People stay shut inside their homes. Streets are deserted. The great market closed. The silence of the Indians surrounds the Conquistadores like a wall.

It is in that critical moment that Pánfilo Narváez, a man in the confidence of the governor of Cuba, reaches the coast of Mexico with a fleet of eighteen ships and more than eight hundred soldiers, and sends messengers to Montezuma telling him that Cortés is an impostor and that Diego Velázquez has not authorized him to carry out any conquest. Thus the very convenient myth (for Cortés) of Quetzalcoatl is going to crash to earth.

In that hour is revealed the spirit of decision, the uncommon audacity and courage of the ex-scrivener from the obscure town of Medellín. In spite of feeling besieged by subterranean hatreds that may at any moment explode into armed revolt, Hernán Cortés leaves Pedro Alvarado in Tenochtitlán with two hundred men and marches with the rest of his soldiers against Pánfilo Narváez and his powerful force. In Cempoala, under cover of a torrential downpour, he falls upon Narváez's camp, captures him and dominates his underlings completely. The part of the warrior finished, the politician enters on the scene. With his golden tongue Cortés succeeds in persuading the other captain's soldiers to come over to his side. Next day he returns victorious to Tenochtitlán with his troops reinforced by more than eight hundred men.

But something very serious has happened in his absence. Pedro Alvarado, whom the Indians called "Sun" because of his blond hair and beard, had stupidly ordered some two hundred nobles murdered. Indignant, the populace is determined to resist by arms. Now all are positive that Cortés is not Quetzalcoatl but an impostor.

An infuriated multitude is gathered in the square in front of the imperial palace, brandishing fists and weapons and roaring threats. Without loss of time Cortés has the emperor brought and tells him to mount to one of the palace galleries and from there to address and appeal to his people for peace. Montezuma does what he is commanded, but he is received with stones. Cortés later related to King Carlos V that ". . . His own people hit him on the head with a stone, so hard that within three days he died."

And he added nothing more about the dramatic event.

The Aztecs of Tenochtitlán now have a new chief in the person of Cuitlahuac.

The Spaniards' position is untenable. Many soldiers have died. Many more are ill. Water and food are growing scarce. The powder is exhausted. And on top of all this the indigenous forces increase in number and fury. There is no alternative to retreat. Cortés sets a night (it is June) to commence the hateful operation. No longer do his soldiers display the arrogant posture of conquerors. They are like highwaymen quarrelling over the spoils. The captain orders the gold, silver and jewels he has amassed divided among his men. The soldiers stuff them into their pockets and packs now empty of munitions.

The retreat is disastrous. It is necessary to cross the canals from which the Indians have removed the bridges. And the Tenochcas give no quarter to the invaders. They attack on all sides like demons, on foot on the causeways or in pirogues on the canals. The Spaniards throw themselves into the water. The weight of the precious stones and metals carries many of them to the bottom. Others, regarding their lives as more precious than riches, empty their pockets. It is a tragic night that will live in history as "the Night of Sorrow."

The survivors reach Tacuba, from which they flee on to Tlaxcala, the republic ally. Cortés is there, but not with back turned on Tenochtitlán, thinking of descending the mountains to the sea. His eye is directed toward the compass point where lies the metropolis of the Aztecs, which he stubbornly plans yet to conquer.


He orders thirteen boats to be constructed in pieces, which are to be carried up the mountains for an emergency attack by water. Still in Tlaxcala, he reviews his forces. He has 550 infantry, forty cavalry, eight cannon and some thousands of Tlaxcaltec allies.

He marches toward the Mexican citadel, which now has a new emperor, Cuauhtémoc. For three months Cortés remains with his army in Texcoco, preparing for the final assault. He puts together the pieces of the ships and with them forms his phantom fleet, which he arms with cannon. He traces out plans of attack, appoints commanders, divides his forces. And one day he makes a frontal advance on the enemy redoubt. Some of his soldiers dash to the Great Temple, scale the steps of the pyramid, but fall. The Spaniards fall back, leaving prisoners. And all that night they keep hearing, from the place where they are camped in the outskirts of the city, the beating of drums and the shouts of the besieged who are carrying their white prisoners to the sacrificial stone, where they tear out the hated hearts.

It is not difficult to imagine what Cortés felt. He was chewing the bitterness of defeat, seeing his great dream of conquest imperilled. It must have been that night that the resolve was born and grew in his mind not merely to take the city but to destroy it. Naturally, he invoked the most noble reasons to his aid. Were not the Aztecs barbarians who ate human flesh and worshipped horrid gods of stone? Destiny had chosen him, Hernán Cortés, to give to His Catholic Majesty, Carlos V, King of Spain, these lands so rich in the three realms of Nature. Yes, and the Church, thanks to the Conquistador, would see her spiritual kingdom also augmented.

Nevertheless, before attempting another attack he sends an emissary to the new emperor, guaranteeing his life and promising to support him in the government if he would surrender his forces and yield up the city. Cuauhtémoc rejects the proposal.

The struggle goes on for nearly four months in repeated attacks under which the city is being gradually, implacably destroyed. Cortés' tactic is to send his Indian allies to demolish all the houses they can and block the canals with the rubbish. And when those allies are counter-attacked and fall back, the Spaniards with fresh troops of infantry and cavalry go in, facing the Aztecs with that advantage.

Foot by foot Tenochtitlán is thus conquered. Taken prisoner and brought before Cortés, Cuauhtémoc at first receives military honours and privileges. But soon the paranoiac dominates the *caballero,* and Cortés demands that the Aztec reveal the hiding place of the treasure of the empire. As Cuauhtémoc refuses to do so, he is tortured, and, years later, assassinated, when Cortés, now appointed by his king Captain-General of New Spain, marches with his men for Honduras, carrying the royal prisoner with them.

In Tenochtitlán no stone is left on stone.

# 6. Puebla and Cholula

A fairly clean and comfortable omnibus is taking us from Mexico City to Puebla, capital of the State of the same name.

It is eight o'clock of a luminous May morning, and the two great volcanoes have never seemed so limpid to us, nor so close. We go climbing, always climbing, slowly rounding Popocatépetl and Ixtac-cíhuatl.

"Once upon a time, many thousand of years ago, there were a prince and a princess," I tell my wife. "They loved each other so much that a god turned them into mountains so that they might never be separated any more."

"Is this tale an invention of yours?"

"No. It's an Aztec legend." I point to Popocatépetl. "Yonder is the prince. In the Indians' language the name of that volcano means 'Mountain that Smokes.' There is the princess, 'The Recumbent woman.' Popocatépetl, the pipe-smoker, tall, erect, is the masculine, active element. Ixtaccíhautl, prone and submissive, is the feminine. Don't you think it's all perfect?"

An oblique, swift glance from my companion informs me she has accepted whatever there is of Andersen in my story but repudiated what I have borrowed from Freud. I shrug my shoulders and gaze at the landscape.

We are in the real *tierra fría*: transparent atmosphere, clean forests of pine and cedar, deep greens against the brown earth. In everything there is that matutinal lightness that does not depend on the time of day, that dry, crystalline cleanness of high altitudes.

The road is first-class, the driver careful, and, for greater guarantee, an image of the Virgin of Guadalupe is hung above his shock of curly, lustrous mane.

The climb continues as far as Río Frío, where there is a restaurant at more than 11,000 feet altitude. In the early years of this century this was a dangerous zone of highway robbers, and anyone who ventured this far had to come well-armed and protected. We get out to take coffee. It is as if we had left an interplanetary rocket on the moon itself. I have the feeling that if I lift a leg to take a step I shall take off in flight. I see passengers moving about, a dog barking, another omnibus leaving, but the sounds made by persons, animals and things reach me only faintly.

Ten minutes later we resume our journey, and thenceforth we descend toward the south-east, bound for the valley where in 1531 the Spaniards founded Puebla as a sort of fortress to protect the city of Mexico.

We pass plantations of maguey, and the frustrated painter in me gets excited at the succession of beautiful pictures. Yonder, for example, are five peasants dressed in white, with their light straw hats, motionless figures sharply outlined against the ochre earth where the magueys thrust up like rigid green plumes in regular rows climbing the slope of the hill, which flees on toward the sky of a cold and fragile glassy blue.

A thought strikes me. Why did Federico García Lorca never visit this part of the world? I do not recall having found in all his work a single poem referring to this country. And yet, certain regions of Mexico can only be described with poetic truth in Lorcan terms, like those of his "August":

AGOSTO

*Contraponientes*
*de melocotón y azúcar,*
*y el sol dentro de la tarde*
*como el hueso en una fruta.*

AUGUST

Counterposings
of peach and sugar,

and the sun inside the afternoon
like the stone inside the fruit.

Very true it is that a man when travelling carries his poets, paint-ers and musicians with him wherever he goes. That earth is by Gauguin. The peasants, by Van Gogh. The crystal sky was born of a sonatina by Mozart. But that fat chauffeur telling anecdotes to the dry, silent sergeant on the front bench—that one, ladies and gentle-men, is mine, all modesty aside.

And here is one of his stories:

Once a poor devil, already half-drunk, went to a wake and stayed there watching over the body lying on a table in the candlelight. There was a thick silence in the air, broken only by the sobs of the deceased man's relatives. The pulque began to make the rounds. The *peladito*, penniless man, didn't hesitate: he tilted several glasses and (with what he had already taken) reached such a state of euphoria that he started dancing and singing. A *comadre* pulled him over to a corner and reproved him:

"Now then, what's this about? Can't you even respect the corpse?"

The *peladito* cast a disdainful glance at the dead man and said, "Corpse? Corpse, that was Juárez. Corpse, that was Zapata. Corpse was Maximilian. That thing there's nothing but a dead loafer!"

The driver bursts out laughing. The sergeant remains serious. I make my diagnosis. The fat man must be a product of the *tierra caliente,* the hot lands. The lean one, of the *tierra fría,* the cold.

"When do we get there?" someone shouts.

The driver responds jovially, *"Ahorita!* Right away now!"

In the neighbourhood of Huejotzingo we pass vast orange and lime groves. Again to mind come bits of a poem of Lorca's:

| | |
|---|---|
| *Limonar.* | Lemon grove. |
| *Nido* | Nest |
| *de senos* | of yellow |
| *amarillos.* | breasts. |
| | |
| *Limonar.* | Lemon grove. |
| *Naranjal desfallecido,* | Swooning orange grove, |
| *naranjal moribundo,* | moribund orange grove, |
| *naranjal sin sangre.* | bloodless orange grove. |

It was here that the Spanish missionaries founded the first monastery in Mexico. I can see its ancient walls, away off, through apple trees. The monks manufactured a cider that was and still is famous in this region. Now here are three words which for me have poetic and pictorial value: monk, monastery and cider. By association I think brown images: earthenware jugs and stills, arcades in patios with patina, Franciscan habits, earth, dark faces and hands.

Along the road's edge we see houses of adobe, infants playing, *burricos* flicking their ears, women squatting, possibly making *tortillas*. Shadows blue, brown, purple. Humid, vivid greens of vegetable gardens, alternating with the yellowish coffee colour of the soil.

We enter the *pueblo*, a town of narrow streets, low and melancholy houses. We pass the *zócalo*, which is like all the other *zócalos* of all the other *pueblos*: church, bandstand, benches with idlers, *portales* over the sidewalks. We stop for several minutes at the bus station, where the gay driver is the first to jump out, tugging at his blue denim trousers that cling to his fleshy hips, sharply modelling them, and passing a dirty handkerchief over his glistening face. *"Vamos, amiguitos, vamos! Tenemos cinco minutes para tomar una tequila y hacer otras cositas más."* "Come on, friends! We got five minutes to drink a tequila and do a few other little chores."

We know from personal experience that those five minutes may stretch to ten or fifteen.


We reach Puebla at noon. A barefoot gamin, with very quick, eager eyes, wants to take us to *el mejor hotel de la ciudad*. I tell him we already have hotel accommodation reserved. But he insists, tries to pull the suitcases out of my hand, dances about us, goes and comes like an importunate blowfly. If he knew the mistake he is making in insistently calling me "Mister! Mister!" he would certainly change to calling me *paisano* or *hermanito*. Because I feel like a brother to these Mexicans, a brother at least in flesh if not in spirit. My wife has already remarked that the majority of these little Indians, with their dark, round faces, their stiff, straight black hair, all look like my natural sons. I accept the paternity with exquisite, tender joy.

I strike a bargain with the urchin.

"If you stop that 'mister' business, I'll give you the bag and a peso."

"Yes, mister."

"No deal."

"*Pero, señor . . .*"

"That's better. Here. We're going to the Palace Hotel."

The hotel is near the *zócalo*. They give us a clean but sadly impersonal room, like those in the majority of provincial hotels.

We lunch in a small room, where we are the only guests at this hour. We ask a waiter, who knows less than we do, for information about Puebla. Through the window I have a glimpse of a cupola with yellow tiles glistening in the sun, amid colonial rooftops that remind me of my Porto Alegre. We have heard so many lovely things about Puebla that we are eager to start out rambling through her streets.

Of Puebla de los Ángeles someone has said: "Made by angels and inhabited by hidalgos." It is the fourth city of Mexico in population and perhaps the most Spanish of all. A city of noble lineage, of lordly ancestry.

The local Chamber of Commerce (there must be one) will inform the visitor that Puebla has some 250,000 inhabitants, and was immortalized by, among other things, having been the scene of a battle in which 2,000 Mexican patriots in 1862 defeated 6,000 French soldiers of Napoleon III; and that in 1847 the Mexicans fought here against the *gringos*. It will say further that Puebla *es muy industrial,* and, in the face of our boredom and indifference, will start enumerating the products of local factories—cotton and wool textiles, fine soaps, leather articles—until a magic word strikes the bell of our imagination. That word is *azulejería*. The painter thrills. The camera quivers. Let's leave the Chamber of Commerce secretary behind and go see the tiles that have made the fame of this lordly city, placidly planted in a vast valley, flanked by four of the most formidable volcanoes on the Continent.

When Puebla was founded as an entrepôt between Vera Cruz and the capital of Mexico, the Franciscan friars discovered the existence of rich deposits of silicates in its environs, which made the new town the most important glass-producing centre of New Spain. The Indians of the neighbourhood made ceramics with a clay of excellent quality, very like that used in the city of Talavera in Spain, famous throughout the world for its ceramics of Talavera de la Reina. The Franciscans sent for several master potters from Spain;

these settled with their families in Puebla and in the course of time produced glazed dishes and earthenware of high quality.

Today the much-esteemed Talavera of Puebla uses clay taken from the soil of three different villages—black, white and red—and mixed in equal parts. For many days this clay is trodden on by barefoot potter's helpers, then washed, pounded, washed again, again pounded and washed many times more. The mixture is then put in a wooden box to "mature." Only after the clay is matured is the shaping done. Once dry, the pieces go into the oven for six or seven hours, at a low temperature. In the old days there was one stage of the process of making pottery at which magic entered upon the scene (magic or faith, as you will) to make the artisan's activity more beautiful still. Before opening the oven after the first cooking, the master potter and the other workers and apprentices stood in the deepest silence, after which they chanted all together: "Praised be forever the Most Holy Sacrament!" They say some Puebla potters retain this custom even today.

At first the ceramic of Puebla followed the Spanish in the use of colours: blue, yellow and white. The Indians and mestizos, however, learned the trade so well that around the end of the sixteenth century they had already modified the designs and colours of their products, and the "Talavera de Puebla" hardly had anything more to do with the "Talavera de la Reina". There are some who say that the earthenware of the Mexican city is more beautiful and of better quality than that of the Spanish.


How to offer in words the image of a city? How communicate to the reader the sensation of *being*—being with all five senses—in a given place? To say that Puebla is ancient, austere and baroque is not sufficient. Comparing her, for example, with Washington, I should say the capital of the United States is like a vitamin-filled green raw salad, while Puebla is in part a fritter cooked in good Spanish olive oil and partly a roast taken off those Indian braziers so widely found in Mexico, the smoke from which, with its characteristic smell, breathes in our faces at every moment, coming from doorways, windows, patios and corridors. I shall explain the culinary image. In these old houses, with tiled façades, warm colours predominate, principally an oxblood red. Almost all these churches, chapels and convents are of brown or grey stone. The persons who walk

along these brown sidewalks seem also taken from ovens: they are
toasted like clay vessels moulded by the local potters.

The Washington salad is doubtless more healthful, but the
Poblano fritter is tastier.

A special circumstance determined the architectural fate of Puebla
de los Ángeles: the coming here, in the early years of the colonial
period, of families from Andalusia. That explains the Andalusian influence in many of the public and residential buildings, where the
use of tile is generous to the point of sometimes becoming extravagant. And as saying "Andalusian" is equivalent to saying "Arab"—
and, if we want to go further back, "Persian"—it is not surprising
that Puebla is also a city of Moorish cupolas and patios rich in
mosaics. Neither must we forget that the Andalusian architects who
came here in the second half of the sixteenth century had to resort
to local labour, so that the first Spanish construction erected on the
soil of New Spain was already undergoing a certain Mexican influence.

During the colonial period there were two great centres of artistic
irradiation in Mexico: the Capital and Puebla. And this exquisite
City of the Hundred Towers began, from the very first years of the
colony, to reflect the thought and the way of life of Seville. Today,
almost oblivious of her Andalusian mother, she is just Puebla de los
Ángeles. And I assure you, friends, that is quite a great deal.


In the field of architecture nothing in this country has charmed
me more than the so-called "Mexican baroque." Puebla and Cholula
—which is only about six miles from here, almost a suburb—are the
two Mexican cities possessing the most churches. Puebla has sixty-
five.

Werner Weisbach has said that the baroque art of the West is the
art of the Counter Reformation, that is, essentially Catholic and
Latin. And, I ask, cannot the Mexican baroque have been an indigenous reaction against the architecture the Spaniards brought to
Mexico right after the Conquest? Cortés and his soldiers razed the
Aztec temples, and the Catholic missionaries, often using the very
stones of the destroyed *teocallis*, built their churches in which there
was much more Middle Ages than Renaissance; temples, in sum,
which in their sombre sobriety of line and tone, said nothing to the
Indian soul, so avid for ornamentation and vivid colours. Even before

the Spanish baroque was brought to Mexico, the Indians to some extent had already anticipated it in their sculpturing of columns, façades, images and altars. And when at the beginning of the eighteenth century the Churrigueresque and the plateresque came to New Spain, the Indian and the mestizo sensed, as it were, in these new styles—unconsciously, to be sure—a road by which to return, even in an incomplete way, to the only architectural and sculptural forms in their opinion compatible with the religious spirit and the supernatural. Now, the friars from the beginning had to use, in the construction of their temples, local labourers, Indian or mestizo (and the mestizo is a being closer to the Indian than to the white in Mexico). The control they exercised over these builders, masons, sculptors, mosaic artisans, stonecarvers, gilders, carpenters, etc., was limited, so that the Mexicans could give almost free rein to their imagination, interpreting in their own way the drawings and models made by the padres. That is why we see on so many of these altars, angels, archangels, cherubim, saints and even Christs with Indian-like faces.

If the Indians had been capable of literary expression, their written protest would have found the formidable barrier of the Inquisition opposing it. Plastic people par excellence, the Mexican found its form of expression in architecture and sculpture. But did not the friars perceive the silent, subtle reaction? I think they did, and not only tolerated but wisely encouraged these innocent heresies as a part of their technique of Catholicizing the people. That tolerance continued through time and culminated in the acceptance, by the Church, of Our Lady of Guadalupe, the Indian Virgin Mary.

It is here in Puebla that the best specimens of Mexican baroque, of the Churrigueresque and of the plateresque can be found.


We are now in front of the *Casa del Alfeñique,* a term, this, that time has deprived of its ironic point to give it a historical patina. *Alfeñique* is the paste, or frosting, of sugar and oil of sweet almonds used on cakes and confections. And the façade of this stately three-storeyed house really does seem more the work of a confectioner than of an architect. Covered with tiles of dark green with white ornamentation, its general aspect is rose-colour. The "icing" or *alfeñique* is in the white carved frames of the windows and in the friezes, in relief, that run along the front as though to indicate the divisions between the storeys. The windows on the ground floor are barred with *rejas,* wrought-iron grills, while the two upper storeys have small iron balconies.

I confess I like this specimen of Poblana colonial architecture. It has the effeminate grace of eighteenth-century hidalgos who danced the minuet, wore their hair powdered and the handkerchiefs of lace, but who for all that were *muy hombres* and knew how to weild their swords with honour and valour. When I used to hear about this house I could imagine myself smiling ironically before a "wedding cake." But not so! Here I am, gazing at and photographing it from many angles, trying in my imagination to eliminate the telephone and electric light wires, pretending we are back in the time of the viceroys and that at this moment a carriage, drawn by four fiery horses (the horses in old romances are always fiery), has pulled up in front of the carved door of the *Casa del Alfeñique.* From inside, a general, a corregidor or an archbishop is going to emerge. Because in the eighteenth century this mansion was a residence designed to lodge high personages. Today it is a regional museum.

We go in. On the ground floor is the section of Archæology and History. The person in charge is a short little woman, withered, fragile and rather hunchbacked. She is modestly dressed and her black silk stockings attract my attention mainly because the little woman has just taken off her black-varnished, high-heeled shoes, placing them under her desk. She comes to meet us, very amiable, and, shoeless, conducts us among these ancient stones and relics, talking not in the automatic tone of someone giving a memorized speech but with calmness, smiles, hesitancies, in such a way that we get the impression the things she says are being improvised especially for us. In her cider-coloured face her agate eyes seem brightened by the glitter of fever. We are so sorry for her that we treat her with an affectionate courtesy and end by being more interested in her life—about which we ask questions—than in the things she says or the rarities she shows us. We give her a good tip and on taking our leave we hear these words: *"Ustedes no son despóticos, a pesar de ser personas de honorabilidad y posición. Acá los ricos nos miran de arriba y nos tratan mal. Muchas gracias!"*—"You are not overbearing in spite of being persons of distinction and position. Here the rich look down on us and treat us badly. Many thanks!"

We are already climbing the stairs leading to the next floor when the little creature exclaims, "You are Cubans, aren't you?" We nod slowly in the affirmative. "I knew it!" she murmurs, her toes wriggling happily.

The keeper of the next section is a Mexican with coppery face, two-day-old beard, rough hair growing long over his ears and down into his dirty collar. His clothes are old, wrinkled and greasy. He looks more like one of those ne'er-do-wells who accost us in the street to beg money than a municipal functionary. Nevertheless, he receives us with great courtesy and shows us, piece by piece, the whole first floor, which is furnished like a residence of the eighteenth century. Purple-red predominates in these curtains, sofas, chairs and rugs. We are particularly interested in the beautiful china displayed in cabinets, product of the "Talavera de Puebla." Before a large shelf of glazed ware the man whispers dramatically, "An American offered me a thousand dollars for this dish. Madam and sir, I am a poor man, I earn a miserable wage, but I told the *gringo* No. Because, the devil! somebody must be honest in this world. This country's works of art are being smuggled out of Mexico and going to enrich foreign museums. It's a shame."

We pass on to the chapel, where the talk turns to human vanity. Our guide philosophizes: "What's the use of all this, if we are to become dust in the end?"

On the top floor we find relics of a more recent story. On entering one of the rooms I am startled to come upon General Obregón sitting talking with another political personage. They are two mannequins modelled, painted and dressed most realistically. The guide assures me that the furnishings are genuine: they belonged to the drawing-room of the general's own home. And he adds further: "They shot him to death in a restaurant."

We stop next before a showcase where the original *china poblana* dress is kept. According to legend, the costume was planned and embroidered in colonial times by a young Chinese woman, Princess Mirra, who had been brought to Puebla by merchants of her country and sold as a slave to a rich family. It is a silk dress with full skirt, full of sequins and fanciful multicoloured embroideries, reminiscent of Oriental costumes.

New Spain was a meeting place for the most diverse cultures: the European, the indigenous, the African and the Asiatic. Arabia arrived here with the Spaniards, and Persia came with the Moorish architecture, in its mosaics. From the sixteenth century onwards

Chinese merchants came with their fabulous ships to Pacific ports, from which they came up, via Taxco, to the central plateau, bringing their porcelains, lacquers, fans and silks. There is a subtle Chinese influence, visible even today, in the sculpture, the ceramics and the textiles of many parts of Mexico, principally here in Puebla.

From the colours of the *china poblana* costume our eyes move on to a mirror splintered and pierced with bullets. The guide says that those were the first bullets fired in Puebla when the Revolution of 1910 broke out. And there now are our faces pock-marked and splintered in the depths of the tragic mirror. For a moment we feel assassinated.


We cross the *zócalo* in the late afternoon when the cathedral bells are tolling the Angelus. Just as the crow of a cock can give perspective to the night or early morning, a bell's voice has the virtue of lending a fourth dimension to the day.

The light, which in the morning was of new gold, has become honey in the afternoon, and now the sun is an orange spilling its juice over Puebla. A smell of fried food and braziers floats in the air. A sad man crosses the street hugging a bass viol as if he were carrying a loved one, a son or a brother. Indians dressed in white are placidly sitting on stone benches with tiles set into the back. And how unreal the tone of their dark skins seems, touched by the light of this last sun of the day! These thick-foliaged trees must be— I won't swear to it, I'm uncertain of it—*calabazas*, calabashes. In the centre of the square, like a huge cage full of birds, we see the bandstand of silvered iron where on Sundays a military band gives public concerts. Children are running around the flower beds, leaning over the railing of the little fountain, playing with the water Arcades, *portales muy castellanos,* surround this *zócalo* on all sides but one, where the cathedral stands. We start over there. The atrium is enclosed by a high, wrought-iron fence.

A Poblano has declared to me that this is the handsomest cathedral in America. Begun in the second half of the sixteenth century, in the reign of Philip II, it was consecrated only in 1649. The style is very good Spanish Renaissance. The material used for this imposing structure? A greyish stone found in the vicinity of Puebla. (Close to the central door someone has written with pitch on the centuries-old façade: *Se prohibe orinar.*)

We enter. Women, with black shawls covering their heads, are kneeling in prayer. Votive candles are burning at the foot of the altars. How to define this immense, echo-filled silence? And the mysterious play of light and shadow? And the all but human presence of those saints clad in garments in which purple predominates?

Yonder, upon a broad platform, is the famous main altar made by Manuel Tolsa: columns arranged in a circle, supporting a cupola under which an image of St. Peter is fixed. The columns are of *tecali*, polished and fire-gilded.

While my wife makes her devotions, I stand contemplating a Christ in a painful posture, the body lacerated and bloodied. A profound sadness overwhelms me. The murmur of the prayers seems to accentuate the silence of the place. I now percieve the presence of an aged padre who is praying on foot a few steps from me. His lips hardly move, his lean and livid fingers grasp a rosary; his eyes are fixed on the agonized Christ. From sheer wear and age his cassock has lost its original colour. White, thin beard covers his parchment face. I imagine his history. Withdrawn from activity by old age, now he is awaiting death. With fear? With resignation? With joy? In what other regions of Mexico must he have served in priestly duties? It is possible that he has been the parish priest in a little village of Chiapas in the days of the religious persecutions, and that only a miracle saved him from the firing squad. The old man's eyes fill with tears. Age or emotion? I try to think how the reflection of the Lord's image must look in those pupils partly covered by cataracts. All this is very sad, but at the same time it has a strange, morbid beauty.

My wife rises, making the sign of the cross, and we go out together to a languid day's end. I inhale the tepid Poblano air. There are purple tones on the horizon. Something oppresses my breast. It is as if I were coming back from the funeral of a friend.

We dine in a restaurant near the *zócalo*. I buy a local daily to see the cinema programme, and discover excitedly that a Spanish operetta and *zarzuela* company is in town. Tonight they are staging *El Gato Montés, The Wildcat*.

My wife thinks, as I do, that we must not miss the show for anything in the world. I ought to explain I was born and have lived nearly all my life in a Brazilian province which has many contacts with a good part of Spanish America. The men of my generation and of the one preceeding it learned Spanish from the clowns of itinerant circuses and from variety artists, popular songsters, prestidigitators and ventriloquists. Many a time Spain would come to our small city in the shape of a poor company that, for the boy I then was, represented the very essence of adventure, a breath from faraway lands half-dreamed but never seen. More than once I have attended exaggerated melodramas like *Los Bandidos de la Sierra Morena* staged in circus rings, in a mixture of Portuguese and Spanish. A little bigger, later on, I would tunelessly hum bits of Spanish *zarzuelas* like *La Verbena de la Paloma* and *La Gran Via* that my father used to play on his gramophone with the morning-glory horn. (Ai-ee! How ancient I am!)

Because of these things I feel Puebla in a very personal way. She is providing me with a re-counter with the Spain I love so much and have never visited. Puebla gives me the smells of Spanish condiments, narrow streets, posters advertising bullfights, inner patios, Andalusian manor houses, arcades, purple churches with sad ladies in black, recalling Holy Week in Seville.

And with all these things I am absent-minded, and because of the tumult of my thoughts I go hurrying along.

"More slowly," recommends my companion. "We're not going to take father down from the gallows. The theatre doesn't start till nine-thirty."

In Mexico no one has lunch before two-thirty in the afternoon or dines before nine. We have been invited to dinners that started after ten, ending close on midnight. That is the schedule of meals in the Hispanic world, where cinemas and theatres customarily offer, among others, performances at six or seven o'clock, before the hour for dinner.

We are sitting in the Teatro Variedades. In reality I find myself at another point in time and space. This is not Puebla, but several cities out of the past fused into one through the work of one of those magicians of my childhood. The year? 1915. They say Pinheiro Machado has been killed in Rio and the situation is very serious. As if that misfortune were not enough, the Great War is continuing in Europe. But what does it matter to me? My parents have given me permission today to come see *El Gato Montés*, and here I am, eager to see the curtain go up, that cloth with the red mouth in the middle of which, in a medallion of feigned relief, cherubim flutter about with wreaths in their fat hands. The curtains of the boxes are wine-coloured. In the air is that smell inseparable from Latin theatres—glue and ink from the scenery, a whiff of cellar odour coming through the prompter's shell and with something vaguely suggestive of immemorial mice.

My companion touches my arm, calling me back to Puebla. She makes a sign toward the left. I look. A large Poblana is giving the breast to a baby, who nurses away at it, producing a liquid sucking sound.

"Imagine," I whisper, "if those cherubim on the curtain got a scent of the milk and hurled themselves on that *señora*. . . ."

"I'd swear she wouldn't be at all bothered, and would give the breast to the little angels."

A child about three years old starts running and yelling down the aisle between the rows of chairs. No one pays the least attention or makes any protest. I believe that in no part of the world—that I have visited—have I found so great a participation by children in the life of adults as I have in Mexico.

The lights are dimmed. The musicians take their places.

In these orchestras there is always a bald fellow with oily skin who plays a flute. And a melancholy man, dressed in black, who affectionately strokes the belly of the bass viol. And a cornetist with a glistening nape. And a cellist who plays disdainfully (because at heart he dreams he is a concert soloist). There they all are. Not one is missing. The tuning-up begins. The trombonist tries out his lungs: he blows three cracked notes from the instrument. The clarinettist practises his mouthpiece: he executes a few flourishes and the clarinet's sounds seem to radiate out into the atmosphere like blue serpentines interlacing themselves with the vivid yellow serpentines pouring from the cornet. Someone strikes a note on the piano keyboard, and the violinists sit nauseatingly tuning their fiddles.

At last the maestro, the orchestra conductor, arrives.

Silence falls. The auditorium darkens. The first chords of the pompous overture are heard. A shiver runs over my skin. The Poblano baby is still nursing away, but the music now drowns out the noise of his sucking. Someone has caught the little girl who was running. The curtain slowly rises.

The first act is in the garden of a residence in the outskirts of a great city. It is a holiday. Soledad (soprano) is waiting for her sweetheart, a famous bullfighter. A gypsy woman (comic high soprano) makes a black prophecy of misfortune for her. Nevertheless, Soledad tries to forget. Rafael el Macareno (tenor) arrives amid acclamations, and the invariable love scene follows. Father Antón (no voice) sings an aria explaining why Rafael is a great bullfighter: he, Father Antón, baptised him. They break into gay dances, and suddenly the orchestra, changing tone, announces something ominous. Trembling all round. All face to the right of the stage. They see Juanillo, El Gato Montés, coming down from the mountains. (Bravo, Juanillo! You are like the Spanish baritones in my memories: middling stature, heavy beard blueing the long cheeks, long nose, Castilian *theta*—ah, you have changed nothing! Thanks, thanks!) With the coming of the Wildcat the bullfighter places himself on guard. The padre frowns. Soledad is uneasy. Great hubbub of voices (sung, because this is an opera, not a *zarzuela*) out of which emerges the information that, because of his love for Soledad, Juanillo has committed a crime and had to take refuge in the mountains, where he is now living like a wild animal at bay. While he is singing, Soledad—a lady of outstanding presence on whose bosom all the Mexican babies in the auditorium must have their gluttonous eyes fixed—wrings her hands. When Juanillo ends his aria, the bullfighter takes the floor. The two get into a duel of words that does not degenerate into hand-to-hand combat only because the good Father Antón intervenes. Juanillo thereupon makes a threat. He knows that Rafael is to fight the bulls next Sunday. "If you do not die on the horns of a bull," sings the Wildcat, "I shall kill you." General commotion: musical *oh's* and *ah's*, crescendo from the orchestra, ruffle of drums. El Gato Montés initiates his withdrawal. Before vanishing from the scene he brandishes his fist and repeats his threat, holding a high note. Soledad falls into Rafael's arms. Father Antón raises his eyes and his hands to Heaven. The curtain descends slowly, to applause.

In the interval we buy and eat *camotes,* the speciality of Puebla, mindful of the good ladies from Chihuahua who recommended them to us on the train.

Again the auditorium darkens. A baby starts whimpering. Heads turn round. A maternal voice is heard: "Hush, Pepito. Why didn't you do it in the interval, stupid thing?" The curtain rises. The scene now takes place next to the gate leading into the bull ring. One can see part of the tiers of seats inside, full of people (painted), and the heads of the brave bullfighters and the horns of the bulls as they charge. On the right, a chapel in which picadores are praying. Soledad comes to meet her fiancé and begs him to be careful. A duet is sung, and finally the sweethearts separate. Rafael enters the arena amid acclamations and begins his work. From the audience we can see his proud head, the movements of the cape, the *banderillas*. *Ovations. Olé! Olé!* Suddenly, a sort of hiatus, followed by cries of horror. Rafael falls. A few minutes later some friends bring him in, dead, in their arms, his abdomen pierced by the horn of a Miura bull. Seeing him, Soledad falls. And with her, the curtain.

Third act, first tableau. It is in a church where they are holding a wake over the body of Soledad, who has not withstood the loss of her well-beloved. The scene is in semi-darkness. A bell tolls for the dead. Father Antón paces from side to side, much downcast. Great profusion of tears. Once more the orchestra announces that something important is going to happen. More bearded than ever, El Gato Montés bursts into the church singing, advances to the bier, takes Soledad's corpse in his arms and runs out with her toward the mountains. The second tableau shows Juanillo's refuge in the heights of the sierra. Soledad, dressed in white and veiled like a bride, is stretched out on the trunk of a fallen tree, cold and motionless (of course she is, she's a mannequin!), as the Wildcat despairingly sings his love. But the police are not asleep. They go out in search of the bandit and succeed in surrounding him. El Gato fights back. Firing starts, and finally a bullet strikes Juanillo in the chest; he falls, and writhing in agony, rolling on the ground, he approaches the late Soledad, pulls her to him and dies embracing her, singing, while the orchestra deafens the air with its *fortissimo* dramatic finales.

Great applause. The curtain goes up and down many times, the artists come out to give thanks, and the honours of the evening fall to the baritone Jesús Freyre, who played the part of Juanillo. Several babies in the audience wake up and burst out crying. Elbowing the Poblanos, we make our way out into the cool, starry night. I feel happy. It is good to discover that somewhere in the world our childhood is continuing, after a fashion. And whistling snatches from the opera that have stuck in our memory, we turn slowly back to the hotel.

A fat yellow omnibus, full of fat yellow Indian faces, takes us to Cholula, which is only six miles or so from Puebla. We spend the day in the "Holy City of Anáhuac," which was formerly the centre of the Toltec kingdom. According to folklore, Cholula has three hundred and sixty-five churches, although statistical truth obstinately puts down barely a scant hundred. I take my oath, friends, I have never counted nor do I intend to count the Catholic temples in the sacred valley. I'll stick to folkloric truth, nearly always prettier than the arithmetical, and hope that my Bahian friends will forgive me the heresy of believing any other city in the world than Salvador may be capable of offering to the faithful a different church for each day of the year.

When the Spaniards reached here in 1520, Cholula had about a hundred thousand inhabitants. In one of his letters to Carlos V, Hernán Cortés stated with his habitual dryness of style that the Toltec capital "is the most beautiful city, externally, in Spain, because it is very full of towers and is flat. And I certify to Your Highness that I have counted from a mosque four hundred-odd towers in the said city, and all are of mosques."

Four centuries after the Conquistador, Aldous Huxley looked at Cholula through his thick, erudite lenses and, after quoting Mallarmé ("Poetry is not written with ideas; it is written with words"), he referred to the fortunes and misfortunes of the writer in his dealing with verbal images, only to ask at last: "Cholula, for example—how to find the words to describe the magnificence, the queerness, the general improbability of Cholula?" And he goes on: "Happy Prescott! He, it is evident, had no difficulties with the place." He then calls on the author of *The Conquest of Mexico* to give, rather in the manner of a school textbook, his description of Cholula. The excellent Prescott was never in Mexico, and this fact furnished him with an indestructible alibi. He could weave all the imaginative fancies he liked, based on second- or third-hand information. But Huxley, posted in flesh and blood atop the same pyramid from which Cortés had contemplated the holy city, felt the tremendous responsibility of the visual, auditory, olfactory and tactile witness. And that is what I am feeling now, if I may be pardoned the immodesty of ranging myself in such illustrious company.

I take some photographs in colour. I recognize, however, that this is not solution but flight. The valley still lies before me, defying the writer.

The landscape is not the kind that makes the observer catch his breath at the first quick glance. It is sober, and whatever grandiose, rare and unreasonably beautiful there is about it is revealed gradually, slowly, like a drug that, ingested through the eyes, slowly but inexorably penetrates into the blood. The colours do not strike the retina like an oil painting in the sunlight: the picture seems, rather, a water-colour. It has no tropical exhuberances, but the gentleness of temperate lands.

We are on top of the pyramid of Quetzalcoatl, which today is covered with earth and vegetation. On the pinnacle of the Great Temple of the Toltecs the Catholic missionaries erected the Sanctuary of Our Lady of Remedies, which is here in the middle of a quadrangular atrium paved with grey stone. Leaning on the parapet, we contemplate the broad valley around us.

All the land appears to be cultivated, and the first image suggested to me by the quadrilaterals of the field is—with the pardon of Cortés, Huxley and Prescott—a patchwork quilt like the one my great-aunt Adelina once made for her eternal spinster's bed. Only the quilt of that magnificent kinswoman who died a maiden held all the colours of the rainbow, while the valley is a quilt of patches in tones of green only: grey-green, jade-green, lettuce-green, sea-green, moss-green—cut here and there by the strong ochre of the roads of hard earth, and occasionally alternating with squares of newly-sowed fields in which the earth stands forth naked and striped with furrows.

In the sky, which also seems lined with tiles from the Talavera de Puebla, an Aztec sun, already quite warm at this hour of the morning, reveals to us bit by bit the details of the countryside. The churches spring up, as it were, from the valley floor, one here, another there, still another farther on, like an animated drawing in colours. First it is a cupola, yellow or pink, among scattered trees of a green that deepens to blue; then we can discern the façade, which in some is of an ochre that can hardly be distinguished from the earth and in others is of a reddish brown. We idle slowly along the four walls of the atrium, but always with eyes fixed on the valley. Yonder is another cupola the colour of egg yolk, shining in the sun. And that wall, battlemented like a fortress—to what temple or monastery can it belong? If we fix our gaze, we shall see, far off yonder against the violet brush stroke of the mountain range, another cupola, which, seen from here, is rather a bright speck than a colour. And all those churches are like soldiers, in their rich uniforms of mosaics, until a moment ago camouflaged in the vegetation, preparing for attack. We feel besieged. But what a beautiful siege! I confess I am already vanquished. I raise the white flag unconditionally.

I point toward the city, properly speaking, of Cholula, which spreads out down there with its brownish roofs, and looking at the Moorish cupolas of the Royal Chapel among trees slender as cypresses, all in a vague climate of desert dryness, I exclaim: "Jerusalem!"

I turn to another side and am inclined to agree with Aldous Huxley, who thought this valley similar to the Roman *campagna*. Yes, but a *campagna* that had suffered—if one may say so—a chlorophyll bleeding, a countryside of soft greens in a Franciscan poverty of water. But no! Now I am facing another point of the compass. I see a field of magueys, a baroque church, burros kicking up dust on a road, led by an Indian in white to the tinkle of harness bells. Afar, the profile of the volcanoes in their eternal vigil. This, ladies and gentlemen, is Mexico, very good Mexico!

Listening to the little bells I imagine the moment when the bells of all these churches start pealing at the same time, creating over the valley a gigantic, sonorous cupola made of voices of the most varied timbre—sharp, brilliant, dull—as they toll for the dead or ring out in festive chime. And why not imagine, too, that the sounds have the colour of the church from which the bells produce them? Yes, the sky would be transformed likewise into a vault of mosaics. I have some suspicion that this is a baroque idea, and that perhaps my prose is already suffering the influence of the style of these Mexican churches.

But wait . . . What are those sounds now really coming to our ears, human voices in a chorus I should term Dantesque if I had not some touch of literary restraint. They sound like howls of despair or hatred. I lean over the parapet. The clamour seems to come from that great building with the look of a barracks, down there at the foot of the pyramid.

Our guides explain to us that it is the Cholula insane asylum. And that at certain hours, principally on windy days, the madmen usually yell like that.

I have not yet mentioned that we have two guides, José and Alberto, Indian boys of eight or ten: round faces, skin the colour of the sapodilla plum, eyes the size of *capulí* cherries (the large kind), stiff, black hair with bristling fringes. They have taken us by assault down there in the city, and want to show us Cholula. They have on the tip of the tongue a speech they have probably repeated to hundreds of other visitors. From time to time when I run a hand over José's or Alberto's head the wrong way, and say, *"Calma,* take it easy, *muchachos!"* they laugh, displaying their strong white teeth.

When we were climbing up here, conquering those hundred-odd steps, halfway up we found, sitting on a stone with a book in his hand, a young Mexican of eighteen or nineteen. He was reading with such concentration, and the moment was so utterly beautiful —the youth, the book, the valley, the cupolas, the sky, the mountain range, Orizaba far off there like a Father of All under his snow-covered head—the picture moved me so much that I could not resist the human temptation to get into it myself. *"Buenos días!"* I exclaimed, trying to start a conversation with the stranger. He closed his book, rose respectfully but without a smile, and came to meet us.

I began: "Excuse me, but will you tell me what you are reading so attentively?"

He showed me the volume, a compendium of biology, and explained: "I am preparing to enter the Medical School and the University of Mexico."

His voice was serene. His features intrigued me somewhat, for I had the impression I had already seen that face somewhere. What was his name? Ramón Jesús. Indian blood?

"Naturally," he answered. "I am a Mexican."

"And after you get your degree, are you going to stay in Mexico City?"

"No, *señor.* I shall come back to practise in my *pueblo."* He smiled for the first time, but almost imperceptibly. *"Mis paisanos* need me more than the men of the capital do."

"And where is your *pueblo?"*

He turned his head and stretched out his arm toward the valley: "Santa María Tonantzintla. It has the most beautiful church in Mexico."

"It has? Why?"

*"Bueno,* that's my opinion."

"More beautiful than the one in San Francisco de Acatepec?"

"*Por supuesto.*"

"More than the Capilla Real?"

"A thousand times more. The Chapel is Moorish. The church in my home town is Mexican."

Then, looking down at his shadow on the dry brown earth, he murmured: "It is where I was baptised."

"You are Catholic?"

He smiled again, knitting his very thick eyebrows: "What else can one be in Cholula with so many pretty churches?"

I asked my companion to take a picture of me with the young man.

"I wish for you a brilliant university career, and that you will be a good doctor, and that some day you will be able to help your people."

"*Gracias, señor.*"

We shake hands. The Indian returned to his place.

My wife and I continue climbing, tugged along by the two small guides, who were laughing at the strange language we were speaking and of which they could understand only an occasional word or phrase.

"You see," I said to my companion, "take that Indian: what a living type, serene and likeable. He is going to be a great doctor. The most important institute of cardiology in the world, note that, *in the world*, is in Mexico. And do you know who its director is? Dr. Chávez, who is pure Indian, as he himself proudly proclaims."

The red kerchief my wife was wearing about her head fluttered in the breeze. I went on: "Benito Juárez was an Indian. Our own Rondon is an Indian. And there are idiots who keep talking about superior and inferior races. Myth, sheer myth!"

I look back. The Indian is still in the same position, absorbed in his biology. I stopped a moment and murmured, "Why is it I like that face so much? It seems to me the boy reminds me of somebody I've known, some friend . . ."

My wife smiled: "Now, now. That's pure narcissism. The boy has exactly your face when you were the same age."

At first I tried to disagree, but then I realized. I had just clasped the hand of the boy that I had been. And I saw myself at eighteen sitting on a bench in the square of Santa Cruz, in the shade of a bamboo, reading in all seriousness a treatise on philosophy.

And as nearly always happens when I feel my autumn sharply, I began to whistle a snatch from Brahms's quintet for clarinet and strings. But I lent the andante a syncopated rhythm it does not have. It's just that the climb was beginning to take my breath.

I looked back once more at the Mexican youth and muttered, "*Adiós!*" In reality it was not to him that I was saying goodbye, but to the other fellow.


We accept our minuscule guides' suggestion and go to visit the interior of the pryamid. We buy tickets and head for a door in the base of the monument. An aged Indian with bronzed skin, bony face, his moustache and hair of a cottony whiteness, leads us through narrow galleries and passages, a veritable nightmare labyrinth. What a fine programme for a claustrophobe like me! My wife communicates her apprehensions, too, in a murmur: "This I don't like at all." The guide talks with a fluency I have not found in any other Mexican Indian. He must be at least seventy. I see his bent back, the white, thick texture of his shirt and trousers, I heard his flutey voice, but without paying much heed to what he says. There is a smell of earth in the rarefied air. Greyish lizards flicker over the walls of these ill-lighted galleries. I know that great hairy spiders and poisonous snakes are marching by the hundreds through my wife's imagination, as her hand seeks mine.

I am convinced we have strayed straight into a nightmare. Why are we walking so far? Where are we going? To the centre of the earth? My beloved, far-off Jules Verne! The remedy is to imagine I am Professor Lindenbrock, author of a *Treatise on Transcendent Crystallography*. I recall the document that launched me on this adventure: "Descend into the crater of the Yocul of Sneffels which the shadow of the Scartaris comes to caress before the Kalends of June, bold traveller, and you will arrive at the centre of the Earth."

Despite the coolness of these interminable galleries, sweat is running down my face, my chest, my back. The Indian's skin, though, is as dry as the earth of the desert.

We reach the centre of the monument at last, where the old man shows us remains of a Toltec mural in which red tones predominate. I can hardly see it, for the sweat is getting into my eyes, blurring my vision. The guide talks incessantly. In an anguish of one buried alive I can feel the whole weight of the pyramid on my chest.

Happily, we are going back. Can the man know the way? After several minutes' walk we catch sight of the luminous rectangle of the exit.

It is good to breathe the free air again and to see once more the great face of the sun. Yes, and the faces of the two little Indians, smilingly waiting to take us as far as the city.


Cholula proper has nothing extraordinary about it except the churches. It is a small city of some ten thousand inhabitants, with its *zócalo*, its *ayuntamiento*, its low houses with ironwork over their windows, narrow sidewalks and many Indians, men and women, in its streets.

There is the market with its stalls under white awnings, everything with an Oriental bazaar look about it. Squatting women sell fruits and vegetables. Others offer toys and odds and ends. Pieces of cloth in many colours are heaped under awnings. Ribbons, also multicoloured, hang from a horizontal stick and swing in the touch of the breeze. On the car-for-hire ranks drivers are napping over the wheels of their Fords and Chevrolets. And patient burros, tied to trunks of trees or to hitching posts, shake their ears to frighten off the flies.

The severe stone front of the church of San Gabriel stands on one side of the square. The atrium is vast, and its thick walls remind one of a fortress. Here we find one of the strangest architectural ensembles in Mexico. It is almost the equivalent of a compendium of history, but a compendium with the pagination in the wrong order, or in no order. Where are we, after all? In the Spain of the Middle Ages, in Arabia or in Mexico? Because the church of San Gabriel is joined, like quite extraordinary Siamese twins, to the Royal Chapel. The church looks like a citadel with its high, bare, battlemented walls, its brutal buttresses, its dramatic medieval atmosphere. It is a synthesis in stone of the historic epoch that engendered it. It seems to tell us that the destiny of man on earth is to pray, to suffer and to await death; there is no happiness possible in this vale of tears. The Capilla Real, with its forty-seven unbelievable cupolas, is reminiscent of a Moorish mosque. We go in. We walk on grey paving-stones through a discreet forest of columns, but I do not find here the expected ogives, the elegant Moorish arches, the colour and the lacy grace of the Mudéjar. The temple is full of the devout. Much light streams in the windows. Sparrows are wheeling in the air, they alight, singing, on the capitals of the columns. Before one of the altars Indians have made a "carpet" of sawdust of several colours, in designs representing flowers, fruits and birds. I see sad, suffering faces here. And always the babies with their velvety tender eyes.

We go out into the maturing morning. In the air floats a fragrance of burned dry branches, which for me has a most evocative power: St. John's Eves with bonfires, balloons, sweet potatoes roasted in the coals, fortunes told, stars, and girls in love. Beside the outer wall of the chapel I see ancient tombs, among which boys and girls are playing hide-and-seek. Lizards of a greenish-brown run over the walls of the church of San Gabriel. The crow of a cock pierces the morning like a lance.

The sun is nearly at its zenith. We cast a last glance at the improbable cupolas of the Capilla Real and go in search of a restaurant.

If there were a cataclysm—a possible though improbable thing—and it were granted me to save only two churches—a thing both impossible and improbable—I should choose the one in Santa María Tonantzintla and the one in San Francisco de Acatepec.

The first is in the little village of Tonantzintla in this inexhaustible territory of cupolas, towers, saints and angels.

The ground of the churchyard, to which some orange trees give a domestic look, is full of stones with inscriptions marking the burial places of town-dwellers and of many of the artisans who aided in building this church, which, in its modest proportions and its colourful grace, seems rather a family chapel. But no one can pass by without stopping, and no one stops at the gate of the atrium without entering, and no one enters without smiling at this specimen of Mexican baroque which, in Huxley's opinion, is "the oddest church in Christendom." The façade, of dark green tiles with designs in light blue, offers among its delightful improbabilities a Moorish door with vertical frame in blue, white and yellow, having on each side two squat columns supporting a yellow cornice which runs across the whole façade and over which are two niches with saints I cannot identify. Between these niches, a window with a balcony. Above the window, another cornice, likewise yellow, and over this another niche with the image of Saint Mary dressed in a blue that seems to have come straight out of the sky of this Cholultec afternoon. Tiles identical with those of the façade clothe the tower, which is of good plateresque style. But unfortunately I know all this wordiness will not succeed in making the reader *see* the church of Santa María Tonantzintla. Patience. The best thing to do, then, is to go into the temple, for when Huxley declared it "unique" it was not for its architectural lines but its interior decoration.

Here inside, the Indian builders, sculptors and painters have given their imagination a field day. One has the feeling that those anonymous artisans applied themselves thoroughly to a kind of catechism in reverse, that is, the Indianization of Catholicism. As some one has written, here "the angels are Indian, the saints are Indian, even God is Indian."

In the middle of the cupola—which to me looks like a luminous outpouring of golden arabesques—is designed a rose window with the dove of the Holy Spirit that only by a miracle escaped being modelled on the likeness of the quetzal, the bird whose feathers the Aztecs prized so much as ornaments.

Upon the white background of the walls and altars the Indian artificers sculptured in bold relief—blue, red and gold—a whole army of angels and cherubim whose features were possibly inspired by those of the village babies. Many a friend, *compadre,* godson and neighbour of the sculptors must have served as model for the images of these dark-skinned saints with prominent cheekbones and slanting eyes, nearly all as stocky as the natives of the region.

The motifs of the decoration of these columns, altars, cornices, retables, all came from Mexican nature: leaves, flowers, fruits, animals; they have nothing to do with the world of the Conquistadores.

We go from side to side, from surprise to surprise, sticking our noses into everything, only with great difficulty restraining exclamations and the desire to caress the plump cheek, the round belly, or other parts of the anatomy of these angels playing the mandolin or the lute, some of them with unangelic faces like this one, on the base of a column, his nose turned up, an expression of disdain on his full-lipped mouth as if he thought himself superior to his environment, wishing perhaps to make us believe he is here against his will. There are moments when one has the impression that these figures, in the midst of which emerge unexpected masks, these groups of dancers—all are details of a Bacchanalia and not of a Catholic temple. The ingenuous and the malicious alternate: the general result is something out of the ordinary.

The crepuscular note of the atmosphere is supplied by a grey Christ with disproportionately long arms and by a *Virgen de la Soledad* beside it, dressed in black and with a sword thrust through her heart.

The silence is complete. We sit down on a bench under the cupola, as one who seeks to refresh himself under a waterfall. I think we are going out of here all spattered with gold. I think tenderly of the serious, silent Indians who sculptured, gilded and painted these wonders.

Like two fallen angels modelled in poor clay, José and Alberto come up to us and whisper that the taxi is waiting outside.


The church of San Francisco de Acatepec stands on top of a hill, solitary in the middle of the countryside, covered with tiles from head to feet. No one should be surprised at the expression "from head to feet," because the tendency of this people is to humanize everything.

Here is one of the most precious jewels of Cholula. The towers are of seventeenth-century majolica; of majolica are its walls, cupola and belfry. I have the feeling I stand before a Chinese porcelain.

The interior is as fantastically rich in colours and designs as the exterior. Here the artists have given the eyes no quarter. There is not a centimetre of wall that is not carved or painted. And always the Indian faces, the profusion of gold, arabesques and pagan ornamental motifs.

Of this church José Moreno Villa wrote:

"The use of tile in this case reaches the point of delirium. The work is a great ceramic toy set up on earth. Confronted by it one no longer thinks whether it is a church or follows some plan of Borromini. We are really in a world of caprice and dreams. Everything in it is colour and brightness. Even the columns, the entablatures, the captials, the cornices and the finials are of tile. If the natives had had mountains of diamonds or pearls within reach they would have erected an edifice exclusively with these elements."


In contrast, I think of the agonized images of the Christs I have found in Mexico. Mexican religious art took the dramatic Spanish theme of the martyrized Christ and made the most funereal variations on it. I recall the Christs in the Catholic churches in the United States, sad but serene, of clean and almost athletic bodies on which there is a minimum of wounds and blood. But the Mexican adores his flayed Christs, his scourged Christs, the Christs that shed blood. There seems a touch of the sadistic in the spirit that engendered these images. It is still the medieval idea that suffering is not only necessary but sanctifying—that the pure and true religion has to be sad, grave and painful, and that life can be worthily lived only in the constant shadow of death. And how that idea found echo in the Mexican soul, so enamoured of macabre images!

In the church of San Agustín in the city of Morelia there is a black Christ. Not long ago in the church of Santa María I saw a grey one. They say there is a red one in the church of San Diego and a blue one in Atotonilco. I have seen in Puebla a series of Christs yellow as that of Gauguin, Christs the colour of verdigris, crucified, sitting, kneeling, bent under the weight of the cross, lying in the arms of the Virgin or upon purple shrouds.

For the Indian who regards himself as the victim of Fate, is not Christ probably the maximum, most perfect symbol of the Great Martyrized One, of "the good man who is the victim of the evil one"? These ideas come to me from reading a page or so of the excellent book *The Skull,* by Paul Westheim, who says at one point: "And the frequency of these sculptures and paintings that are found especially in the humble rural churches in villages of indigenous population, beyond the influences of urban civilization, admits the conclusion that the martyrdom man makes man suffer is an experience profoundly and primordially rooted in the sentimental world of the Indian, and that the Martyrized Christ is so particularly adorable to him because the indigene feels His suffering as something very much his own."

I have found images of saints in the most curious stylizations, but the Christs I have seen up to now have seemed to me startlingly realistic, both in anatomy and in costume, the majority of them displaying "natural" hair, that is, of animal origin. In this country the human frequently shows his intestines, so that I shall not be surprised if some day I come across a Christ slashed open by a centurion's lance, because of gangrenous Christs and cancerous Christs I have already seen more than one.

Yesterday in Puebla, in the church of San Francisco, which is almost as old as Brazil and one façade of which is a pure gem of

Puebla's Churrigueresque, I saw the "incorrupt" body of the beatified Sebastián Aparicio, constructor of the first roads on the Continent. The body is in a glass case of small dimensions, for the *beato* was of small stature. Men, women and children were filing slowly past the body. I stood for some minutes watching the scene. The faces were sorrowful, women with heads covered by dark *rebozos*, men of diverse age, some active, others walking with difficulty, supported on crutches, but all sad with a sadness that seemed to have body and smell. The procession moved slowly, since that appears to be the natural rhythm of chronic adversity. All were silent—always the fishes in the aquarium—and one could tell they were praying only by the movement of their lips. They would stop beside the *beato*, gaze at his mineralized body, kiss the glass of the coffin and many of them would raise their hands to put a nickel coin or a paper peso in an opening in the top of the glass case. It was very queer to see the coins and the worn, greasy banknotes falling on the purple garment of the corpse. And that mixture of misfortune and sanctity, money and mummified flesh struck at my stomach, giving me a desire for fresh air and broad, clean horizons.

It is because of all that, that I—who feel a nostalgia for a religion I have never had, but which I have imagined, half-dreamed, to be gay and fresh as the morning—I see now with affection and gratitude the tiles of the church of San Francisco de Acatepec, whose angels with human faces seem to be playing Vivaldi on their coloured mandolins and lutes of wood and plaster.

Late in the afternoon, on the way back to Puebla, I hear a man telling his seat mate an anecdote which strikes me as representative not only of Mexico but also of the majority of the other Latin-American countries.

On the occasion of one of the many Mexican civil wars there was a "general" famous for his atrabilious deeds and violence. The man simply had a lust for illegality. He would shoot prisoners summarily, he sacked cities, violated women. The faction for which he was fighting won the war and the *caudillo* was officially made governor of his province. In the first weeks he bore himself with the dignity demanded by his position, but after some further time he began to feel such a nostalgia for violence and excesses that he could not contain himself: he sallied forth on new maraudings, liquidating enemies, attacking ladies and maidens, sacking towns. The respectable men of his province sent a memorial to the President of the Republic protesting against the violent acts of the *caudillo*, to whom the Chief of the Nation sent a forceful telegram reminding him that the governor of a State should be the first to respect the law. The general read the President's telegram and, furious, responded with another in these terms: "I resign my post because unfortunately our revolution has degenerated into government."

A burst of laughter is heard in the omnibus, the laughter of the man who told the anecdote. His companion, a large man of middle age, with light skin, well-dressed, with rings on his fingers and a pin in his cravat—that one remains serious, impassive, smoking his cigar.

We have already glimpsed the first houses of Puebla, when the blond youth sitting beside the driver, in white trousers and green shirt, starts singing in his thin but tuneful tenor some classic Mexican songs. When we get out in Puebla the singer passes his hat around among the passengers, asking them for *una contribución*. Some give. The boy approaches the man with the rings, naturally expecting at least *un pesito* from the prosperous-looking gentleman.

"Won't you contribute something, *caballero?*" he asks. He has to repeat the question in a louder voice.

"Why should I contribute, *hombre*, if I heard nothing? I'm deaf."

If the mere sight of a church sufficed to relieve a soul of its burden of sins, I should have mine light and clean, for we have done little since we came to Puebla but visit convents and churches. My wife, however, assures me that the process of purification is not so simple, especially when it's a question of an old, hardened sinner like me.

I am left almost in profane ecstasy in the placid, cool, tiled patio of the Convent of Santa Mónica, which functioned in secret for more than seventy years, because Mexican laws prohibit the existence of convents in the national territory.

We eat *tacos* (Ah, heavens, why must dirt be ever the Siamese twin of the picturesque?) in a shop opposite the Teatro Principal, perhaps the oldest on the Continent, which was completed in 1759. We see pasted on its venerable walls posters announcing the play staged by amateurs last week—*The Shooting of Padre Pro*—based on the dramatic story of the priest who, in the region of Chiapas in the times of the religious persecutions, went disguised as a peasant around villages and farms, secretly fulfilling his sacerdotal functions until the day he was arrested and shot. That impressive mestizo figure, that soul persecuted at the same time by sin and by love of God, inspired Graham Greene's novel, *The Power and the Glory*. The drawing on the poster is of a touching primitivism: Padre Miguel appears in it, kneeling, arms widespread, in front of the firing squad.

Wherever we turn our eyes in the Mexican cities and *pueblos*, we see vestiges of tragedies. It is frequent to hear such things as: "It was there they slit So-and-So's throat."—"See that wall? They shot X there."—"On that corner they put a bullet into General Y."

On the façade of the Jesuit church of the Holy Spirit—where lie the remains of the legendary Princess Mirra, the *China Poblana*, who took the Christian name of Catalina de San Juan—I find on a tile plaque the following inscription: "On the principal arch of this façade was hung by order of the Inquisition the head of Don Antonio de Benavides (El Tapado) false Inspector from Spain and executed 12 July, 1684." Just now, at the door of that same church, an Indian woman, all in black, her dull eyes sunken into bony sockets, begged me for money for "the oil of the Lord." And after receiving the note I gave her, she added in her cavernous voice, "God keeps nothing." Another Indian woman was selling candles *para las almas del purgatorio*. Everywhere we see men and women kneeling, praying. Some penitents cross broad atriums of stone on their knees, arms on high, eyes fixed on the front of the church. Graham Greene wrote that he could never again forget the penitents of Mexico in their mystic postures.

We go out. We stop in the middle of a bridge, lean our elbows on the balustrade. Backs of houses, from the windows of which hang coloured clothes, overlook a stream of muddy, cascading waters. And just as we prepare to appreciate the picture, an unbearable stench rises to our nostrils. There is no doubt: cleanliness seems irremediably to be the price of picturesqueness. We hastily depart from the urological Venice.

At the door of the church of Santo Domingo a filthy Indian, one of the raggedest we have yet encountered, is sitting on the curb playing a curious instrument. I stop to watch him. The man is blowing on a leaf from a tree, extracting from it a sound like ocarina and harmonica mixed, while with one hand he is scratching a gourd to mark the rhythm. What he is playing must be something of his own invention: a monotonous tune of markedly Oriental flavour.

We visit the famous Chapel of the Rosary, which the Poblanos call "the eighth wonder of the world." Ever since we arrived I have had the impression I am eating baroque, drinking baroque, sleeping baroque and dreaming baroque. But I confess I am not yet sated. And the Capilla del Rosario does not disappoint me. In its riches it reminds me of the church of São Francisco in Salvador da Bahia. I think it would be hard to find a chapel with more detailed and delicate work in laminated gold or richer in tile and marble. The Virgin on her altar is quite covered with real jewels.

Outside we find the musician still playing his little tune, as sad and monotonous as his still eyes. We set out along these sidewalks full of people—for Puebla has much life—and stop frequently before old doorways opening upon inner patios (Oh Andalusia that I have never seen!) with galleries and arcades, patios of ancient ancestral homes which today are tenements where underclothes hang out to dry on balustrades, and half-naked dirty children play with patient dogs on old paving-stones.

At six in the evening we enter one of the dimmest churches in Puebla, the church of San Roque. What is going on inside it fascinates me. Elbows propped on the parapet of the pulpit in a rather irritable air, a priest of Indian blood, stiff hair, toasted skin, rosary in hand, eyes closed, is repeating Paternosters and Hail Marys aloud. When he pauses between prayers, a beautiful tenor voice can be heard coming from the choir accompanied by the sound of an organ. It is a round of children, boys and girls between two and six years old, the boys dressed like sacristans or in monkish brown cassocks, the girls in white tunics and wings like angels, walking around the benches singing and scattering flowers—Cape jasmines, roses and red carnations. The whole air of the church is perfumed. (It is the month of May.) The somnolent padre fills the enclosed space with his big voice of good metal but poor in inflections. And again the Mexican tenor, a brunette, warm voice, makes itself heard above the others. And it is a delight to watch the children. They are all very serious, they steal distrustful glances in our direction, walk without rhythm, get out of step, step out of line—back to which they are pushed by the lean woman directing the march—and their tuneless little voices rise in the air not in unison. Among those little black heads of Indians and mestizos I see a blond boy (fruit of whose sin?), perhaps the most timid and alarmed of all. There he goes in irregular skips, slapped and pinched by his companions with such frequency and force that he suddenly bursts into tears.

Just before noon we visit an annex of the convent of Santa Rosa that suggests nothing religious or mystic. It has nothing to do with hair shirts or fasting. It does not evoke ascetic, fleshless saints but fat, greedy abbots.

We are in the kitchen of the convent where in the eighteenth century they prepared dishes that have lived on in the history of Mexican cookery. Ample, clean, with its three vaults it glistens in the Mudéjar wealth of its tiles. At first sight it looks like the antechamber of a Moorish harem. (The difficulty with the writer is that he has to assume the air of one who has been everywhere he mentions in his comparisons.) The floor is of brick with inlay of tile in graceful polychrome designs. In the central vault, or dome, can be seen a circle which—in yellow and more than one shade of blue—contains an octagon and a picture with the roses symbolic of the order to which the convent belonged.

Under the lateral vaults the whiteness of the tiles on the walls is broken by gold-coloured medallions in the form of polygonal stars. A wealth of tiles in many colours clothes the baseboard of this merry kitchen and the uprights of its broad door frames.

The person in charge is a fat woman who comes over to us dragging her slippers and wiping her hands and fleshy arms, of a soft ripe wheat colour like old ivory, with a coarse towel. She has a double chin, thick down and tiny eyes. Everything indicates that she was preparing her lunch, because from somewhere the smell of fried food reaches us. She proceeds to explain how the kitchen "functioned when the nuns were here." She shows us the spring of water, the oven, the cabinets set into the wall, the brazier, the place where the soap was kept, the stone bench built against the wall at the door, the chocolate pot and the wash basin—*aljofaina* is a word I am here using for the first and maybe the last time in my life.

I ask rhetorically:

"Was it here, then, that the famous *mole poblano* was invented?"

The woman lays her open palm on her generous bosom: *"María Santísima! El mole poblano!"*

She tells us that in colonial times whenever a viceroy was to come to Puebla, all the local convents outdid themselves in preparing unusual dishes for the illustrious visitor, whom the Bishop was generally trying to please. Sister Andrea de la Asunción, *gran maestra* in cookery, was in this Dominican convent of Santa Rosa at the time of one of His Excellency's visits. It was a Sunday. According to one version of the legend, Sor Andrea was sitting on her doorside bench of tiles, worried, not knowing what dish to make for the Lord Bishop, when an angel came down from Heaven and whispered a recipe in her ear.

Our woman in charge of the kitchen doesn't believe the story of the angel; she prefers to attribute the whole merit of the invention to the nun's imagination. Be that as it may, after taking communion Sor Andrea sets about her tasks—and I can imagine her running here and there, stirring pots and pans, dipping fingers into pots of spices, grating cheese and chocolate, giving orders to her assistants.

She took several ingredients: raisins, *chile mulato* and some *chilpotles* browned in butter. She toasted over the fire a handful of sesame seeds and then ground up cloves, pepper, almonds, peanuts, cinnamon and aniseed, and mixed it all together.

At this point I feel as though a ribbon of fire is rippling in my stomach, rising through the oesophagus, burning my throat, embittering my mouth. The woman continues:

"Sor Andrea added, then, to all these things two bars of the special chocolate made in the convent, some tomatoes, onions, roast garlic and a few *tortillas* of maize meal, first toasted and then ground up . . ."

"Shades of Montezuma and Cuauhtémoc! How many ingredients in this infernal dish?"

"Twenty-four," the woman serenely informs me. And she goes on:

"The evening before they had killed a *guajolote* (turkey) that had been fed on chestnuts and hazelnuts at the convent. *Bueno,* the Viceroy and the Bishop that Sunday tried out the *guajolote* with the sauce invented by Sor Andrea, and the sauce became known as *mole poblano.*"

I ask an idiotic question: "Did they like it?"

The fat woman fixes her doll's eyes on me.

"Of course, *señor!* And how! And when the story spread round the city, other convents sent to beg Sor Andrea for the recipe, and she, saintly soul that she was, didn't refuse it to anybody."

We emerge into the Poblano sun, nearly as violent as its *mole*. We walk for a time in silence. I think of Sister Andrea, I imagine her Bishop and her Viceroy, both sitting at table in the Casa del Alfeñique. After several minutes I say to my wife:

"Do you know? I'll accept the legend. Except that I think the angel that whispered the recipe to the nun came, not from Heaven, but from the Inferno. It was an angel saboteur. Think it over. . . ."

Noon sharp. The shadows in the streets have vanished. But the intense colours of the store fronts and of the garments of the Indians walking hither and yonder loaded with bundles and children are still here.

I think this is a good time to talk about what Mexicans eat.

It would be possible to recount the social history of Mexico through the story of its most important agricultural product, *el maíz*. Yes, because maize is the basic food of the Mexican. In order of importance the chili pepper, the bean and rice follow. The poor Indian in general eats only *tortilla* rubbed with chili. Where, then, do they get their good teeth? We may find the secret of that calcification in the way the *tortilla* is made here.

First the maize must be softened—it can be any of three types: white, yellow or blue, according to the region producing it—by leaving it soaking for three days in lime water. Afterwards it is ground, using for the purpose the old Aztec system, which consists in placing the still moist paste on a stone, the *metate,* and rolling another, smaller stone, the *meclapil,* over it. From this results the *masa,* or dough, which is pounded until it is transformed into a round, thin sheet, the thickness and diameter of which vary. After taking this shape, the *tortilla* is baked in the *comal,* a kind of flat, earthenware plate, which is set over a bed of hot coals.

The *tortilla,* the bread of the Mexican, is also, so to speak, a sort of "vehicle" for other foods. If we take a few strips of meat of any kind and add to them some chopped onion, slices of tomato and a little chili "for the flavour," and roll the mixture in a *tortilla* just out of the oven, and then fry the whole thing in abundant lard— we shall get the *taco.*

The *enchilada* is a first cousin of the *taco*: take the same ingredients, but instead of frying the mixture boil it in *ranchero* sauce, made of tomato, chili and onion and garlic all ground together. *Enchiladas* are served in a dish with plenty of sauce sprinkled with grated cheese and redundantly covered with minced onion and, in some cases, with a thick coating of whipped sour cream.

Of all these *tortilla* dishes I have a special fondness for the *quesadilla*. Grated cheese is mixed with the raw maize dough and then beaten into the shape of a *tortilla*. The stuffing may be of meat, potato or beans (*frijoles*), but I assure you, friends, that the best and most exquisite of all is the kind made with the yellow flowers of the *calabaza*. And of course a good Mexican *quesadilla* must not lack a few pinches of piquant herbs and the eternal chili. When in restaurants I say, "*Quiero quesadillas de flores de calabaza*," I have the feeling I am reciting a poem, not ordering a dish.

Unfortunately for my Brazilian liver the *quesadilla* also is fried in lard.

There are several types of *tortilla*. The *chalupa*, a speciality of Puebla, is an oblong *tortilla* fried with meat, cheese and chili stuffing. The *gorda* has a greater thickness than the ordinary kind. The *sope* is high on the edges. The *totopo*, made of *tortilla gorda*, is fried in butter, in pieces, and is nearly always seen in company with *frijoles refritos*, described below. The *chilaquiles*, segments of *tortilla gorda* steeped in chili sauce and sprinkled with grated old cheese, are served with slices of onion and radish.

The *tortilla* is used also as a tablecloth, as a napkin, as a plate and even as a spoon—for it is common to see one of these Indians take a piece of *tortilla* in his fingers and with it scoop up the food to carry it to his mouth.

But the utility of the maize does not stop at the *tortilla*. There are still the *tamales*, which are a kind of oval rolls of moist meal stuffed with *mole*, or, more commonly, pork or chicken, and wrapped in the husk of the maize in a fashion that recalls, a little, the old-fashioned crackers at parties. And often one hears this cry in the streets: "*Tamales calentitos!*"

The *elote* is simply the ear of maize roasted or boiled. Yesterday I heard an Indian woman on one of these sidewalks proclaiming "*Pozoles!*" I went over in curiosity. *Pozole* is maize gruel cooked with tomato, bits of lean pork and pungeant herbs. The *pozole* usually comes accompanied by a dish with slices of onion, lettuce leaves and grated cheese.

The onion is intensively used throughout all these *pueblos* and cities where we have been. In the most unexpected places and at the most unexpected hours its active odour assails and envelops us.

The Indians give the impression that they eat several times a day, standing near the stalls we see on the sidewalks or in the recesses of greasy doors. These Aztec, Toltec, Tarascan, Zapotec, etc., stomachs seem to obey no clock. One moment! Look yonder at that Indian woman, almost a dwarf, dressed in dark clothes, her infant on her back. Both are eating, or rather gnawing at something. I draw closer and see that it is *chicharrones,* bits of hog fat fried crisp. The grease smears the faces of mother and child.

Near by, more *chicharrones* are frying in an iron pot over a charcoal fire. In another pot I see a dish much beloved of this people, the *menudos*—tripe boiled in a tomato sauce. The onion and the chili, ever present, are like the chorus of the culinary tragedies in which the *dramatis personae* are the *enchiladas,* the *chalupas,* the *tacos,* the *chicharrones* and the different kinds of *frijoles.* The *frijol,* the navy or the black bean, is prepared in several ways, but these folk seem to prefer the *frijoles refritos,* which are first boiled, to soften them, and then fried. There is, further, the *frijol a la olla,* or "bean in the stew."

Mexican rice in general is dry and not as tasty as that eaten in Brazil. The tomato sauce gives it a pinkish colour which in Puebla harmonizes well with the tiles of the houses. Rice is nearly always served here with fried bananas, slices of onion and sometimes *guacamole,* a salad made of avocado mashed with minced onion and aromatic herbs.

Just as the Americans eat their inevitable turkey on Thanksgiving Day, and in Rio de Janeiro the St. John's Night tidbit is the *rabanada* (slice of bread dipped in egg, then in sugared water or milk, and fried), in Mexico on the same night it is the custom to serve *atole de chocolate,* a sort of sweet rice fluid in consistency to be drunk from a glass. On Epiphany, the Day of the Wise Kings, Mexican comadres and bakers make a special bread called *rosca de los reyes,* or "cruller of the kings." New Year's dish is a sweet salad prepared with several greens and vegetables chopped up with much seasoning, honey and lime juice, and served not in a dish but on a *tortilla.* There is a great variety of breads, cakes and sweet breads. They say that of these last there are more than a hundred different varieties known, all with their household names, usually suggested by their shapes. Thus we have the "policeman," the "ear" and the "horns," etc. Of the dramatic *pan de muerto* I shall have something to say in another chapter.

Of course, the Mexican *cuisine* is much more vast and rich, and I have only touched the surface here, the most popular dishes. We must not forget, however, the *barbacoa*, which is prepared more or less like our *churrasco*, broiled on a spit over the coals, and which originated the American word "barbecue."

It is interesting to note that these folk absorb calcium from the *tortillas*, and their diet of greens and vegetables is quite ample.

The food in this country bears a certain relation to the nature of the land and the temperament of the people. In the Mexican soul there is something brown and dry like broad expanses of the soil— and those rather harsh elements, but no less fascinating for all that, are found after a fashion in the *tortilla*. The "visceral" quality of the Mexican can take as symbol the *chicharron* and the *menudo*. And his ill-contained violence, which at times explodes unexpectedly like his volcanoes, cannot help appreciating the strongly seasoned foods. But not all in Mexico is drama and silence, subterranean or aquarium-like. There are colours, songs, dances. And the people of the hot lands know how to smile. And a generalized tenderness revealed in the use of diminutives, in the comic stories in which the hero is nearly always the *peladito*, the penniless fellow. All this—the colour, the living note—also appears in the food. It is the chilis—red, yellow, mulatto brown, green—the vermilion of the tomatoes, the *calabaza* flowers, the aromatic strong herbs, that make it gay, at least on the surface, enlivening the brown dryness of the *tortilla* and of the other dishes of arid or crepuscular look.

# 7. Oaxaca

Another omnibus, this time silvery and huge; another golden morning, another trip, this time a long one. We are going south and our destination is Oaxaca. When, back in Mexico City, I mentioned my itinerary to a Brazilian, he made a face and repeated incredulously: "Oaxaca?"

"Yes."

"By airplane?"

"No. By bus."

"Travel twelve hours in this heat? But what for?"

"To see some churches, some convents, the market."

The man stared at me for some time and at last exclaimed: "You must really enjoy old stone and dirty Indians!"

Our omnibus is rolling along the Pan American Highway. We go through Cholula and out into the country, heading for the Valley of Atlixco, which is, in Christian language, "on the surface of the waters."

We are uncomfortably seated on the bench at the back. I am squeezed between my resigned companion and a lieutenant of police, an Indian of forty-odd, in khaki uniform. He has a bandit's face, broad, pockmarked, a pair of turtle eyes above which swollen eyelids are pleated. Poor company. To top it off, he sits with legs widespread, occupying more room on the seat than he ought. I imagine him silent and sour. But no! In the first minutes of the journey the man reveals himself. He maintains a loudly bellowed dialogue with a young priest who is sitting on the front seat beside a nun. These two seem to be mestizos, both. Mexican law prohibits their wearing religious robes in the streets. The priest, who is thirty at most, is dressed in black, in a white shirt with soft collar and black tie, with felt hat of the same colour. He looks like a young peasant in his Sunday best, going to the city to have his picture taken. He smiles at the lieutenant's sallies, showing a gold eyetooth.

"Padre!" the policeman exclaims in a voice like a broken reed. "Do you know the temperature went up the day you got to Matamoros?"

The priest turns his head, frowning, and asks: "*Hombre,* why?"

"Because of the heat of your youth!"

The lieutenant's guffaw fills the omnibus. The priest smiles, shaking his head. Beside him the nun, very pale, with something about her skin that looks like a newborn mouse, stares outside. I notice a defect on one of her hands: it has no fingers, and the nails grow from the knuckles.

We are approaching a semi-tropical region, and the countryside that now surrounds us reminds me of the *caatingas,* the wastelands of stunted vegetation in the Brazilian north-east. I see adobe houses, goats, babies and children, burros, little miserable villages where people, in dramatic mimicry, merge into the landscape whose coppery dryness they imitate in skin and clothes.

The omnibus halts unexpectedly in the middle of the road and the ticket-collector jumps out. Shortly afterwards he reappears and speaks to the driver in a tone that hints at something abnormal. What can it be? The lieutenant leaves his seat and goes to investigate. He joins in the dialogue, which grows more and more animated. Finally the driver turns to us and exclaims: "Jump out, all of you! The bus is catching fire!"

"Be calm!" says the lieutenant. "Come out one at a time."

There is no panic. We emerge into the oven of the morning, seeking the shade of the first tree. The lieutenant explains to us, leisurely, that the fire started close to one of the front wheels. The driver and the collector are now attempting to put it out. The passengers are scattered about the vicinity, some of them already half-dissolved into the landscape. On the ground, which is covered with thoroughly dried-out bushes, lizards scurry stealthily. The light is so intense it actually discolours the sky. I try to comfort my wife by murmuring the classic "It can't be anything serious." She shrugs and says philosophically, "After all, if things like this don't happen, what are you going to write about?"

In the thin shade of a tree the nun, the priest and the lieutenant are chatting. The young priest has the floor: "In each of us dwells an angel and a demon. The important thing is to help the angel in his struggle against the demon."

He speaks with no air of a prophet, rather with the joviality of one who at heart does not take himself very seriously—a fact that seems to me very attractive. The lieutenant, with broad stains of sweat on his khaki shirt under the arms, lets out his slow laugh: "Well, padre, I only help the demon."

"You're wrong, lieutenant."

"I'm right, padre. If the angel wins, I run the risk of going to Heaven."

"And where's the harm in that?"

"Heaven's for those stinking-rich Mass-goers in Puebla. I want to go where there are *hombres* like Juárez and Zapata."

*"Buena . . ."*

"And where did people like them go, padre, tell me, where did Juárez and Zapata and Villa go?"

The padre goes on smiling. He lays a hand on the officer's shoulder and says affectionately: *"Pues, quién sabe, amigo?"*

I photograph the group. The priest with his hand on the lieutenant's shoulder. Sitting at the foot of the tree, the nun with her sad, dim look. In the middle distance, the silvery omnibus on the asphalt highway. In the background, a brown hill with spots of opaque green.

The driver announces that the fire has been extinguished and the journey is going to continue, thanks to Our Lady of Guadalupe. *Viva México!*


Now we are travelling through gay green cane fields, motionless under the midday stillness. We stop for lunch at Izucar de Matamoros, whose solid, implacable heat reminds me of Washington's in August. The sanitary conveniences of the hotel they recommended to us are so incredibly filthy and fetid that we completely lose our appetite. No: in spite of our appetite we cannot overcome the repugnance aroused in us by the look of the food, served on a rickety table with a tablecloth heavily spotted with grease under clouds of flies. The soup is too allusive to unmentionable things for us to dare touch it. The rice, hard and tasteless. The bread, old. We cannot forget what we saw, in a fatal glimpse, in the hotel kitchen as we passed. I think of all the black cooks of my life, and honestly I do not recall ever having felt any repugnance for the things they prepared. But with these Indians the matter changes shape. It's just that their dishes remind me too realistically of the colour of their dirty skins and their nasty tatters. We stay in a corner of the open part of the dining-room, gloomily eating some biscuits we bought in Puebla.

The journey continues. The lieutenant, the nun and the priest remain in Matamoros. This is the sugar, coffee and cacao zone. But soon we shall leave the tropical plateau behind to start a veritable toboggan slide, dizzily whirling up and down mountains.

The countryside is full of cacti, some tall and slender, in the shape of torpedoes. Others, the *órganos,* looking like enormous, many-branched candelabra. The soil turns from ochre to red, and the mountains begin taking on unexpected hues ranging from dark red to crimson or scarlet, from jade green to chrome yellow, to purplish blue and to coffee brown.

And once again we are on a plain. The conductor informs us it is the Valley of Nochixtlan. Time passes. We again climb and descend, and it is an amusing pastime to see what the old sun, in its descent toward the West, can do with the shape and colour of these hills, humps and mountains.

Finally, at nightfall, we catch sight of Oaxaca, which, like every Mexican city with any self-esteem, is situated on a plateau and flanked by mountains.


We ask for a room in a hotel whose name strikes my fancy: Posada Marqués del Valle. It sounds like a cloak-and-sword novel. Pretend we are arriving in a stage-coach and I, a musketeer, am here escorting a noble Poblana lady disguised as a peasant woman, who is coming to recover a stolen necklace. It is a matter of life and death. Tomorrow I have to seek out the Bishop of Oaxaca, who will disclose to me the hiding-place of the jewel. For that I shall have to identify myself, showing the fleur-de-lis I have tattooed over my heart. Of course the Viceroy's henchmen are alert, and it is possible that before dawn I may have to cross swords with them. Let them come, one by one!

My wife signals to me. The hotel manager is waiting for me to speak. I request a room. They assign me one. The man warns me honestly: "For two days we have been without water." A sorry piece of news for one just arriving from a journey! We go upstairs. The hotel has no lift. But who expects lifts in the seventeenth century? The place, its atmosphere, is pleasant and clean. The window of our room opens directly on the cupolas of the old cathedral. All will be well if the hostelry is not hand-in-glove with the Viceroy's men. A terrible suspicion assails me. Suppose he poisons our food? I communicate my misgiving to my companion.

"Stop your romancing and try to arrange for a little water."

I load up my pistols, buckle sword to waist, clap on the plumed hat and plunge downstairs in search of my companions. Athos! Porthos! Aramis! *Ma foi!* Your D'Artagnan is come! By the beard of the Prophet, where are you three?


Puebla is a red town: Oaxaca is green. And if it has taken on this colour it was not to gratify the colour-fascinated scribe who is now visiting it. It's just that its churches, convents and mansions have been constructed with that kind of green onyx so abundant in the city and its environs.

Oaxaca of Juárez, capital of the State of Oaxaca, was founded by the Aztecs in 1486 as a military post. Carlos V raised it to the status of city in 1533 and sent a clock with wooden mechanism, as if he wanted life in the new Mexican community to proceed in the rhythm of Mother Spain's tempo, as a gift to its people.

They repeat to me here what I have already heard in Puebla. "This, *caballero,* is the most typically colonial city in Mexico." I nod in silence. "And here you will find the most beautiful specimens of seventeenth and eighteenth century architecture." I repeat my assenting gesture.

Oaxaca is much smaller than Puebla. It probably has no more than 60,000 inhabitants, and it somewhat resembles a city of the same size in the interior of Brazil. The centre of urban life is the main square, surrounded by *portales,* with its kiosk, its benches, its flower-beds and its tall laurels. I see very few modern buildings here, none, I believe, more than three storeys high. Formerly Oaxaca was the centre of the Zapotec and Mixtec civilization. Even today there are more than fifteen different indigenous groups in the state, which boasts that it was the cradle of Benito Juárez. Porfirio Díaz was also a native of the state, a thing I have so far heard no one boast about.

We find the saddest Indian women in Mexico praying in the Santuario de Nuestra Señora de la Soledad, a dramatic church of the sixteenth century, of black stone. The image of the Virgin Patron of the city is sculptured in wood, with her velvet dress embroidered in gold and her jewels set with real pearls. In the church across the way, on the other side of a small plaza in which three idlers are playing the guitar and singing, women are zealously cleaning the altar brasses, and an active, anachronistic smell of gasoline fills the air. A Christ in Death, wrapped in a winding sheet stained with blood, lies in its glass coffin, on the face and hands the scattered peso notes and copper coins left by the faithful with their promises and prayers. We go out again to the little plaza. One of the singers is despairingly proclaiming his love to the four winds. In a thick-foliaged tree birds are furiously chirping and warbling, sabotaging the singer.

We take a taxi to the church of Santo Domingo, whose sumptuousness seemed extravagant to Aldous Huxley, who some twenty years ago wandered through here with his long-legged stride. This temple has been sacked many times. After the Reform laws went into effect requiring the Church to sell its properties, the convent of Santo Domingo, which stands beside the church, served as barracks for a regiment of cavalry. The former refectory of the Dominican friars was turned into a classroom for the soldiers. Echoes of prayers and blasphemies seem still to be floating in the air, here inside. I see on one wall a drawing of a horse in life size, the body divided into sections each labelled with its scientific name. It was here that the cavalrymen learned equine anatomy. But, like the friars, the soldiers too departed, and the monastery today is merely a ruin which attracts tourists. Just as some individuals gain a serene and dignified beauty with age, weather and the centuries have imparted to these stones, both those of the church and those of the monastery, a golden patina with brown and greenish splashes which recall the Aztec mosaics with their incrustations of semi-precious stones. The convent's inner patio, with its fountain, its broken columns and its sundial, which dates from 1639, is covered with weeds.

The caretaker is ancient, an octogenarian with the look of a witch, her skin like parchment stretched over the Indian bone structure. She walks with the aid of a staff, but her eyes are as alive as her gestures and her words.

"I live here with my ghosts," she mumbles. "They are friars, soldiers, bandits and saints. They all know me. The little birds do, too."

She points to the fountain.

"They come every day to drink there. People think I'm in my dotage or crazy. But the old Indian knows. And she don't tell all she knows. The saints in the church are witness. They're mighty old, too, and they know. But they don't talk."

Next morning we attend Mass in the old cathedral of Oaxaca, begun in 1563 and finished two centuries afterwards. Its building of green stone, with a façade elaborately sculptured in low relief, has often been damaged by earthquakes. Its Moorish cupolas display lovely tiles in yellow, black and white checkered pattern.

The sacristan, short, crippled and one-eyed, recalls Victor Hugo's Quasimodo. But the vicar who says Mass, his high tenor nasal, clashes with the severe *ambiance*. He is fair, blond, lean and with a cunning air, when the cathedral calls for a good Spanish padre, dark, with deep voice, coal-black eyes and apocalyptic gestures.


Oaxaca is famous for its market, perhaps the best in the whole country. And for its woven goods, its ceramics, its artefacts of lacquer and leather, its jewels, its knives and daggers. In a tiny shop I examine knives with inscriptions on the blades. One of them reads: *En el hilo de mi dueño, sólo a mi Dios le temo*—At my master's side only God I fear. On another: *Soy de las tierras altas donde habitan los venados*—I am from the highlands where live the stags. And: *Soy amigo de los hombres y acicate de los malvados*—I am friend to men and scourge of the wicked.

The *rebozo* is a kind of mantilla or shawl of wool or silk, in vivid scarlet, but we find green, blue, grey, yellow and white *rebozos*. Oaxaca also specializes in *sarapes*, great thick cloths in more than one colour, which can be used as blankets or as rugs. The Indians used to weave on small horizontal looms. After the Spaniards introduced the vertical loom into this country these people were enabled to make larger *sarapes*. In pre-Cortésian times the natives wove only with fibres of cotton, of the maguey and of an occasional other plant. Only after the Conquest did they begin working in wool.

There has always been a tradition among the Indian weavers with respect to the design and colours of these *sarapes*. A connoisseur in the matter can tell at a glance the origin of a given cloth. The wool used in Oaxaca is particularly soft, which makes possible the use of its *sarapes* more as blankets than as rugs. The traditional patterns here used to represent a light-grey field with a bird in the centre, or an animal or a stylized flower, in blue and white or in black and white. It is said (Exult, you Marxists, exult!) that, owing to the insistence of American tourists, who love loud colours, the Indians began not only to alter their traditional designs but also to accept orders, using more red and blue, and certain patterns like the Mexican eagle or the Aztec Calendar Stone, as the purchaser's whim demanded. Be that as it may, the Oaxaca *sarapes* enchant me. It is common to see an Indian use his *sarape* like a poncho, or roll himself in it. But for their personal use they continue to prefer the tones and patterns that follow a tradition of more than four hundred years.

Today is Saturday, market day. Since nightfall yesterday the Indians have started coming in, alone or in groups, from the country round about. Some have come down from the hills. Others have come from various places in the valley, fetching their merchandise on the backs of burros or in carts.

Nine o'clock. On a sidewalk beside the hotel, under the arcades that face the *zócalo*, we are drinking coffee. I now have a counsellor in Oaxacan matters. It is Juanito. Profession: bootblack. Age: nine. I have gone so far as to have my shoes shined twice a day just to be able to enjoy the company and the chatter of this liveliest of little Indians, whose gaiety is like a sweet-singing bird's. In his smiling face, of an attractive *simpatía*, his eyes look like two obsidian balls. His voice, a reed flute, is rich in melodies. I see Juanito is popular with the hotel guests, among whom he circulates all morning long (he goes to school "on the afternoon shift") bearing his rough wooden box with the tools of his trade on his back. While we drink our coffee, he is running his brush over my shoes.

"Going to the market, *señor*?"

"Of course. That's what we came for."

"That's fine. And the lady?"

"She's going, too."

"She's a *gringa*, ain't she?"

For the third time I explain that my wife, despite her fair skin and her blue eyes, is not an American. Juanito contemplates her for an instant, smiles and shakes his head incredulously.

"What's the best time to go to the market?" I inquire.

"At ten. That's when it starts to warm up."

"Warm up?"

"The activity, the bustle."

"And what is so interesting about the market?"

Juanito knits his brows over a face smeared with black polish.

"*Sarapes*, baskets, fruits, herbs, *rebozos*——" he enumerates like a pupil who has his lesson on the tip of his tongue. "Machetes."

"Machetes? What's that?"

"You don't know?"

"No."

"Word of honour?"

Perplexity on the boy's face. Who doesn't know such a common word?

"Machete—what the bandits use."

"Pistols?"

Juanito laughs: "No! Machete is a big knife." He runs his index finger across his throat in a mimicry of cutting it.

"Ah, a knife!"

"*Ay, ay, ay!*"

For some moments the boy rhythmically whips at my shoes with his cloth. Then he casts another furtive glance at my wife, winks at me and murmurs: "*Pero en realidad es gringa, no?*"

We return to the subject of the market.

"Got to be mighty careful of your money," the lad advises. "Lot of pick-pockets at the market. They're bad men, they come from other towns, they were not born in Oaxaca. People here are honest. Benito Juárez was born in this state."

To protect us against the *hombres malos*, Juanito decides to go with us to the market. Here we go, the three of us, the boy in front, a mixture of guide and bodyguard. It is quite possible that thirty years from now Juanito, like Juárez, may have his name in History. He is the clay of which heroes are moulded in Mexico. And because they are of clay they are born with the wisdom of the Soil. "Cosmic race," José Vasconcelos calls them, he who was born in Oaxaca, too.

The fair is only a few blocks from the *zócalo*. Now and then Juanito turns his head to see whether we are following him. If we had not already seen so many fine things on this trip, it would be worth having come to Mexico only to make Juanito's acquaintance.

The heart of the market throbs under a vast shed with a zinc covering; but the stands spill over, as it were, and spread out for blocks along the sidewalks and gutters of the adjacent streets. The conglomeration of people is already considerable at this hour. I don't believe it possible to give in words any idea of what the great fair of Oaxaca is like. When I started this book, I thought many times about this moment, just like a tenor who waits, harassed and apprehensive, for his great aria, which only ends in a chest note. The image is terrible. I detest opera. I can't stand heroic tenors. And the chest note has always seemed to me a sin against nature. I have never cared for *morceaux de bravoure*. All my life I have avoided "anthological pages". Now I find myself here on this tumultuous stage, in the midst of a numerous and heterogeneous cast, or mob scene, and I can already hear the orchestra chords heralding the great aria, "Il Mercato di Oaxaca" from the opera *Messico*. You can go on playing, maestro. I refuse to sing it. Uproars of protests? Tell the manager to refund the audience its money. I don't care if they go out spreading the word that I am a decadent singer. I want to amble slowly among these stands, listen to the merchants talk with their customers, and, little by little, unhurriedly, give my reader some notion of what this fair is like. For that it is necessary to forget I am writing. Don't look at your watch. We've plenty of time. Let's take some snapshots first. The night is magical. In Mexico nobody bothers to hunt unusual angles, because all angles are out of the ordinary. Close your eyes, aim the camera at random and press the button. There! You can be sure you have taken an artistic photograph. I know no country more pictorial than this one. Photographers have the greatest time of their lives here. Painters are left as though in hallucination before these persons, landscapes and still lifes. Mexico exudes drama. Here even the fruits resemble the people that cultivate them and consume them, and the soil that produces them.

Can there be a fruit that looks more like the earth than the *mamey*? It is an elongated oval in shape, like one of the smaller mangoes. The rind, the colour of dry soil, reminds me of the savannas of the North, the adobe houses, the hands of the old Indian selling this fruit in the market. I split the fruit into halves and the contrast shrieks aloud: its interior is the burnt, rich red of Tahiti to be seen in some of Gauguin's pictures. No juice runs over my fingers. The pulp of the *mamey* is compact, a little like that of our Brazilian persimmon, and must be eaten with a spoon.

Flies are swarming round fat, succulent slices of pineapple piled on a huge tray, over which a serious Indian woman dressed in black mounts guard. We pass it by, for the pineapple, an old acquaintance, offers no novelty for us. Its sweet fragrance, though, pursues us like a voice calling after us.

We stop short to look at some green fruits the size of peaches.

"What is that?" I ask.

"*Zapotes negros*," says Juanito, and the words pop out of his mouth like so many gleaming, round fruits.

"Why 'black,' when the fruit is green?"

"The flesh is black."

The flesh of the black sapodilla is so hard that it has to be pounded first to make it eatable. I have read in the *Historia Antigua de México*, by Francisco J. Clavijero, S.J., that the pulp of the *zapote negro* when boiled and chilled with sugar and cinnamon has a most delicate flavour. The white *zapote*, with pale flesh, is equally tasty and has soporific qualities.

The ghost of Van Gogh must have been wandering around here today, flicking yellow brush strokes right and left. These mountains, or rather, these ranges of mangoes must have been painted by poor Vincent.

We eat warm mangoes—*la gringa*, Juanito and I—and smear our faces with its "broth." Mexican mangoes do not taste of turpentine, they are extremely sweet and their filaments are less bothersome to the teeth than are those of the Pará mangoes in Brazil.

The *aguacates*, avocadoes or alligator pears, show their black ugly faces; their rind, wrinkled and rough as the hide of a pachyderm, contrasts with the pale, fluid green of their pulp. And there are the *capulí* cherries, which in shape and colour, if not in flavour, are so like the European cherries.

The impassive Indian woman, with haughty eyes, amid her trays, with a jade-green *rebozo* over her shoulders, might well bear the title "Queen of the *Chiles*." Because chili peppers of all varieties surround her, some so glitteringly green and red they look polished; others yellow as a ripe cashew; and there, too, is the *chile mulato*, withered, half-dried, of a rather sombre look, in a vague threat of gastric disturbances. And that little fruit with the innocent aspect in the middle of those gaudy pimentoes? Take care! Let's not be fooled: it is the terrible pepper of Tabasco to which the Indians give the name of *xocoxochitl*. I want to photograph the Queen of the Peppers, but she makes a negative gesture with her hand, ordering us away. I wave a peso at her, but the woman doesn't even look at me.

We walk along rows of squashes that look like fat, tranquil *señoras;* rows of *camotes* displaying the twisted, distorted shapes of modern sculpture; and of *huacamotes,* a sweet root, a kind of yucca, to be eaten cooked. Yonder are the radishes, the turnips and the carrots, which experts on the subject say were brought from the Canary Islands by the Spaniards. We bow to the onions—there are various sizes and shades of colour—a subject of controversy. Some assert that the onion came from Europe and others declare it is native to Mexico, where the Indians called it *xonacatl*. (I recall that in one of his letters to Carlos V, Cortés said he had found onions on sale in the market of Tenochititlán.) We cast swift glances at a quantity of edible roots, unknown to me, of aspects a little suggestive of parts of the human anatomy.

The papayas, sometimes called papaws or pawpaws, with their deep yellow splashed with green and black, contrast with a dark mound of smooth-shell pecans, looking rather like nutmegs. And now we are among the tomatoes. The large ones here are called *jitomates*. I don't think they differ, either in taste or in appearance, from our own kinds.

I do believe I am giving the impression that each fruit, vegetable or green has its separate place in this fair, as in the ancient market of Tenochtitlán. Not at all. Order is what is utterly lacking in the Oaxaca market. If there were orderliness, it would not be Mexico. Of course, in an over-all way there are several sections in this huge shed: foodstuffs, draper's goods, fruits and vegetables, flowers, birds, rugs, ceramics. . . . The boundaries of these provinces, though, are not neatly delimited. And inside each of them reigns a disorder that is perhaps one of the greatest charms of this and of other fairs.

In the stall before which we are standing amulets and medicinal and aromatic herbs are sold. Among the latter we recognize rue, citron, cress, fennel, rosemary, quassia, camomile. Juanito tells us the names of others, *azocopaque, santo-domingo, rosa-de-castilla,* explaining their magical virtues. He recommends that we buy "stag's eyes," which will protect us against the evil eye. And can there be a more alarming eye than that of the very Indian woman selling these roots, herbs and talismans? She looks like a witch. Her reptilian eyes are cold and viscous. I'll go so far as to accept the hypothesis that she is dead and mummified, for her immobility is absolute. Her hands are like roots. The witch must know dark secrets, be acquainted with decoctions and potions of terrible powers. Unfortunately, it is impossible to get into conversation with these Indians. One has to extort words from them with pincers, or pliers, and as a result such words come out piecemeal, unintelligible. The mestizos are more communicative and lively, but not easier to talk with for all that.

Let's go into the flower section, where masses of colours seem to form vivid mosaics. Fragrances are floating in the air, which seems cooler here because of the presence of those corollas and leaves bedewed with water. I find old acquaintances: roses of various kinds, Cape jasmines, red and white carnations, gladioli; but what intrigues me is the flowers I have never seen and that for me have no names yet. "What's in a name?" asks the bard. Indeed the name tells little or nothing about the person or thing it designates. I consult my technical adviser. I indicate a mound of flowers of an intense yellow and ask: "What is that?"

Juanito frowns, hesitates an instant and, suddenly, his face lighting up, says: "Flowers, *señor.*"

"Ah!"

Isn't it enough to inhale these perfumes enveloping us, which seem to hold all the colours of the flowers or the leaves from which they emanate? A young mestiza woman with toasted skin is tying a bunch of lilies, humming. It is the first pretty face I have found in the market. (*Mejorando los presentes*—present company excepted—as they say around here.)

A tourist buys an armful of red carnations, and, while her husband pays, clasps the flowers to her breast and smiles as if she were being photographed. I feel like crying, "Those carnations, *señora,* call for a brunette face, Mexican eyes, hair the colour of roast chestnuts. You are fair, you have freckles on your cheeks, and your hair looks like cornsilk. May I suggest a bouquet of tea roses? Or those modest little blue flowers whose name I don't know?"

I see a withered, quiet little old man, dozing in the middle of the flowers of his stall; they cover him as they might the corpse of someone important.

The tireless Padre Clavijero has spoken charmingly in his book about the flowers of Mexico. There was the floripondio, "which merits first place for its great dimensions," a white flower, lovely, strongly scented, produced by an elegant bush the branches of which form a kind of cupola. The *yelloxochitl,* or "heart flower," white and pink or yellow inside, is also showy and large, and endowed with so powerful a scent that one of them is enough to perfume a whole house. And the *coatzontecoxochitl?* It is the "viper's head flower" with five petals, purple on the inside, white in the middle and pink at the extremities, the whole spattered with white and yellow dots. The jaguar flower has sharp-pointed petals, scarlet, with white and yellow patches simulating the pattern on a jaguar pelt. The *cacaloxochitl,* raven flower; small but perfumed—white, red and yellow—was used by the Indians to adorn altars; the Spaniards discovered that exquisite conserve could be made from it. Where are all those rare flowers with the long and difficult names? Have they vanished, or changed name? I don't think so. Can they belong to other regions? Perhaps.

Here we go now with the impression that we are walking inside a gigantic boot smelling of tanned leather, for this is the zone of leather goods. On shelves or tables stand rows of footwear of various shapes, sizes and colours, from the cloth *alpargata* through the traditional *guarache*—a species of leather sandal, speciality of Oaxaca—and through the high-topped, elastic-sided shoes to the shoes of modern type, nearly all of rather crude shapes and styles. I invent an interesting game: to look at one of these articles of footgear and imagine the face and clothing of the person who is going to buy and wear it. That *guarache* will be acquired by an effeminate young man from New York, a painter of bohemian temperament. He detests the United States and is living in Oaxaca, where he paints street types and churches, and in his idle hours reads Gide and Cocteau in Spanish translations. I can imagine his chestnut-brown corduroy slacks, his shirt of printed silk, his swaying gait, his light, dancer's step. Now, an *hombre malo* is going to buy those black, elastic-topped boots, which will be stained with blood from the *compadre* he will knife one Sunday at a cockfight. The yellow boots? I can see them splashed with pulque. A commercial traveller from Jalisco who has a girl friend in the *zócalo*. The *alpargatas*. . . .

Juanito pulls us out of the enormous boot, interrupting my game.

We are in the region of the foodstuffs. It looks like a vast kitchen: grease on the floor, on the tables, on the faces, the hands and the clothes of the men and women preparing and selling things to eat. An active smell of garlic, onion and aromatic herbs fills the air, making it seem thicker. The temptation is to pass quickly by this section, but something holds us, seduces us and, despite our sense of repugnance, leads us to examine carefully the cooking vessels, big-bellied bottles, jugs, wooden mugs and platters. It is a delirium of fried food. In veritable lakes of hot grease, hog fat cracklings and tripes are sputtering, *quesadillas* and *tacos* are turning brown. Charcoal fires burn under ribs of beef, mutton or pork. In great earthen-ware pots, *ollas*, I see white beans, navy, brown or red beans swimming in lard. I walk up to an Indian woman sitting in Oriental fashion on the floor, and look into the caldron at her feet, which is filled to the top with a maize dough of sombre aspect.

"Why has that stuff so dark a colour?"

Without raising her eyes, she responds in a hollow voice: "Blood."

Heads of roast pig (victims of what Zapotec Salomé?) repose upon heavy platters, and their still eyes, looking like glass buttons, reflect our likenesses. Viscera of animals unidentifiable by the naked eye are hanging from hooks, some still dripping blood. A fat, jovial Indian woman is chopping tripe with a machete, while at her side, on the floor dotted with puddles of viscous liquids, a two- or three-year-old baby, completely naked, is sucking at a pink ice frozen on a stick. Standing in front of the stalls, Indians are eating. They look like rodents. They are pacas, coypus, squirrels, hares, in the middle of this forest, indifferent to the passing or the proximity of other beasts. I notice that these stocky little men and women always walk in a straight line, they never turn aside and they go sweeping before them anyone they encounter on their way, even the enormous, broad-shouldered tourists who, with bursts of laughter, jump aside in order not to be trampled on.

Here inside there is not so much noise as I was expecting and perhaps wishing for. Human voices are heard, yes, but in a vague hum, and also the chirping and squawking of birds, but in a general way the fair is not as noisy as the famous Oriental bazaars. These Indians do not advertise their wares by shouting. They conduct their negotiations mutedly: their economy begins with their words. And the truth is, they don't seem much interested in selling.

Now we are in something like a great hatchery. It is the section of birds. In cages of the most varied sizes little birds flutter about. They are finches and linnets and singing canaries, thrushes that imitate human voices and are the object of Juanito's special affection. And there are house-sparrows, too, which seem to wander through all the world's climes. And calanders singing like nightingales, of plumage spotted with yellow, white, grey. I see one beautiful bird with yellow beak, black head with green glints, breast and belly red, tail white and blue. Juanito recognizes in that one the *tzinizcan*. Then seeing two common sparrows whose upper bodies are white and the lower grey, he informs me that when they grow old these birds change colour: the male's head turns red and the female's yellow.

Parrots and macaws stain these cages with bright colours. And now it is we who have to drag our small guide out of here, for he has got into an interminable dialogue with some turquoise-coloured parakeets.

We pass on to the *sarapes*, hanging from ropes, solemn as banners. They are tempting. We purchase a white one with red stripes and a blue and black lozenge in the centre. Juanito intervenes in the transaction to bargain with the vendor, who shoots a glance of ill-will at him but ends by giving us the discount the small Indian suggests.

Just as there is a museum fatigue, there is a Mexican market fatigue, which is perhaps worse. I say worse because aggravated by bad smells and confusion. Well, that's the fatigue we are seized with now. And the colours and designs of the *sarapes* surrounding us contribute to our greater numbness. We emerge from the great market building into the sun of the streets, where the shops and the stalls and the come-and-go of the customers continues. An ambulant jazz-band of Indians is playing *rancheras* and *huapangos* on a corner. A tiny Indian girl of about seven passes, carrying on her back, like a knapsack, her months-old brother.

We cross an open space where a veritable battalion of burros is lined up, motionless. Juanito explains that the Indians park their burros here while they are working at the market. A burro parking lot!

It is really a pity that we have left for the last what is perhaps the most important part of this market: the ceramics. We stroll among the shops where articles of earthenware and glazed crockery are of an extraordinary richness. We see tea and coffee sets, tableware, decorative platters, trays, compotes, pitchers, glasses and vases, decanters, ashtrays, dolls—all in the loviest colours and shapes. We are particularly interested in the famous black ceramic of Oaxaca, made in the town of Coyotepec, which has soil containing a very plastic black clay rich in lead oxide. After being baked, the pieces made from this clay take on a black, metallic colour. The *mezcal*, a powerful drink from the distilled juice of the maguey, is usually sold in decanters or jugs of this material, with thin neck and with bottom so rounded it is hard to stand them up.

And here we are, finally, in front of the celebrated sirens of black earthenware we so much wanted to see and buy. They are fat and their bodies resemble hens' more than fishes' bodies. Their faces, in comic design, seem to smile at our weariness, our lassitude. On their rough shelves the black sirens of Oaxaca are playing the lyre.


I am convinced that Sunday is not a day of the week but a state of mind. It is urgent to find a word to describe that "listless, paltry sadness" that generally overpowers us on Sundays. *Chateação* is a low term. Dullness is weak. Ennui, besides being a Gallicism, is finicky. Tedium, too literary. If English has the expression "boredom," why not give it a Portuguese form, transforming it into *boredão*? Weigh the word well: *boredão*. See whether it doesn't sound like an enormous, sonorous yawn. *Boredão*. It has the colour and the weight of lead.

On this, our first and last Sunday in Oaxaca we do not feel the slightest *boredão*. In the morning my wife goes to Mass in the old cathedral, and I stay sitting on a bench in the plaza reading Ramón Xirau's essay, *Tres poetas de la soledad*.

He is, as it happens, discussing my three favourite Mexican poets: Octavio Paz, Xavier Villaurrutia and José Gorostiza.

Looking at the face of the old clock on the cathedral, I understand better this verse of Paz:

"The clock gnaws
at my heart,
a vulture
with the patience of a mouse."

The clock, pawn of time, is indeed a vulture working for Death. But there is so much sun, so much gold in the morning that such black thoughts lose a little of their force. Curious: not long ago I read an anthology of contemporary poets of Mexico. I found it singularly empty of native subjects and landscapes. Indeed, there was a notable quantity of nocturnes in it. Can it be the Mexican sun tires these poets so much that they constantly seek the refuge of night? Or is it that they prefer the night because it is the sister of Death, a theme that reaches the point of obsession in many of them? Of these three admirable poets the essayist says that "they penetrate deep into the paths of their own consciousness and paradoxically renounce communication." They live in an ivory tower, in a formalistic poetic world.

Sitting on a bench a few steps from me, four Indians, all in white, all four with legs crossed, motionless and silent, look like quadruplet figures in a picture, in a frieze. I have the impression that they are sitting for an invisible muralist. (Or are they really the paintings themselves?)

Gorostiza's poetry seems to deny itself, and his poem "Death without End" is, in the last analysis, a return to silence, to the essential nothingness. For him, man lives in solitude, "that emptiness that clutches us in islands of echoless monologues." Hence his distrust of the word:

"That word, yes, that word
that coagulates in the throat
like a cry of amber."

I look at the white frieze of Indians and sense in it a mysterious, invisible colour: amber. Have they perchance discovered, like the poet, the uselessness of the attempt to communicate?

And when Gorostiza finds the word and wishes to give it form, to preserve it living, he feels it in the end only *exact*:

"Look at it, ah, touch it!
Look at it, now!
Look at it, utterly absent from words,
Without voice, without echo, without language, exact. . . ."

As a miserable prose writer who has so often tried futilely to describe dreams, I encounter this gem in Villaurrutia:

"To dream, to dream the night, the street, the stair
And the cry of the statue turning the corner.
To run to the statue and only encounter the cry,
To try to touch the cry and find only the echo,
To wish to catch the echo and encounter only the wall,
And to run to the wall and come up against a mirror."

Juanito catches sight of me, waves, crosses the street, and I have no help for it, I yield up my shoes and my feet to him.

How many times, awakening in the middle of the night, have we felt assailed by a nameless anguish, so hard to describe in words? This devil of a poet solves the problem in four lines:

"Because the night carries with it on its low tide
Anguished memories, frozen fears,
The thirst for something that, tremulous, we drank off one day,
And the bitterness of what we no longer recall."

The secret is in the last line: "The bitterness of what we no longer recall." But in the little bootblack's face I see the high tide, the sun of day. What would become of the world in this hour if Juanito did not exist?

Octavio Paz freezes my blood with this poem:

"I sought to go out at night
And at dawn take communion with those who suffer,
But, like the lightning on the solitary wayfarer,
A livid certainty caught my mind by surprise:
The sun had died and an eternal night was dawning."

I ask Juanito: "Is it true that the sun has died?"

The boy looks at me startled. I repeat the question. He smiles and at last responds: "*Pero, señor, está ciego?*—Are you blind?" And with his dirty finger he points to the sky. Comforted, I return to the book. But the poet gives me no quarter:

"Silence and solitude surround me.
Outside, the night increases, indifferent
To the vain dispute of men."

I confess to being charmed by that indifference of Nature and all her elements to our quarrels and passions.

"After Time, I think, comes Death,
And there shall I be, when I no longer am.
But there is no after nor before and Death
Does not await us in the end: it lies within us,
And with us it dies away in little sups."

I close the book. The old cathedral bell strikes, and the faithful begin coming out from Mass: ladies with their heads covered with black mantillas, girls with blouses of vivid colours, burghers in their Sunday best, Indians with their eternal, melancholy uniform. I catch sight of my companion in the midst of the crowd. And Juanito, who sees her, too, smiles and murmurs affectionately, "*La gringa.*"

At five o'clock in the afternoon the municipal band gives a concert in the bandstand in the plaza, around which the sidewalks fill with youths of both sexes. At eight tonight the same band returns for a special concert, this time under an awning (courtesy of Pepsi-Cola) and in a square enclosure to which only the *personae gratae* of the place seem to have access. In the afternoon the musicians wear a light uniform of khaki drill. At night they appear in dress uniforms of heavy stuff, dark blue, with gilt buttons and collars as crimson as the ribbon on their kepis.

Sitting at a table under the arcades of our hotel, we delightedly watch the spectacle, which awakens in us memories of our cities in the interior of Brazil. The other *portales* are illuminated by the light from many cafés and *pulquerías*. Under our arcades the fauna is rich. A tall, bearded American, the likeness of Ernest Hemingway, is drinking his whisky at a table in the company of an elderly woman, her hair completely white, her shoulders covered with a scarlet *rebozo*. They are chatting animatedly in English. A fellow with the aspect of Joseph Conrad's outcast is sipping, solitary, a tequila. A lean man with drooping moustache and tender eyes is methodically drinking beer. A plump young brunette, smelling strongly of jasmine, is humming something, I can't hear clearly what, while her companion, a middle-aged gentleman, gazes at her with eyes at once greedy and sad.

The band breaks into a medley from the opera *La Bohème*, and the sounds from the little brass group roll out into the *zócalo*, mount through the branches of the laurels, bound for the stars. On the sidewalks of the plaza the girls walk in one direction and the boys in the other. There is a thing Anglo-Saxons do not understand: the Latin *namôro* or, in Spanish, *enamoramiento*, the long looks these young people exchange as they pass each other. *Namorar, enamorar,* is a verb not found in an English dictionary. If in the United States a boy takes an interest in a girl, he asks her for a date; they go out, go to a cinema, to a restaurant, they skate, they go for a drive in the car, and it may well be that nothing in the way of love comes of that date, the whole affair remaining on a level of companionship at sports. But to keep one's distance, in the street, at a dance or in a cinema, exchanging long looks with the loved one, is a thing the American cannot conceive. But in Oaxaca—I verify with nostalgic joy—the *enamoramiento* survives still. *Viva Oaxaca!* When he was here, Aldous Huxley wrote: "Yes, Oaxaca is a fine place. Fine and, as gaiety is reckoned in the provinces of

Mexico, positively gay. There are two or three cafés in the plaza; and at night a band discourses from the kiosk at the centre. The Indians squat on the pavements to listen, their dark faces melting into the night—invisible. High-heeled, in every tender shade of artificial silk, the flappers stroll giggling under the electric light. There is a rolling of eyes, a rolling of posteriors. The young men stroll in the opposite direction." Accustomed to the blonde English girls, surely, neuter in the matter of hips, with pale eyes incapable of rolling, Huxley must have been a little shocked at what he saw in this plaza. The scene has not changed much. There are the Indians sitting on the ground, on the benches, or standing with arms folded, outside the square enclosure where the important personages, evidently members of the local bourgeoisie, take their seats in folding chairs (also by courtesy of Pepsi-Cola). And in their statue-like postures they listen to the concert. Automobiles are rolling slowly along the street, at the pace of a stroll.

A tall, spare old man with an exceedingly sharp Adam's apple crosses the street, completely drunk, and comes to sit at a table near us. Two steps away from him, at another table, two men are playing backgammon in silence. A swarthy, stocky fellow, dressed with great care but rather in the manner of a Mexican film villain, comes to settle himself a few yards from us, and, after ordering a beer, casts conquering glances about him. He is dressed in grey, with a red cravat, the brim of his felt hat pulled down over his nocturnal eyes. From time to time he caresses his shiny moustache. Another type, equally pretentious, soon takes a seat at the same table. I hear the first say in a voice loud enough to be heard round about: "No. I'm a bachelor. The one who's married is my wife." Both men burst into laughter.

An old Indian in white passes among the tables with a tray full of flowers, timidly calling: *"Rosas! Rosas blancas! Rosas!"*

In the middle of the street other Indians are offering *sarapes* to the tourists. The police prohibit them from coming up to the *portales*. Indian women display blouses of maguey fibre with fanciful embroidery. And a boy with one leg, supported on crutches, waves lottery tickets at us.

In a delirium of cymbals, ruffle of kettle and snare drums, and thunders of the big bass drum, the band finishes the medley. Great applause from the conservative classes. The Indians remain impassive. The maestro bows gratefully. The band disperses to relax.

There is a warm smell of burning dry branches floating in the night. Far off, rockets are popping. Where are we? In what year? What part of time and space? A ridiculous but enjoyable nostalgia sweeps over me, carries me back to the city where I was born, where I had sweethearts, where I strolled in the plaza listening to the concert by the Eighth Infantry Regimental Band, under the baton of Sergeant Aparicio. Wait . . . Yonder he is, soloing on the saxophone a selection from *La Forza del Destino*. This is an important Sunday in my life because I am wearing my first suit of tussore silk for the first time. Yes, my straw hat is also new. White tennis shoes: *le dernier cri* of local fashion. Knitted tie. Perfume? *Fleur d'Amour*. Age? Seventeen.

The musicians have returned to their places. The maestro raises his baton. Now it is a Strauss waltz. Moths flutter about the electric lamps in the plaza. The promenade of the *enamorados* continues. In the middle of the street an Indian opens a *sarape*: on a red background, stylized birds in white. And like a bullfighter inciting a bull, he stands there trying to attract the tourists. One of them charges down upon him with the zest of a Miura bull. The encounter is swift and of few words. The tourist hands a banknote to the Indian, receives the *sarape* in exchange and comes back, covered with glory, to his table and his whisky.

But the silent, patient *torero* remains, another *sarape* unfolded: white, black, green and yellow. This time the bull is I. I rush out and buy.


My wife and I are making plans. We shall go tomorrow to visit the ruins of the pyramids, temples and sepulchres of Monte Albán, relics of the Zapotec and Mixtec civilizations. Many people come to Oaxaca exclusively to see them. It was there that Alfonso Caso, one of the most illustrious anthropologists in America, discovered in "Tomb 7" a marvellous collection of jewellery of gold, silver, turquoise and coral, which we saw yesterday in the museum of the city. Yes, we must see Mitla, too.

We go to sleep late, long after watching the plaza empty itself of musicians, Indians, bourgeois and *enamorados*. We wake so late next day that we miss the bus that was to take us to Monte Albán. It doesn't matter. We idle about the city with gusto. At night we sit in the *portales* where the old men play backgammon, always in silence, where the twin of Hemingway is drinking his whisky and chatting with the elderly woman in the scarlet *rebozo,* and the old Indian goes round with his basket of flowers, crying in his sweet, grandfatherly voice: *"Claveles,* carnations, *claveles rojos!"*

And entertained with these aspects of Oaxaca, we gradually forget about the ruins of Mitla and Monte Albán. Until the day comes to go back.

We climb into the long, silver and blue omnibus, which twelve hours later spills us out into the City of Mexico.

# 8. Colloquies
# with José Vasconcelos

I believe Alfonso Reyes and José Vasconcelos are the two most widely known and respected names of Mexican literature in their own country and outside it. In Mexico perhaps Reyes is a less controversial and more universally accepted personality than Vasconcelos.

I cannot say I know them very well, but from what I have read of theirs and about them, and from the contact I have had with both— more repeated and prolonged with Vasconcelos—I have gained the impression that, although men of the same generation and companions in many campaigns in the past, in temperament they are almost antipodal and in ideas rarely find themselves nowadays on the same side.

Alfonso Reyes is the classic type of pure humanist. A man of insatiable intellectual curiosity, he has cultivated all literary genres, accumulated a considerable culture, travelled extensively abroad, less as a Mexican than as a citizen of the world. Where Reyes has the scholar's caution and doubt, Vasconcelos will compromise himself immediately, leaps from the library or the tribune to the barricade, from the classroom to street action. He is, as Leopoldo Zea has well observed, at once statesman and professor, thinker and revolutionary.

If Reyes is a poet, Vasconcelos is a prophet.

A man more of tenderness than of passions, the former is like a Mediterranean flower miraculously flourishing in a rough country-side of cacti. A new incarnation of Prospero, Don Alfonso survives uncontaminated in a land which—if we give credit to Vasconcelos himself—has always been and still is being dominated by Calibans.

Now, Professor José Vasconcelos seems to me to have a little of the nature of the cactus, which has allowed him to survive with physical and intellectual vigour in this violent land where *el hombre malo siempre vence al bueno*—where the evil man always conquers the good.

I heard this phrase from the mouth of Vasconcelos on the occasion of our first meeting, at a diplomatic luncheon, when I asked him whether in his opinion Mexico has a good body of fiction.

"How can it have?" he exclaimed quickly, gripping his fork as one might a sword, ready for the duel. "For good art to exist in a country, it is necessary for goodness to exist also. And what can be seen in Mexico but the triumph of the wicked?"

The talk took another turn. Vasconcelos told me that he had been, until a short time before, in a spiritual retreat in one of those eighteenth-century Mexican convents:

"The preacher, a Dominican friar of powerful eloquence, talked to us for three days on the horrors of hell, on the temptations of this world, and about the obstacles to a sinner's entering Heaven. One day I went to look him up in his cell and said to him, 'Padre, I'm leaving. You have painted the torments of hell and the strictness of God with such realism that I regard myself as already hopelessly lost.' The friar smiled and replied, 'Wait. Tomorrow, in my last sermon, I shall speak of Mercy.' I did stay, and I'm not sorry I did!"

When a youth, Vasconcelos read Schopenhauer passionately, an explosive fertilizer for a young Oaxacan cactus. Later, when he was converted to Catholicism, he came to see God from another angle, developing a philosophy according to which human life must be action and the world must be the result of an active principle that keeps bringing about qualitative changes, from matter to spirit.

In the strength of youth he belonged to the famous Generación del Ateneo de la Juventud, that is, the Generation of the Athenaeum of Youth, and fought the positivist materialism of the Porfirian era by setting against it the spiritualist intuitionism of Bergson and Boutroux.

In the eternal quarrel between Indianists and Hispanists Vasconcelos is, so to speak, the high priest of the latter group, which does not mean he is a racist, for his book *Raza Cósmica* is a eulogy of crossbreeding. In his opinion we Latin Americans are the only people capable of creating an authentic culture, new insofar as it is universal, for Iberoamerica stands before the world as a crucible of races.

He argues: "The so-called Latin peoples, because they have been faithful to the divine mission, are called to consummate it. And that fidelity to the occult design is the guarantee of our triumph."

José Vasconcelos, already well along in his seventies, is a short man with white hair cut *en brosse*, a round, pink, full face, and dark, lively eyes. He dresses like a bourgeois, but a careless *petit bourgeois*. With his cane, a medal dangling from his watch chain, he looks like a retail merchant. When, however, he begins to speak, his interlocutor immediately senses that he has a *man* facing him, and a rare man, of extraordinary vigour and lucidity, of an infectious enthusiasm—gay, restless, frank, the best of companions.


I intentionally start off on the wrong foot:

"Reading the letters of the Conquistador to Carlos V, and the chronicles of the Conquest, I have come to a diagnosis of Hernán Cortés. Paranoia."

Professor Vasconcelos starts laughing, a slow, patient laugh, shaking the glass of whisky and ice just handed him by Vianna Moog, in whose apartment we find ourselves this warm June evening.

My sole function in these colloquies will be to stir up the Professor, to prod him into talking. I continue: "Cortés was left so bedazzled on seeing the riches of Mexico that he dismasted his ships in order to make his men's return to Cuba an impossibility and the Conquest a necessity. He turned then to fostering a great dream: to be Captain-General of the lands he was going to conquer for Spain. When he found himself with Montezuma and the latter gave him to understand that he saw in Cortés a new incarnation of Quetzalcoatl, that is, a supernatural being, Cortés accepted the situation with every naturalness as something to which he had the right. Note that well, Professor. His whole conduct proclaims the paranoiac. Nothing is too good or too great for him. All measures are licit to him. He relates to his king with the greatest coolness that he had fifty Indian warriors' hands cut off and later that his soldiers succeeded in easily killing some three thousand Cholultecs in a few hours. When Cuauhtémoc refuses to reveal the hiding place of the imperial treasure, Cortés subjects him to torture."

I leave the sharpest dart to the last:

"All these cruelties seemed just or justifiable to him because he perpetrated them in the name of two tremendous absolutes: the Church and the Empire. He was going to augment the dominions, the glory, the power of Spain, as well as bring the Indians to the Catholic faith."

I had kicked off. It was my hope that the Professor would take the ball and hang on to it for the rest of the game.

"What chroniclers have you been reading?" he asks with his boyish smile. "Prescott? He was a sentimentalist and he was never in Mexico. It was he who invented that myth of Cuauhtémoc. He and the North American historians, indirect agents of Protestantism who would like to extinguish the whole mark of the Spaniard in America!"

He gets up, comes over to me and lays his hand on my shoulder:

"The gravest harm those imperialists have done to us has been to accustom us to see in Cortés a stranger. Whereas Cortés is ours in a greater degree than Cuauhtémoc can ever be. The figure of the Conquistador covers the fatherland of the Mexican from Sonora to Yucatan, and goes beyond, to the territories he conquered and we later lost. While Cuauhtémoc may be, at most, the ancestor of the Indians of the meseta of Anáhuac, with no relation to the rest of the country."

I want to ask him how he justifies the cruelties of Cortés, but Professor Vasconcelos gives me no time, as he continues: "Spain destroyed nothing in Mexico because nothing existed here worth preserving when she came to these regions, unless one considers sacred all those soul weeds such as the cannibalism of the Caribs, the human sacrifices of the Aztecs, the brutifying despotism of the Incas. Fortunately the Spaniards were the first to arrive here, and thanks to that the history of this region of the New World is rich, unlike that of the zone occupied by the Puritans. Ever since we appeared in the panorama of universal history, we have figured in it as an addition to the oldest, wisest, most illustrious culture of Europe: the Latin."

Vianna Moog smiles at me and, in the best Brazilian fashion, says: "Now get out of that!"

"I don't doubt," I say, "that it was better for Mexico to have been colonized by the Spaniards than by the English, the Dutch or the Turkish. But I was talking about the unnecessary cruelties of Cortés. . . ."

"Cortés was the most humane of the Conquistadores," replies Vasconcelos, sitting down again, "and the most selfless. Spiritually he binds himself to the conquered in converting them to the Faith, and his action leaves us the legacy of a fatherland. Whatever the race he belongs to, every one who feels himself Mexican owes to Cortés the map of his country and the first idea of unity of nationality. Before the Conquistador, Mexico did not exist as a nation: it was a multitude of tribes separated by mountains and rivers and by the more profound abyss of its three hundred dialects."

"Agreed," I answer, "but the cruelty with which the Conquistadors treated the Indians is repugnant and revolting to me."

Vasconcelos lifts his arm in a gesture so abrupt that the liquid from the glass overflows and runs through his fingers.

"The Spaniards oppressed the Indians and we Mexicans continue to oppress them, but neither type of oppression can be compared with the sufferings that the caciques and other indigenous chieftains inflicted on their subjects. We shall doubtless find iniquities in the history of the Conquest. It is one facet of the Spanish concept of maleness not to deny or even dissimulate their errors, but rather be the first in condemning them. The habit of confession undoubtedly influences that frankness . . ."

I interrupt: "Cortés spent a night in prayer and on the following morning ordered several Aztec warriors burned alive in front of the imperial palace of Tenochtitlán. It is possible that after this he confessed to the chaplain of his army, obtaining full absolution. . . ."

As if he had not heard me, Don José proceeds:

"When one compares the history of Mexico with that of the sister nations of the continent, one concludes that a special curse weighs upon our territory. It isn't that the people here are worse than elsewhere, but because our broad periods of pretorianism have made ignominy the rule. As long as we continue to be drunk on patriotic lies, hope will not show itself in our sky. One resplendent truth is the prerequisite of every resurgence. When I wrote my *Breve His-*

*toria de México* my principal intention was to clarify the truth. I know I irritated many people."

Through the broad windows of the apartment I can see the dark profile of the skyscrapers and a little of the Paseo de la Reforma, with its coloured neon-gas advertisements.

"What objections were made to the book?" I ask.

"Nobody questioned its veracity. But someone said that in destroying myths of more than a century's existence and in baring the muck in which we are struggling, I had left youth without hope for the destiny of the fatherland."

"And what is your answer to that criticism?"

"To that I reply that neither is there hope for those who live in lies. There exists no more despicable spectacle than that of a people intoxicated by its own ineptness, like the disillusioned sufferer who takes delight in his own sores. On the other hand, history teaches us that the effort of redemption of the country is not initiated without a radical revision of the dubious values. The worse optimism is that which trusts to time without sowing a seed in the furrow, without counting on the grain capable of germination and cultivation."

"What is your message to Mexican youth?"

"Nothing can be got from nothing. Civilization is not the fruit of miracles but of genius. Every society that crushes its cultured class and lets itself be guided by lack of conscience, by dishonesty, is a condemned society. I am one of those who believe in the enslaving power of acts of the spirit. In the pain of the Mexican people is rooted our hope. There is not in all the earth a race more forsaken, more oppressed, more deceived. But in the long Calvary of our people I see a sign of promise."

He pauses an instant, takes a swallow of whisky, and adds: "It is the constancy of the spirit of rebellion. The day it dies, the fate of Mexico is sealed."

And with these words he ended the first colloquy.

I know no history more sanguinary and painful than Mexico's. After all the violence of the Conquest, the colonial period lasted three hundred years. The "Black Legend" depicts the Spanish domination as an era of injustice, cruelties and rapine. The defenders of Spain reply that the lot of the Indians of America in no way worsened with the coming of the Conquistadores. Were not the tribes living in a state of barbarism, many of them addicted to cannibalism and constantly decimated by interminable wars? Could there be a more monstrous thing than the sacrifices with which the Aztecs propitiated their frightful gods? One can also say, with José Vasconcelos, that the cruelty of the Spanish colonizers never surpassed that of the Aztec and Maya caciques and emperors themselves. Also, that the average Indian was not happier or more free before the arrival of the Europeans. Also, a phrase from Salvador de Madariaga may be invoked: ". . . In history there are no villains, there are only men, wicked enough but much more complex than any demon." It is possible, too, to adduce other reasons in defence of the colonizers. The territory was too vast, means of communication difficult, the problems complex and the inter-tribal rivalries continued, while a cross-breeding—Negroes, Europeans, Indians—was going on that did not help the situation at all. Besides this, Spain had her problems in Europe, many and serious, which prevented her from giving greater attention and care to the colonies in America, and from thinking more about the well-being of her Indians and mestizos. Finally, the high, the definitive argument arises: however it may have been, the Spaniards brought the religion of Christ to America, indoctrinated the Indians, gave them an awareness of their own souls and of the existence of the One God.

I am not interested in denigrating or justifying the Spanish colonizer in America. When we attempt to comprehend the Mexico of today, what seems to me important with regard to the colonial period is to bear in mind what Samuel Ramos wrote: "To our lot fell the destiny of being conquered by a Catholic theocracy which was struggling to bring its people by degrees into the current of modern ideas stemming from the Renaissance. Hardly had the colonies been organized in America when an isolation was imposed upon them to preserve them from heresy, closing the ports and prohibiting trade with non-Spanish countries. So the only civilizing agent in the New World was the Catholic Church, which by reason of its pedagogical monopoly modelled American societies within the framework of a medieval sense of life."

The observation, which strikes me as excellent, has sufficient force to shed a revealing light on the Mexico of our time. The Church prolonged the time of the Middle Ages in the space and time of the New World. This explains in part the colour, the atmosphere, the medieval savour which we still encounter today in some corners and in some souls of this prodigious country.

On the 15th of September of 1810 Father Miguel Hidalgo addressed his parishioners of the town of Dolores in the State of Guanajuato, calling for the independence of Mexico. On the day following that political discourse, which has passed into history as *El Grito*, the cry for independence, a small group of revolutionaries kindled the flame of the War of Independence. A curious thing: the two greatest heroes of the Revolution were Catholic priests. When Hidalgo was captured and shot by the Spaniards, he was succeeded in the command of the rebel armies by another padre, José María Morelos, who having been captured later, too, was stripped in public of his priestly robes and shot in the back as a traitor to Spain.

The war lasted more than ten years, during which the tragic Mexican earth was soaked with much blood, and ended with the victory of the patriots and the expulsion of the Spaniards.

At first the Mexicans seemed not to know what to do with their victory. What type of government to adopt? Then began the rosary of absurdities of the history of Mexico. It was decided that the country should be an empire, and the emperor was chosen in the person of General Agustín Iturbide, who mounted the throne as Agustín I. His reign lasted only ten months, however, for, incapable of ruling in the face of chaos, Agustín abdicated and was sent into exile. Having returned to Mexico the following year without the government's permission, he was arrested and shot. Thenceforth the history of Mexico can be compared to a *corrido*—those ballads narrating long stories which are born and sung among the common people—but a *corrido* marked by the rhythm of shots from firing squads.

The Republic having been proclaimed, Mexico adopted a Constitution. Guadalupe Victoria was the first president elected. He was succeeded by Antonio López de Santa Anna, in my opinion the most picturesque, most refined scoundrel in American history.

The place? Vasconcelos' study in the old Public Library, of which he is the director. The room is huge, and of a monkish simplicity. The initial dialogue gives me an idea of my interlocutor's state of mind. The Professor is having one of his best days today.

"Are they true," I ask, "all those terrible things they say about General Santa Anna?"

"Yes, my friend, unfortunately they are. That contemptible man represented all the vices of the military caste dedicated to ruling and not to defending the country."

"But was Santa Anna a professional soldier?"

"He went into military service with no technical preparation of any sort. Through sheer influence he obtained, at one stroke, the post of cadet. And do you know what his first military exploit was?"

I shook my head. Professor Vasconcelos thrusts his head forward and says: "To combat the insurrection of Hidalgo and his patriots! Later, when he saw the royalists were being defeated, he turned coat and went over to persecute his former comrades with the same fury with which he had previously fought the minority insurgents."

"And how was it he came to be a general?"

"Thanks to his treachery to Iturbide in the Plan of Casa Mata, Santa Anna emerges promoted to general, preparing himself for the series of infamies that were to sully the life of the nation."

I remember having read a letter in which a pro-Iturbide colonel wrote to Santa Anna: "You have abandoned your family, maltreated your brothers and failed to succour your needy relatives . . . and to the falsification of a signature, and to your abusing your leader's trust, you owe your first promotion in the military career."

"And that same Santa Anna who protested against the tyranny of Iturbide," the professor goes on, "offered himself a thousand times to the Emperor to destroy the Congress, his own words being 'with uproar, scandal and even blood'. That is what Santa Anna was like before becoming president."

"But didn't the man have at least a more or less coherent norm, a constant in regard to political ideas?"

Vasconcelos laughs.

"Made president by the uprising against Bustamante, and after having raised the federative banner with Gómez Farias, Santa Anna joins the revolution that had been initiated against him and remains in the presidency as a centralist."

"How was a man like that able to administer the country?"

"Administer? The persecutions, the riots, the administrative disorder, the personal wasteful spending of every kind of funds, the forced loans, the bare-faced confiscation of property to buy granges and to pay his gambling and Don Juan debts, such are the features of what they called 'Santa Anna's administration'. He was so inept and lazy a man that he left any hanger-on in charge of the presidency while he went out to put down uprisings in long, costly campaigns or to enjoy the company of his prostitutes."

"But how could a type like that keep himself in power?"

"The voracious generals, the starving bureaucracy, they expected everything of the dictator *de facto* that Santa Anna was, and for lack of heroic deeds to attribute to him they invented eulogies the reading of which gives an idea of the degradation of the time. Imagine, a newspaper, *El Censor* of Vera Cruz, went so far as to call him 'human deity'."

"And the case of Texas?" I inquire. "Just how guilty of the loss of that territory was Santa Anna?"

"It is a long story. The Texas colonists were the advance guard of Yankee imperialism. They were farmers and ranchers, but they had cultured men as their leaders. Houston, aware of the mission he was called to carry out as a soldier, had begun, like all great soldiers, by being an educated civilian with a university degree. The future captains of Texas read Homer and revered Cortés. Houston even imitated Cortés in his methods, winning the friendship of the Cherokees. Not even marriage to an Indian maid, daughter of an influential chief, was lacking to make the imitation perfect."

"Then you believe the uprising headed by Houston did not begin merely as a local adventure?"

"Of course not. It was, indeed, the result of a well-matured plan, one of long standing. The juridical bases for the occupation of Texas had been prepared with the complicity of the blind governments of the Mexican Republic. The colonization of Texas made it possible to justify the right of possession. The abuses of Santannism gave the pretext. The colonists declared themselves autonomous in the name of the rights of humanity outraged by the Santannist troops. And the United States were enabled to realize their purpose of taking possession of Texas without the need of direct conquest."

"But didn't the U.S. Government aid the Texans?"

"Without any doubt. Arms in quantity, volunteers of every sort, together with capable leaders, began arriving from the North. In brief, the scant and ill-equipped garrisons of Mexican troops began to be attacked and beaten by the men who created the new Texan state."

"What was Santa Anna doing in the meantime?"

"His Most Serene Highness, the man who considered himself Napoleonic without knowing with any certainty what Napoleon had been, only very slowly comprehended the situation, and his first step was a ridiculous fanfarronade emphatically pronounced before the minister from France: 'If the Americans don't behave themselves, I shall march through their country to plant the Mexican flag in Washington.'"

It is unnecessary to repeat here what is already known, the marches and the countermarches, and the many battles that culminate in the independence of Texas. But there are points on which I have doubts or curiosity. And many of them interest much more the teller of tales than they do the student of history.

"And that adventure they tell of Santa Anna and a beautiful Texas girl?"

"Ah! Castrillón, one of the officers Santa Anna had ordered to knock down the roofs of some Mexican houses near the Alamo, found in one of them a respectable lady and her daughter, a girl of extraordinary beauty. Castrillón took the news to Santa Anna, who immediately asked him to fetch the girl to him. In a gesture of dignity Castrillón replied that he obeyed only military orders. But one Colonel Miñón had no objection to playing the pander. The girl's mother declared she would yield her up only in marriage, for the child was the daughter of a former officer in the Mexican army, whose honour she expected his colleagues to respect. Between Miñón and Santa Anna the abominable plan was arranged to feign a wedding, and for the purpose a third officer disguised himself as a priest. The false wedding was consummated in Santa Anna's own quarters."

"And the Battle of the Alamo the Texans talk so much about?"

"There were hardly 160 Texans inside the mission, besieged by 6,000 Mexican soldiers. The attack was ordered to the savage signal of '*degollar*—cut their throats.' One of the officers had told Santa Anna: 'That is going to cost us many lives.' To which His Excellency replied: 'It matters not what it costs.' We can seek in vain through all history for a general more brutish and contemptuous of the lives, the comfort and the honour of his soldiers."

"And the taking of the Alamo really did cost many lives . . ."

"After several bloody assaults our men entered the old mission building as conquerors. In one of the rooms was the American, Travis, wounded. He asked to speak with the Mexican general, Cos, while our General Amador was reproving a soldier for not having liquidated Travis. Cos appears and hurries to the wounded man, explaining to his friends that he owed Travis his gratitude from the time when he had been Travis's prisoner. He begs his colleagues to join him in asking pardon for Travis and for another Texas leader, Crockett. When they went to Santa Anna, the latter merely said, 'Kill them.' And in front of Santa Anna both were executed."

"Well, look here, I've always been inclined to think all that was a pure invention of Paramount or Metro-Goldwyn-Mayer."

"Wait, there's still more. At the moment the firing squad was discharging the volley, from one corner of the building came the bullets of some desperate Texans who had not been disarmed. His Highness started running, seeking refuge among the ruins. And afterwards, to avenge himself on the corpses, he had a pyre kindled on which all were burned. It was then that Almonte, less imbecilic than his chief, exclaimed: 'Another victory like this and we are ruined!' "

"How do you explain such cruelty?"

Professor Vasconcelos shrugs his shoulders:

"Some American historians think Santa Anna hated the rebels because they were American invaders disguised as colonists. I think the reason is different. Collective murders were the usual practice of war in the army of which Santa Anna was representative. It is natural that an army in which the worst executioners are retained as leaders, an army in which the soldiers fear their superiors and do not love them, should make the peaceful populace tremble with terror, but should not be apt for war with the foreigner."

"Is it true that Santa Anna was a coward?"

"In a meadow of New Washington, surrounded by his officers, Santa Anna received the news that Houston was approaching. He mounted his horse and, yelling like one possessed, dashed away, trampling on women and children, crying: 'The enemy is coming!

The enemy is coming!' It is not impossible that this access of persecution madness is symptomatic of a temporary loss of mind, a thing that happens to all who persist in killing unarmed people for a long time. Remorse torments even the cretinous. Spilled blood intoxicates worse than alcohol. Fear castigates the murderers."

"My question has not been answered, Professor. Was Santa Anna a coward? Is it true that in one battle in which he was defeated and taken prisoner, on seeing the enemy soldiers he flung himself on the ground and covered his face with a blanket?"

"So goes the story. It is said further that the enemies kicked him to his feet. And His Excellency took a Texas soldier's hand and kissed it humbly. On coming into Houston's presence, Santa Anna straightened up to say that the other ought to feel proud of having vanquished the Napoleon of the West. To which Houston, still feeling the pain of his wound and irritated with Mexicans, used the same term that Cambronne did at Waterloo. Santa Anna begged for mercy, alleging that he was not guilty of what had happened in the Alamo."

"What surprises me is that this was not the end of Santa Anna. Only in the wildest of adventure novelettes could such canaille remain in power in his country after that series of failures, weaknesses and degradations."

Vasconcelos smiles, toying with his watch charm, and goes on: "The explanation is simple. Santa Anna was sent north. They needed him in Washington. A man of that ilk was necessary to the Yankees on the eve of the war they were preparing against Mexico."

"And to use him better it was first necessary to rehabilitate him."

"Precisely. And Santa Anna was rehabilitated. But there is something worse than Santa Anna, my dear fellow, and that is the epoch that admired him, petted him, had him as its representative!"

"I have read, I don't remember where, that President Jackson in Washington amused himself at the expense of his prisoner."

"Evidently! That one was a real soldier, the finished type of conqueror."

"And how was the Napoleon of the West received when he came back?"

"It is shameful, but he was received in Vera Cruz by the authorities, who declared a holiday when the traitor returned. Santa Anna, in Washington, had signed all the papers they laid before his nose."

"Wasn't it about that time the incident of the pastries occurred?"

"Yes. The incident proves that Santa Anna's colleagues were no better than he. The officers of one of the corps in the capital gave a sample of Santannism. Gathered in a pastry shop and house of amusement in Tacubaya, after getting drunk and beating the French proprietor, they set fire to what they had broken up. The consequent legal suit, added to others by French subjects, gave rise to what has been called the 'War of the Pastries.'"

"Who was governing the country then?"

"Don Anastasio Bustamante. He could not handle the French claims, even the pastry one, and with the world's blessing, for foreigners and Mexicans alike were suffering at the hands of the soldiery, the French blockaded Vera Cruz, which capitulated. The government, however, did not approve the surrender."

"And it was there that Santa Anna came on the scene again."

"Exactly. In that battle he lost a leg."

"Which was enough to be transformed once more into a hero."

"Of course. The government lost the case with France. It signed a shameful treaty, obligating itself to pay more than it ought. But that fellow was rehabilitated."

At this point in the conversation I am beginning to feel rather annoyed with myself for not having invented Santa Anna as a character in a story. But if I had, who would have believed me?

"In March, 1839, Bustamante leaves office on the pretext of going to stamp out a revolution in Tampico, and hands over the presidency to, no more, no less, the traitor of the war with Texas, General Antonio López de Santa Anna. President Jackson was well served! The American General Staff had completed its plans. Polk was now President of the United States and was continuing, like his predecessors, the expansionist policy."

Then came the war between the United States and Mexico. Zachary Taylor commanded the invading American army. Vasconcelos sums up the situation:

"The outcome of the war was already plain to see in the faces of the leaders. It is enough to look at the portraits of Taylor and compare his strong, Roman conqueror's head with the narrow head, the perverted eyes of Santa Anna, to divine the inevitable result. Besides, Taylor was commanding an army. The officialdom of ours was Santannist, that is, like the one which provoked the 'War of the Pastries' for having robbed a public establishment, a body of officers accustomed to make targets of the unarmed civilian populace."

"How did 'our hero' behave?"

"In the battle fought at La Angostura, when the victory was swinging toward the Mexicans, Santa Anna ordered retreat and fled, saving his skin. After other failures he took refuge in the capital, where he managed to gather 18,000 men. But in reality he did not want to fight. On the contrary, he sent to ask the Americans under Scott for a million pesos in exchange for handing over the capital to them. Scott accepted."

"Are there proofs of that proposal?"

"Yes, there are copies in the Austin library."

"But when such ignominy was revealed, didn't it discredit Santa Anna?"

"Wretched people! He never lacked a sycophant to define as shrewdness the worst infamies of that degenerate. The truth is that Santa Anna fulfilled his promise and afterwards tranquilly watched the taking of Chapultepec and the sacrifice of the cadets without moving a single one of the 20,000 armed men he had in Mexico City to save them. Poor country! An Anglo-Saxon flag was actually flown on the palace of the viceroys."

"And Santa Anna?"

"He had to hide, not because anyone in Mexico wanted to kill him, but for fear of the Texans, who kept repeating the slogan, 'Remember the Alamo!' Among Yankee soldiers Santa Anna departed for Vera Cruz, where they put him on a ship. He remained in safety far from the country, thanks to his American friends. Hardly, though, had the withdrawal of the invading troops been effected, when those same friends took advantage of the fact that the soldiery missed their general (however absurd it may seem), and through their Intelligence Service managed to get Santa Anna back into the Presidency. And when they saw His Most Serene Highness once again in power, it occurred to them to propose the Treaty of Mesilla, by which Santa Anna sold them the region of Southern Arizona, pocketing the money. And that negotiation was proclaimed as a diplomatic triumph for Mexico."

"What were the last days of Santa Anna's government like?"

"An unbelievable public farce. With no concern whatever for the future the Conservatives adhered to the personality of His Highness, and we suffered the humiliation of seeing a man who had constantly betrayed his country, a soldier who had repeatedly

dishonoured his sword, attain through public adulation a place in
the strophes of the National Hymn, composed by a wretched hack,
one Bocanegra, repeated by I don't know how many generations
of Mexicans with servility or incomprehensible imbecility."

Vasconcelos falls silent for a moment, and then, with his tireless
enthusiasm, rounds off, as it were, the chapter of Antonio López
de Santa Anna:

"The liberal revolution which overthrew Santa Anna had the
support of the whole country. It represented a hope, but above all
it was the means of putting an end to all that plague of people
which not even the cholera morbus, which laid waste to the republic about that time, had succeeded in rooting out."


Same locale, another day.

I open the talk with a question I know is capable of kindling
Vasconcelos.

"What have you to say about the *Reforma?*"

I see no sign of impassioned reaction in his face. He responds
with the natural air of a professor of history in ordinary classroom
routine.

"The Mexican revolution called the 'Reformation' was initiated
in March, 1854, with the proclamation of the Ayutla Plan, which,
disregarding Santa Anna, created a provisional government and
convoked a Constituent Assembly."

"Don't you think the measures proposed by the Reformation were
good ones?"

"On the surface, yes. But let's see what was behind those apparently good purposes, and who were the men supporting them."

Professor Vasconcelos is beginning to show animation.

"The loss of Texas, New Mexico and California was complete.
But another chapter in the history of the Yankee conquest was
lacking: the destruction of the Mexican Catholic Church to the
benefit of North American Protestants, or, as the United States
writers say, the extension of the work of the European Protestant
Reformation."

"I confess, Professor, I find no difficulty in believing in the truth
of that 'plan.' Do you mean that the Mexican Reformation, in the
final analysis, is nothing but an episode, somewhat lagging in time
and remote in space, of the Protestant Reformation?"

"Precisely. The initiators of the movement abstained from giving it the frank character of a war of Protestants against Catholics. Liberal laicism was the mask. The fundamental purpose was the destruction of the Catholic Church, and, in passing, the liquidation of the rich families, heirs of the Colony, for the benefit of the foreign caste which was gradually taking possession of the mines, the commerce and the lands of the Mexicans."

"How is it possible to believe that the Mexican conservatives lent themselves to such a thing?"

"They did so without knowing one iota about Calvin. They carried forward the offensive directed toward the aim of destroying the sole Mexican institution which had survived the storms: the Catholic Church."

"I confess I look on the Reformation with great sympathy. It has always seemed to me that, despite the many errors committed in its name, fundamentally it was necessary."

"We are not arguing the legality of certain aspects of the *Reforma,* nor its necessity. It is evident that the clergy, as well as the State, needed purification. The censurable part is that the *Reforma* was carried out under the direction of a foreign programme and with an anti-religious sense."

"If my memory doesn't fail me, the famous Lerdo Law called for the freeing from mortmain of properties owned by 'corporations,' alleging that 'private corporations could not possess property.' "

"The term 'corporations' was used to dissimulate religious hatred, but in the certainty that nearly all corporations were ecclesiastic in nature."

"But don't you think Benito Juárez protected himself in legality, sought to re-establish the prestige of the vote, of the national will?"

"Nobody denies him that intention. It is a pity that exigencies of social and religious nature unsuitable to Mexicans were mixed with his programme. Were it not for that, we could praise unreservedly the liberal movement which for the first time opposed the Santannist and Iturbidist methods of armed uprising with the civilized methods of popular election as the origin of power."

"What about the Juárez Law?"

"It did not even speak of transference of property but of confiscation and nationalization of property of the clergy. Besides that, the monastic orders were suppressed, an absolute blunder against civilization, and the Civil Register was created, which was all right for non-Catholics and should have been done, but in such a way as to harmonize the new method with the old, not in a barbarous fashion, refusing to recognize Catholic marriages and registers of baptism."

"I remember having read in Justo Sierra that 'the liberals represented the light and the conservatives the shadow, the former, the day, and the latter, the night.'"

"As a good son of his time, Don Justo Sierra, instead of judging, goes off on the tangent of the common literature of his day. Why say that atheism is the day and faith the night? Where does contemporary civilization get its origins and its strength, in the atheistic negation of the Stoics or in the light and clear vision of Christianity?"

"What can you say of the accusations made to the effect that the Church was rich and corrupt, and had a corrupting influence on national politics? Don't you find that the Church has supported illegal and cruel governments? And don't you think poverty might have been a benefit to the moral health of the Church in Mexico, where it went so far as actually to practise usury?"

"Even if we admit those accusations, I must say to begin with that a statesman ought to see that all of them together were no reason to destroy the Church but, at most, to demand its cleansing."

"But wasn't the *Reforma* aiming at that cleansing?"

"Up to a point, yes, and within those limits I am with the liberals, for I regard the measures dictated as inevitable. Nevertheless, it is indispensable to distinguish between purification and destruction. It is against destruction that I take a most decided stand."

We are interrupted by a young man who comes to ask the professor to autograph one of his books. When the youth withdraws, happy, a volume of *Ulises Criollo* (the autobiography of Vasconcelos) under his arm, the latter turns to me and proceeds: "The laws of the Reformation, in the form they were written and enforced, constitute a unique case of sectarian intolerance and of economic downfall."

"I don't think they were vigorously enforced."

"That is true, and only because of that have they subsisted. Juárez himself vacillated, and during his presidential term from 1867 to 1872 a certain benevolence prevailed. For example: he considered religious marriages valid, and refused to deprive parish priests of the church-owned houses used as their homes."

"And during Porfirio Díaz's dictatorship?"

"The *Reforma* laws were carried out only in part. Under Carranza and Obregón, about half. Plutarco Elías Calles is the one who started imposing them to the letter. With his Turkish hatred for all that is Christian, he loosed religious war once more. There can be no peace in the Mexican family while the Reformation laws remain in force."

"Don't you think the Juárez Law up to a point is in accord with the spirit of the religious regime existing in modern countries?"

"The Juárez Law was innocent only in appearance. It contains the absurd assumption that the Church does not exist, since no juridical personality is recognized in it. This is called a 'lay state', but in reality the lay state always recognizes the fact that a Church exists in its bosom. You who live in the United States know that very well."

José Vasconcelos gets up to answer the telephone. When he comes back, he fires these words at me with passion: "So then, my friend, as a consequence of the Reformation laws Mexico has been left as the only officially atheistic country on earth!"

I want to get back to a theme that interests me:

"What can you tell me, Professor Vasconcelos, about the wealth accumulated by the clergy and of the necessity to put it into circulation in order to help a distressed public economy?"

"It is incredible," he replies, "that that humbug is tirelessly repeated in a country which, after its religious Reformation, still has lands transferred to enrich hundreds of foreign companies today profiting from the best part of the Republic's property!"

I can see that my esteemed interlocutor is continuing to use attack as a weapon of defence, for he cannot deny that the Mexican clergy had accumulated riches in a land of starving population and deficit economy.

"Even supposing the necessity of reducing the territorial property of the Church had existed," he goes on, "that should have been not by radical measures of total confiscation but by rational methods. However it was, they ought to have left the Church in possession of its temples and parish houses and beneficent foundations. It is fitting to the simple economy of a people that many citizens be established on untouchable properties. Every priest was the centre of a small Mexican family and in every priest's home unmarried women found lodging, aunts, sisters, nieces . . ."

"Lovers . . ."

"Lovers, if they will! But they were Mexican mouths with their living assured. And with the confiscation and closing of the priests' homes, gardens and orchards, thousands of Mexicans were left in the street. Moreover, it is known also that certain religious orders devoted to culture and to material labour, like the Benedictines, the Franciscans, the Dominicans, etc., are incomparable factors of production, and represent an economic element of stability which cannot be advantageously replaced. And no one with an atom of patriotism will deny that those gardens were better in the hands of Mexicans, together with certain lands annexed to the convents, than in the hands of anonymous companies which send their profits out of the country or use them in the country but for the benefit of foreign colonies."

Through the open door I see a group of young students passing, on their way to the reading room. Their steps resounded on the pavestones of the old corridor. For an instant José Vasconcelos remains silent, hands laced over his stomach, eyes apparently fixed on his own shoetips. Then, raising his eyes to me:

"First came the general confiscation from the clergy. Then, the general confiscation from Mexican proprietors, consummated later by Carranza's revolution, always to the benefit of the great companies, the great proprietors from the United States."

He makes a gesture of discouragement.

"The treasures of the Church, priceless artistic treasures, because of the unpremeditated, disorderly, savage confiscations, went to swell the museums of the United States and fill the houses of that country's millionaires. The three best centuries of Mexican art were thus turned into ruins, and nothing that is being done today can hope to replace what is destroyed."

Discounting the exaggerated enthusiasm of Vasconcelos for the Church, which makes him too tolerant toward the defects of the Mexican clergy, I cannot help concluding that my friend is right in nearly all he says. But the aspect of the *Reforma* that attracts me most and about which I have the greatest curiosity is the agrarian problem, perhaps the core of the question.

"How much was the Mexican *campesino* benefited by the Reformation?"

"The indigenous communities which had enjoyed separate lands for their work since the time of the Colony were obliged to split them up. Just as today the theoretical exigency of collectivization prevails, the false economists of the *Reforma* were enamoured of 'individualization.' They thought they were achieving progress by dividing the lands of the community among the members of it. The result was that those members began to sell and transfer their *fondos.* And once the community lands were on the market, the swiftest got possession of them, the nearest landowner bought them for practically nothing, and the situation of the Indians worsened. As a result, not only were the Mexican priests proletarianized, but the Indians, too. The wise Spanish institution of the *ejido,* which had borne such good fruits for more than three centuries, was undone, to the benefit of a latifundian element that, beginning with the Reformation, gradually became predominantly foreign."

And the last words of José Vasconcelos in this third colloquy were: "By a painful irony it was Juárez, an Indian, who deprived of their lands his compatriots whom Spanish law had elevated to the category of proprietors!"

Lunch in a genuinely Mexican restaurant. We are first served *quesadillas* stuffed with *flores de calabaza.* Then comes a delicious soup the name of which I do not ask, for here I am not in the mood for culinary research but to ask Professor Vasconcelos, whom I have sitting defenceless across the table, to give me his opinion about several figures of his country's history.

"Talk to me about Maximilian," I beg, "and the strange empire Napoleon III 'invented' for Mexico."

Professor Vasconcelos utters his little throaty laugh, prolonged and jovial. I don't know why just then it seemed to me I was facing a *caudillo* from the interior of Rio Grande do Sul. Yes, a political leader from our common border with Argentina. Let's call him "Colonel José Vasconcelos of Uruguaiana."

"Spain, England and France sent ships of their fleets to Vera Cruz. Europe was not resigned to the absolute domination of Mexico and the rest of the Continent by the United States. The English and the Spanish had no programme, and limited themselves to claiming payment of debts and indemnities. But Napoleon III conceived the magnificent dream of taking Mexico as a point of support for a Latin resurrection in the world."

I smile, perceiving the course the professor is taking.

He continues: "It was the moment to recover for New Spain her central position in the Continent, and for France to play the rôle of Philip II's Spain, that is, the rôle of head of the Latin civilization."

"And if the fantastic empire had lasted," I ask, "what would have happened?"

"The empire of the Anglo-Saxons would have been broken forever if we had accepted the support of France in constituting a nationalistic government. We might even have reconquered Texas and California."

"Justo Sierra actually wrote that if Maximilian had come a year earlier, which he could have done had it not been for the French defeat at Puebla, he might have arrived in time to make an alliance with Lee's Southern forces, in which case the secession from the United States would have been effected."

"Yes, but what Don Justo Sierra did not understand, as he should have done, was that such a secession suited our country and the Latin continent. Because without Lincoln's triumph Juárez would not have returned."

"God writes straight through crooked lines . . ."

Don José gives me an inquiring glance. I do not explain, for not even I know just what meaning to offer for my own words.

"*Bueno*," he continues. "Maximilian arrives in the capital amid great rejoicing of a people accustomed to applauding success without worrying about its masks. Instead of devoting himself body and soul to the conservatives, the Emperor ratified Forey's liberal measures and surrounded himself with a council of young and moderate men. His intention was to govern according to the civilized system that recognizes and reconciles the interests of the parties most opposed to one another. Maximilian understood that he was not going to found a dynasty, exotic in America, but to encourage the creation of a national government which, with the disappearance of the Emperor from the scene, would once more become a republic. It was, as Maximilian himself said, a democratic monarchy."

"Like the one we had in Brazil with Pedro II, who resembled Maximilian a little, even physically. Our emperor was an educated man, too, with modern ideas."

The waiter comes and goes with plates.

"The year 1865 saw the Empire consolidated. But unfortunately the Civil War in the United States ended that same year with the victory of the Unionists, and the first thing they did was to invoke the Monroe Doctrine, threatening us with the invasion of Mexico by Grant's troops."

"And by that time Juárez had come back across the frontier and was beginning to gather men . . ."

"Yes, and to receive arms and money from the agents of the Union. It was thus that the liberal armies blossomed forth."

"And meanwhile, Napoleon was contending with the Prussian threat."

"Exactly. He did not feel capable of declaring war on the United States. He was obliged to yield to diplomatic pressure. He ordered the withdrawal of the French forces and advised Maximilian to abdicate."

He pauses to give his attention to the fresh plates that the waiter brings us. For some moments we forget the tragic prince of the Hapsburg house to sample the delicious dishes Professor Vasconcelos has ordered.

"Maximilian then," he goes on, "performed the most selfless act of his life. Considering probably that it was not chivalrous to abandon his Mexican partisans, he decided to remain in the country with no other protection than that of the native imperialists. In the year 1866 the revolution grew in the North. The Indian Juárez was finally going to be the wedge that would disintegrate the profound, painful but creative work of the Colony, splitting it into pieces. Mexican society would dissolve, to the benefit of Lincoln's compatriots. The rest is known. On March 15, 1867, Maximilian and his generals Miramón and Mejía surrendered. After a trial that was nothing but a farce, the three were shot, to the scorn of the most generous opinion of the country and of liberal Europe, which had counselled pardon. That useless shooting is one of the stains on our history."

Lunch over, we go out to stroll idly along one of the streets in the old part of the city. From time to time Don José stops and points with his cane to a building, tells a story apropos of it, cites a date, a name, an anecdote. Then we resume our way.

I wish to settle a doubt.

"In all these colloquies of ours, I have noticed on your part a great animosity against the United States. Am I to consider you anti-American?"

Professor Vasconcelos utters his rather hoarse little laugh.

"I confess that the whole plan put into practice by the United States to attain the hegemony of the New World strikes me as admirable. I only lament the fact that we have been its victims. I recognize, too, that in the conflict of nations nearly always the better one wins. As the Saxons say: 'Let the best man win.' Yes, the best man wins. Between a Taylor and a Santa Anna I do not hesitate for a moment; I execrate Santa Anna and I admire Taylor. I admire him for having conquered Mexico with 25,000 men almost as much as I admire Hernán Cortés who conquered it with nine hundred. But at the same time I believe every conquest harms both the conquered and the conqueror. The conquered, because it degrades them, and the conquerors because it develops in them the militarism that ends by corrupting the best nations."

"I don't think one can accuse, with any justice, the United States of today of corrupt militarism. Their sins are probably of a different nature."

Professor Vasconcelos does not respond. He surprises me with his further observation: "The Yankee has done well to try to extend his empire. It is an ineludible law of history and human advantage that the most virtuous race be the one to predominate. And we have to recognize that fact above the humbug about theoretical international law. Civilization would be wiped out in the world if, in the name of intangible local sovereignties, social states like Mexico under Santa Anna or Calles, or like Venezuela under Gómez, should be perpetuated."

"Or under Pérez Jiménez," I add.

We stop on a corner. Don José catches the lapel of my jacket: "There is a law of humanity that is above the abuses of barbarism. Every time the level of a people falls, descending below the level of animals, every time men resort to the cannibalism of periodic firing squads, to brute force as a system, to wickedness as a norm, every time that happens a kind of divine law imposes itself and foreign conquest cleanses the corrupt society with fire and blood."

I see that José Vasconcelos is still defending Spain and Hernán Cortés.

When we take leave of each other, clasping my hand he says these final words: "So it always happens that in any region of the earth the case of Sodom and Gomorrah or that of powerful but debased Babylon is reproduced."

And on this point we part.

I commence the fifth colloquy by giving my impression of Oaxaca, his natal city, to Professor Vasconcelos. He listens in silence, and when I finish he says:

"In Oaxaca one of the firmest crystallizations of the Spaniard and the indigene was consummated. The typical Mexican is a mixture of Spaniard and Indian. The Valley of Oaxaca has from the start been a Hispanic island in the midst of mountain ranges densely populated by aborigines."

We are alone in the corner of a salon full of people, at one of those parties that Vasconcelos, if he wishes, can offer as another expression of American imperialism: the cocktail party—a meeting at which one drinks and talks and in which the confusion, the crowding and the heat, the babble of voices, are all so stunning that at the end of the party no one knows what he has eaten and drunk or about what or with whom he has talked. I only hope they will leave us, Don José and me, untroubled in this providential corner.

"The best people of the Conquest," he continues, "Hernán Cortés himself and many of his men, chose the Valley of Oaxaca as a marquisate. The houses, the churches, the palaces of Oaxaca display the blazon of the robust Spanish romantic and baroque architecture. There the old names proclaim lineage from Castile. The mingling with native blood took place long after the Colony. In the period of the Reformation the Oaxacan capital was still white. In it the indigenous mass was educated. Santa Anna's tyranny found in Oaxaca the old resistance of the Spanish caste against the abuses of public power. The old Castilian piety flourished there in the hearts of fighters and mystic. There human contact was not reserved, after the indigenous temperament, but plain and affable in the old genuinely Spanish fashion. In that refined, masculine environment the character of Porfirio Díaz was shaped."

"That was what I was coming to. What sort of man was the Dictator?"

"He was a man in whose strength there was something of the native rock, which became a work of art under the chisel of the artificers from Spain. What Díaz lacked was the polishing, the finishing. But his soul was the block around which a diseased nation found the unhealthy peace of thirty-five years of dictatorship."

"Was there in him any conflict of ideas, so peculiar to the mestizo?"

Don José makes a grimace of doubt.

"In Díaz there was no conflict of blood or of ideas. In his make-up the Mixtec blood fused with the Spanish, creating a firm equilibrium. And his ideas were too scarce for there to be any conflict between them."

"How would he come out in a parallel with Juárez?"

"His Spanish blood defended the Dictator from the pitfalls into which Juárez fell, the pure Indian who, not being able to see in his mind the advantages of the Iberian conquest, unreservedly yielded himself up to the Nordic influence. Through being a mestizo Porfirio Díaz is Mexican, while Juárez was only an Indian. His lack of education and his incapacity prevented Díaz from comprehending his people's problem. But the fact that he sincerely embraced the policy of religious conciliation is a proof of how repellent, how repugnant to him was the Yankee plan, which the other, the Indian, adopted without scruple."

"Is it not true that Díaz did plunder the treasury?"

"He was an honest man. But because he was a dictator (and a dictatorship cannot moralize) he allowed his friends to steal."

I inform Professor Vasconcelos that in my home state we had Dr. Borges de Medeiros, who governed for twenty-five years, a dictator, to some extent, of Don Porfirio's type. It was a dictatorship inspired by the political ideas of positivism, practised by an honest, austere man, in whose shadow, however, many outrages and cruelties were committed.

"And the curious thing," I say, rounding off my parenthesis, "is that if Don Porfirio was overthrown by a revolution of *campesinos,* landless men, our Borges de Medeiros was thrown out by a revolution provoked and conducted by members of our rural aristocracy, lords of vast estates."

"As a clan chieftain," my interlocutor proceeds, "Porfirio Díaz is the ablest of the Republic's rulers. He never perceived that the material progress invading Mexico was part of an evolutionary process which not even Turkey or China escaped. That is why he did not know how to utilize that progress for the benefit of his compatriots. On the contrary, in the most ignorant and servile fashion he placed himself at the service of foreign capitalism, which made him the policeman, the guardian of their own properties."

"Of that, happily, we cannot accuse our Borges de Medeiros."

"And so, under the government of Porfirio Díaz, a whole nation of sixteen millions of people was despoiled of its lands, of its waters, of its petroleum, of its mines and of its future!"

Now here is a statement that calls for a drink. I snatch a glass from the tray of a waiter passing within reach of my arm.

Other people come over and surround Professor Vasconcelos, making it impossible to continue our colloquy.


When, at the age of twelve, I used to see photographs of the Mexican Revolution of 1910 in old numbers of the Parisian magazine *L'Illustration,* to which my father was a subscriber and of which he was a voracious reader, what most fascinated me in the whole sanguinary story were the figures and the feats of Pancho Villa and Emiliano Zapata. Later came the Hollywood films in which the role of the *hombre malo,* the villain, was always Mexican, and Mexico was depicted as a sort of no-man's land infested by bandits, volcanoes, long siestas and drunken Indians.

I confess that when I passed through Mexico in 1941 for the first time, remaining in the capital little more than twenty-four hours between planes, the mature man that I was still looked at the country rather with the eyes of the boy who leafed through the pages of *L'Illustration* and went to the Cine Ideal to see Triangle and Vitagraph films to the tinkling of Dona Gabriela's piano.

The city seemed to me as sombre as its populace, and I had the impression that a smell of corpse and blood was still in the air.

I have read articles or books dealing with the Mexican Revolution of 1910 from the most diverse angles. There is the point of view of the Porfiristas, that of the Catholics, that of the Zapatistas, that of the Maderistas. There is also that of the United States. And, naturally, that of the Communists.

I think that all that Mexico is today, all that is represented in the lines of the University City, in the murals of Orozco, Rivera and Siqueiros, by the vigorous new literature inspired by native themes, and—why not?—in the Compañía de Petróleos Mexicanos and principally in the reconciliation of the race with its Indian past; all, in short, that is called "contemporary Mexico," began to take form, slowly, with the Revolution set afoot on the 20th November, 1910.

At first the movement did not differ much from its predecessors. It was a matter of deposing a tyrant who perpetuated himself in power and who, an octogenarian and surrounded by a Cabinet nearly as decrepit as he, was still thinking of re-electing himself. Francisco I. Madero, the spiritual leader of the Revolution, was a member of a rich family of landowners and had been educated abroad. The men about him were also intellectuals. It can be said that the immediate objectives of the Revolution were political in nature. It was a question of putting young men in power and re-establishing honesty, justice and a democratic regime in the country. The real chiefs of the Revolution were men like Pascual Orozco, Pancho Villa and Emiliano Zapata, who commanded armies of ill-armed peasants, barefoot *campesinos,* and who, seeking to avoid pitched battles, by preference adopted the tactics of ambuscade and surprise attack. And the victory, coming too soon, in a way stunned the intellectual leaders of the movement. The affair had turned out better than they had imagined. The delirious enthusiasm of the people on the day Madero took office gave the idea that they were expecting great basic reforms. Much to his disgust, Madero found himself transformed into an Apostle. An honest man, of good feeling, he nevertheless lacked the qualities of a leader. Having conspired and fought to rid his country of a tyrant, he found himself now with a social revolution on his fragile, patrician's hands.

Yes, because the real character of the movement was defining itself now in victory. Even after Madero took office, Zapata refused to disarm his *campesinos.* He demanded that the government go back to the system of the *ejidos,* restoring lands to the villages.

Gradually a nationalistic idea emerged from the chaos. The Mexican people, which ever since the Conquest had been separated by barriers of language, race, culture, seemed now to seek its unity. There was more than that. The Indian, the *peón,* the *pelado*—the have-not—all lifted their voices, sued to recover their civil rights in a land which until then had been governed by the Spanish white man or the *criollo*—the man born in America of Spanish parentage —demanded participation in the government of a country where the quadruply centenarian idea prevailed that the Indian is an inferior being, incapable of raising himself above his miserable condition, a poor devil destined to be eternally the servant of the upper classes—of the military, of the clergy, of the politicians, of the great landowners.

As Frank Tannenbaum very well observes, Mexico was not a nation but a land of "born colonists," who for all effects considered themselves in a foreign country and looked for their inspiration beyond the borders of their natal land, especially in France. Everything was imported: painting, literature, architecture, sculpture. The rich landowners sent their sons to study abroad. And it was to the interest of the ruling classes that Mexico continue to be an archipelago with the many islands of diverse tribes, plus the island of the mestizos and that of the *criollos*. The Revolution now wanted to build bridges, *chinampas,* to link those islands to each other, in the hope of some day forming the Mexican Continent. The Indian, the *campesino,* the people, in short, had countless times been summoned to take up arms, to fight and die to decide the wars that were always being started, not for their interest or well-being but for the interest and happiness of the different politicians or institutions that were fighting each other. But whether it was monarchists against republicans, State against Church, federalists against centralists, the people wanted to be heard, wanted to share in the government and most of all in the land.

Examined closely in time, the Revolution of 1910 gives us the impression of a bloody failure, of just another killing. (I knew a *gaúcho,* a Rio Grande do Sul *caudillo,* who used to say that every slaughter had its usefulness.) Many of the very leaders of the Revolution had caused this, detracting from its spirit. The desired and hoped-for agrarian reform did not take shape to the degree dreamed of by the revolutionary peasants. *Caudillos* of the old school succeeded each other in power, and everywhere in the country uprisings, corruption, political murders, organized banditry, economic ruin continued; and as if all this were not enough, foreign intervention was repeated.

Seen, however, from our point in time, the importance of the great Mexican social insurrection, which gave a new physiognomy to the country, stands evident. With it was born, or at least fortified and affirmed, that spirit of rebellion which makes of Mexico a unique case in America. The famous nationalistic pride, that exacerbated "Mexicanism," comes mainly from the spirit. In sum, the Revolution gave the Mexicans the consciousness of a destiny to fulfil and the desire to recover the land they had lost even before they had been born as a nation.


Having finished the lecture I gave this afternoon at the University of Mexico—"Parallel between Latins and *Gringos*"—I go to Vianna Moog's house with some friends. I manage to get Professor Vasconcelos off to a corner of the room.

I go straight to the point: "What can you tell me of Francisco Madero?"

"He was of pure Spanish blood, of small stature, with bearded face and large, luminous eyes, noble head, kindly and energetic bearing."

Don José's advantage over the majority of historians—I reflect—is that, from the time of Porfirio Díaz to date, he has known personally and close up the personages of Mexican history. Yes, and he himself has been in the cast of that great drama, in rôles of decided importance.

"Madero was a man of simple and affable address," he continues. "His clear, profound thought was expressed in precise, nervous, rapid sentences. Seeing him move across a cinema screen, we are reminded of the type of French politicians who impose themselves by dint of talent and honesty."

"It is strange that a man like that was unable to govern."

"With him was born and extinguished the hope that a Mexico would arise that would be directed by the mind, governed by intelligence at the service of patriotism."

"Don't be so pessimistic. You can't deny that the situation has improved."

Paying no attention to my interruption, my interlocutor continues: "Madero aspired to more than his own happiness. Love of his compatriots motivated him. He was the first in power who did not begin by shouting '*mueras.*'"

I remember the remark of a character in D. H. Lawrence's *The Plumed Serpent*: "Whenever a Mexican shouts '*Viva!*' he ends by yelling '*Muera!*' When he says 'Long live . . . !' in reality he means 'Death to this or that man!' "

"Madero did not try to set one class against another. He was not of the breed of destroyers. He initiated a campaign of truth and frankness. Porfirio Díaz arrested him. Madero fled from the jail, took refuge in the United States and from there incited the people to rebellion."

"In your opinion, what was Madero's mistake on taking office?"

"One of his major errors was to have continued the disarming of the irregular forces which had brought him victory, leaving himself thus at the mercy of the old Porfirist army in consequence."

"How did the Press behave, which he had freed from the dictatorial gag?"

"Freedom of the Press turned into licence. It not only magnified the government's mistakes but also employed calumny, trying to discredit the administration."

"Who and what was behind that campaign?"

"The foreign advertisers, of course!"

"Through what special motive?"

"Because Madero abolished monopolies and undercover business deals. In the time of Don Porfirio all government typewriters had to be bought at a surcharged price from a certain foreign company which paid commissions to the functionaries."

(Oh, God—I think—how all this is the same, the day before yesterday, yesterday, today . . . and for how long?)

"Madero ordered all purchases to be made through public bidding. And the business man who lost by it, the owner of the principal English-language newspaper in the city, became a leader of the anti-Madero gang."

"In a way, that technique is still going on throughout Latin America."

"More still! The American Embassy was later turned into a centre of the conspiracies, irritated by the first agrarian act of Madero: the prohibition of transferring national lands to a single individual or enterprise of an area greater than 5,000 hectares, or 13,355 acres."

"There is one thing I don't understand," I say. "Wasn't there a newspaper or two that accused the Madero Revolution of having been financed by the American oil people?"

Professor Vasconcelos makes a vivid gesture and replies:

"The truth is that American oil interests failed in attempting to carry out a pipeline contract. On the other hand British firms which had made millions in the shadow of Porfirianism, seeing that they would no longer gain concessions of great unexplored zones, put their influence on the side of Madero's enemies."

"In the meantime, what was happening about the agrarian question?"

"To solve the problem, to give lands to those who needed them, and to restore the confiscated lands to their owners, Madero appointed a committee which, if it had lasted, would have solved the problem in practical, just terms, without arbitrary confiscations and avoiding the subsequent chaos. And yet the wicked accuse Madero of having betrayed the agrarian programme of the Revolution!"

"What was the position of the clergy with regard to Madero?"

"It held aloof. Not because Madero took action against the benevolent practices we had won under the protection of the Porfirist policy, but because he did not repress the anti-Catholic preachments of certain agitators."

"So Francisco Madero's government was just, benevolent and democratic."

"Yes; but that did not suit Mr. Henry Lane Wilson, Ambassador of the United States. The Embassy continued to be the centre of conspiracy. It was not possible to overthrow Madero by arms. The country was at peace. People were beginning to think about the President's successor. He had to be a cultured man, educated in the learning of the schools and in the experience of the world. Mexico had now left barbarism behind, creating a civilised nation's regime. Oh! But the picture did not please those who were still profiting from great fortunes and the dishonest business of the Porfirian era. Resentful politicians and ambitious military men were also discontent with the situation."

"Do you think American opinion was against Madero?"

"No. In the United States the majority opinion, always generous, inclined toward Madero and the new regime. North Americans of good will instinctively understood that a regenerated, progressive Mexico would be a better neighbour and friend than a savage Mexico subjected to cruel despotisms."

"I am glad to see, my friend, that you do not blame the *whole* United States people, as many do, for the policy of the financial and industrial groups, of 'big business,' in short."

I speak of the treachery of General Victoriano Huerta, who took office and then ordered the murder of Madero, of whose forces he was commander-in-chief.

"Huerta," says Don José, "that indescribable drunkard, wrote one of the blackest pages of our history."

"What was the Mexican popular reaction to Francisco Madero's murder?"

"Armed protest was not long in coming. There was uprising in several parts of the country, and Governor Venustiano Carranza placed himself on the side of the people. In the South, Zapata was under arms with his *campesinos,* ready to fight for the Ayala Plan. In the west a *caudillo* appeared: Álvaro Obregón. In the North Pancho Villa had raised an army and was inflicting defeats on Huerta's troops."

"What effect had the election of Wilson in the United States on Mexican events?"

"It favoured the cause of our legality. Wilson was a man of ideals. He removed the American ambassador who had conspired against Madero. He also refused recognition to Victoriano Huerta's government."

"All of which, if my memory serves, led Huerta to resign."

"Understand this, though: Wilson lent no material aid to the rebels. Huerta was driven out by the guerrilla troops of Carranza, Villa, Zapata, Obregón and others."

"I gather that General Venustiano Carranza remained, at least in the capital and vicinity, master of the situation. What sort of man was he?"

"A man of extraordinary capability dominated by a lust for power. But his envy of his most capable subordinate led him to intervene in unimportant matters to the prejudice of the administration."

"And do you think Carranza's ineptitude is due to the lack of any defined meaning of the so-called Constitutionalist Revolution?"

"Of course! Each one of its leaders interpreted the Constitution in his own way. In the South, Emiliano Zapata refused to obey the authority of Carranza, whom he called bourgeois and reactionary. He carried out the Ayala Plan in his own fashion, that is, by taking over the granges, the country estates. Villa and his soldiers wanted elections called, to eliminate Don Venustiano."

"And Carranza's *compinches,* his chums, wanted to maintain a long period of pre-constitutional dictatorship before the elections."

"Exactly. The Zapatistas advocated an indigenous republic and a division of lands . . ."

"According to a Communistic plan?"

"No! According to the Ayala Plan. There was no talk yet in Mexico about Communism or Collectivism. At bottom, each of the three factions was paying court to Washington, that is, seeking recognition of a state of war, which would permit open trading in arms."

"Whose idea was it for a Revolutionary National Convention?"

"A group of patriots who wanted to avoid the shedding of blood."

"What sort of agreement was reached in that Convention?"

"A revolutionary programme fairly advanced in the agrarian and labour fields. The agrarian clauses were introduced by the Zapatistas. On the political plane the Convention found that the moment had come to free the country from the military *caudillo* system which had soiled the whole history of the nation, and also determined that, for the same reason, personal mandate, Carranza's as well as Villa's and Zapata's, should cease. The forces of these three *caudillos* were to be subordinate to the Ministry of War of the Provisional President, whom the Assembly immediately elected."

"How did Carranza receive those decisions?"

"Ah! He paid no attention to them. Villa and Zapata offered their arms to the Convention government. And war was officially declared between the Carranzistas and the Convention."

"A thing that has always intrigued me is the behaviour of General Obregón, the man of rural tradition. It was to be expected that, heading the troops from Sinaloa and Sonora, he would support the Provisional President, Don Eulalio Gutiérrez."

"Yet he preferred to join Carranza, whom some days before he had formally refused to recognize."

There followed a period of Mexico's history which bewilders me by its very confusion. Carranza is expelled from the country by force of arms. Gutiérrez occupies the capital and does everything possible to avoid acts of vengeance and needless killings. On the other hand, Zapatistas and Villistas, united in their hatred of Carranza, kill each other over irrational rivalries. Gutiérrez signs a decree dismissing Villa from the command of his troops. But his weakness prevents him from enforcing the decree. He abandons the capital with his government to set himself up at San Luis Potosí. Villistas and Zapatistas improvise a Convention, declare Gutiérrez dismissed, and appoint a crony of Pancho Villa as Provisional President. So Mexico is left with three Presidents: Roque González García, Villa's puppet; Venustiano Carranza, self-candidate; and Eulalio Gutiérrez, elected by the Aguascalientes Convention. Woodrow Wilson held the political fate of Mexico in his hands when he decided to close the border to trade in arms and munitions, declaring that he would recognize only the faction that set up a government through the vote. Shortly after, forgetting that decision, he recognizes Carranza. Villa was an outlaw and his deeds of banditry had ruined his prestige. Obregón routed him, making him withdraw to the North, where he found refuge in the mountains, always pursued and harried by enemies and with the closed American border at his back. Zapata took refuge in hiding places in the South. Carranza was enabled to organize his government with the blessing of the United States.

"What sort of government did Carranza administer?"

Professor Vasconcelos, who for some minutes had turned his attention to the Uruguayan diplomat who had come over to him, then responds:

"His first really important law was that of January 6, 1915, on the restoration of the *ejidos;* it was the work of Don Luis Cabrera, the illiterate Dictator's principal adviser."

"What were the provisions of that law?"

"It nullified the concessions of land made during the dictatorship of Don Porfirio Díaz to the prejudice of indigenous villages and communities, and re-established communal ownership of those lands."

"Then Zapata's ideas triumphed?"

"Yes, but the political purpose of the measure was to leave Zapatism without a platform. And it was curious, you'll note, that a revolution calling itself radical should commence by reviving the Spanish system of the *ejido,* contradicting the Juárez Law."

"Then came the Querétaro Convention."

"Yes, and it promulgated the Constitution of 1917 which, on the political side, retains the guarantees or rights of man contained in the Constitution of 1857. But as for the Executive, the new charter augments its powers to the point of turning the President into a legal dictator."

"Possibly Carranza had a special interest in that article. . . ."

"And he knew how to make very good use of those prerogatives. His government was constantly bombarded with diplomatic protests, occasioned not only by hasty, irresponsible laws, by confiscations, but also by the outrages committed in rural districts and cities by officials whose impunity Carranza guaranteed. As for Customs, Carranza revived Santannist methods, issuing licences for the free importation of many articles. Those licences, with the signature of the Chief of State, were sold and resold."

Oh, Brazil!—I exclaim mentally—Oh, distant land of mine, your sons were not the inventors of the system of selling import licences!

"Carranza never would confess the number and value of the issues of paper money he ordered. His refusal to recognize the paper money he himself issued and his plundering of the coffers of the banks of emission caused total devaluation of all forms of paper money and the bankruptcy of a whole generation, the loss of a whole people's savings. And, naturally, the poor classes were the worst hurt."

He pauses, and then resumes: "The state of insurrection became chronic in Mexico. A famous bandit, Chávez García, made a public march for months through the centre of the country, conquering towns and cities, sacking homes, violating captured women. Carranza ordered Emiliano Zapata killed by ambush and promoted the officer who committed that treachery to the rank of general."

We step out on the apartment balcony and stand there looking at the night and the city. A neon-gas advertisement, blinking on and off, casts alternate blue and red reflections on my friend's face.

"It was natural that after all those excesses, scandalous robberies and acts of banditry, Carranza should think about an obedient successor who would stand guarantee of his impunity. But the opposition launched the candidacy of Álvaro Obregón, who made a campaign tour throughout the nation. The best men of the Revolution joined the Obregón party."

José Vasconcelos smiles. Red now, his face looks like an amiable demon's.

"Thank God, dictators always commit a fatal error. Don Venustiano Carranza, fearful that the controversy of his government would go on and wishing to destroy the enemy at birth, ordered Obregón arrested. One of Carranza's Cabinet Secretaries, General Calles, abandoned his leader to go stir up the auxiliary forces in Sonora. Other military commanders rebelled and Carranza was obliged to flee from the capital."

Now blue, the professor's face has an almost angelic expression.

"As he was making his way into the Puebla mountains in his flight, Carranza was assassinated by an escort pretending adherence to him. Next day a document was signed declaring that Don Venustiano had committed suicide."

Arms resting on the railing, Don José looks down at the street, where automobiles and human forms are moving.

"Be that as it may, Carranza fell by an ancient law. 'Who lives by the sword shall die by the sword.' And the country felt relieved, since at least one of its tyrants had paid with his life for a whole chain of iniquities."

I cast a glance at the immense metropolis. The idea that all those dramas have taken place here actually causes a kind of shudder in me.

With the election of General Álvaro Obregón and his assumption of office, at least a simulacrum of peace returned to the Mexican nation. Ten years after the deposition of Porfirio Díaz the country seemed to have a constituted and generally accepted authority.

In my next encounter with José Vasconcelos I ask him what sort of man Álvaro Obregón was. We are strolling along a street in the old part of the city, and Professor Vasconcelos is walking slowly at my side.

"He was tall, fair, with grey eyes, of robust appearance, with an intelligent head, the typical *criollo* of Spanish ancestry."

I remember the wax figure of Obregón I found in the Casa del Alfeñique in Puebla.

"He possessed an extraordinary natural talent, though he had never left his native village and his higher culture was nil. Devoted to rural affairs and to local politics, Obregón had the education and preparation of the provincial middle class that reads the newspapers from the capital and a half-dozen books, principally of history."

"Can we consider him an idealist?" I prompt him.

"The revolutionary ideas which in some other generals produced a mental chaos left Obregón serene. He was a practitioner of moderate methods and his most profound aspiration was to imitate the opportunistic systems of Porfirio Díaz. That is why he never applied the barbarous laws of the Constitution against the clergy. Neither did he set about reckless experiments in agrarian matters."

"And yet," I interrupt, "I have read that Obregón encouraged the formation of labour unions, gave government posts to his leaders, financed the labour conventions, actually gave them free passes on the trains . . ."

"Yes, he did all that. But he did not court the labour element as Plutarco Elías Calles was to do later. Obregón was a born soldier, without doubt the best in Mexico after Hernán Cortés. And like all real captains he was a strict soldier on campaign, but one who liked civilian forms in ordinary life."

"But isn't it true that he also committed acts of cruelty?"

Professor Vasconcelos is pensive for an instant and then says:

"Yes, in reprisals he showed cruelties that dishonoured his victory. But his personal dealings were affable and gained him friends. In the first three years of his government, national progress was evident in all activities. The Obregón peace was not the fruit of terror but of tranquility of spirit, of mind, which was not true of Carranzism."

Suddenly I recall that the José Vasconcelos I have here with me was Secretary of Education in the Obregón government. And a great Secretary! Under the influence of Tolstoy he revealed himself an apostle of peace and equality. To those who came to him with the old song about the inferiority of the Indian, the then young professor would reply: "They all have souls, all human beings are equal. After all, that is the doctrine of Christ and I am a Christian!" At first Obregón appointed him Director of the National University. Don José declared that he was not seeking to assume direction of a "monument in ruins" for the purpose of cultivating foreign models. He regarded himself as a delegate of the Revolution, he was going to organize an intensive and rapid educational system that would include all Mexicans. What would it profit to teach French in the University when there were abandoned babies all over the country? He thought the first responsibility of the government was to protect and educate children. It was in that spirit that he sought out Obregón and convinced him of the need to create a Secretariat of Education.

Vasconcelos's plan at the head of the new Ministry had a magnificent breadth. It was not enough to teach the public to read. It was necessary to carry music and art to the masses. A popular choir was organized. Free night schools were established. A most vigorous campaign was launched against illiteracy, teachers were gathered—whoever they might be, it was sufficient that they could read—who taught not only in schools but in their homes; and if they had other obligations, they received their pupils on Sundays, holidays and saints' days. The campaign, received with enormous enthusiasm, brought together hundreds of volunteer teachers and awakened the greatest interest throughout the country.

Vasconcelos's plan, however, was not limited to the primary course. He thought the Ministry of Education he had created ought to have a fine arts section, not to supervise or to judge artists, for in his opinion (which is mine, too) "the State cannot judge the work of the artist, no one can but the artist himself," but to encourage them. So it was that José Vasconcelos handed over the walls of important public buildings to artists like José Clemente Orozco, Diego Rivera and David Alfaro Siqueiros for them to paint murals on them.

Vasconcelos never attempted to deprive education of its secular character. What he did was to make it, besides secular, free and compulsory up to the age of fourteen. And when the official Press was incorported into his Department of Education, he ordered classics published with the aim of disseminating them through the whole country. The great Secretary probably nourished the hope of some day seeing the Indians with books of Homer, Goethe, Plato or Cervantes in their rough, dirt-encrusted hands.

I remind José Vasconcelos of all these things. He smiles, saying merely:

"Our nationalist programme of public education, completely free from religious hatreds, came to cost us fifty millions of pesos a year. When Obregón's term expired, the budget for education was reduced to twenty-seven millions under the Calles government."

"Let's get back to our *caudillos*," I say. "At some point in his career Obregón must have committed a blunder. What was it?"

We sit down on a bench in the Alameda a few steps from the monument to Benito Juárez.

"What ruined Obregón was ambition. He had waited out Carranza's term to become President, and the four years of his own term seemed short to him. The Constitution strictly prohibits re-election. So Don Álvaro's course was to govern through a figure-head. For that purpose he chose the most unpopular, the most discredited of his friends, the one with the worst antecedents, Plutarco Elías Calles."

I remember that for the election the armed forces were divided between two candidates: Adolfo de la Huerta and Calles. The former succeeded in stirring a good part of the army to revolt and Obregón was able to suppress the rebellion only thanks to the support of the Zapatistas (whom he had courted during his government) and of the labour unions. Of great help to him also was the indirect aid lent him by the United States. The elections were held and Calles elected.

José Vasconcelos traces on the pavement, with the tip of his stick, some invisible designs.

"One of the boasts of the Obregón administration was that it had been able to maintain itself for more than three years without the express recognition of the United States. But as soon as Don Álvaro divorced himself from the people through his whim of imposing Calles on them, the need for Yankee recognition became imperative."

Don José glances toward the statue of the Indian who admired Lincoln, and then continues:

"It was on that point that Washington took revenge. It imposed conditions to the recognition of Obregón's government. For example, the derogation of the agrarian laws insofar as they touched American interests, and recognition of the non-retroactivity of the laws on petroleum insofar as they affected foreign companies. They got all this. And more: it was stipulated that in case of expropriation of lands of North Americans the payment to the expropriated owner would be in cash and not in bonds of the agrarian debt. This meant that the lands of the Yankees in Mexico would never be expropriated, because we should never have the money to pay for the expropriation. So it was Obregón who took the first step for the total transference of the natural wealth of Mexico to the profit of the North Americans."

"But did the Senate approve the agreement?"

Don José utters a short, dry laugh.

"About that time Obregónism was contending with the military campaign against Adolfo de la Huerta's rebels; Obregón, from Ocotlán, intimidated the Senate. One day several senators were kidnapped right in the capital of the Republic. One morning Senator Field Jurado, who had taken a stand against the treaties, was attacked in front of his home and murdered with impunity by government agents. Obregón won a victory on the battlefield and the Senate did not debate the treaty with the United States."

"And the Council of Ministers?"

"It was not consulted. Nor was the Press informed. The agreement was approved in the shadow, under the terror of martial law."

After a pause, Don José goes on: "And on the first of December, 1924, General Plutarco Elías Calles began his regime of murders and lies."

I recall a passage from Frank Tannenbaum's book, *Mexico: the Struggle for Peace and Bread,* in which the American sociologist states that the survival of Mexico as a country in those four agitated years of the Calles administration was a miracle and a proof of her inner vitality. "In spite of his many faults, his arbitrary temper," writes Tannenbaum, "and his complete ruthlessness toward political opponents, Calles crystallized the ideas of Mexican nationalism and saved the Mexican social revolution from internal disintegration and external pressure." He goes on to say that Calles supported the Mexican Regional Labour Confederation, gave an impulse to the distribution of lands, disciplined the army with iron hand, launched an irrigation programme, built roads, stimulated the system of rural schools, and founded the National Bank of Mexico. I remind José Vasconcelos of all these things, and he only says:

"Tannenbaum is, of course, an apologist for Calles. He was rewarded with the Order of the Aztec Eagle, a decoration created by the Yankee-Mexican President Abelardo Rodríguez."

The Indian Juárez remains motionless, seated in his stone chair on top of the monument. In front of him, in the street, shining automobiles pass. And on the sidewalks Indians, mestizos, *criollos* and foreigners pass each other and repass.

"In an atmosphere of terror," Professor Vasconcelos proceeds, "the term of the administration passed. But the whole country felt relief on learning that Calles was no better than a prisoner."

"What do you mean?"

"The whole Cabinet had been appointed by Obregón. To Calles was left only a shadow of power. But such situations are very dangerous even for him who plans to derive benefit from them. At first Calles conformed to his status as puppet. But shrewdly he made the most of Obregón's weakness for money and let him make great business deals: vast areas of land in Sonora and a whole railway passed into Don Álvaro's hands. There were other shady transactions, too. Generally speaking, a contest of crime and lowering of prestige was held among the men who ran the country, which was really the loser in the end, in ruin and blood, in that antipatriotic struggle."

"Is it true that Calles stamped out public liberty?"

"Without the slightest doubt. A daily paper of the opposition was attacked by government henchmen disguised as workmen. One of the editors was shot to death and part of the machinery destroyed. The police, as usual, arrived late. In several parts of the country political assassination continued. So usual became the practice of shootings carried out by the authorities, imitating the President, that on one occasion a lieutenant, commanding a garrison detachment in an Oaxacan village, hauled all the town councilmen out of their homes and shot them in the local cemetery."

"And the persecution of the Church?"

"That began on a ridiculous pretext. Hoodlums of a government organization attacked the church of Soledad, profaned altars, chased away some devout women. Immediately, on the pretext that 'public order had been disturbed,' the church was closed. A week later it was turned over to a renegade priest who said he had a plan to create a Catholic, but Mexican, Church independent of Rome, something like the Anglican Church of Henry VIII. This reprobate priest, however, was left with an empty church. But attempts on ecclesiastic property followed, and the expulsion of more than two hundred Spanish priests was effected. The private schools in which the Catholic religion was taught were closed; the number of priests was so limited that whole regions were left without parish priests. The outrages were so considerable and so irritated the people that a general uprising in the centre of the country was not slow in appearing. To the cry of 'Viva Cristo Rey!' ill-armed *campesinos* declared against the dictatorship of Calles, which, solidly established and well-armed, massacred the rebels. This rebellion was at the same time a pretext for government attacks to take the most savage forms throughout the country. Women of the best social class were publicly whipped by generals of the Calles faction. Others were turned over to the soldiery to be violated. Among the captured men there were coldly calculated tortures and mutilations worthy of Africa. Never has more blood flowed in all the country, and never has opprobrium reached such a point!"

"Excuse me if I insist on the agrarian restorations. But what did Calles do along that line?"

"To his own profit and to content his greedy friends, Calles initiated a series of occupations of lands and expropriations which caused real panic. The despoiled proprietor who would not meekly yield was accused of being a *cristero*—rebel against Calles—and was shot. In the provinces the *caciques* imitated the conduct of their leaders in the capital. And every man who owned anything had to sell it to preserve his life. All, that is, but the foreigners."

José Vasconcelos refers to the machinations of the American ambassador to Mexico at the time, Dwight Morrow, who declared Calles one of the great statesmen of his day.

"It is just that all Washington's demands had been satisfied by Calles. The man who held the power, in the last analysis, was Don Dwight, ex-partner of Morgan, diplomat, lawyer, millionaire and banker."

As the 1928 elections drew near, again the country was disturbed by armed movements. As Álvaro Obregón set himself up again as candidate for the Presidency, part of the army presented a candidate: General Arnulfo Gómez. Calles himself urged him to be a candidate.

"That Gómez," Professor Vasconcelos explains, "was an accomplice of Calles in the killings. On the other side, an Obregónist group offered the candidacy of Francisco Serrano, ex-Minister of War, a degenerate type, morbidly depraved, intelligent when he was in his right mind, with a clownish talent, for he had been a circus artist. When he was drunk, however, he was extremely dangerous. For sheer pleasure he would kill chauffeurs, public women, friends and enemies. And as these two candidates had strong support by the army, talk of uprisings started. That was exactly what Obregón wanted, for he was also thinking about standing as candidate."

False friends took Francisco Serrano to Cuernavaca and killed him. On the other side, the division commander Escobar murdered Arnulfo Gómez.

"Obregón was confident of the Catholic vote," continues Vasconcelos. "He declared that, although respecting the Constitution, he had known how to keep all parties satisfied during his term of office. That statement ruined him. From the time of its publication all forces supporting Calles because of his anti-Catholic mania took the field against Obregón."

Vasconcelos falls silent, as though weary of remembering so much misery, so much violence. Then, in a calmer voice, he says: "Obregón was killed in July of 1928, in a restaurant where he was dining with some friends."

Here end my colloquies with José Vasconcelos, whom I have not seen again. But obviously the History of Mexico does not end here.[1]

The five or six years which fell between the murder of Obregón and the assumption of power by Lázaro Cárdenas were a dubious period in the history of Mexico. During that time three men occupied the Presidency. Calles appointed them to the post and Calles

[1] Although not taken down in shorthand, all these colloquies reproduce with absolute fidelity the words of Jose Vasconcelos, who has permitted the author of this book to use the passages from his *Breve historia de México* that refer to persons, ideas and facts discussed in the dialogues. (Author's note.)

protected them. First came Emilio Portes Gil, whom the National Congress selected as Provisional President from 1928 to 1930. In the words of Vasconcelos, Portes Gil was "graduated in law by an illegitimate school, an ex-deputy, ex-agent of Victoriano Huerta, converted to the Revolution via Calles, and, naturally, a radical, socialist, Callista extremist." This was followed by an armed revolt of a great part of the army, put down by Calles with the aid of the agrarianists and the unions. The Presidency was taken over, with the blessing of the United States, by the diplomat Pascual Ortiz Rubio. His opponent in the election, as candidate of the independents, was our José Vasconcelos, who accepted the candidacy not because he had any hope of free elections but "to set an example and to prepare the ground for a national rebellion that would expel all the Calles bastardy from government." The electoral farce was consummated. Vasconcelos's electors were intimidated by the agents and forces of the government. Violence and fraud ruled, and the official candidate, as always, won.

Popular indignation, nevertheless, was tremendous. On the occasion of the assumption of office by Ortiz a patriot shot him in the face, leaving him an invalid for a long time, while Calles dealt the cards in the government. In 1933 Pascual Ortiz Rubio was obliged to resign. General Abelardo L. Rodríguez took over the government, serving until the election of Lázaro Cárdenas.


Here is a President for whom I have always had a pronounced sympathy. Great things happened in Mexico during his term of office. I have the impression that he gave special attention to the "common man," to the *peón,* to the Indian, to the small rural proprietors. He used to hold public audiences and listen to the complaints, claims and requests of the people. It was a parade in which the pathetic and the comic alternated. Ladies came to complain of their husbands' infidelity, *peones* accused neighbours of having stolen a hen or a head of cattle. They attribute to Cárdenas the admirable statement: "They need so many things! Patience, at least, I can give them." And, rare fact in Mexican politics, Don Lázaro was a man with great respect for the lives of his fellow men. When someone was surprised that he travelled through the country without a bodyguard, he said: "It is better to die trying to do good than to keep oneself alive by practising evil."

He was a silent man (and on this as on some other points he invites comparison with Brazil's Getulio Vargas), and nothing seemed to him too small to merit his attention. Not only great projects attracted him. He thought it important to open a little school here, a public hospital there, and so on.

Don Lázaro was not merely a kindly man. He was also—an extremely rare thing—a man of courage and energy. His first act on taking office was to confront Calles and the Callistas. Several gambling houses which had enjoyed federal concessions were operating in the country. Cárdenas had them closed. He gave special attention to the agrarian problem, accelerating the distribution of lands among the villages. He turned his eyes, too, to the proletariat. He supported labour unions and demanded that industry treat its employees like human beings. And finally—courageous decision!—he confiscated the foreign petroleum fields in order that "they might not influence the outcome of the forthcoming presidential election."

The expropriation of the oil fields occurred in 1938 when the foreign companies exploiting them refused to obey a decision of the Mexican Supreme Court. Their attitude was tantamount to rebellion. The situation was aggravated by a public declaration of the aforementioned oil companies, which was an insult to the nation: they would not take responsibility for what might happen in the country. Lázaro Cárdenas showed himself a man equal to the situation, taking the only decision appropriate at that juncture. In my opinion it was an act of the most legitimate common sense. The question was not merely social and economic, it was also a moral one. There was the opportunity to say "That's enough!" to the intervention of foreign companies in Mexican public affairs.

The people of Mexico enthusiastically supported their President. The matter seemed to make national unity stronger than ever. It was touching to see barefoot Indians bringing nickels, pennies, even pigs, chickens and other products of their poor lands "to help pay the expropriations." The Catholic Church itself allowed collections to be taken up for the purpose in front of its temples. (Cárdenas had used his personal prestige to end the persecutions of Catholicism.)

Throughout the country there was an atmosphere of optimism and hope that seemed to announce better days. Cárdenas nationalized the railways, turning them over to their employees to run. He created a National Bank of Credit to stimulate the *ejido* programme. He gave new impetus to the irrigation project. And, like a Great

Father, he continued the public audiences in which he received and heard practically everybody, however silly or ingenuous the complaint, the request or the cause.

But no one can work miracles. One man, however good he may be, cannot change by decree or personal example a situation resulting from more than a hundred years of errors and vices. Cárdenas surrounded himself with capable, respectable collaborators. But the nation's bureaucracy remained corrupt. And as the new President had put an end to the practice of liquidating enemies, they continued to enjoy excellent health and naturally were left with their appetite for money and blood whetted. Moreover, the railway employees to whom he had turned over the railroads and the oil workers to whom he had entrusted the administration of the oil wells did not reveal in their new tasks the competence and integrity that were to be expected and desired.

Problems of another nature arose. The Civil War in Spain brought on the birth of a Falangist movement of clearly Fascist character in Mexico, at the same time that Nazi groups were being formed in the country—an eminently strategic point—and by means of intrigue, bribery and propaganda they sought to win positions and influence in the government. A man of democratic spirit, Lázaro Cárdenas placed himself from the start of the Spanish Civil War on the side of the Republican Government, to which he lent aid; and when the struggle was over, he opened the doors of Mexico to the exiled Republicans.

His attitude toward the oil companies had not been a gesture of irrational patriotism or a primary expression of anti-Americanism. When the Second World War broke out, Don Lázaro informed the United States that, in case of war between that country and Japan, all the human and material resources of Mexico would be at the disposal of the neighbouring nation.

In 1938 General Cedillo, a *caudillo* of San Luis Potosí, rebelled against the central government. It was the only armed uprising to take place during Lázaro Cárdenas's government. And the presidential elections of 1940—thanks to this President who wanted to teach his people that it could be governed without cruelty—were held without any revolt or uprising, although there were sporadic acts of violence.

General Manual Ávila Camacho succeeded Lázaro Cárdenas and governed from 1940 to 1946. The next elections were much less marred by violence than all the foregoing ones, and brought to power a civilian, the first since Francisco Madero—Miguel Alemán, who governed until 1951. My hopes for the political regeneration of Mexico rest on the fact, among other symptoms, that all the Presidents who came after Obregón have managed to leave office alive. It is the fate I wish for Ruiz Cortines, who is occupying the Presidency at the moment I write these lines.

# 9. Once Again, The Capital

We are back in Mexico City, in the same hotel, and Tito comes to take us for a visit to the Convento de San Angel and to the Baron von Wuthenau.

We get into a taxi which speeds out the Paseo de la Reforma, dizzily circling the *glorietas,* toward the old quarter of San Angel.

While I, hypnotized, stare at the hairy neck of the driver, Tito traces a brief biography of the baron:

"He belongs to an old family of Saxony. He was in the diplomatic service of the Third Reich, but he abandoned his career when Hitler came to power. He settled in Mexico, where today he is considered one of the greatest authorities on colonial art. He lost his wife, whom he loved and admired very much, and by whom he had many children. He married, not long ago, his wife's niece. It is the most bohemian family I know. The children, I don't know how many boys and girls, are growing up in freedom like lovely plants. The father spends part of his time here, in his residence in San Angel, and when he is not off visiting churches and ruins, he is to be seen in the city of Taxco, where his second wife keeps a *pension* in the house where Baron von Humboldt lived in the nineteenth century."

It is not necessary to say more. I am already interested in that family, whose members I am beginning to visualize. The baron must be tall, corpulent, blond, with round face, pink, full cheeks.

He has a trombone voice that contrasts with the gentleness of his blue eyes. I can see around him a collection of golden heads, a forest of thin, restless legs.

We arrive. We dismount in front of the church of San Angel. We enter the walled atrium, in the centre of which stands an old well; we walk across the grey paving-stones; we enter the dark, cool temple, where Tito whispers in my ear: "You are now going to see the most unexpected, the strangest 'ensemble' in the world."

He takes me by the arm and leads me forward. Yoly and my companion follow us. We enter the convent of San Angel, which is now a museum; we walk along its stone corridors; we visit its cells, where we see hair shirts and other instruments of penance; we look at the paintings on the walls; we descend into the underground portion where we find, in their little coffins, mummies of nuns who once lived here.

"Where's the baron?" I ask.

"Be patient. We have already seen part of the convent. What do you think we are going to see now in the other half of this building?"

"A factory?"

"Wrong."

He calls me over to the window of one of the cells that is boarded over, and has me look through the cracks between the planks.

I see a patio with arcades, peopled by human figures. Nuns? Friars? No. It is like a strange congress of marginal creatures. *Pelados* —penniless men—Indians, mestizos, one or two whites: all men, all dirty, all barefoot, all ragged, all unshorn.

"What's all that?" I inquire.

"A municipal jail."

"Here, beside the convent?"

"In the same building."

"And what kind of prisoners do they send here?"

"Vagrants, thieves, drunks. . . ."

He goes on to tell me that those poor creatures have the habit of thrusting their hands through the crack under the great iron door, and there they stay for hours at a time, palms extended, hoping that some charitable passer-by will place on them a cigarette, a cigarette stub or —*quién sabe?*—a coin.

"But that's not all. This same convent where nuns used to live in the odour of sanctity, has other surprises in store for us. Come on."

We go down to the atrium, gain the sidewalk, go forward a few steps, and stop in front of the great central doorway that opens on a vast patio.

"Here we have a series of apartments occupied in general by artists, poets, writers, painters. But the best part is in the other wing."

We head for that wing.

"But where the devil does that baron live?" I insist.

Tito smiles.

"We have to walk carefully, and I'm going to explain why. The baron bought one wing of the convent, but a crazy American woman who occupies the apartment next door is suing von Wuthenau, for she thinks that she, only she, has a right to all this part of the historic building."

"You spoke of walking carefully. What has that to do with the matter?"

"The American woman has the custom of sicking her Great Danes on the people who come to visit the baron."

"Oh! Oh! Oh!"

The women halt and refuse to go farther. Tito calms them down. He may perhaps have exaggerated a bit. Maybe all that story is nothing but fabrication.

We climb some steps and enter a corridor.

"Better not make any noise. Silence, then. That's the barmy *gringa's* apartment." And he points to an old door.

We walk on tiptoe, mute. We stop beside the entrance to the residence of the Baron Alexander von Wuthenau.

Tito whispers: "Do you know whom that American is living with? A drunken German she took out of the neighbouring jail."

I am enchanted with the convent of San Angel. To see all this it is worth risking being torn to bits by the deranged American woman's Danes.

Tito raps softly at the door. Some seconds pass, it opens, and its rectangle frames a figure that seems to have stepped out of a Grimm tale. It is a girl of about thirteen, lean as a greyhound, very fair, with grey eyes, straw-coloured hair in long braids. She is dressed in white and holds in one hand a freshly bitten apple. As the light is coming from behind her, her head is aureoled in gold.

"*Buenas tardes.*"

Her voice is water and wind. Her name must be Gretchen. Her father? A miller. Mother? Spinner. When she is not at school, the little girl looks after a flock of ducks. There she goes, wand in hand, barefoot through the field, prodding on white ducks of yellow beaks and feet waddling toward the lake. The wind, cloud-herder, urges on great flocks of cotton in the sky.

How is it that so many images can pass through our minds in a mere fraction of a second?

The girl has us come in. The baron comes to greet us with two more blonde and skinny infants hard on his heels.


He is not as I imagined him. Of medium stature, he only seems tall because he is thin. He has an angular face, hair of light chestnut, blue eyes. He is clad in a modest grey suit, with a rustic plush shirt. He looks more like one of those German electricians of my childhood than a noble of Saxony.

He receives us with an agreeable, natural cordiality. The introductions over, he makes us welcome and we move about the little apartment, which is stuffed with images of saints, crucifixes, ex-votos, pictures by primitives, candelabra and old parchments. The bedroom is also a study for work. Alexander von Wuthenau tells us that at the moment he is building a residence in colonial style for a very rich Mexican. With those heads, arms and legs of statues tossed into the corners, this looks like Frankenstein's workroom.

The room charms me. With the presumption natural to a novelist, I go over to look more closely at the portrait on the little bedside table at the head of the great iron bed. I see a woman with girlish features, the intense eyes of the tuberculous, facing the photographer with a sad smile. I recognize death in the pallid face, in the feverish glance. She must be the baron's first wife. Possibly this is the bed in which she died.

I approach an oil painting in which a mediæval tower can be seen. The baron explains to me: "That fortified tower was constructed in the year 935 by my ancestors to defend themselves against the Slavic invasions. Today that part of Germany is in the hands of the Russians."

Von Wuthenau has a sharp voice. His Spanish is fluent but with a heavy accent betrayed principally in his throat-rasping R's.

He takes my arm and leads me to a covered area, with arcades, and points toward the street. I see a mound of ruins.

"Do you know what used to be there? A building of the colonial era, lovely. They tore it down, probably to build in place of it one of those horrible pseudo-modern apartment houses."

He is a man of nervous gestures who talks with a passion that his voice, not at all theatrical and somewhat cold, does not succeed in conveying.

"Half-culture is killing this country!" he exclaims, flinging his arms up in the air.

My companion and Yoly pass the time looking at pictures, trinkets, tapestries and rush mats. Von Wuthenau's children are playing in the area-way and, like acrobats, are perilously walking along the edge of the parapet, with arms outspread, giving me cold shivers. A fall there would be fatal. But the baron apparently pays no attention to it.

"On account of barbarities like that," he continues, "I resolved to write a memorial in verse to the President of the Republic, protesting against demolitions like that. Because to misprize national artistic treasures is the same as to violate one's own mother!"

"Have you published the memorial?" I ask.

"Of course."

"And what was the result?"

"They put me in jail for thirty days!"

We all burst out laughing. The baron shoves back the lock of hair that has fallen over his eyes and points to a stone saint on a table.

"Yonder is a beautiful image carved by an Indian. It has nobility, beauty, meaning. But what do those society women want, those rich gentlemen. They want prettily made images, saints that look as though they had come out of a hair-dressing salon! They want nasty things made of mud. Mud? Phew! Mud is noble material. Of *mierda!*"

And he begins jumping up and down, agitated, repeating frenziedly—"*Mierda! mierda! mierda!*"

The long-legged acrobats continue their dizzy evolutions. Now they are leaping from the parapet of the arcades to the old aqueduct that runs parallel to them. The women are apprehensive, wide-eyed. The baron, however, remains indifferent.

"Do you know who lives in the cellar of my house?" he asks. "Two indigent nuns and a family of Indians. A total of fourteen persons."

I think of the church, the convent, the jail, the mad *gringa*, the indigent nuns, the family of Indians, the baron and his blond offspring—I attempt to add all that up; I feel dizzy and reach no result. I line up the fractions again and finally find the sum: Mexico!

The duck girl is now driving her siblings to the lower storey where the dining-room is. It is time for lunch and there goes the lass with her blond ducks. The baron follows them with his blue, vague eyes and murmurs:

"I have three more girls who are in Taxco with my second wife."

If we ask ten Brazilians what is the first word that comes to mind when they read the name "Mexico," it is possible that eight will say, "Revolution." And yet I have always associated with the name of this country the word "mural," which immediately projects in my mind the figures of Orozco, Rivera and Siqueiros.

I do not believe there is any other country in the world that can boast of possessing a group of muralists of that stature. All that is plastic, telluric, tragic, grotesque, horrendous, absurd and startlingly beautiful about Mexico is, one way or another, contained in the hundreds of murals not only of those three painters but of many others, in frescoes which decorate the walls of hundreds of public buildings of the country.

Orozco died in 1940. Rivera—I saw and listened to him last week in a lecture on modern architecture. But I have talked at length with Siqueiros, with whom I have become good friends.

Mural painting in Mexico already existed before the Christian Era, and examples of it are known in the frescoes of Bonampak, Chichén-Itzá and Tulún, and in the murals of Teotihuacán. After the coming of the Spaniards countless frescoes were painted on the walls of convents, churches and private homes, now under a European and Catholic influence. (On passing by the Convent of San Agustín de Acolmán several days ago, I saw on its crumbled walls vestiges of one of the most ancient murals of pre-Cortésian Mexico.) During the Porfirio era Mexican paintings declined to the point of becoming merely a pale and unimportant reflection of European academic painting. At the beginning of this century Dr. Atl returned from Europe with his eyes and heart full of the works of the Renaissance artists, principally the decorations of the Sistine Chapel and the frescoes of Benozzo, Gozzoli and Tintoretto. His enthusiasm infected the young Mexican painters who, with José Clemente

Orozco at their head, founded the Artistic Centre, whose principal aim was to obtain walls to paint. "Walls! We Want Walls!" With their Mexican tenacity and their youthful ardour they are on the verge of gaining their objective when the Revolution breaks out and all the hopes of the young artists are swept away.

Dr. Atl, however, with his paintings, was far from heralding plastic artists of the power of today's muralists. He was still painting fat pink angels, garlanded nymphs and parodies of the figures of Michelangelo.

That was when, without fanfare, a singular artist, of folkloric nature, so to speak, emerged from the people. He was Guadalupe Posada, an engraver, a political caricaturist, castigator of customs, who—a novelty in Mexico—gave to his work a purpose of social criticism. His *Calaveras* ("Skulls") became famous. He was one of the greatest critics of the Porfirian regime. He portrayed with cruel realism the social panorama in which aristocrats who dreamed of Spain and thought in French were supporting a despotic dictatorship, watched with indifference the passing of the country's mineral deposits into the hands of foreigners, while the *campesinos* were despoiled of their lands and the workers were treated like "things" in the factories. In a certain way—not for the form but for the content of protest in his works—Posada was a precursor of the Mexican mural painters of our time.

If the idea of the young men of the Artistic Centre was the seed of that muralist movement, the spirit of the Revolution of 1910 was the land, the sun and the water that the seed needs in order to germinate. David Alfaro Siqueiros attributes great importance also to the student strike of 1911, as a precursor of the movement for the renovation of Mexican painting. That student strike in the Academy of Fine Arts was an act of rebellion against the pedagogical methods then in vogue, products of the Porfirian mind. "The Army of the Revolution," Siqueiros still says, "gave us the geography and the archæology, the whole tradition and the man of our country, in his most direct, complex and dramatic social problems. Without that participation, it would not have been possible to conceive and animate, later, in all its integrity, the Mexican pictorial movement."

When Obregón rose to power, bringing a period of reasonable peace to the country, the old dream of the youths of the Centro Artístico—now mature men—became a reality. José Vasconcelos at last was giving them the walls they were asking for.

That was the moment in which many plastic artists of Mexico

exchanged the easel for the wall and began to work on the Escuela Preparatoria. At first they are still confused, they do not know exactly what they want. A few years before, Siqueiros had published a *Manifesto to the Plastic Artists of America,* clamouring for "a monumental, heroic art, a human art, a public art, with the direct and living example of our great and extraordinary pre-Hispanic cultures of America." But what Rivera produces on the walls of the Preparatory School is still far from that revolutionary ideal.

In his "Creation," in the Bolívar Amphitheatre of the aforementioned school, we see in gigantic proportions the Christian symbols, Faith, Hope and Charity, mingled with the pagan figures which represent Justice, Strength, Wisdom, Prudence, the Dance. Rivera himself, referring today to that work, classifies it as "a definite Italo-Byzantine creation."

And meanwhile, what was Orozco doing? He was first paying his tribute—the last!—to the Renaissance, painting in Botticelli fashion a "Motherhood" in which not even the classic nymph with a bunch of grapes is lacking. But later, as if an inspiration had struck him with the force of a lightning bolt, nourished by his deep Mexican roots, he produces three admirable paintings: "The Trench," "The Farewell" and "The Trinity." With these works Mexican muralism took on body, meaning, course.

Siqueiros, who during his stay in Spain had come into contact with radical ideas, in 1923 and with some colleagues founds the *Sindicato de Pintores, Escultores y Grabadores Revolucionarios de Mexico,* or the Union of Revolutionary Painters, Sculptors and Engravers of Mexico, and publishes a manifesto addressed to "soldiers, workers, farmers and intellectuals not in the service of the bourgeoisie." The Mexican artists are no longer struggling just for the ideals of the Revolution of 1910—a bourgeois democracy, a Mexican capitalism, the agrarian reform—they are now agitating, arguing, writing and, above all, painting in the light of the ideals of a proletarian revolution. Many of them—like Orozco, Rivera and Siqueiros—go so far as to join the Communist Party. I have the impression that Orozco soon was disillusioned with Marxism and really never came to accept the socialization of art. Rivera, undisciplined, wavered between Trotskyism and Stalinism, broke several times with Moscow only to return willingly afterwards. Of that trinity, I think Siqueiros had been the most constant and the most actively revolutionary.

José Clemente Orozco was perhaps the most pessimistic of the three. Diego Rivera permits himself some humorous and satiric tones in his murals. David Alfaro Siqueiros is a man of optimism and strength that know no flagging; his, as the Mexican poet Carlos Pellicer has said, is "the fist that splits the horizon in twain."

Graham Greene, who has written about this country a book of undisguisable prejudice and incomprehension (although highly readable and interesting), speaks thus of the great muralist: "Orozco —however valueless we may consider his ideology—knows himself and knows his world." Aldous Huxley, another Englishman who seems not to have liked Mexico, saw Orozco's murals in the Preparatory School and wrote: "These have a queer merit, even when they are most horrible—and some of them are about as horrible as anything could well be. Their unsuitability as decorations in a school for adolescent boys and girls is almost absolute. But they are real pictures, by a man who knows how to paint. The formal inventions are often extraordinarily felicitous; the colour subtle; the modelling, for all the ferocious brutality of the subject, very sensitive and alive. They are pictures that remain rather disquietingly in the memory."

Can it be possible—I have asked myself many times—to like Orozco's paintings without liking Mexico, the Mexican people, the Mexican drama that his pictures represent? Perhaps it is, because the Indians in the murals do not smell bad, and because the blood of the dead from gunshot is dried colour and—of course!— because in those frescoes all the violence, all the tragedy and all the harshness of Mexico are transfigured into art.

If Rivera makes us smile with his satires or think with his epigrams; if Siqueiros sweeps us off our feet with his paintings that seem to start off the walls, aggressive, three-dimensional—Orozco produces in us a shudder of horror with his flayed men, his tremendous hand-to-hand melées in which the dead are heaped upon one another, their faces contorted, their necks, their breasts pierced by bayonets and already visibly putrefying. Gravediggers, skulls, mummies, inhumanly maltreated *peones,* battlefields where after the fray skeletal women wander in search of the corpses of their husbands—these are some of the tragic motifs of his pictures. Here I am, in the Escuela Preparatoria, in front of his picture "The Farewell." Sitting on the ground, an old woman dressed in white, her eyes vacant, is lifting her hand, which a bareheaded man is kissing reverently. No legend is needed. It is the son who is off to war. Is not that the destiny of men—to fight for the possession of the land? And what else can the woman do but wait, survive, in order to look after the wounded or to bury the dead?

A curious trait of this almost sadistic creator of apocalyptic nightmares is his tenderness for the woman who suffers, keeps silent and waits, that great forgotten one of the art and the literature of our Latin America, our masculine world of mediaeval colouration. I have never seen a gay theme in any mural or canvas from the brush of this great stylizer of cataclysms. He prefers dark and neutral colours, and if he uses red frequently it is because in no other way could he paint the blood that runs from the bodies of his martyrized figures.

Whenever I was asked for a physical description of our poet Ascenso Ferreira I used to say, "He's a big fellow who reminds one of Diego Rivera." It would be silly if, describing Diego Rivera, I should now invoke the image of the Pernambucan poet. Anyway, it is hard to find anyone who has never seen the portrait of this extraordinary Mexican artist who, thanks to his sayings and doings, is nowadays almost a folkloric figure.

Born in Guanajuato in 1886, Rivera went as a very young man to Paris, where, friend of Apollinaire, he was known as "the Mexican of Montparnasse." He was a bosom companion in the experiences of Braque, Picasso and Juan Gris. In art he could have chosen the path he wanted and would have won success in all genres, for he is an admirable draughtsman, I believe as great as Picasso. He could also have made a fortune painting academic portraits of bourgeois, but, on returning to his own land, the indigenous past spoke more strongly in him. He adhered to the revolutionary artistic movement, of which he shortly became a leader.

The body of anecdotes about him is vast, and his matrimonial experiences multiple. If I am not in error in my count, Rivera is now with his sixth or seventh wife. (He will forgive me for having increased or diminished the number of wives.) When someone once asked him about his plans for the future, the painter responded: "I've never thought of devoting myself to the life of a hermit. My grandmother used to tell me that my grandfather had the most glorious death to which a *caballero* can aspire. He, who had been on so many battlefields fighting on three continents, died at seventy-four poisoned by a young woman of twenty who was jealous of his legitimate wife. I haven't the insensate pretentiousness to believe that I am like my grandfather, but I am certain I retain in my constitution a great part of his vitality."

Another time, interviewed by an American reporter, the latter asked him: "Is it true that you once ate human flesh?"

And Diego Rivera, with his oboe voice so unexpected in such a big man, responded softly: "Yes. It tastes sweet."

The rivalry between Rivera and Siqueiros, which explodes into written or oral polemics, is widely known. I suspect that these two men, telluric at heart, respect and possibly admire and even esteem each other. But the truth is that, actors both, even if they do not admit it, they have to carry on the picturesque comedy of rivalry, which has actually become a part of Mexican folklore.

We are in the Department of Public Education, in front of Rivera's mural called "La Maestra Rural." There is the little school-mistress in the middle of a circle formed by Indian pupils, men, women, adults, children. The teacher holds an open book in one hand. In the middle distance a revolutionary on horseback can be seen, with his carbine in his hand, his bandoleer of cartridges slung about his neck; in the background, men working the scorching earth with ploughs.

The murals of this artist nearly always tell a story. The *Corrido de la Revolución Proletaria* presents a series of pictures such as "La Orgía," "En la Trinchera" and "En el Arsenal." In the first appear bourgeois figures, rural lords, aristocrats in frock coat and high hat, drinking champagne with semi-nude prostitutes; on the right, in the foreground, a young man in dinner jacket is crumpled in a state of coma, with a glass and a bottle of champagne overturned at his feet. In the background, behind an arch, three revolutionaries with car-bines and bandoleers are holding conference. In this picture, in the figures representing the bourgeoise, the features are caricatural and the tone frankly sarcastic. But the treatment of the figures of the rebels is serious and dramatic.

In the "Arsenal" we see workmen engaged in the manufacture of arms and munitions for the Revolution that sooner or later is to bowl over the personages in the orgy and all their world represents—and in that arsenal, where one can see the hammer and the sickle, in the midst of machines and cases of cartridges, men, women and chil-dren are fraternizing. Paying more attention to the details of the picture, I see in the background *peones,* mounted warriors, one of them gripping a red banner with the hammer and sickle and this legend: *Tierra y Libertad*—Land and Freedom. Can it be that my eyes deceive me? In the middle distance to the left rises, behind an armed labourer, the head of David Alfaro Siqueiros, with a grey hat on the crown of which stands forth the red star of the Soviets. "La Trinchera" represents the struggle, the barricade, the soldiers of the Revolution, almost all with the workman's denim uniform, operating a machine-gun. And the curious thing is that all these frankly Communistic allegories were painted on the walls of the Department of Education of a country whose government, these past years, has been tending, if not a little toward the right, at least toward the centre. And the man who offered these formerly empty walls to the Marxist painters was a man who today is a fervent Catholic.

Of all the murals I have seen the most *populous,* the ones with the greatest number of personages and the greatest wealth of details, are Diego Rivera's.

Here I stand, half-stunned, before the mural of the title "La Formación de México." At the base of the enormous picture soldiers of Cortés, in their steel armour, are fighting hand-to-hand with Aztec warriors, and in the midst of the tangle of bodies, arms, faces, lances, swords, rise masks of the Tiger and the Jaguar. Above, in the centre, against the Calendar Stone, an Aztec priest grasps a human heart, and over his head an enormous eagle, perched on a nopal cactus, is holding a snake in its beak. Then I lose myself, confused, amid historical faces. There is Hidalgo, and the other heroes of Independence, and Iturbide, the first and last emperor of Mexico, and the contemptible Santa Anna, and Obregón, Calles, and a series of anonymous *peones.* High up at the top, Zapata with his broad *sombrero* and his drooping moustaches, and a frieze with the distich *Tierra y Libertad,* surrounded by figures of workmen that my ignorance does not succeed in identifying. I appreciate the perfection of the drawing of this great fresco, I respect the intention, but on my word I cannot manage to feel any artistic emotion as I contemplate the whole. Perhaps the trees do not permit me to see the forest.

In this same palace there is still another work of Rivera's—"La Represión Reaccionaria"—in which Indians, Communists, agrarians appear hanged, throats cut, tongues hanging out of their empurpled mouths, workmen shot down because they are on strike, and always the bent, humble Indians, working the land for possession of which they fight and suffer.

I go wandering along the galleries of this old palace from the first years of Cortés's time, and finally I begin to regard the murals the way one ought. Diego Rivera, the giant with the boy's voice, between 1929 and 1946 devoted himself to the gigantic task of portraying the epic of his people in a triptych which begins with the solar and human myth of Quetzalcoatl and which represents the struggle of the Mexican against foreign domination under various aspects—the military, the economic, the political—reaching its denouement in the full conquest of freedom. The first pictures of the triptych are, from the decorative point of view, the most interesting, like the one, finished in 1946, which reproduces the Market of Tenochtitlán.

Of all the Mexican muralists, Rivera is perhaps the one who has the vastest work, the one who is most attached to the classic processes of painting murals and the one who draws best. Orozco was indisputably the most tragic, although the least spectacular. I have the impression, nevertheless, that none possesses as does Siqueiros the spirit of mural painting, the plastic sense of the monumental.


What immediately attracts attention in David Alfaro Siqueiros is his imposing head, which seems to have been painted by himself, and which makes this artist give the impression of being taller than he really is. His thick hair is black and curly, with extremely rare white threads. In his olive face, long and fleshy, two features stand out: the vigorous nose with its flaring nostrils and the magnetic eyes with their dark-flecked pupils: beryl and obsidian. Taut, with the look of an athlete and the elastic movements of a young man, at sixty David Alfaro looks at most like a well-preserved fifty-year-old. Capable of every violence and of every chivalric act, he is a mixture of Renaissance artist, *caudillo*, political agitator and prophet.

I lunch one day with him and his wife Angélica, a pale brunette with long eyes, in a genuinely Mexican restaurant. And, eating *quesadillas* with exquisite stuffing, I listen to the romantic story of this muralist.

At fifteen David Alfaro takes part in the student strike of the Academy of Fine Arts. At seventeen he shares in the conspiracy of his colleagues against the government of Victoriano Huerta. A little later he joins the Army of the Revolution, in the same year that the First World War was to break out in Europe.

"How long did the civil war last?" I ask.

"Four years. But four years of armed fighting."

"Siqueiros rose to captain," Angélica informs me.

In 1918 David finds himself in Guadalajara with his companions, taking part in a Congress of Soldier Artists.

"What was the result of that meeting?"

"It meant the beginning of the end of the traditional artist-bohemian in Mexico, to give life to the artist-citizen."

And, changing tone, Siqueiros tells me:

"Try that *quesadilla* and tell me what it's stuffed with."

I obey. The taste is delicious, but I cannot identify the stuffing. It is a very fine paste, of a purplish black. I raise an interrogative eye to my host. He throws his head back and laughs.

"Strange as it may seem, it is a sort of rotting maize . . ."

And he pronounces an Indian term that I am unable to retain.

"But go on with your story," I beg.

"*Bueno.* In 1919 I went to Europe with my captain's pay. In Paris I met Diego Rivera. That meeting, which I consider transcendental, represented the contact between an important period of European formalism, the post-Cézanne, and the aspirations of the young Mexican painters who participated actively in the Revolution and were partisans of a new social art."

In 1921 Siqueiros publishes his *Manifiesto a los Plásticos de América.* In 1922, with Orozco, Rivera and others, he initiates the Mexican mural movement.

"In '23 I was Secretray-General of the Revolutionary Painters', Sculptors' and Engravers' Union. In '24 I founded and edited *El Machete,* official organ of the Union. In '26 I became a union and political leader, I organized the miners' union, I directed strikes. . . ."

"And were arrested several times," I prompt him.

"Yes, many times," he assents, smiling like a boy recalling a piece of mischief. "And I understood that a leader art can only be the work of leader artists, in the broadest sense of the term."

In 1923 Siqueiros was "judicially secluded" in Taxco, where he painted more than a hundred canvases, nearly all on social themes. The following year he is exiled to Los Angeles, where he paints three murals that must have shocked the Californians: "Street Meeting," "Tropical America" and "Present Portrait of Mexico."

"It was the contact with that great industrial country, the United States, that made me see how archaic and anachronistic were the material means then used in the execution of mural painting in the whole world. Right there begin my experiments and achievements in the field of a modern technology for contemporary social art."

I know that the technique of mural painting owes to Siqueiros innumerable innovations. He was the first to turn away from the classic process—the mixture of lime and sand—used in fresco by the Egyptians, by the painters of the Middle Ages and the Renaissance, and by the majority of the muralists of our time. He was also the first to use the pneumatic gun for his new type of fresco with cement base. In 1933, in Uruguay and Argentina—once more in forced exile—he produced his first paintings on a background of pyroxyline. He returns to Mexico the following year and is elected President of the National League Against Fascism and War. And the artist gives me a picturesque explanation of that political activity:

"Even at the cost of temporary loss of professional exercise and gymnastics natural to the artist-painter of realistic social inclination, it is a good thing for him to refresh his militancy from time to time."

He flings back his head, utters a laugh, with mouth closed, that comes out in a snort through his nostrils. He is like a pony.

In 1935 Siqueiros founds an Experimental Atelier in New York in which he studies modern materials and tools more profoundly, as well as dynamic composition in mural painting.

"If my memory doesn't fail me," I say, "you fought in Spain, too."

"Yes; in 1936, with some companians from the Experimental Atelier and some Mexican military men, I joined the Spanish Republican Army."

In that civil war Siqueiros rose to lieutenant-colonel, commanding different units through three years of military action.

From 1939 to date he has devoted himself to an incessant search for new forms and techniques, having painted hundreds of studio works and principally important murals on public buildings.

Lunch over, Siqueiros invites me to go look at some of those works. I can imagine no greater pleasure.

We leave Angélica in the centre of the city, intent on shopping, and get into a taxi that takes us to the Preparatory School.

"An art without ideological function," says Siqueiros on the way, "despite the genius of its creators, or, more exactly, of its fabricators, is transformed progressively and inevitably into society juggling for 'ladies and gentlemen.'"

His strong, expressive hands are lying on his thighs. But they do not stay in that position long, for the next moment both are waving in the air as though helping to give body and colour to their owner's words.

"A more and more integral realism, growing ever more complete and real, is what identifies the artists of all important periods of the history of art. And the loss of that aspiration leads inevitably into decadence. It is because of all this that our modern Mexican movement can be considered the healthiest in the whole world!"

We are now in the Preparatoria looking at a fresco painted in the traditional manner. It is called "The Burial of the Sacrificed Workman". Three workmen with indigenous features (the face of one, the one in the foreground, strikes me as a crude version of Siqueiro's own face) are raising to their shoulders a rustic coffin on the lid of which are painted a hammer and a sickle.

Hands in his belt, contemplating his work, Siqueiros says: "I painted that between 1922 and 1923. The period of my artistic life that commenced in 1922 is characterized by a search for pre-Hispanic, colonial and folkloric bases that form the national artistic tradition of my country. And as this mural proves, I was already starting my political militancy, too."

It is not hard to interpret the meaning of the mural. The workman must have been killed in a strike.

We leave the Escuela Preparatoria and walk several blocks. I remind Siqueiros of a picture of his that deeply impressed me, although I had seen it only in a black-and-white reproduction. It shows a seated Indian woman, her face sad, her eyes empty, her arms hugging her knees, with a little child hanging on each side of her shoulders, while a third, smallest of the three, is lying at her feet in an attitude of agony. I had the impression that the children, in spite of their size, had a look of the foetus about them, and that both they and the mother were as though wrapped in a viscous placental atmosphere.

Siqueiros smiles and says: "It is called 'Proletarian Mother.' An oil, painted in 1929."

He tells me that from 1932 to 1938, discontented with the pre-

Hispanic, colonial and folkloric forms, which he came to consider archaic and anachronistic, he devoted himself to seeking a public function, a social meaning, for painting—all this without abandoning his revolutionary political activity. It was during that period that he painted, among many canvases and murals attacking war and Fascism, an impressive and prophetic "Explosion in the City." Upon a vast plain can be seen—from the angle of an eagle in full flight—the destroyed city from which rises toward the tragic sky an enormous, frightful cloud of smoke which takes almost the shape of the famous mushroom which much later was to be produced by the explosion of the first atomic bomb on Hiroshima. (The picture is dated 1936.) Of that phase, too, is the "Echo of the Weeping." Amid the ruins from an explosion looms the great head of an infant crying, and from its black, wide-stretched mouth emerges a full-length reproduction of the same baby, also crying. The figures, like the rest of the picture, have the shocking look of "carbonized things."

From 1939 to 1950 Siqueiros ends the technico-experimental stage and enters theoretically and practically into a new realism whose end and aim—and the words are exactly the ones he used—is "to give a better civic function to art." Of that period is his "Portrait of the Bourgeoisie," painted in the building of the Mexican Union of Electricians, an enormous mural in which appear English and American capitalists in fine clothes, but with their faces hidden by gas masks, which gives them the aspect of repellent beasts. On the other side we see Hitler and Mussolini, also with masks, and a quantity of other figures symbolic of American and European capitalism, as well as of Fascism, which is also represented in the background by its soldiers, marching with the regularity and uniformity of automata. Naturally the workman is also present, not only in his sacrifice to the masters of capital but also in his hope of the Revolution. Of all the murals of Siqueiros this is the one I like least, because of the excess of allegorical figures, and principally because of the circumstantial character of many of those symbols. I find it very dangerous for the artist to deal with the political mythology and symbology of our own time. I think the Aztec or Maya symbols and myths offer fewer risks, for I do not believe that time can change their meaning. A clear and concrete example of what I am saying is the portable mural that Diego Rivera painted in 1952, called "Signatures for Peace," in which appear, besides Fascist soldiers shooting or hanging proletarians, two enormous figures, those of Mao Tse-tung and Stalin—handsome, great and noble in contrast with the sorry, ridiculous caricatures that represent the United States, France and England. The two leaders are signing a treaty of peace of which they are to be the major guarantee. What will happen to that mural now, after Khrushchev in his famous speech has presented Joseph Stalin to his people not only as a paranoiac, cruel and arbitrary, but also a man who was leading his country into war?

A *libre* takes us to the Palacio de Bellas Artes. We climb the inside stairs of the Porfirian edifice and take up a stand in front of the Siqueiros mural, "The New Democracy," painted in 1943. The picture measures nearly forty feet in length by more than sixteen in height. The New Democracy is represented by a gigantic figure, a beautiful, vigorous, full-breasted woman, naked from the waist up, her arms outstretched before her, showing her chains broken and holding in one hand a luminous torch. One had the impression that those arms are leaping from the wall and striking his solar plexus, such is the brutal force and the sculptural relief of the figure. Beside the central figure are others of fallen men. One of the things I admire in Siqueiros is the boldness of his perspectives and foreshortenings. I tell him so, and he remarks:

"It was I who introduced the use of the camera into mural painting, to fix the human document. Thanks to photography we can employ a more integral realism. The camera also helps us to analyse masses, space and the movement of those masses in space."

Here on these marble landings are murals by Diego Rivera and Rufino Tamayo. The latter began by painting frescoes in the manner of the "three greats," but lately has been devoting himself more to easel painting, revealing himself more permeable than any other Mexican artist to American and European influences.

Knowing that Siqueiros cannot stand him, I prod him: "What can you tell me of Tamayo?"

"If Rivera in his painting speaks a Frenchified Náhuatl, Tamayo expresses himself in a French of bad construction and worse pronunciation, as all our painters do who truckle to the Museum of Modern Art in New York."

The Mexican revolutionary artists cannot forgive Tamayo his popularity in the sophisticated circles of the United States. In spite of not liking the abstract mural Tamayo has painted here, I consider him a plastic artist of great importance, a restless, tireless seeker for new forms of expression, like Portinari and Picasso. And as for his indifference to the social function of painting, I do not think the artist must make *engagé*, political, interested art; I think he *may*, if he will, follow that path. And if he has talent, he will succeed in harmonizing art with propaganda, although that is not at all easy.

We pass on to another gallery, where we stand for some time before other Siqueiros murals, the central figure of which is Cuauhtémoc. In one of the pictures the last Aztec emperor is depicted at the moment when he is being tortured by the soldiers of Cortés, who are burning his feet. In another the *Cuauhtémoc Redivivus* rises sword in hand, in brand-new Spanish armour, with a huge horse, feet up, on the ground in the back. In all these pictures Siqueiros' colour has an extraordinary vivacity that almost gives his figures the sonorous quality of a shout.

Another *libre*, a Plymouth manufactured in a country where Siqueiros could only with difficulty find a dramatic subject in the factories where every workman owns a car as good as this one and earns a wage that permits him a standard of living better than that of the Mexican middle class—a swift taxi takes us to the Hospital de la Raza, an imposing structure of modern lines, not yet completely finished.

I see in a great vestibule two admirable frescoes by Rivera, of fascinating drawing and colour. The first represents the magical medicine of the time of the Aztecs, and the second the medical science of modern Mexico.

Siqueiros waits patiently for me to examine the works of his rival and then takes me to see his own unfinished murals, saying:

"Formerly muralists painted only on rectangular surfaces. I thought it necessary to paint also on 'active surfaces,' concave, convex, composed of concavities and convexities, as well as on flat or broken surfaces, etc. Those surfaces make optically possible the dynamic phenomenon dreamed of by the painters of the past."

I remember having read the following words of Tamayo in an interview given to the journal *Arte Vivo Mexicano*: "To say that the painting of murals on curved surfaces is a transcendental event is nothing but a demagogical assertion implying the statement that mural painting has been done solely on rectangular areas. No one who has even a slight knowledge of the history of art can swallow so enormous a millstone. Mural painting ever since its origins has been subject to the geometric conditions of the surfaces on which it has to develop; and it is obvious that from prehistoric times, passing then through all architectural styles to the present moment, mural painting has been produced on surfaces of every kind."

Siqueiros raises his arm and points to the vaulted ceiling: "Look at that figure yonder, on top. Now tell me one thing: where is it looking?"

"At us."

"*Bueno.* Come with me."

He takes me to the opposite side of the vast salon: "And now where is the figure looking?"

I discover with surprise that the gigantic creature is again looking in our direction.

Siqueiros perceives my perplexity and says: "That is what I call 'dynamic composition.' The spectator is not a statue that presupposes curvilinear perspective, but a being who moves over the whole surface of a given architectural topography. The classic muralists used static, academic composition."

These walls are covered with parts of a mural which will bear the title *Por una Seguridad Completa y para Todos los Mexicanos— To a Security Complete and for All Mexicans.* Siqueiros has succeeded in giving new forms and dimensions to this salon by creating the illusion of fathomless depths, by producing fantastic perspectives, re-entrants, angles, vaulted arches that architecturally do not exist, for they are products of the magic of the painting of this indigenous Michelangelo here beside me, with his urban air, his grey suit flecked with colour, his gentlemanly manners—things which at first sight make it difficult for us to associate this man with the author of the fabulous mural. Of all the unfinished whole, there is one detail that impresses me. The assembly line of a factory (in the background a gigantic turbine symbolizes the impersonality, unhumanity, monstrosity of the machine) is bringing forward to the foreground the body of a workman killed in an accident. Here he is, with his face covered with blood. Three companions gaze at him in grave sorrow.

A little tired, my chest physically painful from all the blows it has borne from the formidable fists of Siqueiros' murals, I go out with the artist into the afternoon sun.

One night, in Vianna Moog's apartment, we again meet Siqueiros and Angélica. The painter, who is full of verve, relates two interesting stories to us.

He was about eighteen when one day his father, having read in the papers the news of the arrival in Mexico of a local painter who was returning from Paris with a certain reputation, asked his son: "Why don't you show him some of your paintings? Maybe he will encourage you."

David Alfaro was a little reluctant, but as the old man insisted, he decided to accept the suggestion, went up to the attic and searched among some old canvases he had painted, many of which he had forgotten completely. He picked out two that seemed to him the least bad and took them to the recently arrived artist, who examined them, liked them, and next day in a press interview referred to his "discovery of a young painter of talent," specifying in great detail the canvases he had seen. On reading the interview and identifying the pictures, Siqueiros' father put his hands to his head and exclaimed:

"David Alfaro, *hombre!* The canvases you showed that man were not painted by you but by your cousin Enrique!"

Only then did Siqueiros realize his mistake.

When he finished his story, I cannot resist the curiosity of asking: "And what became of that talented cousin Enrique, who painted so well?"

Siqueiros takes a swallow of whisky and responds: "He was murdered in Chicago in 1932. He was a gunman for Al Capone."


The second story Siqueiros usually calls "The Loss of Courage." It's a pity I can't retell it in the narrator's words, and in his expressive Mexican Spanish.

During the revolution against Huerta a platoon commanded by Siqueiros captured a suspicious-looking civilian who was wandering around the revolutionary camp. The prisoner being interrogated, it was learned that he was a colonel of the loyalist army who was trying to cross the rebel lines to join his own men. Tried by a summary court, the man was condemned to be shot. The colonel did not defend himself, did not ask for clemency, did not speak a word during the trial. He received the sentence without moving even a muscle of his virile face. He walked firmly out of the room, head up, bearing erect. In the prison where he awaited with other condemned men the execution of the death sentence, he refused to receive his wife, who, having been informed of what had happened, had come in despair and in tears to beg the revolutionaries to spare her husband's life. "Go away!" the latter shouted without looking at her. "I do not ask for, nor do I want clemency. Go back home!"

One morning, very early, the guards went to get the colonel and the other condemned prisoners to take them to a hill on the outskirts of the town, where they were to be shot. The mothers, wives and daughters of the prisoners were waiting at the gate of the prison. When the men appeared, a clamour arose. And the poor women, all dressed in black, followed the sinister group in the cold light of dawn. As they had to go through the town, the cortège gradually grew larger, and other women—some of whom had nothing to do with the condemned—joined their tears to those of the others. The colonel's wife walked beside her husband, hung on to his arm, to his neck, kissed his hands, which were tied behind his back, but the man walked on imperturbably as if she did not exist, his eyes fixed on the horizon. The march, however, was long. Siqueiros, who was accompanying the group, watched the changes that before long began taking place in the colonel's face, as the cortège approached the top of the hill. The man now was not walking stiffly; his head was drooping over his chest and his steps were less firm. Now he was looking at his wife with a mixture of tenderness and sorrow. But that expression turned into terror when, at the top of the hill, he saw the first prisoner fall in front of the wall, riddled with bullets. They had left him to the last, and he had to witness or at least *hear* the shooting of the others amid the women's cries of despair.

The bar of the horizon was growing lighter. Cocks were crowing. A cold breeze was blowing. A new volley was heard. The executed man fell. His blood spattered the wall. The lieutenant went up to the body, drew his revolver and gave the *coup de grâce* to the dying man's head.

At that moment the proud colonel uttered a howl and threw himself on the ground, weeping like a baby, and started bellowing pleas to them not to kill him. He kissed, he slobbered on the platoon commander's hand; he clasped the latter's knees like a spurned female mad with passion, and ended by rolling in the dust, his body doubled up, knees against chest, head between his hands, refusing to stand up and march to the wall like a brave man.

At this point Siqueiros paused. And when one of us asked him whether they had to tie the colonel to a post, he replied: "No. He was shot right there on the ground, like a worm."

Now, when at this distance in time and space I recall our last days in Mexico City, memories throng in a jumble into my mind, in Mexican indiscipline, with not the slightest consideration for the clock or the calendar. Some rise up in me whole and clear. Others outline themselves vague as phantoms. I wonder whether it is worth while to set them in order. Is it permissible to touch up the pale one with artificial tints?

I close my eyes and see myself on a certain corner of the Avenida Juárez, one sunny morning. I feel on my skin, in my nostrils, over my whole body the buoyancy of the air. I can see the faces of houses and of persons. (Images from the past are clearer when we shut our eyes.) I breathe like a convalescent who has just come down from the mountains, from a sanatorium for tuberculous patients where they have removed a lung. I can see from here *El Caballito* and the great Arch of the Revolution, a monument which has always seemed horrible to me and for which there is no distance or nostalgia capable of improving its absurd structure.

Now we are in a car with friends, rolling down the Paseo de la Reforma. And when we pass by a house with a front of glass, someone says to us: "In that café Victoriano Huerta used to get drunk. On such occasions, when the general was in a state of coma, they would put out all the lights so that the habitués of the place would not see the President being carried to his automobile in the arms of his cronies."

We were walking, my companion and I, in the suburbs. We are now collectors of signs, posters and window legends. We have already discovered a butcher's shop with the name of *La Atrevida*— The Bold Girl. A pulque bar called *Las Ilusiones*, and another, better still, on the indigo-blue façade of which we read *La Purísima* —a term usually signifying the Virgin. Stuck to a windowpane on a pink shack with doorframes of white, we see a large card with an advertisement that makes us stop, read and smile: *"Se hacen batas para carnicero y doctor"*—"Smocks made for butcher and doctor." We expect to find at any minute the famous sign: *"Recuerdos de su Porvenir"*—"Memories of your Future."

My companion declares she is fascinated by the sonority of certain names of Mexican places. Guadalajara—Jalisco—Cuernavaca—Acapulco—Querétaro—Churubusco—Chapingo—Hermosillo—Manzanillo—Polanco—Xochimilco.


Xochimilco! There isn't a tourist who doesn't thrill with joy on hearing that name. To go to Xochimilco in a "must." There the floating gardens are, the Aztec *chinampas*. Gondolas bedecked with flowers glide along the canals of blue water between banks of a festive green. And if the tourist is a music-lover he can take along in his boat two or three velvet-eyed and moustached *mariachis,* with their *charro sombreros* and their guitars. Can there be a more romantic and beautiful way to spend a Sunday?

Now I am a man who has always fought, and will fight, for the freedom of thought, word and locomotion, not to speak of others that do not come into the case. But among these civil liberties, there is one that has been much neglected. It is the right *not to go.* The older I get, the more I understand the importance of this right.

There is so much talk about Xochimilco, such marvels are told about the *jardines flotantes,* so much insistence on the "must" character of the excursion, that we decide positively *not* to go.

And when, back in Washington, some woman tourist who has visited this country asks me, batting her eyelids and rolling her eyes: "Did you see the marvellous, the fabulous floating gardens of Xochimilco?" I want to have the great, the enormous, the indescribable joy of responding: "No, madam!"


We did visit Chucho Reyes, folk painter. A bachelor, he lives in the middle of the city in an old house, with a sister, also unmarried, who looks after him. The artist's studio is small and stuffed with easels, pots of paints, brushes, sculptures in chalk and wood, images of saints, old colonial furniture. A delight, in short.

Tito introduces me to Chucho. I had been told that the painter is already in his sixties, but the impression he gives is that he is much younger. Of average height in Yankee terms, but considered tall by Latin American standards, he is a slender man with hair still black, ivory skin, thin face, courtly manners. He is wearing dark grey trousers and a black wool sweater, which gives him the look of a young university student.

Chucho Reyes does not paint canvases, but "decorative papers." He is a most personal artist, and his speciality is Christs, clowns and cocks. And are these not, perchance, subjects intimately, "viscerally" Mexican?

Just now I stated that Reyes is a folk painter. Latest style! Writing about this artist, David Alfaro Siqueiros has said: "Folk painter? Not at all! Jesús Reyes Ferreira is an authentic, great creator with roots in the people. But a creator who does not invent a popular or retrospectivist style like all the formalists of today. . . . The popular style comes out of himself, from inside, from his body, from his emotion and not from his intellect or his head. Thus he is Mexican in an integral way, an example of aesthetics for us all."

Chucho has a soft voice and is a man of few words. Indifferent to wealth and fame, in his retreat he keeps on painting his papers, in which stand out some singular purples, some aniline blues, some gildings and silverings as from a baroque church, some startling scarlets.

Chucho Reyes' pictures are to the murals of Rivera, Orozco and Siqueiros as a haikai is to an epic poem in hundreds of cantos.

Master Reyes shows us some of his work. His long pale hands delicately take up the fragile papers. Here is a cock with scarlet crest, head erect. Then comes—mallow against a blue background spattered with roses—an animal, part horse, part boar. Now it is a St. Francis of Assisi with a crucifix in his right hand and a skull in his left. The saint's head, yellow against the brown cassock, suggests a skull. Blood drips from the crucifix and from the wounds in the saint's hands. The artist shows us gayer figures, other cocks and horses. But there comes a clown, tragic in spite of his shrieking colours. After, against an olive-green background, a strange skeleton with bloodstains, as though completely demounted. Finally, the most impressive of all the papers. It is called "The Black Christ of the Candles." In the foreground, ten yellow candles, lighted. Behind them, seated, a lean, injured Christ, with a touch of the demoniac, his whole body black, full of holes and striated with red. On his head a crown of thorns of a vivid yellow, dripping blood. The

Saviour's face wears an expression that does not translate suffering, sorrow or resignation, but wickedness. The background of the picture is a sky blue, serene as the painter's eyes.

When we come out and pass through the little inner patio, where goldfish are swimming in an old fountain among motionless tortoises, I think as I go:

"In what other place in the world but Mexico could a painter like Chucho Reyes exist?"

On taking leave of us beside the almost ruined gateway, the artist gives my wife, as a present, a paper rose.


We emerge from the atrium of the Church of San Felipe, where we have watched some sculptors working with hammer and chisel on statues of saints. A young Indian is putting the finishing touches to the feet of an angel taller than he. A good smell of fresh-cut wood permeates the air. And it was strange to see so many Christs and angels stacked under the rough shed in front of the temple.

We are now in the Calle Francisco Madero. Indicating the façade of the Jockey Club, Tito tells me: "Into that club one day Zapata entered on horseback, frightening the bourgeois who were there."

Suddenly a gust of wind springs up, and a wave of dust so strong that we have to seek shelter in a café. The air is brown and gritty with dust. Newspapers, bits of paper, *sombreros* fly about. Women scurry along holding down their skirts. Men hurry with hands to their hats. Doors slam. The fine fingers of the sand scratch the glass of showcases and windowpanes.

Tito smiles and explains: "This happens frequently. It is the north-easter, which blows late in the afternoon, bringing the sand from Texcoco, the dry lake."

A few minutes later the wind ceases, the dust falls. And life goes on. The luminous signs begin to come on.

Emiliano Zapata!—I exclaim to myself. The meteorologists may explain the phenomenon as they wish or can. But in my opinion those storms are stirred up by your white horse, which fled off to the mountains when you were assassinated. He is still looking for you, Emiliano, everywhere, with all fury. It was he who came in here just now at the gallop, on the wind. What will there be in Mexico the day that you two meet again?

One scene has remained in my memory with inextinguishable clarity.

Standing on the curb of a sidewalk in the Paseo de la Reforma, I watch the passing of the funeral of a fireman who committed suicide. The drums, covered in crêpe, are muffled and sound dully. Not even a trumpet call is heard. Behind the drums march several platoons. The soldiers, in black uniforms with red collars, crêpe on their arms, march in cadenced silence. And on a wagon also covered in black lies the grey coffin enveloped in the Mexican flag.

*Plan-ra-ta-plan! Plan-ra-ta-plan!* There goes the cortège, bound for the cemetery. Can there be another country in the world where a wake is more wake, a funeral more funeral, and death more death?

*Plan-ra-ta-plan!* Farewell, fireman! I never saw you. Your name I do not know. But it will be difficult, impossible for me to forget your funeral. *Plan-ra-ta-plan!*

Corpus Christi Day. We enter the cathedral. In the mystic atmosphere is an extremely sweet fragrance that comes from the flowers covering the steps of the altars, flowers in profusion—lilies, gladioli, roses, red and white carnations, Cape jasmines. We move with difficulty through the multitude that fills the temple. Votive candles are burning. Mothers bring little girls dressed in typical costumes: *chinas poblanas,* peasant women's dress from Costa Chica and from the Sierra Zongólica. There are small boys in white clothes and red neckerchiefs, with straw hats, like Chantales de Tabasco peasants. Each child brings an offering to the saints: armfuls of flowers, cages with birds or baskets of fruits.

At the entrance a priest asperges those who come in with holy water. "Asperge" is not quite the word, because the poor father, who must already be tired of the gesture, is now, as it were, hurling holy water in gouts over the faithful, in quantities nearly diluvian.

We make our way among these gilded twisted columns, looking at the suffering images, stumbling at every step over Indian men and women kneeling in prayer. The murmur of the prayers fills the air like the humming of an enormous swarm of bees. A lady in black is on her knees beside a confessional: an old priest with a Sonotone hearing aid in his ear is listening to her with a bored air.

They say that this cathedral possesses two Murillos, one in the chapel and another in the choir. But I wonder whether there is a better painting than this living one we have before our eyes.

The faithful continue to enter in long files. The sounds of an organ fill the place, solemnly. (Ah! Johann Sebastian Bach, why weren't you born a Catholic?) The offerings accumulate at the foot of the altars. I remember a description I have read about this same feast day in the church of the Jesuit mission of São Miguel, in Rio Grande do Sul, in the eighteenth century. There are impressive analogies and the principal one is the pagan aspect of the solemnity. I find it strange, this mixture of the Middle Ages—suggested by the temple, by the images, by the priests, by the devout women in black—and the twentieth century, Europe and Asia, Spain and the Aztec world. Yes, and—why not?—the mixture of Catholicism and paganism. The Aztecs tried to feed their gods. Now these Catholic descendants of the Indians of Tenochtitlán come bringing presents for the saints of their devotion in order to placate them or to purchase their sympathy and liking.

We come out into the luminous Mexican morning. In front of the church some Indians are dancing, clad in costumes of a colouring that we regard as an incitement to our camera. There is a dancer of imposing aspect. He is young, with a thin face, his muscular body covered by a red cloak with yellow decorations, a headdress on his head, yellow shield in his hand. Women dressed as in the days of Tenochtitlán also take part in the dance. I am fascinated by a shield decorated with positively Greek motifs. One of the dancers approaches to beg money from me. While I am taking out my wallet, my wife takes a snapshot of the beggar. And from then on she surrenders to a photographic delirium. To the sound of a mandolin, the rounded belly of which is an armadillo's shell, and to the music of various kinds of lutes, Indian men and women dance, surrounded by curious spectators.

We go back to the hotel satisfied with the opportunity we have had to photograph the exotic dancers. But Tito throws cold water on our enthusiasm:

"That's a show prepared for the tourist. Those Indians receive pay from the municipality to dance. They are public employees."


From our base of operations in Mexico City, we make several short trips to interesting places in the vicinity.

Vianna Moog is taking me today in his car to the ruins of Teotihuacán, some twenty-five miles to the north-east of the city.

As soon as we start off, he grumbles: "If another tourist turns up that I have to take to those ruins, I'll go crazy. I've been there a thousand times already. I'm fed up to here. . . ."

The most important thing en route is the ruin of the convent of San Agustín de Acolmán, which dates from the sixteenth century and has a handsome façade in plateresque style.

We arrive at Teotihuacán. On this tepid Anáhuac morning we are the only visitors in the ancient city of the Toltecs, if we don't count a burro, grazing in reserved silence at the foot of a pyramid.

When he wandered around here, Professor F. S. C. Northrop was impressed by the urban sense of the Indians who constructed this symmetrical city, which seems to have been the work of architects assisted by priests, artists, astronomers and geometers, for everything apparently pivots around the Pyramid of the Sun. Teotihuacán in a way reproduces the solar system as the Toltecs saw it. The whole—this can be seen from the top of the greatest pyramid—must have been a prodigy of harmony and logic of city planning. Some anthropologists believe this was a ceremonial city, not properly a residential one. Here the temples were located, the houses of the persons who occupied themselves with religious functions.

A certain mystery surrounds the tribe of the Toltecs, their customs and doings. Such contradictory things are said concerning those Indians that there are those who actually doubt their existence.

It is known that they were great architects, carpenters and mechanics, as they were also able agriculturists.

It is beyond doubt that they came to the Valley of Mexico long before the Aztecs.

Situated in a valley, Teotihuacán occupies an area something less than four miles long by two miles wide.

The converted Indian Ixtlilxochitl, referring to the religion of the Toltecs, mentions a Supreme God: Tloque Nahuaque. But it is quite possible that the inhabitants of this part of the valley worshipped the Sun God and the Moon Goddess, to whom they erected these monuments.

The Pyramid of the Sun, although lower than the Great Pyramid of Egypt, has a broader base. We climb to its apex. Vianna Moog is bareheaded, and the morning light sets fire to his hair.

"Pedro Alvarado!" I say.

"Who's that?"

"Cortés's captain whom the Indians called 'The Sun' and who committed some outrages in Tenochtitlán."

"Is that the way you repay the sacrifice I've made in bringing you here?"

I look at the truncated Pyramid of the Moon, smaller than that of the Sun. Vianna Moog extends an arm toward the west:

"As you see, this pyramid is in the south, but not facing toward the true west. It is a little turned to the north. The anthropologists tried to learn the reason for that. They finally concluded that these two monuments, to the Sun and to the Moon, are not oriented exactly toward the west but toward the spot where the sun sets on the days it passes through the zenith. This proves, they think, that this pyramid was dedicated to the Sun God."

"And have you noticed the analogy between these two pyramids and the two volcanoes that dominate the valley?"

"How?"

"The Pyramid of the Sun, the larger, corresponds to Popocatépetl, a masculine symbol. That of the Moon, smaller, corresponds to Ixtaccíhuatl, 'The Recumbent Woman,' a feminine symbol."

"Leave old Freud in peace and let's walk a little."

We descend the stone steps and, once more at the base of the pyramid, we take the Way of the Dead, bound for the Citadel, where the Temple of Quetzalcoatl is.


Friday. We are in Toluca, capital of the State of Mexico. We have come to see the famous market where the most beautiful baskets in the country are sold.

Hardly do we get out of the car when two dirty, barefoot ragamuffins run toward us, shouting, *"Guatiucá? Guatiucá?"* It takes us some time to understand what they want. They are asking in English, or what they think is English, whether we want them to watch our car: "Watch your car?" Two round, swarthy, merry faces are lifted to us, receiving full the morning sun, which lends a glassy brilliance to the great black eyes, of a gentle and rather sad expression, like that in the eyes of the *burros* we have encountered in *pueblos* and on roads.

Vianna Moog leaves the car in the care of the two *Mexicanitos* and leads me in the direction of the market. Midway we are assailed by fat, taciturn Indian women who want to sell us objects of wood carved with penknife: jewel-cases, cigarette cases, ashtrays. They ask one dollar per piece, a mere nothing, for it is a matter of delicate work that must have occupied weeks of the craftsman's time. I buy three or four, and my pockets soon grow fatter and fatter.

Situated in the valley of the same name, this city is higher even than Mexico City. Thin and cold is the air of the June morning. Like nearly every Mexican city, Toluca has a private volcano, El Nevado, with an altitude well over 13,000 feet.

The market does not differ much from the others we have seen. It is dirty and its basic colours are black—the clothes of some of the Indians, the sooty pots and pans—and various shades of brown. But above that sombre base leaps gaily the colour of the baskets, in the most varied shapes, sizes and patterns. I have never seen more beautiful ones. I start buying, over the protests of Vianna Moog, and shortly we are both loaded with them, like ambulant vendors.

The art of basket-making is one of the oldest in the world. Some archæologists think that it was through it that the primitive peoples accidentally learned to make pots of clay.

It is possible that the first baskets were made of rush or reed, or of some thick and durable straw. And may it not also be possible that the basket maker's technique—weaving the rushes—suggested the idea of making textiles?

In this market is an indescribable collection of baskets. I see one, quite large, its bottom of chestnut colour with designs in red, canary-yellow and egg-yolk yellow: deer, eagles, and pyramids. I cannot resist the temptation to buy it, and here I go more loaded than ever. How is it possible—I ask my friend—that these sad, dirty, illiterate Indians can produce such beauties? Moog reminds me of a passage in Samuel Ramos's essay on the Mexican: "Today the indigenous popular art is the invariable reproduction of one same model, which is transmitted from generation to generation. The Indian nowadays is not an artist, he is an artisan who manufactures his works by means of a skill learned through tradition."

"Be that as it may," I say, *"Viva México!"*

A lean Mexican who is passing by and hears me, takes off his *sombrero* and says, very seriously: "And why not? *Viva México!"*

Moog bursts out laughing. And together we start off, stopping here and there, down a long aisle edged with stalls where, besides the baskets, mats and purses and bags are exhibited, an endless series of small objects of straw for domestic use.

I see in front of his stall a motionless Indian, his eyes closed, and I ask him: *"Yqué tal, amigo? Cómo le va la vida?"* "How are things, friend? How's life going for you?"

The Indian half-opens his eyes, gives me a cold glance, thrusts forward his lower lip, barely lifts his shoulders covered by a bi-coloured poncho, and gives the best, the most philosophical of responses:

*"Pues*—Well . . ."

And he closes his eyes once more.


Metepec is a *pueblito* situated at a short distance from Toluca. We have come here because I know that in this village pottery figures are manufactured. We go directly to the source, avoiding the middle-man.

Master Timoteo is a short mestizo, with a reserved air, who lives in a little house in the centre of the old village. I look at his workroom with a certain emotion, at the clay with which he works and at many figures still unpainted, just out of the oven.

The craftsman takes us to a small room where, lined up, are the works ready to sell. My interest is caught—love at first sight—by some absurd little horses rearing on their hind legs, with red mane and green wings, their bodies decorated in blue, purple, deep red and scarlet.

"What animals are those?" I ask, ignorant of this mythology.

*Mestre* Timoteo looks at me gravely, and after a brief hesitation says: *"Caballitos."*

I buy two of them and another animal, a mixture of ox and elk. And also a Tree of Life, a sort of candelabrum and incense burner of earthenware, in vivid and varied colours; on it I see cherubim, flowers, fruits and birds. The price of all these things is very low. I beg the craftsman to autograph one of his works for me. He accedes. Delightedly, I watch him make under his name all those capricious flourishes that were customary under signatures in the eighteenth century.

We go out into the streets of the village, where Time seems to have stopped. Today, here, is Friday, yes, but in what century?

Midday exactly. The sun is falling upon the narrow streets and deserted alleys, from which shadows are absent. Grass is growing between the irregular stones of the walkway. What strange, indecipherable but disquieting murals has age been painting on these walls with the paints of the wind, the earth, the rain and the sun?

Much moved, I stand contemplating the old, dry Indian yonder on the sidewalk, wrapped in his poncho, in a statuelike immobility, as though posted on a corner of Eternity, waiting for nothing and nobody.

After the visit to Metepec it is good to see again the Avenida Juárez, the Calle de Francisco Madero and the Paseo de la Reforma. Our hotel room now looks like a museum of popular art. Master Timoteo's *caballitos* lend colour and warmth to the formerly cold, dull place. And there are baskets, mats and rugs in all the corners.

We go to Cuernavaca one Saturday. The road is first-class, but the landscape strikes me as harsh and dun-coloured. An hour later, though, we catch sight of the valley of Cuernavaca and everything changes. There are the richest greens and the most beautiful flowers in this section of Mexico.

Alfonso Reyes has written: "God created the world in six days and rested on the seventh, so He invented the week. To spend the week-end we don't know how He managed. Now, according to what they say, He spends the week-end in Cuernavaca, which possesses a privileged climate. Some residents of Mexico and some from the neighbouring country are of the same opinion as God's."

Stars of the American and Mexican cinema come to pass their holidays in this beautiful garden, much sought out also by those whose hearts, weary from the altitude of the capital, feel better in this city, nearly 2,000 feet lower. Cortés built his summer palace in Cuernavaca, and Maximilian and Carlotta also used to spend the summers here. Joseph de la Borde, a Frenchman who grew rich with silver mines in the eighteenth century, constructed a residence surrounded by a fabulous garden with Moorish and Andalusian touches, which today is still one of the tourist attractions of the place.

Cuernavaca is an artists' centre, too. Writers, sculptors, painters and actors live in this place of colonial flavour, with houses painted blue, yellow and pink, a lively small plaza, mansions with inner patios and arcades, irregular streets, many of them full of ups and downs.

The *zócalo* enchants me. I stroll among its trees and benches, in the midst of an animated crowd. Because of Cuernavaca, at least in this centre, it always seems to be a holiday.

I see some men sitting at tables in front of strange machines. Who are they? What are they doing? The gadgets are typewriters of the most primitive type, the forefathers of those we use today in our studies. Those men earn their living by writing letters for illiterate persons. Yonder is an Indian dictating his missive. I can hear only these words: "Very Beloved Eusebia. . . ." The scribe beats on the keyboard, producing a noise as of old iron. Farther on a woman in black dictates: ". . . And they carried off a cow and two pigs of ours." What sort of letter can the young mestizo be dictating, the one in the avocado-green necktie and electric-blue felt hat? I draw near, recklessly, and hear him say in a firm voice: "If you don't answer me, I'll kill myself, word of honour."

The cafés and hotels are full of people. In front of one, in the middle of the street, three *mariachis* are singing, strumming guitars.

In front of the Palacio de Cortés a small band starts playing a military march. Rockets zoom up and burst in the air: the echo responds—where?

We set out, curious, for the great building and discover that a popular oratory contest is going on. We go in and take a seat. We hear only the last orators, for the tournament began early. The winner is an Indian of about twenty, heavy-maned and serious. In shirt sleeves, facing a solemn jury, he makes a fiery speech exalting the agrarian revolution and frequently quoting Pancho Villa and Zapata.

We lunch in the garden of a hotel, in the shade of the jacarandas, tamarinds and bougainvilleas of purple flowers.

And in the early afternoon we contine on, to a city I am eager to know.

# 10. Taxco

With little more than ten thousand inhabitants, Taxco is the oldest of the mining cities of Mexico. I see it first from the bottom of a valley through which the highway from Cuernavaca runs, and I feel I am encountering the city of my dreams. It is one more case of love at first sight. Of course, I came prepared for this moment and this affection. Anyone who has lived a little must have concluded that, just as there are bodies predisposed to tuberculosis, there are hearts predisposed to love. In the former case a puff of wind suffices. In the latter, a simple exchange of glances.

Well, my love affair with Taxco was born the day I saw the first photograph of this old city of the State of Guerrero.

Here we go with Aurélio and Marina in the car belonging to a *simpático* Brazilian agronomist who is taking a course of special training in Mexico. The highway—ever the Mexican theme of the serpent—has made dizzying swoops, climbing, descending and rounding stony hills covered with vegetation of a velvety, vivid green.

The first comparison that occurs to us when faced with Taxco is with a crèche. But it is so obvious, so facile, that I refuse to make it. The houses are mounted on the slope of a hill. The streets are narrow and some of them so steep that they are closed to vehicles, and it was necessary to build steps on them to aid the pedestrian. They say Taxco is reminiscent of Toledo. But I, who have never been to Spain, find it rather like Ouro Prêto. Let's say it is a rosy

Spanish version of Ouro Prêto. Here, too, it is prohibited to demolish old houses or to construct new ones in modern style, so that Taxco, according to the connoisseurs, has changed little from the eighteenth century to this day. The government maintains it as a historic and artistic monument.

We leave the car on the skirt of the hill and set out on foot with our light baggage (for we shall spend only a day and a few hours here) for the centre of the city. In the outskirts is a fine hotel of American type, with a night-club and swimming-pool, but it would be an ignominy to lodge there. The Baroness von Wuthenau expects us at the Casa de Humboldt, a mixture of inn and museum, a building from the late sixteenth century where merchants' caravans from Acapulco with their precious cargoes, bound for Mexico City, used to stop overnight.

We climb slowly for two powerful reasons. The first is that both Professor Aurélio and I have long-since passed our adolescence. The second is that we cannot resist the temptation to stop now and then to read the name of some shop or to look inside some *pulquería* or a patio. Now, for instance. Yonder is a handsome fat cock with scarlet crest, golden plumage with feathers of a black with green lights in it, strutting proudly atop an old wall, with the air of king of the walk. In a neighbouring yard hens are scratching away at the ground where exceedingly filthy pigs are napping, their hairy, shiny bellies half submerged in the mud. Clothes—red, blue, yellow—are hanging from a rope, and ripple like banners.

We continue the climb. The name of that *pulquería* is *"Mi oficina"*—"My Office." Farther on, a teasing advertisement: *No te apures, calentura, que aquí está tu Mejoral*—Don't fret, fever, here's your Mejoral. Then it is a church, possibly quadricentennial, wholly of blackened stone, with one of the most dramatic façades I have seen in this or any other country. We pass several houses painted rose-colour or light blue; colonial lamps, windows barred with *rejas*, patios with arcades, wells and tiles. I begin to feel irritated with the automobiles which, brand-new and anachronistic, are rolling along these one-way streets, and irked by the wires and lighting poles. Were it not for these signs of progress it would be possible to preserve the colonial atmosphere in its purity.


We reach the heart of the little city. A moment of rest and silence to hear it beat. Are you listening? Aurélio assures me that the beating is from our own hearts, for the city's heart, mute and of stone, does not pulsate. We sit down on a bench in the small square, where tall, thick-foliaged *calabazas* flourish. In the middle, a kiosk with yellow roof. Ah! Yonder is the famous church of Santa Prisca. All pink, with its slender towers and its Churrigueresque façade, it looks like the enlargement of a jewel made by a skilful craftsman of the colonial era. The tiled cupola is far to the back, which led Aldous Huxley, who passed this way, too, to compare this church with a hunchback and to say that he had never seen a building in which each part, even the tiniest, decorative detail, was so coherently out of proportion. "One of the most sumptuous churches in Mexico— one of the most sumptuous and one of the most ugly." ". . . An inverted work of genius." I remember the phrases well. Now, I disagree. Santa Prisca may rest easy: this Brazilian who has just arrived in Taxco likes its church, has no objection to its proportions and is even touched (or can it be sheer weariness from the climb?) by the laciness of its front, by its great, carved wooden door and by its Moorish cupola.

The Frenchman Joseph de la Borde who came here in 1716, poor but full of ambition, found so much silver in the neighbouring mine of La Cañada that, in a moment of enthusiasm, he declared that if His Catholic Majesty would deign to visit New Spain, he, de la Borde, undertook to pave the whole road from Vera Cruz to Mexico City with silver coins.

The rich miner, now with his name Mexicanized—José de la Borda—had the church built which is here in front of us, but when the silver vein in his mine was exhausted, he asked the priests to give him back the jewel-studded tabernacle which he had donated to the temple. The request was granted. De la Borda moved to Zacatecas, in the north, where he rebuilt his fortune. It is said that his only son entered a monastery, and on dying, de la Borda left his whole fortune to the Church, on condition that Masses be said for his soul.

I look at the old, irregular stones of the pavement which de la Borda must have trodden so many times when, with tricorn on his head, breeches fastened at the knee, buckled shoes, lace cuffs, he went to church, where he probably had a reserved seat. At the moment for the collection he would surely toss several silver coins into the sacristan's purple velvet bag. Silver from his mines, in which the poor Indians were treated like animals.

I hear the sound of other phantom footsteps in the street. There goes a young man dressed in late sixteenth-century fashion. It is Juan Ruiz. He was born here by chance, as his father is a mine superintendent. The boy's head is full of dreams. He wants to go back to Spain, he wants to study, to read, to write. He is already scribbling things, half in secret. A visionary? No. From this point in time I can make a safe prophecy. The world will some day know this youth by the name of Juan Ruiz de Alarcón, playwright, whose plays *El tejedor de Segovia* and *La verdad sospechosa* will sweep over a world and mark an epoch.

But the church clock tells us it is noon. The hostelry is a few steps from here. We direct our steps that way. I feel light, in holiday mood. Because Taxco is outside of time. And man will lose more than half his worries and cares the day he succeeds in forgetting the clock.


We are housed in the Casa del Barón de Humboldt, so called because at the beginning of the last century the famous German naturalist lived here.

The façade, of faded rose, has a vague similarity to the Alamo in Texas, and an air of illustrious ruin. Will I be committing a heresy to say it has something plateresque about it? Seen from the street, the house seems to be all on one floor, but, constructed over a ravine, it actually has three. I don't much like the great living room, where they recently built a hearth which gives the hostelry a Tyrolean flavour that is absolutely inappropriate. The rest of the old house is a delight, with its thick, whitewashed walls, its many galleries and stairs of stone, a terrace garden with colonnades and arcades, the venerable garden, some mysterious alcoves, some vaulted corridors that lead us inescapably to think of duels, ambushes and amorous intrigues. Our room has a pleasant rusticity about it and is immaculately clean.

We five lunch with the baroness and her stepchildren in a cool room on the lowest level, its floor of flat paving-stones. Señora von Wuthenau prefers us to call her Trixie, a name which suits this tall, slender young woman with light chestnut hair and faded blue eyes. She looks more like a colonist of Picada Café, in Rio Grande do Sul, than a German baroness. And when I say this my intention is obviously complimentary.

Trixie talks little. Her voice is gentle. Her whole person seems a dim drawing on a Dutch tile. Her gestures are vague. According to gossip, years ago a young Arab lodged here and fell in love with her, and at mealtimes spent the whole hour with elbows on the table, face resting on his hands, his eyes languidly fixed upon the lady of the house, forgetting to eat, sighing, unhappy, suffering his unrequited love in silence.

This is a moment to remember. The rustic table, the shallow wooden bowl with tomatoes, lettuce and carrots; the earthenware pitcher of limeade; the colourful dishes of Puebla china; the children with the faces of Nüremberg dolls. And the friends, the blurred image of Trixie with her long arms, her long fingers, her long silences.


A colony of artists exists in Taxco—painters, sculptors, writers—among whom are many Americans who detest their country and have come to stay, to live with and like the natives. We encounter the most improbable types in the streets and cafés. There comes one. Skinny, tall, blond, of some fifty years of age, he strolls through the square dressed like an Indian, in white cotton clothes, folded poncho over his shoulder, straw hat. That elderly woman sitting before an easel, trying to reproduce on canvas the image of the church, also looks like a foreigner.

We visit silversmiths' establishments, for here there are great numbers of them. They say a *gringo*, a Mr. Spratling, came down here, and he has the best shop in the town. This Mexicanized American is a retired architect who has succeeded in creating a tin industry in Taxco. He makes ashtrays, small pitchers, mirrors, an uncountable series of tin objects, besides furniture in colonial style. He has followers, has created a school, and has won fame.

The local jail is alongside the church. They say the municipality doesn't feed the prisoners, leaving that to their families. All this has an exquisite mediaeval flavour.

We climb to the top of the hill on which the city is located, and on the way we encounter many burros. One of the few sympathetic observations Aldous Huxley made about Mexico refers to these patient brothers of ours. He remarked that when a Mexican meets one of the beasts he feels obliged to yell, "Burro!" with all the force of his lungs, "not because that gains anything, but for the pleasure of shouting." I think there is something more than pleasure: a kind of shamed tenderness, a masculine way of saying to the animal, "I'm with you, I recognize your presence, I like the name 'burro,'

I'm your friend." There are burros of the most varied markings. They climb or descend hills with baskets across their backs. Their eyes, as always, are sad and tender. "Burro!" we greet them. And every time he pronounces the word, Professor Aurélio turns to me, serious, makes a bow and murmurs: "No allusion intended. . . ."


On this Saturday afternoon little bands of musicians wander through the streets towing signs asking for contributions. In front of the group an Indian is setting off rockets. Boys follow with trays on which passers-by drop copper coins or peso notes. Behind, the band playing furiously: six musicians, all in the characteristic dress of the man of the people. Bass saxhorn, trombone, trumpet, clarinet, snare drum and bass drum. They go out along these narrow streets to the sound of *pasodobles* and marches, and when they have disappeared in the distance one continues to hear for a long time the bursting of the rockets and the ruffle of the drums.

At night we sit on a bench in the plaza to listen to the *mariachis* who are singing on the balcony of a café. The air is cool and still. The church towers are silhouetted against the violet sky riddled with stars. (In a country where the phrase *murió acribillado de balas*—he died riddled with bullets—is heard so frequently, it cannot fail to be a delightful novelty to use the word *acribillado* in connection with the sky and the stars.)

The breeze brings us the scent of honeysuckle. The voice of the *mariachis* fills the plaza, where figures are strolling in the scanty illumination of the street lights. Someone shouts, *"Taquitos calientes!"* To top it off, it is a night with the moon at the full. A sentry paces up and down in front of the jail. A cricket starts chirping. The *mariachis* moan: *"Ando volando bajo!—*I'm flying low!"

It is very strange, this sensation of being in Taxco, in the very heart of the Sierra Madre, on a June night in 1785.


We go back to the hostelry at midnight, and I should be the worst of miserable men if I went straight to bed, closed my eyes and fell asleep. The moon, the piquant night air, the perfume of the jasmines—everything invites me to go to the terrace, lean on the parapet wall and stand gazing at Taxco. I accept the invitation. Dogs are barking in the distance. Thanks, friends! What my soul was lacking was precisely that. A Latin night with a whole horizon of dogs. And the cock's crow still missing, a few minutes later flashes luminously through the night like the firework called "nigger chaser."

The inn is silent. But if we whet the ear of fantasy it is possible to listen to the sound of conversations on the lower storey. Whose strange voices are those? What language are they speaking? Now I understand. We are in the nineteenth century. Down there, drinking and talking, are the merchants who have come up from Acapulco, where two days ago a Spanish galleon arrived from Manila with a cargo of Chinese silks, bundles of muslin from India and bags of spices and exotic perfumes. This is a night like many in the early part of the past century. Yesterday a mounted messenger passed through here on his way to Mexico City to announce the arrival of the galleon. Why such haste to carry the news? Simple. The merchandise just arrived is in great demand. In the capital the richest merchants, the members of the aristocracy and even members of the clergy combine their resources into a common fund to buy up the whole valuable cargo of those Spanish ships to resell it in Mexico with a fine profit. This operation is called "the Chinese fraud."

And that same galleon on its return to the port of origin will carry a load of silver in coins and bars, and oil, wine, wool and cochineal. How many men will be murdered tonight in their rooms, to be robbed? Trixie will be safe, because more than a hundred years separate her from that night of bandits, merchants and pirates. Yes, among the phantom guests there are also Chinese. Chinese who came with their vessels from Macao and Canton, loaded with tea and raw silk.

Who is this figure I see beside me, also leaning on the parapet. It is the Baron von Humboldt, the friend of Goethe. He is looking at the stars, since astronomical observation is necessary in the exact calculation of geographic co-ordinates. The baron has decided to make a map of Mexico. He is also a devotee of Taxco. And anyone who thinks he is preoccupied solely with the formation of rocks and the classification of plants will be much mistaken. Humboldt has already shown his horror at the inhuman treatment given to the Indians in the silver mines; he has also criticized the antiquated methods of exploitation of those mines. One day he will write that "men of over sixty and boys of twelve crawl into ill-ventilated tunnels, a horror of powder smoke and dust, hot as hell." He will compare the latifundian and mining aristocracy of Mexico with that of Czarist Russia, and will prophesy the independence, within a short time, of the Indo-Spanish nations. More than that: he will even go so far as to predict the Mexican Revolution. "I am absolutely convinced that this nation is destined to advance by means of education, in a challenge to the Church and to the autocratic governors."

From afar now comes the rattle of gunfire. Six detonations in rapid succession. Afterwards, silence pricked by the barking of dogs. Someone must have been killed somewhere. The crime statistics of the State of Guerrero are the highest in the country. But I cannot really associate the idea of violence and death with the placid beauties of Taxco.

I return to the room, I undress, I get into the bed, on its hard mattress (we buccaneers are accustomed to these discomforts) I think of the barons—von Wuthenau and von Humboldt—of Trixie and her stepchildren, of the church of Santa Prisca with its enormous image of a Pope paternally cradling in his arms a Christ just taken down from the Cross, drained of blood. Then my thought goes to Brazil, via Washington, to the church of Cruz Alta where Padre José, with his dark red face, like ripe strawberry, preaches indecipherable sermons. And I see myself as a child in a house in my natal city, playing with a tin ship with a curious name painted on its side—*Nimrod*. And then the *Nimrod* is at Acapulco, discharging bales of silk which are revolver bullets which *acribillan* the breast of the night sky the breast of the *china poblana* Taxqueña baroness. . . .

Of course all this is taking place in a dream, for I am fast asleep in the perfumed, evocative Taxco night.


Sunday morning, with sun, bells, birds and clouds.

Marina and my wife have gone to Mass with Trixie. I have decided I don't ever want to leave Taxco for long. My dearest project at the moment is to rent a quite ancient little house and stay here painting and writing, with a *charro* hat on my head, and clad in Indian clothes. And why not? Why go back to an office of steel and marble to sign papers and more papers that no one will ever read, in the shadow of an implacable clock? Why go back to committee meetings, to the parties, to the ambassadors and the generals, in a country which travels at supersonic speed, when here I have discovered a city which, because it drags itself along with the charming slowness of a rosy snail, has not yet got out of the eighteenth century?

I sit for a long time looking at a *callejón*, a very narrow street of green, white and blue houses, with colonial lamps, and burros tied to hitching posts. Then I go out to photograph Taxco from all possible and imaginable angles. I go up to the terrace of one of the hotels, I catch a general view of the city with a flame of red bougainvilleas in the foreground. In the plaza I ask an Indian woman sitting on one of the benches for permission to take her picture. She assents with a slight movement of her head, and I needn't ask her to sit still for an instant, because these Indians are motionless by nature. She is a pretty woman, still young, with an oval face of prominent cheekbones, her hair smooth and black, a millenary sadness in her dark, liquid eyes. Over her shoulders she has a *rebozo* of turquoise blue. Only now do I perceive that she is pregnant. What most impresses me about her is her air of calm dignity. She has not licked her lips, has not adjusted hair or shawl, has not made the slightest gesture of coquettishness when she saw I was going to photograph her. To tell the truth, she has not even paid any attention to the photographer. And when I move away, she sits there with her basket of yellow fruit, her muteness, her immobility and her mystery.


Professor Aurélio returns from a stroll through the streets of the silversmiths, and is here beside me telling stories of the Brazilian north-east. The morning band concert has begun. The musicians in the bandstand are playing a little serenade waltz. All of them are in straw hats, coatless, and have that touchingly serious look of the amateur. The old man on the clarinet must be an octogenarian. The youth on the baritone saxhorn can't be more than fifteen. The light-skinned maestro looks like an Italian, but is dressed like the others. They are only seven musicians, which does not prevent the band—after playing *huapangos, rancheras, pasodobles*—from attacking with bravura von Suppé's "Light Cavalry." And one of the liveliest parts of the piece coincides with the exit from Mass: the bells ring and the church doors spill out into the plaza a festive crowd in Sunday best which soon fills the benches. Infants run about in the shade of the great trees whose rough, knotty trunks look like limbs of antediluvian animals. And the band finishes its piece in a ruffle of drums and clashing of cymbals. Applause.

Through the bars of one of the little windows of the jail a sad-faced prisoner is watching the plaza.


After lunch we return to Cuernavaca.

*Adiós,* Taxco! *Adiós,* Trixie! *Adiós,* Nüremberg dolls! *Adiós,* Sunday that will never return!

We leave the silver city of la Borda behind, among its water-colour hills, with its terraces, narrow streets, bells, burros, bougain-villeas, slopes and lamps.

It is very hot, and the sky, which dawned so bright and blue, now turns harsh, with cocktail cirrus clouds, in a threat of rain.

Professor Aurélio, his voice pitched high and tremulous, imitates an orator of Pernambuco who one day, in a municipal ceremony, referring to the São Francisco, warbled: "That river which passes singing to the mandolin of the sands!"

Mandolin of the sands! We burst out laughing. Other stories come. The women talk of silver and rugs. And, driven by a safe chauffeur, the auto speeds along the "writhing, serpentine road-ways," as the north-eastern orator would have said.

How long have we been travelling? It is hard to say, because the company is pleasant and Taxco predisposes us to find everything good.

Suddenly our car stops. What's the matter? In the middle of the road we see a woman waving to us. She is corpulent, with rich hair, and her white blouse is stained with blood. Crime? A trap? We see an old Chevrolet with its snout bashed against the bank of the gully, at the side of the road. And a few yards from the car, in a ditch, a man in shirt sleeves lying with his head all over blood in the lap of a woman dissolved in tears. On the hard surface of the highway we can see in a whitened trail the zigzag trajectory of the Chevrolet—a sort of graph of the accident. Sunday drunkenness—I diagnose.

The unknown woman runs toward us crying:

*"Virgen purísima!* Help, *señores,* help! A horrible disaster!"

Panting, she points to the figures in the ditch, from which the weeping woman lifts supplicating eyes to us. We consult each other in an exchange of glances. Our agronomist remarks that in Mexico it is regarded as a crime to pick up persons injured in highway accidents without awaiting the arrival of the police. But as it happens, I have always had a vocation as Good Samaritan, and I am not going to let this magnificent opportunity pass.

"Shall we go help the man, professor?" I ask.

"We can't let him die."

Aurélio jumps out of the car and we follow him. I grasp the injured man under his arms, aided by the agronomist, while Aurélio lifts his legs. He is a stout fellow, forty-odd, bald, with thick black moustaches and unshaven. We succeed in placing him with great difficulty in the front seat, to which the lean, tearful woman also mounts. The other, the one with the bloodstained blouse, wishes to get in, too, but we find there is a serious problem of space.

"Stay here," I tell her, doing all I can to sound like a Mexican. "We'll send somebody to find you and take charge of the automobile."

"Is there any town near by?" asks Aurélio.

"Yes," says the woman, "Puente de Ixtla. It's five minutes from here."

The injured man is muttering unintelligible words. Blood is running down his forehead. I examine his head and see on the crown a cut the depth of which I cannot estimate, and over which the blood is beginning to coagulate. The small woman passes tremulous hands over her man's cheeks, murmuring: *"Pobrecito, pobrecito"*—"Poor darling, poor dear."

"Is he your husband?" Marina asks with feminine malice.

The *muchacha* shakes her head in a negative and explains: *"Es mi amigo"*—"He's my boy-friend."

"Ah!"

Everything is clear, the picture complete. Our car starts off, bound for the pueblo. Five minutes? We take nearly fifteen. The injured man groans and mutters: *"Conchita, dame una pistola, méteme una bala en la cabeza"*—"Give me a pistol, put a bullet in my head." Conchita confines herself to tears, which roll down her bony, ill-painted face. We can do nothing. We look at the road and can see no town. *Dame la pistola, Conchita!* The auto speeds on. Conchita's perfume is sweet, cheap and nauseating. *"Madre mía,"* whimpers the man.

At last we come in sight of Puente de Ixtla. The car turns off the road to enter the town. We ask the first Indian: "Where can we find a doctor?" He shrugs his shoulders: *"Pues, quién sabe?"* We have better luck at a *gasolinera*, a filling station, where the employee points out the home of a doctor. We knock at that door. A maid opens. We tell her what we have come for. She goes to the back part of the house, is gone for an eternity, and comes back with the message: "The doctor is in the bath and says he is not in the habit of attending patients on Sundays."

"But it's an emergency case," I insist. "We have a seriously injured man in the automobile."

The Indian woman stands silent and motionless. We have no other recourse than to ask, "Where is another doctor?"

She points out a yellow house in the next block. We start for it. At this point a small crowd of curious folk is following our car. From inside a café come the strident sounds of an electric music machine: Pedro Infante is singing a *bolero*. Flies are circling about the fruits on a market stand on the corner.

We knock in vain at the second doctor's door. A neighbour puts his head out of the window and tells us: "The doctor has gone fishing."

The procession moves on. I go to the car to see how the injured man is. I verify that he is breathing and incessantly muttering, saying his head aches, he can't stand it, and the only thing to do is for somebody to give him a pistol so he can blow his brains out.

We are directed to another doctor's house three blocks away. Aurélio and I head for it on foot, followed by the rest of the caravan in the car, which in turn is surrounded by an increasing number of the curious. Behind us marches a mestizo with a likeable face, wearing a broad-brimmed hat. I have the feeling that he has been following us for some time, at a distance.

Finally we get a doctor. He is a stocky fellow, swarthy and not very cordial. "Bring in the injured man!" he says rather harshly.

We carry our *hombre* into the consulting room, which is quite clean and pleasant-looking. "There!" exclaims the doctor, indicating a sofa. We lay the patient on it. Conchita, who has not left him, caresses his cheeks. The patient whimpers: *"Madre mía, dame la pistola!"*

Aurélio and I gaze mutely at the tableau. The doctor, who is over at the lavatory basin washing his hands, says ill-naturedly: "What are you waiting for? Strip the patient for me to see whether he's broken something."

The two Samaritans approach the injured man. Aurélio lifts his body, I loosen his belt, and a moment later I am holding the stranger's trousers in my hands. The underclothes worn by this corpulent fellow of so unprepossessing a face are an innocent sky blue. Aurélio and I look at each other.

At that moment the man who was following us comes up and says: "I'm from the local police. What happened?"

We tell him the whole story, which to our surprise he accepts without question. We ask him to send help to the woman in the white blouse who was left on the road. The investigator takes down our names and addresses in a notebook.

"May we go?" we ask.

"Of course. A pleasant trip!"

The doctor finishes his examination. And when we ask him about the condition of the patient, he informs us, without looking at us: "He hasn't broken anything."

"And the head injury?"

"It's not serious."

He says this and turns his back on us. Conchita thanks us. We depart from Puente de Ixtla, headed for Cuernavaca, where we have a dinner engagement. We arrive two hours late, but with the joyous heart of travellers who have done a good deed.

As we re-enter the paved highway we meet a burro. And to blow off steam I let out a bellow: "Burrrrro!"


There is a word the Mexicans use to designate a boon companion. It is *cuate*. It corresponds to the French *copain* and the English "pal." I have a Mexican *cuate* whose name is Ermilo Abreu Gómez, my colleague in the Pan American Union. He is one of the important writers of Mexico, author of pieces for the theatre, novels, short stories, and a delightful autobiography in four volumes. Ermilo achieves the miracle—perhaps a secret of the Maya Indians of his native province—of looking a youthful fifty when in reality he has already entered his sixties, three years ago. He is a short man, with sober, gentle gestures. When I see him in the marble corridors of the Union, I imagine him clad in a Franciscan habit, pacing under the arcades of a conventual patio. But let no one be deluded by that monastic appearance. Ermilo is a man with a ferocious capacity for irony, with a sharp satirical mind. In his writings he has attained a clean economy of style which we Brazilians are not accustomed to associate with the literature of the Spanish language.

Of his humorous vein here is a sample:

Once Ermilo and I were travelling together, and in a South American airport we went up to the immigration officer, who examined my friend's passport and asked him: *"Cuál es su destino?"* (Now, *destino* means both "destination" and "destiny" in English, which lacks a single word for this word-play.) Unhesitatingly my friend replied, "Of the blackest."

I write these words not only to call the attention of my readers to a writer I consider important, but also to recall that when we said goodbye in Washington Ermilo recommended to me: "Don't fail to go to Yucatan. It's the other Mexico."

I did not go to Yucatan, as I did not go to Jalisco or to Vera Cruz or to Morelos. Friends and books assure me that in those hot lands the people are gayer, the land less arid, life more amiable.

Speaking of Mexican contrasts, Mariano Picón-Salas, in his excellent *Gusto de México,* asks whether the differences between the highland Mexican and the Yucatan Mexican do not correspond a little to the differences between the warlike Aztec, crushed under his pessimistic, tragic theogony, and the Maya, more imaginative, sensual and expressively naturalistic.

In many ways the Maya civilization was more important than the Aztec, besides being more ancient. The ruins of Chichén-Itzá give an idea of the grandeur of the Maya cities. Their monuments rivalled those of the Egypt of the Pharaohs, those of ancient India and those of ancient Greece. Someone has said the Mayas are the Greeks of pre-Cortésian America.

I have the impression that Yucatan is to Mexico as Texas is to the United States: a province apart, peopled by folk of special and psychologically separatist temperament. In the case of Yucatan, however, the isolation is not just psychological but geographic. As to Nature, the Southern Mexican state resembles Guatemala more, a country with which it shares the vigorous Mayan tradition.

But I continue to affirm—until someone convinces me of the contrary—that the most expressive zone of Mexico is that of the central highland, not only because the majority of the country's population is concentrated there, but also because what that people is, does, thinks, feels and says seems to me to represent the Mexican character best.

Ermilo, my dear *cuate,* forgive me for not having been able to visit your Yucatan.

# 11. The Mexican

Between the day we left Mexico and the exact moment I am beginning to write this chapter, two years have passed, during which I have sought not to lose sight of that country and its people. In spite of all the personal, direct observations made during the journey narrated in this book, and the many readings to which I have devoted myself before and after it, I find myself still intrigued and perplexed before the mystery of the Mexican character.

Among the many essays that seek to unveil the mystery, three at least seem to me indispensable as a compass or guide for anyone who ventures into the *terra incognita* of the Mexican soul. I refer to *El laberinto de la soledad,* by Octavio Paz; *Perfil del hombre y de la cultura en México,* by Samuel Ramos; and *Mito y magia del mexicano,* by Jorge Carrión.[1] To these three admirable books I owe, in the main, many of the ideas, theories and information and suggestions which have made possible the present chapter, in which— *cum grano salis*—I try to discuss, since I cannot explain, the social character and the psychology of the Mexican.

First, however, it would be interesting, even at the risk of going

[1] The three titles would be in English, respectively: *The Labyrinth of Solitude, Profile of Man and Culture in Mexico,* and *Myth and Magic of the Mexican.* No English translation of any of these is listed in the Library of Congress.

back over much ground already covered in this narrative, for me to say something about the configuration, the climate, and the most serious problems of the land of Mexico.

CONFIGURATION.—As Frank Tannenbaum has very well observed, the physical geography of Mexico is of such a nature that it seems to have been made especially for the purpose of isolating the Mexicans from each other and the entire nation from the rest of the world. In this country there is scarcely a place where the observer is not either surrounded by mountains or at least in sight of some mountain in the distance. The more or less flat zones comprise not more than a third of the total area.

The chains of the Sierra Madre Occidental and the Sierra Madre Oriental, which flank both seacoasts—from which they are separated by fringes of lowlands—form the buttresses of the central plateau. These two cordilleras, which come together south-west of Puebla to merge into a single chain ending abruptly in the Isthmus of Tehuantepec, are barriers which separate the central mesa from the Pacific and from the Gulf. In that rapid plunge of the land toward the South the valleys narrow, the ravines deepen, the climate becomes modified and cities grow scarce. The terrain rises again in the State of Chiapas, comparable in altitude with the plains of Chihuahua, but, as happens with Lower California, is separated from the central part of the country by the lack of roads. Many travellers are amazed to find, in relatively small areas, communities which live separated from each other, with their perculiar customs and traditions. The mountains are responsible for these separations and isolations, which themselves explain why certain tribes of old succeeded in maintaining their own language, at times so different from those of neighbouring groups living only a few miles away but on the other side of the mountain.

CLIMATE.—It its customary to divide Mexico into three climatic zones: *Tierra Caliente,* or Hot Land, with vegetation from tropical to desert in type, and corresponding to areas of altitudes less than some 3,300 feet; *Tierra Templada,* Temperate Land, or subtropical, in altitudes between 3,300 and 6,600 feet; and *Tierra Fría,* or Cold Land, which comprises the highest parts of the central plateau and the lands between 6,600 and 10,000 feet. In this last zone it never gets really hot, nor can one say that there are severe winters.

As if all the topographical difficulties were not enough, Mexico further suffers from poor distribution of rainfall. The land in the north is calcined and dry. The humidity of the central part of the country barely permits vegetal life. In the south, however, there is too much water. The parts of the country where rain falls in sufficient quantities are tropical and thinly populated. There is a small basin, running from the federal capital to Aguascalientes, in which agriculture is possible without artificial irrigation, since during the summer it rains in abundance, though with no regularity. One who crosses Lower Calfornia and passes through the north-western zone of Sonora—tremendous sandy wastes of cracked, arid earth—can hardly imagine that in the lands of the south and southeast, in Tehuantepec and Vera Cruz and Tabasco, there is so much water, so much swampland and so much humidity in the air, that life and work there become all but insupportable. By a sorry irony, in Mexico water is lacking where it is most needed, and that lack constitutes one of the principal obstacles to the economic life of the country. The rivers either vanish, sucked up by the deserts, or pour into the sea in untamable torrents. The populations of the desert zones, which in summer have to endure an infernal heat, in winter shiver with cold on the still burnt, dry earth, lashed by freezing winds which produce sand storms.

It can be said that the history of Mexico has been summed up in a struggle for possession of the land. As a setting with pictorial qualities, there are probably few landscapes in the world that can equal the Mexican countryside in beauty and grandeur. But as a source of food, of well-being and security for its people, it is not excessively imaginative to compare Mexico's Nature with a splendid woman of majestic but sterile aspect, of erect but dry breasts. And the Mexican peasant loves, with a silent, stubborn passion, that stepmother who denies him sustenance, and who now and again explodes in excesses of fury manifested by seismic tremors and volcanic eruptions. It is true that from the breast of that stepmother oil has been spouting for some time, but only the future can tell just how much the black milk has contributed to satisfying the hunger and to improving the conditions of the life of the masses.

Barely seven per cent of all Mexico's territory can be used for agriculture. And I think it no exaggeration to assert that the Mexican, who lived ill-fed in pre-Cortésian times, entered the colonial period hungry, continued to be hungry after Independence was won, and in a way is still hungry in our own time.

Incurring all the risks inherent in simplifications and assertions of any absolute nature, I shall say that, in Mexico, if the land is chronically thirsty, the people are almost chronically hungry.


RACIAL GROUPS.—Mexico is a nation in which Indian blood predominates. Nearly thirty per cent of its inhabitants are racially and culturally Indian. The minority of the population—some ten per cent—is composed of whites (I always write that word with doubts and reservations), of *criollos,* that is, offspring of Spanish parents but born in Mexico, and of a good number of persons from various European countries and the United States. The other sixty per cent are mestizos.

The Indian is the passive element of the population, "the hinterland of the Mexican," as Samuel Ramos calls him. He constitutes a kind of silent, motionless chorus in the national tragedy. His capacity for effacing himself is not merely psychological or sociological but also physical, for by a curious defence mimetism, like that of certain animals, the Mexican Indian can dissolve into the landscape.

The ten per cent who are or consider themselves white, live and think more or less like the whites in any other country of America, and their dramas and neuroses do not arise, I believe, from the fact of being Mexicans but from their belonging to a certain social class and living in this century and at this hour.

Thus, what in my opinion best represents Mexico is the mestizo, that is, the man of Spanish and Indian blood, not only because he constitutes the majority of the population but because—and this is the main thing—he furnishes the tonic note in the life of the country. To understand him, therefore, will be to understand Mexico.


THE MESTIZO.—"Begotten with violence and without joy, the mestizo comes painfully into the world." The phrasing, which strikes me as expressive, is by Fernando Benítez. The mestizo, like the Mexican nation itself, is a product of the violence and the cupidity of the Spaniard. Appearing on the Mexican scene from the earliest days of the Conquest, this hybrid type gradually came to be a sort of bridge, a hyphen, between the European and the diverse racial groups of Mexico; he was also a transmitter of European culture to the natives. If we consider the pre-Cortésian Indian as representative of a chaotic world without national unity, divided by differences of language, customs, interests in conflict, and other rivalries; and if we regard the Spaniard as a figure strange to all that barbaric environment, we shall have to recognize that the mestizo was actually, from the first of the Colony, the most important element in the Mexican population, perhaps the only one really to have the idea, or, rather, the *desire* to be a nation.

The Indian was too reticent and uncommunicative and drawn into himself, as was natural, as a consequence of the psychological and physical mutilation inflicted on him by the Conquest. The *criollo,* in spite of having his feet planted on the soil where he was born, did not really love his country or his people, kept his eyes turned to Spain, whose life, customs and ideas he sought to imitate. But the mestizo, without ever losing contact with the land, without ceasing to be tellurically Mexican, had an awareness of the rest of the world, knew of the existence of other countries, other peoples, other cultures—an awareness, this, which gave him the desire to build his own fatherland.

Condemned to subordinate activities during the colonial epoch, when he was denied access to government positions and the opportunity to improve social and economic condition, that centaur—half-Indian, half-Spaniard—insofar as what depended on the *criollos* and the Spaniards was concerned would be destined to remain eternally a marginal. His first opportunity came with the movement for the independence of Mexico, a period in which his presence began to make itself noticed on the national scene. The Revolution of 1910, kindled at least apparently for the purpose of giving lands to the Indians, had as its spiritual chief a *criollo,* Francisco Madero, but it was commanded and directed militarily by mestizo chiefs like Zapata, Huerta and several others. But mestizos, too, were many of those who later betrayed that same Revolution. This seems to confirm a current idea about the mestizo character, viz., that he has two facets: personal ambition and lack of scruple. I dislike the idea not only for its assertive and over simplified content but also for its slight tincture of racialism. Personal ambition seems to me a trait of human nature and not an exclusive quality of the mestizo. What there seems to be in the latter is the desperate desire to define himself in his dramatic dichotomy—Indian, or white?—to free himself from the sense of inferiority born of the scorn with which other members of society regard him and treat him. And as he can find no way of changing the colour of his skin or of eliminating from his blood whatever touch of Indian it has, that is, its "inferior component," according to the ruling concept in the so-called white societies, the remedy is to rise in social position. Now, this eagerness to rise, to impose himself, to become notable or at least noticed, to gain prestige, wealth or political power, leads him inevitably not to be selective about his means of ascent. His conduct is ruled now by the European's scale of values, now by the Indian's, and not infrequently by a confused mixture of both.

I have the impression, therefore, that in Mexico the mestizo has solved his problem in great part by means of a reconciliation with his Indian past. In the country there is no shame in having Aztec or Maya or any other Indian blood. Nowadays that is actually a motive of pride. Sometimes a fierce pride which itself cannot fail to be a source of new problems.


THE COUNTRY AND THE CITY.—It may be said that in Mexico the European element predominates in the cities and the Indian in the country. The northern part of the country is, in a general way, markedly mestizo. The south, as a whole, is culturally and racially Indian. It has always seemed to me—and this journey has confirmed the impression—that here, as in several other Latin-American countries, is a population which, though it cannot be considered Indian, lives on an Indian cultural level. It is calculated that in Mexico there exists perhaps some five millions of persons whose habits, instruments and techniques of work, domestic utensils, family and social organization, basic aptitudes and ideas about the world are more Indian than European.

The increase in the Mexican population has been slow. It has never been possible to estimate with any accuracy the number of aborigines living in Mexico when Hernán Cortés disembarked in Vera Cruz. What is known with certainty is that from the day of disembarkation on, the slaughter of the natives began. There were, besides epidemics, deaths caused by unfavourable working conditions in the mines, and by ill-treatment; and we cannot forget the forced migrations.

From the moment I entered Mexican territory one thing has caught my attention. It was the scarcity of population in the vast savannas of Chihuahua, in contrast to the zone of the federal capital and the regions surrounding it. The population of Mexico is really badly distributed. It is very dense on the central plateau and scanty on the littoral and on the borders with the United States and Guatemala. Mexico is in reality a land of *pueblitos*. The rural population is not scattered in the country on granges, small farms, ranches, but grouped in hamlets, villages, towns and small cities.

Prestige and political and economic power are concentrated in twenty-one cities, more or less, with populations of 25,000 or more each. I do not know how far one can trust statistics, but it is stated that sixty-four and nine-tenths per cent of Mexicans live in rural districts. Ninety-nine and two-tenths per cent of all inhabited places in Mexico had, in 1940, populations of less than 2,500. Only seven-tenths of one per cent were living in urban areas.

LANGUAGE.—If the Spanish of the Caribbean Islands has the sweetness and the consistency of syrup, the Spanish spoken in Mexico is equally fluid and sweet, but much clearer. It is a Castilian with honey and a pinch of chili pepper. Whoever has heard Cantinflas probably has an idea of the speech of the Mexican of the people, with its musical intonation, its abundance of diminutives, its pyrotechnical quality, and its emphasis on certain very long vowels.

It must have been principally the Negro who sweetened the Spanish of the Caribbean Islands (and the same was done by that extraordinary race with the Portuguese of Bahia). But from the Aztec and the Maya the Mexican could expect no sweetness either of language or of character, so that it seems to have been the mestizo who gave to the Castilian spoken in Mexico that music, that plasticity and that familiar grace.

It is asserted that, if a dictionary of the real Mexican national language should be made, we should see that half of its words are of indigenous origin. The truth is, we find them at every step, giving names to places, domestic utensils, animals, fruits, plants, foods. Two-thirds of the geographic names are of indigenous origin. Happily, the tongue of the Spaniard and that of the mestizo to some extent "Christianized" many or the majority of these words, making them more pronounceable. *Cuauhnáhuac* became Cuernavaca. *Huexolotl* (turkey) turned into *guajolote*. *Chokolatl*, luckily for us, was reduced to chocolate, and *petatatl* (mat of rust or straw) to *petate*, and so on.

The idea, ventured by some, that the Spanish spoken in Mexico resembles the Andalusian does not find many adherents. What most charms me in the Mexican language is the use of diminutives, the thing a stranger least expects to find in the mouth of a people with so much capacity for violence and so little inclination to tenderness. Many a time I have stopped in the street to listen furtively to dialogues between individuals of the people.

Now let's imagine a rapid conversation between two *pelados* in a *pulquería* called *La Compañerita* (Little Companion).

"*Quieres un poco de tequila, amiguito?*"

"*Sí.*"

"*Cuánto?*"

"*Un naditita.*"

"*Un tantito así?*"

"*Eso! Gracias, hermanito.*"

"*Cuándo vuelves a tu casa?*"

"*Lueguito. Y tú?*"

"*Nochecita no más.*"[1]

When a Mexican says *ahora* (now), in reality he does not mean "at this moment," for his notion of time, I repeat, is different from the usual one. But if he says *ahorita*, or simply *orita* (right now), we may expect the promised thing to happen within an hour. If, however, compressing his lips and prolonging the *i*'s, he says *ahoritita*, the prospects of more immediate action become better.

There are phrases heard with great frequency in everyday talk. If we are relating something to someone, it is possible that the someone will exclaim: *Qué bueno!* If we ask a favour of him and he accedes to it, it is quite likely he will say: *Cómo no!* or *Pues sí.* The use of *pues* as a kind of expletive is quite general. *Dónde estás, hombre? Estoy aquí, pues.* (Where are you, man? I'm right here.)

---

[1] If the above could be adequately put into English—which is really impossible—it would convey the tone of the *-ito* diminutives, which do not always signify small size but very frequently lend an affectionate colouration to words. The inadequate meaning of the conversation is, in English: "Want a drop of tequila, old pal?" "Sure." "How much?" "Oh, just a touch." "About like that?" "Right! Thanks, buddy." "When're you going home?" "Right away. How about you?" "Not till night."

When a given person or thing displeases the Mexican, he will say: *Me cae mal*. But when he sees a beautiful woman pass by, it is probable that he will toss her a compliment, which may be one (or both) of the following: *Qué chula! Qué mona!*—meaning approximately "What a doll!" "What a cutie!"

If the person we speak to did not hear, or failed to understand, what we said, he is almost certain to say: *Mande?* with a rising inflection, meaning in English "I beg your pardon" with similar inflection.

The use of *mero* (and its feminine form *mera*) is curious in Mexico. I ask a youngster where such-and-such a building is, and he informs me: *"Muy cerquita, señor; en la mera ciudad*—Right close by, sir; just downtown (right in the main part of town)."

When two friends take leave of each other, it is quite common to hear one say: *"Bueno. Nos vemos."* And the other: *"Nos vemos, pues."* Literally they are saying, "Well, we see each other," and "We see each other, then." And no obligation is sealed and delivered unless the parties add, *"Vaya, pues."*

In sum, the Mexican strikes me as a hard man with a soft tongue. Hard? But isn't there a lot of talk about Mexican courtesy?


COURTESY.—Just as the vivid, festive colouring of the flowers, the regional costumes, the rugs, mantles and baskets we see in Mexico do not alter the essential brown of its soil, so the courtesy of the Mexican is a surface iridescence which does not succeed in disguising for long the crepuscular aspects of his character.

Up to a point that courtesy is a holdover from Spanish chivalry. It is obvious that the Creole aristocracy, which predominated during the Porfirian era, Spanish by blood and French in spirit, should have created a tradition and a code of courtesy which the mestizo ended by imitating and absorbing. That tradition and that code have remained on the surface of the life of the country in literary formulas, words, gestures and attitudes.

I have received letters from Mexico beginning: "Esteemed true friend." When a Mexican tells me he is going home, he uses the expression *su casa*, not *mi casa*, because his code of chivalric courtesy requires him to say that his house is mine. Once, on saying goodbye, a Mexican *caballero* told me, *"Póngame a los pies de su señora*—Place me at your lady's feet."

Octavio Paz has written that "if our courtesy attracts, our reserve chills." Grahame Greene, in *The Lawless Roads*, refers in a rather drastic fashion to what he calls "Mexican hypocrisy."

Studying the bourgeois of his country, Samuel Ramos comments on his not infrequently exaggerated courtesy, which at any moment may give way to an explosion of insults which reduces him to the level of a *pelado*. The same essayist remarks that one of the traits of the middle-class Mexican is his tendency to imitate in his land the forms of European civilization, in order to feel that he is the equal of the European man, forming in his communities a privileged group which considers itself superior to all the other "uncivilized" compatriots. Now naturally the first thing to stand out in the model imitated is that surface courtesy which is usually attributed to a "European upbringing."

I am inclined to think that the Mexican's courtesy is a defensive attitude, an advance guard of his reserved character, a product of his hermetic tendency—in short, a fence, gilded if you will, but hard and cold, which he erects between his person and other men to keep them at a distance. Always the trench, the barricade. Because courtesy, friends, is far from being cordiality.

Octavio Paz also said that the Mexican, be he *criollo* or mestizo, in his surly solitude is thorny and polite at the same time, and that "everything serves for his self-defence, the silence and the word, courtesy and scorn, irony and resignation."

GESTURES.—I have a special interest in these folkloric, popular, gestures. In Mexico I have observed some I have not encountered in any other of the countries I have visited up to now.

I must explain that the Mexican in general is a person who gesticulates little; as for the pure Indian, he sometimes seems no richer in gestures than a statue.

With what mimicry do we Brazilians designate money? By rubbing the index finger repeatedly against the thumb. I believe it is a nearly universal gesture. Well, money in Mexico, the peso, is designated by forming a circle with the same two fingers, in the shape of the coin.

Many times when one Brazilian invites another, from a distance, to have a *cafèzinho* or a drink, it is natural for him to stick out his thumb and index finger, forming parallel lines, and the distance between the two fingers indicates the quantity of coffee or other liquid. The Mexican uses the same gesture to give an idea of time or volume. If from a distance I shout to a friend, "Come on, man!," he may make the same gesture to mean "Wait just a little for me." And he will employ the same gesture, too, to show the amount of tequila he wants in his glass.

There is a gesture of courtesy, of gratitude, which consists in raising the open hand and giving it a quick quarter-turn, holding it in the latter position. It means "Thanks!"

In his delightful book, *Cornucopia de México*, José Moreno Villa refers to the three ways with which the Mexican indicates the height of persons, animals and things. In the first instance he folds the middle, third and little fingers, aiming the index finger resting on the thumb as though reproducing the outline of a revolver. In the second he opens his hand wide, all the fingers together, and hacks it through the air as if it were a knife or a saw. In the third case—a question of things—he uses the hand in the same way but palm down, as if he were going to lay it on a flat surface.

All these gestures perhaps have little importance and may not aid in understanding the Mexican better; I mention them because I find them curious. Possibly another, more astute than I, may be able to discover in them a hidden meaning, the key, or rather, one of the many keys, to the uncountable secret coffers of the Mexican soul.

CANTINFLAS AND THE PELADO.—Is there anyone nowadays who doesn't know Cantinflas, the great clown of the cinema and the Mexican theatre, whom many consider as great as Charlie Chaplin? Cantinflas symbolizes the *pelado*, that is, the representative of a very low social category: the marginal, the refugee of the great city, a type which, according to the definition of Samuel Ramos, is at once economically less than a proletarian and intellectually a primitive.

The great comedian's costume—trousers perilously fastened below the waist, always on the verge of falling, greasy hat with brim turned up on the sides like a *sombrero de dos picos* (a two-cornered hat) white vest crossed by an inexplicable, touching baldric of dirty cloth, his swarthy face under a thin beard—is a very good synthesis of the *pelado's* manner of dressing, for he permits himself, even in the blackest misery, a few pretentious touches and a few parodies of elegance. But it is fitting to note that Cantinflas represents principally the more amiable and humorous aspects of the *pelado,* his false pride, his desire to appear what he is not, to make himself felt, to impose himself, his capacity for simulation and, mainly, his abundant, confused language, which is like a "nigger chaser" in its uncertainty, unexpectedness, sparkle and veering about. All this is tempered by some traces of chivalry and quixotism which at times come to give the figure a pathetic air.

Cantinflas as a symbol is occasionally compelled to betray the class he represents, for not always is it possible for him to keep on thinking, speaking and acting like a *pelado* in the generally rather infelicitous stories of his films, in which the psychology of the hero has to be subordinated to the narrative, to the action. But even so *El Gran Pelado* succeeds in maintaining some admirable constants.

Studying the *pelado,* Samuel Ramos says that his explosions are principally verbal. He asserts himself in aggressiveness, in coarseness. "He has created a dialect of his own whose lexicon abounds in words of current usage but to which he gives a new meaning. He is an animal that constantly uses pantomimes of ferocity to frighten others, making them believe he is stronger and more determined."

There is a type of "literature" which has always captured my attention for its revelation of the psychology of the people producing it. I refer to the inscriptions, words, phrases, verses—often suggestively illustrated—found on walls of public lavatories. What one finds most in Mexican toilets is insult. Insults addressed to whom? To him who may read. To others. It is the mural journal of the *pelado.* In the United States this type of literature is poor, unpicturesque. In Brazil, where the spirit of such phrases and verses is more mischievous than insulting, not infrequently the allusions and satires bear the name or the initials of the person whom the "writer" wants to reach.

Samuel Ramos refers to the abundance of sexual allusions in the terminology of the *pelado.* They reveal a furious phallic obsession. For a long time I have been calling my friends' attention to an identical tendency. I have noticed in the Brazilian, especially in the *gaúcho,* the man of Rio Grande do Sul.

When a *pelado* quarrels with another, the first thing he does to assert himself as a he-man is to yell: *"Yo soy hombre, tengo muchos huevos*—I'm a man, I got lots of eggs!" One often sees, in Mexico, a man casting doubts on the masculinity of another out of spite, to get even. Samuel Ramos says that as the *pelado* is a being without substantial content, he tries to fill his vacuum with the only value within his reach: that of the male. With the *gaúcho* the explanation must not be so simple. His scale of values is richer, his social and economic position better, not to speak of his pedigree.

But it would not be fair to judge the Mexican by that riff-raff. Let us go on, then, to examine other aspects of the mestizo's character.

DISTRUST.—When I visited Mexico for the first time, I expected to find in this country a joyous, communicative and uninhibited populace. I was surprised by the coldness, the dryness and the reserve of the inhabitants of its most representative region, the central. But above all, the distrust of the people threw me off balance.

Where does it come from? Samuel Ramos thinks it is from the lack of confidence of the Mexican in himself, which leads him to an erroneous perception of reality, which in its turn is translated into distrust of everything and everybody.

In my opinion that distrust is a trait inherited from the Indian and sharpened by the Conquest and by the many deceptions, swindles, violences and humiliations the nation has suffered from the first years of its independence down to our day. How is it possible to be optimistic and trusting in a country whose rulers do not keep their promises and live by resorting to fraud, theft, political murder, violence and arbitrary authority? How trust neighbours who have snatched away the better part of our territory, and who more than once have invaded and crossed our border with military force and aggressive intent? How look with innocent eyes on the foreigners who enter our country to take over our mineral wealth with the connivance of our own government men? How trust a land in which a peaceable patch of maize may at any moment give birth to a volcanic mountain? Because the Mexican feels surrounded by perils and possibilities of violence. The national atmosphere is constantly saturated with menace. One frequently hears expressions like: *"Mira que te van a matar"*—"Look out, they are going to kill you"; or, *"Me querían matar"*—"They were trying to kill me." One gets the impression that in Mexico no one dies a natural death. In popular songs the words occurring most are "traitor," "villain," "he stabbed me in the back," "I was betrayed," "faithless friend," "ungrateful woman," etc.

And when the distrust of the Indian is combined with the susceptibility of the Spaniard, the result is more distrust and more reasons for susceptibility.


SUSCEPTIBILITY.—Count Keyserling has said that in South America there is a "primacy of susceptibility." I know no people more susceptible than the Mexican. There exists in Latin America a sort of "primadonnaism"—and Brazil is no exception—a thin-skinned sensitiveness which makes it difficult to get along with people. We have to watch our words and our gestures, walk gingerly among those sensitive points as one walks in a glassware shop.

When it was announced that I was going to write this book, a Mexican newspaper writer published in his journal an item filled with indignation which said in other words: "What right has this gentleman, who hardly knows us, to write a book on Mexico, when even we who have lived here all our lives still do not know ourselves well, have not yet said the definitive word about our people?"

What the journalist seems to ignore is that only by giving literary form to his impressions of a land and a people, only by setting his memories in order, can a writer *begin* to understand that country and that people. And also that it will not be just because I have spent little time in Mexico that I am going to refrain from telling what I thought, felt and observed there. And also that only a hopeless idiot can deem himself capable of saying the final word about a human group—or about any other subject.

That little newspaper piece is revelatory of many traits of the Mexican character which I have been stressing in this chapter. It is a product of sensitiveness and distrust, as well as of the fear of seeing his land and his people *once more maltreated by a foreigner.* It has not even passed through the journalist's head that I might have liked and—through a miracle of the Virgin of Guadalupe—even understood Mexico.

PATRIOTISM.—The Mexican is a man of exacerbated patriotism.

I have read in Octavio Paz (and other friends have called my attention to this orally) that on national holidays it is common to hear the Mexican shout: *"Viva México, hijos de la chingada!*—Hurrah for Mexico, you sons of. . . !" But who are these "sons of *la chingada"*? They are imaginary enemies, anyone of any race who may be saying or even thinking "Down with Mexico!"

The journalistic piece I alluded to in the preceding section is equivalent to a *Viva México, hijo de la chingada* hurled in my direction.

Alvaro Moreyra is wont to say that Brazil is the only place in the world where "mother" is an ugly word. But who is that Mexican *chingada* to whom the man in the street attributes the maternity of all his enemies? It is not a question of a mother of flesh and blood—Paz explains—but of a mythical figure. I should say she is the same eternal mother of illegitimate sons in our Brazilian folklore. *Chingar* is a verb difficult to define. *Chingar* can be "defecate." It also means "to fail, abort, frustrate, botch," etc. One says *"empresa chingada"* for an undertaking that has "gone haywire, been frustrated, failed." A rocket that has failed to go off, a firecracker that has not exploded, is a *cohete chingado,* and so on. *Chingar* is also to fornicate, the first meaning which, by analogy, occurred to me when I heard the expression *hijos de la chingada.* The *chingada,* then, is still another important figure in the Mexican mythology, like the *gringo* and the *gachupín.*

Once a Brazilian in Mexico City went to visit Aurélio Buarque de Holanda and parked his locked car (for he had left a piano accordion inside it) at the writer's door. He stayed a little over ten minutes on his visit, and when he came out he had the unpleasant surprise of seeing his car had been broken open and the accordion stolen. Days later, telling the story to a Mexican, he was amazed at the latter's reaction: the Mexican exclaimed, his face lighting up: "In ten minutes? Ah, Mexican thieves are the best in the world!" My Brazilian friend assures me the man was talking seriously, without the slightest humorous intention.

Another time—the same compatriot told me—when he referred to the central plateau of Brazil, his Mexican interlocutor retorted: "Don't come telling me tales. Everybody knows Mexico is the only country in the world with a central plateau."

In the intellectual sphere the patriotism of the Mexican is revealed in a tremendous "will to power," in an insistence on "winning them all." During the three years I have worked in an inter-American organization I have had the opportunity to verify the fact that the representatives of Mexico were always the bravest fighters, the most fanatic polemicists, and the hardest losers. (I must make it clear that I am far from considering all these traits as *defects.*) There is always in them the desire to take or bring to their country the greatest possible number of international institutions, and, once that objective is attained, the slow but implacable process of Mexicanization of those organizations commences.

I was present at a dialogue which marvellously illustrates Mexican patriotism and its aggressive attitude toward the United States. The scene took place in Washington, at the headquarters of the Organization of American States, at a luncheon where an American librarian was expressing to an illustrious representative of Mexico his anxiety about the fate of the public library of the Federal District, the books of which had just been transferred from the old building in the centre of the city to the library of the new University City which, because of its distance, was beyond the reach of the public.

"What can we do here," the American asked, with his missionary air, "to remedy the situation?"

The Mexican pulled on his pipe, emitted a puff of smoke and said: "Nothing. Don't worry. What use are all the huge libraries in the United States if this country has no art of its own? But look at Mexico. Men like Orozco, Rivera and Siqueiros never went to universities and yet they are among the greatest painters in the world."

The American smiled patiently. I lowered my head to the plate of salad. The Mexican continued his attack for some minutes, getting farther and farther away from the subject that had brought us together.


FIESTAS.—The Mexican is a being whose solitude continues even when he is in the middle of a crowd, at a fiesta or in any other public gathering. The calendar of this country is full of holidays and saints' days. There is nothing noisier, more violent and startling than a Mexican fiesta. If it is a religious one, the Mexican prays, lights candles, goes out in processions with his saints, gives himself up to traditional celebrations—some of which have almost the quality of a dance or an auto-da-fé. And he eats, drinks, gets drunk, invokes the Virgin of Guadalupe, yells, whistles, fires shots, fights and not infrequently kills or dies. But he does all that joylessly. What at times gives the impression of gaiety is fury. What seems joy is violence. I have observed a curious predilection of the Mexican of the people for fireworks, mainly for the rocket and the nigger chaser. Both of them have two predicates which the Mexican admires from the bottom of his soul: they are both explosive, sparkling and colourful. *En la fiesta nos disparamos,* says Octavio Paz.[1] In their fiestas the Mexicans discharge pistols and their emotions, they throw bombs, hurl hats into the air. At bottom, a fiesta resembles a revolution. It is an escape valve for their suppressed violence. One who observes it from afar—the fireworks, the coloured balloons, the multitude singing, shouting, dancing, amid the explosion of the rockets—has an impression of gaiety. But let us not be deluded. If the forest is gay, the trees are sad.

Someone told me that once, in a stadium where a football game was being played, some individuals on the highest rows of seats in the cheap section amused themselves by setting fire to strips of cloth soaked in gasoline and tossing them down on the people below.

It is not surprising, then, that one of the favourite pastimes of the Mexican is the *corrida de toros,* the bullfight.


BULLFIGHTS.—Just as I did not go to Xochimilco, I did not see a bullfight, another commonplace in the life of Mexico. The fact is, our visit did not coincide with the season. Now to my mind comes the description D. H. Lawrence makes of a bullfight in his novel *The Plumed Serpent.* It is the moment when a bull charges down on the *picador's* horse and with his horns rips the animal's belly. Horse and rider go down. The *picador* succeeds in extricating himself and runs to find refuge. The old horse, dazed, struggles to get up, with precisely the stupid look of a person failing to comprehend what is happening, and the bull, which the *picador* had wounded, stands glaring about him in the same attitude of hopeless

[1]Being a poet's statement, this connotes as much as denotes: "We hurl ourselves into the fiesta (with the violence of a projectile, heedless of consequences)."

stupor. But his wound hurts and is bleeding, and, seeing the horse getting up, the bull, smelling blood and intestines, again charges blindly and once more thrusts his horns into the other animal's belly, from which the bloody intestines are dragging in the dust of the arena.

Blood and intestines—what an admirable sight! The crowd roars. Then comes the matador, moments of glory and emotion follow, the passes with the cape, the placing of the *banderillas,* and then the final sacrifice of the bull.

It has already been asserted that the Mexican has no spirit of community, of solidarity, and that these two sentiments are revealed only in religious acts and in the bullfights. The spectacle of the supernatural or the presence of violence (in both, of course, the idea of Death is latent) draws them together and unites them. They lift their voices in chorus in prayers addressed to God or to the Brown Virgin. And those same voices, in another tone, mount in the luminous air of the bull-ring to applaud, urge on or vituperate the bullfighters and to incite the bulls.

The psychoanalysis of the bullfighter and of bullfighting has frequently been done. The bull symbolizes the masculine element, strong, aggressive—and I need not say what the horns represent. The bullfighter, in his effeminate costume, represents the feminine element. It is the bullfighter who dances in front of the bull, inciting him with colourful gestures and dress. Faithful still to the feminine psychology (at least to the psychology accepted by the Mexican folklore) he swerves aside when the bull charges, denies him his body and, as if that were not enough, wounds the animal with the *banderillas* and, at the end of the tragicomic dance, kills the bull. But the great, the rare moment is when the male, the bull, gains possession of the female, tearing her flesh, producing blood. It is the great, the final moment of consummation.

I have the impression that in the arena the Mexican never solves his ambivalence. He is now for the bullfighter—for courage fascinates him—now for the bull, since brute force and violence hypnotize him. And before that show of blood and sun he never remains neutral. If the bullfighter is brave and skilful, he applauds him. But if the bull shows himself sullen or fearful, he hisses him, enveloping the bullfighter also in his fulminations.

Can there be a spectacle in the world more apt for the mestizo than the bullfight? His love of them must have come to him on the current of Spanish blood. Fascination for the bloody spectacle of death and sacrifice is an inheritance from his Indian ancestors.

But the truth is that for one who has never attended a *corrida de toros,* I am dwelling too much on the subject.


TIME.—It was Vianna Moog who first called my attention to the "intemporality" of the Mexican. In the mind of this singular people yesterday, today and tomorrow seem to intermingle in an absence of perspective that rather reminds one of a similar lack in Aztec drawings.

They hate Cortés and venerate Juárez with such intensity and *actuality in present time* that one gets the impression those two historic figures are not only contemporary with each other but continue to live. It is as if the Mexican did not know the difference between *since* and *until,* between *from* and *as far as.* It is not surprising, then, that a *pulquería* exists in this country under the name of "Memories of the Future."

This strange concept of time is owed to the Indian. Lévy-Bruhl says in his book *La Mentalité Primitive:* "The concept of time (and also of space) that we deem innate in the human mind, almost does not exist in the primitive mentality, which sees the immediate causal nexus between the given phenomenon and the extra-spatial occult force. To them the visible world and the invisible form only one single world, and the supernatural becomes the natural."

To the American, who loves simplifying formulas, no word better defines the psychology of the man of the Mexican people than *Mañana.* Yes, everything is left until tomorrow. Why do today what can be done tomorrow or later? It is an eternal transferring— a mixture of laziness, fatalism and it's-not-worth-whilism. And the classic expression *Quién sabe?*—in which there is not even an interrogative inflection, which would be a sign of interest—is nothing but a procrastination, also, not only in time but in space. I recognize all the perils of making categorical statements when we are studying the character of a people. Of course not all Mexicans live under the sign of *mañana.* There are many who go as fast as their Anglo-Saxon neighbours. On the other hand, who can say that the idea of time of an inhabitant of the Ozark Mountains or a hill-billy from Oklahoma or Alabama is identical to that of a business man from New York or Chicago? There is, then, a "Mexican time" also in certain regions of the United States.

But it can be said in a general way that in the latter country the Western concept of time predominates, and in Mexico—as, for that matter, in nearly all Latin America—the Oriental.

"Time is money!" exclaims the Yankee. The Latin American shrugs his shoulders and replies that he won't make the day break any sooner by getting up early.

STOICISM.—It is not surprising that one of the virtues most esteemed by the Mexican is stoicism, both in war and in peace, in public life as in private. The national heroes are figures like Cuauhtémoc, who even under torture did not confess where the treasures of the Aztec empire were hidden. Heroic is Zapata, who died like a man for his agrarian ideals. And Juárez, the imperturbable.

And what then of Jesus Christ? The man who suffered on the cross without complaining could not fail to move the Mexican soul.

An anecdote is going around Mexico—although I cannot swear it originated there—which is indeed a humorous exaltation of stoicism.

An army captain goes out walking over a battlefield a few minutes after the battle is over and the enemy completely decimated. Walking among corpses in the most horrifying postures, he comes to the spot where one of his soldiers is still alive, with his chest spitted on a bayonet. The captain squats beside him and asks, pointing to the bayonet: "Does it hurt very much?" To which the soldier responds with cavernous voice, blood running from his mouth: "No, captain. Only when I laugh."

HUMOUR.—*Chistes*, jests, of every kind circulate in Mexico, but there are two types that predominate. The anecdote about sex (as is true all over Latin America in greater or lesser degree) and the sort based on macabre motifs.

Of the first I shall give an example. Two *peladitos* are chatting on a corner in Mexico City. Says one:

"Want me to explain the difference between plutocracy and democracy?"

"*Bueno, hombre, explica pues.*"

"Imagine us two talking here and a bourgeois passes by in his Cadillac, he spatters mud in our faces and goes on without looking at us. That's plutocracy."

"*Bueno.* And what's democracy?"

"Imagine this: The bourgeois orders the driver to stop the Cadillac, invites me in, shakes my hand, gives me an *abrazo*[1], kisses me on the cheek, takes me home with him, serves me champagne, gives me the finest meal, presents me with clothes and jewels and, finally, winds up inviting me to live with him."

The other frowns and inquires:

"Has that ever happened to you, pal?"

"To me, no. But to a sister of mine it did."

The anecdotes of macabre flavour are legion. There is one whose mechanism is repeated, clothed in the most diverse garments.

A man meets an acquaintance and asks him:

"You like flowers?"

"I certainly do!"

The first pulls out a pistol, puts a bullet in the second, and remarks:

"Tomorrow you'll get some!"

Or:

"What's your name?"

"Carlos."

Bang!

"That *was* your name."

It may seem strange that death is a motive of humour to the Mexican, but the truth is that, just as the time of that strange people is not our time, their death is not our death, or, if it is, it shows different faces from ours. The poet says,

"La muerta toma siempre la forma de la alcoba
que la contiene."
(Death always takes on the shape of the bedroom
that contains it.)

---

[1] An *abrazo* is an embrace. Between men the ordinary, friendly *abrazo* consists in each man's putting his right arm under the other's left, his left over the other's right shoulder, and patting the other's back. If greater emotion is appropriate to the meeting, after this procedure the two reverse right and left to repeat the *abrazo*; and on ceremonial occasions, of course, a kiss on each cheek may be added. It seems superfluous to attempt description of an *abrazo* between man and woman.

DEATH.—In Mexico death is a sort of concubine, a companion that every man carries with him everywhere and at all times. The Mexican displays his death as an adornment, a jewel. Jorge Carrión writes that death is the only consecration possible. "Only in its expressive silence does the essence of the civil or military hero rise transcendent, as only in the amorphous, stratified substance of myth and popular legend does the historical consciousness of the Mexican take shape." That is why Santa Anna, shrewdly knowledgeable about his people, buried the leg he lost in battle at Vera Cruz with full military honours. "This is equivalent to dying a little and to attaining while still alive something of the immortal substance of heroicity."

"Our death illumines our life," Octavio Paz has said. It is not just a phrase: it is a truth. And the word "illumines" is well taken.

In our world the awareness of death generally casts a shadow over our lives. In the Mexican world it is different. The idea of dying has something luminous about it, and sometimes something humorous. Because to these people death is also a toy, a plaything.

Where does this queer attitude toward death come from? Not from the Spaniard, because he, though he may carry on some flirtations with the Fates, does not look on death without fear and never fails to regard it as a sort of annihilation, despite his Catholicism.

I think the Mexican owes this tendency to the Indian component of his character. For the pre-Cortésian Indian what lay beyond the tomb did not promise torment or castigation. The Aztecs accepted the idea of immortality. For them the vital force continued after death. Was not Nature's own procedure a token of that? Did not the seasons succeed each other? The Sun—symbol of strength and life—did not the Sun, which disappeared swallowed up by the night, appear again the following morning? And that is not all. Quetzalcoatl, the god destroyed by fire—did he not re-emerge transformed into the planet Venus, precursor of the Sun, herald of a new day.

Death, therefore, did not mean destruction, but transformation; it was one phase of an infinite cycle. Death, therefore, is not eternal but ephemeral. It is a perennial rejuvenation of life. That explains the joyousness with which the handsome youths sacrificed to Tezcatlipoca, God of Eternal Youth, marched to their death. The Mayas called new-born infants "prisoners of life."

The poet Xavier Villaurrutia has written: "Here in Mexico there is a great facility in dying which is the stronger in its allure the more Indian blood we have in our veins. The more Creole one is, the greater his fear of death, seeing that is what they teach us."

If death is the greatest source of man's anguish, and if the Mexican does not view it with horror, whence comes the drama with which the life of this people is saturated? I should say, from the very anguish of living, from the fatality of life. There is one variety of death the mestizo fears: social death, the horror of not triumphing, of not climbing, of being left in low estate, ignored and nameless.

If an ordinary Christian fears the demons of Hell, what the Mexican fears are the demonic forces of this world full of magical influences, most of them maleficent. Death—he seems to say—is certain; the uncertain is life. In one of the chapters of this book I mention a song that says *"La vida no vale nada."*[1] Another phrase often encountered is: *"Qué me importa la muerte si no me importa la vida?"* —"What does death matter to me if life doesn't matter?"

According to the indigenous legend of the Suns, or epochs, the first men were created from the bones of the dead. The sexual act, procreation, is represented in Aztec codices by a scene in which the man is seated facing the woman, clasping her hands, each holding in his mouth an obsidian knife like the one used by priests to tear out the victims' hearts in sacrificial ceremonies. As Paul Westheim keenly observes, the *tecpatl,* the flint knife, symbolizes the blade-edge, the cutting, and thus is a symbol of death at the same time that obsidian is the stone which produces the spark, the life-giving fecund flame. Thus we have yet another evidence that the Indians associated the idea of procreation with that of death. In one of his historical works the Indian Ixtlilxochitl describes the nuptial ceremony of an Indian prince, in which the priest, standing before the altar on the temple pyramid, covered the newlyweds with very fine blankets on which death was painted.

Here a question is pertinent. What transformation has this concept of immortality, held by the Mexican Indian, undergone in these four hundred years of Catholic influence? I believe it has not

[1]The statement is susceptible of variously shaded interpretations: "Life is of no account," "Life is worth nothing," "Life is of no avail," "Life is (in itself) no good," etc. Much depends on the context.

been very easy for the aborigine to exchange his vertical and horizontal heavens for the single Heaven of the Christians and its entrepôt, Purgatory. As for Hell, the idea of eternal punishment can only have contributed to making the poor Indian wretched. On the other hand, I can see many points of contact between the magical thinking of the Indian with reference to the "beyond," and the Catholic ideas of resurrection of the body, of the transitoriness of earthly life, and of the conviction that this world is a vale of tears.

There is an Aztec poem which expresses the transience of life on earth:

"We have only seen sleeping,
We have only seen dreaming;
It is not true, it is not true
That we have seen living on earth."


THE DAY OF THE DEAD.—After all that has been said, wouldn't it be interesting to see how the Mexicans commemorate the Day of the Dead?

Paul Westheim, in his valuable book *The Skull,* says that on the second of November "a certain carnival freedom" reigns. On the eve of it the women prepare the *pan de muerto,* a kind of bread decorated with a skull of sugar and the name of a person beneath it. Indeed, the skull is a very popular decorative motif in Mexico. The figures in the majority of the political or social (or merely humorous) sketches by Guadalupe Posada, as well as those by others like Manuel Manilla and Santiago Hernández, were skeletons. In the section where I have offered some aspects of the pre-Cortésian world I mentioned the skull as one of the themes of Aztec sculpture.

*Flores de muerto,* flowers for the occasion, are also prepared, with tissue paper garlands and images of saints. The house is decorated with flowers, principally *cempazúchiles,* which from the time of the Aztecs have been regarded as the *flores de muerto* par excellence. In the principal room of the house an altar is improvised, at the foot of which offerings for the deceased person or persons of the family are laid (much as their Indian ancestors did at the tombs of their dead): a series of tidbits in which predominate the dishes preferred by the deceased while living. The infants of the house wander about eating death's heads and skeletons of chocolate and sugar, some of them decorated with papers of vivid colours or glittering spangles —everything, naturally, in proportion to the imagination and the economic resources of each family.

On the morning of the first of November pamphlets commence appearing with *calaveras*, death's-heads, generally containing political satires and criticisms, with legends in prose or verse.

On the Day of the Dead begins the pilgrimage to the cemeteries. The graves are bedecked with flowers. Candles are lighted around them and by night the cemetery gives the impression of being covered by a legion of will-o'-the-wisps. Family groups begin their night's vigil, eating and exchanging recollections of the deceased. The jug of pulque or tequila commences its rounds. It is possible that someone may sing a muted song in native tongue. It is almost certain that long silences will fall.

In Tonantzintla, in the Valley of Cholula, and in other towns like that in which old customs are still observed, the Indians usually strew the path from the tomb of the dead to the door of his house with carnations or leaves "so that the deceased won't get lost." On the island of Janitzio in Lake Pátzcuaro (the description is from Carlos González, quoted by Paul Westheim), at six o'clock in the afternoon on the eve of the Day of the Dead the tolling for the dead begins, and with half-minute intervals the bell continues tolling until daybreak. Shortly before midnight the families leave their houses for the cemetery, the women wearing their Sunday clothes and their gaudiest necklaces. All the people carry burning candles to light the way. And so the strange procession moves toward the city of the dead, where each group turns to the graves of the family dead, covering them with flowers and candles. At midnight the women kneel down and the men begin to intone funereal eulogies of the dead, while the bell continues its tolling. At intervals the women pluck off the petals of *cempazúchiles* over the tombs, afterwards lapsing into their mournful, contemplative silence. And thus the hours pass, the candles burn down, amid sighs and moans of grief or sad songs in a language the whites cannot understand even though they may hear and sense them.

Near the cemetery, in the atrium of the parish church, a Mass is celebrated in honour of the dead, attended by the families that have no dead or whose relatives have been buried for more than three years. They confine themselves to lighting candles on a much-bedecked arch erected in front of the church, where they deposit their trays with offerings.

What is the explanation of this ceremony? It has roots in the indigenous belief that for three years something of the deceased remains in the sepulchre, and that is why offerings are carried to the tomb. But when, after three years, the spirit of the dead person ceases to have a personality of its own, it merges—curious similarity to the monistic theory—into the Great All, into a single immense spirit to which that arch is erected.

It is interesting to note that this pre-Cortésian concept—one feature of which is that the dead man must make a long hard journey, undergoing various tests, before attaining his definite dwelling, Mictlan—existed parallel to and harmoniously with the Catholic doctrines and ceremonies.


RELIGION.—During the Conquest, and even after it, while the soldiers of Cortés were bent on the liquidation of the Aztec Empire —decimating its tribes, demolishing its temples, destroying the images of its gods—the Franciscan friars were beginning the difficult work of the catechization of the people. Only a fanatic Indianism or a pure literary diabolism could induce a man of our time to assert that the Christianization of the natives was an error, or that the Indian has lost in the exchange of his barbarous gods for the God of the Christians. And only a blind anticlericalism could lead us to say that the Church's influence was merely injurious in the times of the Colony. I neither can nor want to forget that there were priests who individually committed grave wrongs, and that the Church itself was guilty of political and social errors in more than one instance during the colonial era and in the years which followed the Independence of Mexico. In the first decades of the Conquest several Indians were burned alive for sins of idolatry. In Yucatan, Bishop Landa tortured some Mayas and a chief was executed in Texcoco for having bowed before gods of stone. But it is only just to recognize that many a time the Franciscan friars and their convents and churches were the only refuge the Indian could find to flee the fury of the Conquistador. More than one prelate excommunicated functionaries of the Crown and encomenderos who refused to treat the Indians as humans. In the early years of the Spanish domination it can be said that the priests were the only advocates the Indians could count on. And thanks to religion, as

Octavio Paz well remarks, the colonial order "was not a mere super-imposing of new historical forms but a living organism." The Church, in fine, was the centre of the life of the Colony.

Catholicism, in a way, filled the void in the indigenous soul which the death of the gods and the chieftains had reduced to a deplorable state of orphanage. A primitive people dominated by magic thinking, the Indians of Mexico found even in the Catholic Church the atmosphere of magic and the supernatural to which they were accustomed, and without which it would have been harder for them to live. The Catholic faith gave them a new mother in the person of the Virgin Mary. To that people accustomed to bloody sacrifices to the gods, the friars must have explained that Christ had sacrificed himself *once and for all* to save all humanity. And I hope it is no mere literary image to say that the habit of ritual anthropophagy has found some satisfaction in the sacrament of Communion, in which converted Indians were given the Body of Christ to eat. For many of them Jesus must have seemed a new incarnation of Quetzalcoatl, symbol of love and wisdom, the god who sacrificed himself for his people to rise again thereafter and go to heaven. And there was, further, the fascination of the Catholic ritual, the gold of the altars, the chants, the smoke and smell of incense, confession, the processions, fasting, penance, the tolling of bells. And the gold monstrance: did it not correspond in the popular mind to the image of Tonatiuh, the God of the Sun who appears in the centre of the Calendar Stone?

But that exchange of religion must have been neither rapid nor easy for the natives. It is natural that in the early colonial times the Indian should be a withdrawn, mournful, frightened being. Catholicism offered him mainly masculine symbols like the Holy Trinity which must have corresponded in the Indian's subconscious to the feared or hated image of the Spaniard, the Conquistador, incarnation of violence and arbitrary authority. What the native, with his childish soul, wanted were feminine symbols. It is understandable, then, that the aborigine should have turned to the Virgin Mary, who, as F. S. C. Northrop has very well observed, represents what Plato called the feminine *eros* (the emotional, passionate, metaphysical principle which exists in the nature of things), in contraposition to the masculine *logos* (the rational, doctrinary principle, formalized explicitly in orthodox Catholicism by Saint Thomas Aquinas). That may explain the prestige of the Mother of God among the native population, which in the early times of the Conquest took refuge in Her miraculous lap.

In spite of all, she was still a white, *foreign* saint, brought by the Conquistadores, a goddess, in short, with no roots in the Mexican soil. Between Our Lady and the Indians no racial link existed. Just as the mestizo was later to be a link between the *criollo* and the Indian, the latter needed an intermediary partly or entirely of their own race to establish contact between them and the One God of the religion offered to them by the Franciscan friars.

The mediator appeared. She emerged from the place where she ought to have emerged: the land.


THE DARK VIRGIN.—Between the 9th and 12th of December in the year 1531, to the Indian Juan Diego, on the hill of Pepeyac, a vision appeared and told him: "I am the Virgin Mary, Mother of the true God." And she ordered the Indian to tell the Bishop of Mexico, Fray Juan de Zumárraga, to build her a temple on the site of the apparition. Now, the bishop received the message with scepticism and asked the Indian to give him proof, a token that what he said was true. Advised by the Saint, Juan Diego cut roses and other flowers on the hill and took them to the prelate. And when in his presence the Indian unrolled the cape in which he was carrying them, on the cloth was painted, in an oval, the image of the Saint venerated today in Mexico as Our Lady of Guadalupe.

I believe this was the most important event in the religious history of the country. There came a time, even, when the Virgin was actually identified with the very image of the fatherland. It was the democratic ideas of Voltaire and Rousseau that in some degree inspired the movement for independence in Mexico, but it was the image of Our Lady of Guadalupe which served as banner for the revolutionaries, urging them on to victory. Later, the agrarians of Zapata were to fight in the name of this same Mexican saint. Today her painted or sculptured image is seen everywhere in Mexico, in private homes and in public buildings, in *pulquerías* and in *tiendas*; and there is not an omnibus in which there is not to be seen, over the driver's head, a lithograph of the *Virgen Morena,* often with this inscription: *"Nuestra Señora de Guadalupe, Reina de México, Emperatriz de América"*—"Our Lady of Guadalupe, Queen of Mexico, Empress of America."

According to not only the testimony of Juan Diego but also that of the image miraculously depicted on the cloak, Our Lady of Guadalupe was dark, a detail which made her immediately appealing to the Indians' hearts. The apparition took place exactly on the spot where formerly the Aztec temple of Tonantzin (also a virgin and known as the "Little Mother"), the Goddess of the Earth and of Maize, had existed. The destruction of that temple caused tremendous turmoil and sorrow in the inhabitants of Tenochtitlán.

At all events, the Indians now had a Mexican Mother of God in whom they could confide and in whose shadow they sought refuge in moments of peril or misfortune.

The popularity won by the Virgin of Guadalupe from the very first, her universal acceptance among the Indian elements of Mexico, created problems for the Church. In the beginning there was even a certain rivalry between this Indian saint and the *Madona de los Remedios,* the patroness of the Spaniards.

And the best of it (or the worst—this depends on the observer's point of view) is that the Indians accepted the idea of the mediate divinity of their Virgin, divine, that is, in her own right without needing the intermediary of her Son. I have never encountered any image of the *Virgen Morena* with the Child Jesus in her arms. She appears alone in the niche of the basilica which was erected to her in Mexico City, a short distance from the place where, according to tradition, she appeared for the first time. Of course the priests will declare—as they could not fail to do—that the virtue of the Dark Virgin is mediate through Christ. This point, nevertheless, is not discussed, and, as far as I know, there has never been a serious attempt to explain the problem to the Mexicans.

I visited the basilica of Guadalupe one fine sunny day and stood perplexed on seeing the faithful, mostly women, crawl the whole distance from the gate of the atrium to the Virgin's altar, inside the temple, dragging themselves on their knees over the rough stones. There is one wing of the basilica the walls of which are completely covered with ex-votos containing thanks to the Queen of Mexico for graces obtained. And the Mexicans most learned in religious matters inform us that the temple is not a cathedral, but a basilica, the third-ranking in all Catholic Christendom. A guide, taking me aside with a conspiratorial air, told me, "I assure you, *señor,* the Basilica of Guadalupe is more important than the very Cathedral in the *zócalo.*"

CHURCH AND STATE.—How to explain the Catholic Church's having suffered so many persecutions and restrictions in a land of people so profoundly religious as Mexico? Well, the subject requires a whole book, and I have only a few lines at my disposal here.

In colonial times the Church was identified to such an extent with the Spanish crown, thanks to the royal patronage, that it would be impossible for the Mexican to revolt against the latter without incurring the hostility of the former. During the three hundred years of the Colony's duration, the Church grew so rich that it became the greatest proprietor of latifundia in a country whose starving peasants were continually clamouring for a bit of land to cultivate. It was natural that this wealth, plus the privileges and immunities enjoyed, should make the Mexican Catholic Church a natural target for the patriots who suffered under the Spanish yoke, and who, under the influence of the ideas of the Encyclopedists, wanted to create a free and liberal nation.

Obviously, the Indian, the mestizo, the man of the rural districts had no idea of the existence of a universal church, with a Pope in Rome and a millenary tradition on both the spiritual and the temporal planes. For them there was just the church of their *pueblo,* with the priest and, mainly, the saints of their devotion, which in some cases were almost like members of their own families. Priests never have existed in Mexico in sufficient quantity to attend to all the parishes. It can even be asserted that there have always been more chapels and churches in the country than priests.

When the struggle for Independence was set afoot, the Mexican clergy divided. The high dignitaries, the monsignores, bishops, archbishops, in their majority Spaniards by birth, took the side of Spain. The poor priests, almost all Mexicans and in many cases with their touch of Indian blood, the village priests who lived in intimate contact with the miserable masses—these took the side of the insurgents. It is well not to forget that two of the great heroes of that insurrection—Hidalgo and Morelos—were Catholic priests.

The war over and the representative of Spain expelled, the friction between the Church and the new State began, as a natural consequence of the position taken by the former in the struggle.

Did the Indian and mestizo peasants turn, then, against the Mother Church? No. They continued mute and aloof from the religious contention. Those who were hostile to the clergy were city folk, the literate, the learned, the liberals. Their objective was to snatch from the Church the privileges which royal patronage had given it in the colonial period and thanks to which the clergy had an absolute control over education and the greatest facilities for augmenting the material wealth of the religious communities. It was said that half the Mexican land belonged to those confraternities, and that, besides practising usury, the Church held mortgages on lands it did not own. Furthermore, for the greater guarantee of all these liberties and advantages, the Church was beyond the jurisdiction of the courts. It was not surprising, then, that it had such great political power in Mexico, often constituting a serious obstacle to the administration.

In 1833 the Mexican government secularized education, suppressed the University for being under the domination of the clergy, and also declared that the payment of the tithe to the Church was not a civil obligation.

In the colloquies with José Vasconcelos we have had the opportunity to hear from the lips of that illustrious man of letters the dramatic enumeration of the restrictions imposed upon the Mexican Catholic Church and the persecutions which priests and the faithful endured in various periods of the history of the country.

In 1910 the Church declared against the Agrarian Revolution, remaining on the side of the conservatives and the foreign companies that had interests in Mexico. Mexican Catholicism was once more divided. The Catholic *peón* who went to Mass and who lived under the protection of Our Lady of Guadalupe, whose image served him as a war flag, rose in revolt. But the high clergy remained faithful to the dictator Porfirio Díaz, who, during his government, had restored to the Church some of the great freedoms and advantages lost to it. The gravest thing, however, was that Mexican opinion once again identified the Catholic Church with the foreign interests in the country: first it had been the Spaniards, and now it was the English and the Americans. Later that same clergy favoured General Huerta and refused to obey the Constitution of 1917.

On taking office in 1926, Plutarco Elías Calles revived the anticlerical campaign, rigorously enforcing the Constitution of 1917 and carrying the struggle to reprehensible excesses by virtue of his atrabilious temperament and his personal hatreds, as we have seen through Vasconcelos's depositions. About that time the relations between the United States and Mexico reached a point of great tension over the agrarian and mining legislation. Once more the

Church gave the impression of applauding foreign intervention in Mexico. The religious wars which followed, with the bloody episode of the *cristeros* and other manifestations of violence, are a consequence of all these politico-economic facts combined with the Mexican temper, which knows no half measures, and with the interests and idiosyncrasies of the political leaders of the states.

We have already seen, too, how the personal influence of a moderate, kindly man like Lázaro Cárdenas succeeded in putting a stop to the campaign against the Church, without the necessity of altering the federal law for the purpose. It can be said that today there are no more religious persecutions in Mexico, where the Church maintains its temples, colleges and hospitals, and where its priests exercise their functions freely in the whole national territory.

To me it seems that the moral health of the Mexican Catholic Church can only have benefited from the loss of its privileges and immunities, principally its latifundia and its right to collect the tithe and to practise usury.


DIALOGUE.—In the book I wrote about my second visit to the United States I invented a personage who was to the author what Dr. Watson was to Sherlock Holmes. Tobias—that was his name—is the providential interlocutor, who may be alternately innocent and malicious, lucid and stupid, all depending on the convenience of his creator and the course of the dialogue.

Let's call up the excellent Tobias and talk with him about Mexico. Let's suppose the dialogue is held within four walls in the strictest intimacy, which will leave both participants completely at ease to give voice to all the absurdities that may come to their minds.

Here is our Tobias, this time with a *charro* hat on his head and a tricolour *sarape* over his shoulder. It is he who begins the chat.

"If you had to do the psychoanalysis of the Mexican people, how would you explain that anguished sensation of insecurity and disquiet in which it seems to live?"

"Tobias, you know I'm a layman."

"If the analyst invades the field of fiction so frequently, why shouldn't the novelist have the right to do the same in the province of psychoanalysis?"

"Even in that case, old friend, I'm afraid I'd lose myself in labyrinths."

"Come on, take courage. Lose that fear of the labyrinths."

"Very well. A birth trauma, which deeply marked the collective subconscious of this country, must be responsible for the anguish neurosis dominating the Mexican people."

"What are the symptoms of that anguish?"

"An afflictive sensation that something evil, something terrible is always about to happen. The birth of the Mexican nation was difficult, dilacerating, bloody, painful."

"And how has the newborn child behaved?"

"The Indian who survived the Conquest has not adapted to the cold, hostile environment created by the invader: he has desired to return to the maternal womb, that is, the earth."

"And the mestizo?"

"He, perhaps even more unhappy, has hesitated between the desire to return to the maternal womb and that of reconciling himself to his own birth."

"But time has passed. The nation has grown up."

"I have the impression that even today the Indian seeks to disappear, lose himself in the countryside. What is the classic posture of the Mexican?"

"*El hombre acurrucado*—the squatting, crouching man."

"That's it. The squatting man. His bust bent forward, hands clasped across his chest, knees against his hands, head against his knees. In sum, almost the foetal position. He spends long hours in that position, sleeping, thinking, dozing, trying to warm himself in his own heat or in the heat of the sun or of the earth."

"And what has happened in the mestizo's case?"

"He has struggled in an ambivalence, undecided between the desire to return to the womb and that of reconciling himself with having been born. Everything indicates that, the second tendency having prevailed, he has sought to assert himself, which he did in a violent way, in accord with his nature and conditioned by the other national traumas."

"Are you referring to the foreign invasions?"

"Exactly. While still in her adolescence as a nation Mexico suffered the trauma of the American invasion. She was also the victim of a castration: the loss to the United States of the greater part of her territory. Because of these humiliations and diminutions, to date the Mexican has been trying to assert himself in an exacerbated 'Mexicanity' which at times actually becomes xenophobia, in

an aggressive assertion of masculinity and in an indiscriminate distrust which includes both foreigners and his own compatriots. And
the proximity of a strong, white, and to a degree racist nation has
contributed not at all to relieving him of that anguish neurosis."

"And how do you explain the Mexican's hatred of the Spaniard?"

"Oedipus complex. The Mexican, after the Conquest, hated the
stepfather (and in the case of the mestizo, the legitimate father) in
the figure of the Spaniard who violated his mother, the Mexican
earth. Jorge Carrión has written that the Conquest took on a clearly
erotic character. It is the impression I have. It was an act of lecher-
ousness. The attitude of the Spaniard toward the Mexican earth
was that of a lusting male before a young and beautiful female.
And few rapes in the history of the world have caused so much
pain and so much blood. After that act of violence the Mexican
came to see in the Conquistador a symbol of the law, of arbitrary
authority, of all that restricts and causes discomfort and pain. There
came a moment when this Mother Earth was incorporated in Our
Lady of Guadalupe. And so that the maternal symbol might be
more perfect, the image of the Dark Virgin, in whose bosom the
Mexican psychologically seeks refuge, always appears against a background which reminds one of the ovular germ."

"But hasn't the Mexican probably overcome that complex?"

"Up to a point. I'm told that on the occasion of the date of the
national Independence there are Mexicans who get drunk and go
out looking for *gachupines*—Spaniards—to beat. It is a species of
annual and symbolic castigation of the father."

"I don't believe that hatred is still very strong today."

"A time came when that dislike was transferred to the *gringo*."

"Who in this case would represent . . . what?"

"Not the father, but the neighbour who breaks down the door of
the home to violate the mother, and who doesn't hesitate to sacrifice
the young children who oppose his aggression: the cadets of Chapultepec. But obviously we long ago left the mysterious province of
psychoanalysis to enter the limitless realm of fiction."


MEXICO AND THE UNITED STATES.—Once more I resort
to Tobias, suggesting that he ask me this question:

"How are relations between Mexico and the United States nowadays?"

"Officially very good. Mexico is finishing the payment of the debt contracted with her neighbour by the expropriation of the oil companies. At the moment there is no serious question pending between the two countries."

"And on the popular level? Is there hatred of the *gringo* in Mexico?"

"I would not use the word 'hate.' It is too strong. Sometimes I even think the *gringo* is as necessary to the Mexican mythology as the devil is to Christian mythology."

"A kind of scapegoat?"

"That's right. The theory of the scapegoat has a folkloric character, but in my opinion it also possesses a certain sociological value. The scapegoat of the Mexican is the *gringo*. The scapegoat of the Russian is Capitalism symbolized by the United States. The Americans' scapegoat may very well be (or is it already?) Russia, the day when their country undergoes some serious economic or social crisis. I need not recall that the scapegoat of the Nazis was the Jew."

"But is there, or not, distrust, prejudice, dislike on the part of the Mexican for the American?"

"It does exist. The difficult thing is to determine the degree of that dislike. At some point these collective sentiments lose their force, heat and even reason, to become merely a habit."

"In 1847 the Mexicans were defeated in military action by the Americans. Half their territory passed into the hands of their neighbours. In 1914 and 1917 the United States intervened again with arms in Mexico. Have no resentments been left in the Mexicans over these facts?"

"Yes, resentment must have remained in the collective subconscious. But I do not believe that there is any desire to get even, or any hope of recovering Texas, California and New Mexico left in Mexico."

"Then you think there is perfect understanding between the two peoples?"

"By the ashes of Montezuma, no! Far from it. Friction also exists. The differences persist."

"How are they manifested?"

"One people will not accept the other's way of life. The Mexican is irritated by the haste, the mania for standardization and mechanization of the American. The latter, in his turn, hasn't much patience with his swarthy neighbour's notion of time, his slow rhythm of life, his improvidence; he doesn't understand his explosions, or the contradictions of his character. (On the plane of human relations, have you ever seen a poor man *love* a rich man? Or a rich one treat a poor one as equal to equal?) The Mexican in a certain way cannot forgive the American in his prosperity, his physical comforts, his financial easy circumstances. The American gets a little uneasy with the presence of his turbulent, unstable neighbour. I shall repeat what I have been suggesting through this whole book: the American is a logical people, the Mexican a magical people. They live within different co-ordinates. From time to time one feels fascinated by the other's way of life. The magical one seeks the logical world and the logical one loses himself in the magical world. As they have more money, the logical ones travel more. The attraction exercised by the magical world is very powerful. At heart the Americans feel a nostalgia, to them sinful, for a bohemian and carefree life, the symbol of which seems to be the melted watches in the famous painting by Dalí. While the fascination which the logical world exercises on the mind of the man of magical thinking is tinged with fear—fear of the machine, of the discipline, of the obligation, of the schedule, of the dehumanization . . .'

"And to what point does the tourist contribute to a better understanding between the two peoples?"

"He doesn't. Sometimes he even worsens the situation. The continual presence in Mexico of the free-spending, carefree Yankee tourists, with that arrogant air of one who thinks he can buy everything and everybody (which I, who think I know them well, consider more an ingenuous and juvenile trait than a malicious one), that annoying presence irritates the Mexican. And then, my dear fellow, a man is a man and a nation is a nation. I find the German better as an individual than as a nation. Now with the English just the reverse is true. Individually the Latin American, as a general thing, gives a very good impression, and with his gentlemanliness, his picturesqueness, his keen intelligence, he tends to give the foreigner the impression that his country as a whole possesses all those qualities—which in reality is not the case. Now with the American it is just the opposite. Those overgrown boys, ignorant of geography, those naïfs of over-conditioned conversations and reactions, those irremediable specialists form a formidable, productive, intelligent, lucid nation where one lives marvellously well. I speak *ex cathedra*. I have lived six years in the United States. I assure you the American tourist doesn't give even a faint idea of what the United States represents as a nation."

"Suppose the Americans should suddenly completely leave off visiting Mexico?"

"The Mexicans would yell 'Boycott!' And their dislike for the *gringo* would increase."

"What is the idea the American gets of the Mexican?"

"Unhappily, it is not very flattering. For every ten educated, cultured Mexicans who visit the United States, giving an excellent impression of their country, there are at least two hundred—five hundred—farm labourers, generally illiterate and of sorry physical aspect. Unfortunately it is by that majority of *braceros* that the Yankees judge the neighbouring people. In short, for them the Mexican is a swarthy, hairy, evil-looking type, with criminal tendencies. (Other than this there is the silly, false idea offered by Hollywood: the gay *caballero*, the romantic *charro*, etc.) But I think it no exaggeration to state that for the American the Mexican, taken as a whole, is a physically, intellectually and morally inferior being."

"And how does the Mexican judge his neighbours?"

"Rich but stupid. '*Los gringos tienen plata, pero nosotros tenemos sensibilidad y cultura*'—'The *gringos* have money, but *we* have sensitiveness and culture.' They are good husbands because they wash dishes, look after the children; but they are awful lovers. '*Los machos somos nosotros*'—'We are the *he-men*.' Jorge Carrión says that the manifestations of energy and the libido through which the Mexican channels part of his resentment against the United States can be condensed into the sentence written by that American woman reporter: 'Every Mexican always dreams of the amorous conquest of three or four *gringas*.' And the same author cites other symptomatic sayings: *All* gringas *are libertines. The* gringos, *on the other hand, are sexually weak. The former, therefore, desire Latins—romance—and like the latter the Mexicans have a high virility.* This supports the thesis of Samuel Ramos about the *pelado*: the man of the people in Mexico seeks to insult his adversary by raising suspicions of his virility."

"What other important difference exists between the two peoples?"

"The one that corresponds to the difference between two verbs: *to be* and *to do*. For the Americans, a people of action, the important thing is *doing*. For the Mexican, a people of emotion, the important thing is *being*. 'Our body exists,' Octavio Paz has written; 'we suffer it and enjoy it.' While the American seems to have more confidence in his gadgets than in his own body, of which he appears to be somewhat ashamed, a feeling revealed often in a prudishness about the emotions, that is, about the things the body feels, solicits or repels. This may be a vestige of the Puritanism of colonial times, therefore an Anglo-Saxon, Protestant trait. In the Catholic countries —where the Church promises the resurrection of the flesh and prohibits the incineration of corpses—there is a sharper awareness of the body, not entirely, it must be confessed, devoid of shame and the idea of sin."

"Can that difference be a source of conflicts?"

"Of opinion, perhaps. The devil of it is that in the Latin-American countries which, like Mexico, are more inclined to being than to doing, the middle class, or, rather, the classes that have some acquisitive power are finding it harder and harder to *be* without the aid of the things the American *makes*, manufactures. I refer to those machines and apparatus which, by their use, materially improve our lives while at the same time creating financial difficulties for us, for how can peoples of low economic level have the comfort and the facilities which a rich nation like the United States enjoys? As for the man of the people, well or ill, he continues, in Mexico and in other parts of Latin America, to use the most perfect machine yet invented: his body. To improve those machines, to give them fuel and adequate care, to make them work properly and fully—here is a whole social programme."

"Now another question. To what extent is Mexico being modified under American influence?"

"On the surface of her life there are visible signs of that influence. The famous 'manifest destiny' which led the Yankee pioneers first to conquer the West and then to grab lands away from Mexico, seems now definitively satisfied on the geographic plane. It still goes on, however, on the economic plane. It is natural that the Americans export, along with their merchandise, their customs and their philosophy of life. I am, and always have been in favour of a policy of friendship between our countries and the United States, in favour of a *modus vivendi* based on mutual respect and interests. I think we can import automobiles from the United States (since we are not yet producing them domestically) without having perforce to lose our national characteristics and accept the way of being and living of the Americans."

"But it is undeniable that Mexico is becoming Americanized."

"Well, the new generations are too exposed to the allure of the life and customs of the neighbour to the north, through the cinema, the radio, magazines, books and the actual physical presence of American tourists. In the Mexican bourgeois class there is a certain pedantic desire to imitate the Yankees. On another side, the purpose of attracting and pleasing the tourist leads them to create in Mexico hotels, night clubs, bars, restaurants, drugstores, department stores, etc., of the American type. The Mexican cinema is at once one of the best and one of the worst in the world. For every film of artistic and folkloric value like *Raíces* (*Roots*), *María Candelaria* or *La Perla* (*The Pearl*), there are hundreds of bad imitations of Hollywood which present a false, ridiculous Mexico, which in reality either does not exist or else constitutes an unimportant minority."

"Do you believe that influence is very profound?"

"Waldo Frank, a sincere friend of Latin America, thinks it is, and that disquiets him. I believe that it is not *yet*. I sincerely hope it isn't. However much I admire the American way of life, I do not want to see the rest of the world Americanized. It would be sad and absurd, besides being monotonous."

"What elements of resistance is Mexico offering?"

"First, the Indian element, the core of the nation. That will remain untouched, intact, impenetrable, irremediably Mexican, in an invincible passive resistance."

"And as for *active* resistance?"

"It can only be maintained—and I think it is being—by all that represents Modern Mexico, which, I repeat, was painfully born of the Revolution of 1910, and which is expressed in art, literature and life. Modern Mexico is its extraordinary mural painting, its architectural audacities so well consubstantiated in the new Ciudad Universitaria. It is its literature of Mexican root and inspiration. It is a rational nationalism, conscious of its potentialities, proud of its Indian roots, confident in its cosmic force, animated by the certainty that, for good or ill, Mexico is a nation different from all the others in the world, mistress of a character and a style all her own."

"Do you think a complete understanding between those two neighbouring countries may some day be possible?"

"Complete, no. Peaceful and dignified coexistence, based on mutual respect, yes. To that end we have to count on the best in the élites of the two countries. I refer to the liberal groups on both sides of the Río Grande, to the men of humanist thinking free of commercial and financial bonds and of any racial or social prejudice. Speaking of the liberals of his country, the admirable Mexican essayist Daniel Cossío Villegas has written: 'And, happily, the Mexican liberal is not entirely alone: he is accompanied by the North American liberals, who are not few, and all the Yankees who are, without being overtly so, understanding and upright. They are even more abundant in the United States. Of North American public opinion we can expect, certainly, great aberrations, but also the purest justice.'"

# 12. The Return

The holiday is drawing to its close; we have to go back to Washington.

As we still want to see Guanajuato and Querétaro, which are to the north of the capital, we decide to go to those two cities by omnibus. We commission Tito to put our luggage on the train which is to leave here in three days for the United States and which we intend to catch at the second of the two cities.

A doubt, however, arises. We wonder whether the *Internacional* stops at Querétaro. We cannot get definite information. Some say it does; many say it doesn't; others murmur, *"Quién sabe?"* A prudent friend advises us to desist from the excursion. My wife says she is ready for anything. And I, who have been absorbing a little of the Indian's fatalism during this visit, am disposed to run all risks, even that of missing the train. Well, then, let's go!

We went. I have some unforgettable impressions left of that trip, among which I remember particularly passing by night through mysterious *pueblos* which seemed merely a product of the magic of the omnibus headlamps. It was their bright, sudden light which sketched in the darkness those narrow streets, those walls, houses, faces, forms, a whole town, in short, leaving in our somnolence the impression that, once the bus had passed on, the ghost *pueblito* was again vanishing into the night of time and space.

Another unforgettable scene was the one which took place in a hamlet on the outskirts of Guanajuato, when our bus was rolling slowly and heavily between adobe houses with the look of ruins and in which no living soul could be seen. Suddenly my companion and I, who were sitting on the front seat, saw looming up in the roadway a woman in black, running in front of the vehicle, trying to flee the light of its headlamps. She would turn her head from time to time and—imagination or reality?—we thought we could see an expression of fright on her face. The whole thing suggested a drama. The creature was fleeing from something terrible. She had killed someone, or had just witnessed a crime. For a few seconds she veered like a distraught hare in the luminous glare. Suddenly, she vanished, as though extinguished in the air. Before us nothing remained but the road of beaten earth. And a little later the lights of Guanajuato began winking in the distance.


In another chapter of this book I have spoken of "museum fatigue" and "journey's end fatigue." It is a weariness which inevitably attacks every traveller, however tough he may be and however much he may be enjoying the people who are entertaining him. We feel that weariness in body and mind. In the stomach it makes itself felt in a burning sensation and a slight nausea. It is the result of continual diet violations, of exotic, highly seasoned foods which, out of courtesy or curiosity combined with lack of character, we eat at uncertain hours and in unexpected places. (A Mexican ulcer? Ah! What a decoration!) The fatigue of our members comes from the many walks—sometimes runs—a fatigue not rare in high altitudes; from engagements without pause for rest; from that eternal getting in and out of automobiles, from that endless jolting over dizzying highways; from the interminable sleeping in strange beds. Above all, we feel a weariness of mind, a kind of aversion, arising from an excess of things seen in too short a time and too hurriedly—here churches, there markets, now museums and cities and towns and monuments. . . . It is quite possible that on this page my reader may be feeling—if he hasn't already—a "book's end fatigue."

But the reader has a remedy. He can close the volume and lay it aside for several days, or forever. But we don't want to "close" our trip. We have to make the most of this opportunity to the end, for

I don't know when we shall be able to visit this country again. And we want to see Guanajuato, which passes for a rival of Taxco in regard to colonial traditions and charms.

The manager of the Posada de Santa Fe, where we take a room, explains that the name Guanajuato comes from the Tarascan *Quanaxhuato,* meaning "Hilly place where frogs abound." In 1550 Juan Rayas, a muleteer, discovered the first silver mine here. Four years later the Spaniards founded the city.

Guanajuato is surrounded by hills of indescribable beauty, in their light greens splashed with pink and grey-brown. The atmosphere of the streets is delightfully colonial. We notice a Moorish tinge in many buildings. The thing is, Andalusian colonists came here, too, with all their burden of Arabia in blood and eyes. The streets are narrow, tortuous and frequently steep. I have not yet found any that followed a straight line for any considerable number of blocks. Here is a gently, gracefully curving street. Farther on we find an alley of a street which breaks in an obtuse angle. I'll bet there are acute and even right angles in the trajectory of these streets. I fall in love with certain little blind alleys with romantic names: *Callejón del Beso* (Lane of the Kiss), *del Campanero* (of the Bell Ringer), *de los Cantaritos* (of the Water Jugs), *de las Crucecitas* (of the Little Crosses). We climb with special care the lane of *El Resbalón,* the Bad Slip. The streets, too, bear pleasing names: *Calle Matavacas* (Cow-killing Street), *del Sol* (Sun Street), *del Cerero* (of the Wax Chandler).

I am delighted by the audacity with which these people paint their houses. Yonder is a front all mustard yellow. Facing the *Fuente del Baratillo* (Fountain of the Second-hand Shop, or, of the Bargain Counter) we find a wine-coloured wall in which white-framed windows open. The pink houses and the blue leap out at us with every step. It is not surprising that a man was born here who, as few do, knows how to handle colours: Diego Rivera. But the great muralist evidently has nothing to do with the Teatro Juárez yonder in the plaza, a heavy edifice of the past century with a portico sustained by twelve columns, and an elaborate platband above which are aligned six stone figures in natural size. (If they are the Muses, as a passer-by informs me, I don't understand why three are missing.)

Mexico has been teaching us, among many other things, to appreciate the beauty of old stone. Let's interrupt our stroll for an instant to contemplate this centuries-old wall. It seems to tell a story. At first glance it looks like only an old, unkempt thing. Gradually, however, with the complicity of the sunlight and the shadows of the lane, it reveals to us its more profound facet. Its stucco dressing, painted light blue with a rust-coloured "baseboard," is peeling away from the stone, forming blisters and cracks in labyrinthine patterns, so that the whole gives the impression of a lunar landscape with its mountains, craters, valleys and channels. There is something indescribably fascinating—I should say almost human—in this ancient wall against which my wife insists on taking my picture. I know I don't deserve this beautiful backdrop, but I have no help for it but to lose myself on the Moon. I am photographed.

We find old acquaintances in these blind alleys. We greet them with effusive cordiality: "Burro!" They respond by waving their hairy ears, and there they go at their tiny, beaten trot.

This placid Guanajuato—where we keep on walking despite our fatigue—has bits which recall now Salvador da Bahia, now Arabic cities, with its white, cubical houses with no eaves, climbing up the slope of hills. That great, two-storeyed house with iron balcony could well be in Recife. A Spaniard has assured me that he knows corners of Guanajuato that resemble Toledo. And this alleyway we are now entering, couldn't it be an uneven alley in the Kasbah?

And what the deuce is that big house yonder on the very crest, squat and massive with the important air of something traditional? It is the *Alhóndiga de Granaditas*, the Granaditas Grain Exchange. (These names together, one Arab and the other Andalusian, are worth a chapter of sociology.) It was in colonial times just a warehouse for cereals, but it gained historic stature because, in the War of Independence, the loyalists took shelter behind its thick walls and there offered resistance to the rebels. A patriot, José Barajas, also known as Pipila, dashed to the doorway of the building and set fire to it, which permitted the insurgents to win their way into the citadel, conquering it. For a long time on the four corners of this building were exposed the heads of four revolutionary leaders: Hidalgo, Allende, Aldama, and Jiménez. The enormous statue to Pipila, with a torch in his hand, today crowns the hill which rises in the very centre of the city.

We continue our stroll along the sidewalks which, being so narrow, hardly allow two persons to walk side by side. We spy into houses, and see tailors who remind me, I don't really know why, of those in the *Thousand and One Nights;* reception rooms where the image of Our Lady of Guadalupe reigns; workshops of goldsmiths and silversmiths; barbers' salons where Biblical manes and Zapatista moustaches are trimmed. That footwear shop has a name I like: *El Botín Rojo*—The Red Boot. I utter a cry of triumph on reading the name of a bookshop: The Pythagorean Cock.

An old and famous university is in Guanajuato. At night we attend a student parade in which girls ride through the streets sitting on the mudguards of automobiles, led by a band and followed by a noisy cortège of young men on foot, carrying lanterns and banners with legends. It's about the candidate for the title of Queen of the Students. We are informed that the elections will be held tomorrow. Who will win? Rosario? Amparito? Sol? Gregoria? Pía? Rosita? Dolores? By the light from the lanterns I see attractive, smiling faces. As always, the Indianlike, swarthy type predominates. But now and then we are offered the surprise of a blond head, a white, Nordic face. (Some *gringo* lost his way?) The procession loses itself in the twisted streets. For some time we hear the music of a *pasodoble* and the noise of cheers. Afterwards, silence and the night. And infrequent forms in the half-asleep streets. And the colonial lamps which seem to whisper to us stories of the times of the viceroyalty. I should not be surprised if the *sereno,* the nightwatchman, should emerge from one of these lanes, lantern in hand, shouting the hour.

At long intervals we pass by cafés and *pulquerías* from which come the sound of voices and the music of guitars. And in the light, antique silence which accompanies us, our steps resound without actually breaking it, for now they are a part of it. In the silence, as in a dead sea, our tired bodies are floating.

Suddenly, in the sky framed by the end of a street, we come upon the luminous great face of the moon. *Buenas noches, señora!*

More or less in the time when Miguel de Cervantes was writing his novels, plays and *entremeses*—one-act interludes—in the city of Guanajuato was erected, thanks to the prosperity of its silver mines, a temple which was to be dedicated to San Roque. Upon the stones of its atrium, in a little plaza which would also bear the name of the saint, a stone cross was set up, surrounded by lamps of black iron—which was to lead the people of the place to give the little square also the name of the Plaza of the Street Lamps. No one can explain to me why they have not finished one of the towers of this simple, severe church. I observe that the posts of these lamps are not straight, but twisted—always the Mexican theme of torture, agony, suffering. Anyone coming into this *plazuela* has the impression that he is stepping into the sixteenth century. It is not surprising, then, that the local University Theatre, under the direcion of Enrique Ruelas, has had the idea of performing the interludes of Cervantes in this atrium. Rough tiers of seats, like those in a circus, have been built in front of the temple. The first performance was given some two years ago. The district judge and some miners and merchants of Guanajuato, as well as students, took part in it.

A student is now describing to me, with passionate enthusiasm, the performance in February of this year, when three Cervantine interludes were staged: *La guarda cuidadosa* (The Picket of Love), *Los hablodares*[1] (The Two Talkers) and *El retablo de las maravillas* (The Marvellous Pageant).

The seats are filled with people of all social classes. The places of honour are occupied by the delegation sent by the President of the Republic to represent him at the festival. Among the crowd are tourists come from Europe, the Antilles, the United States. They say even an Icelander is present!

Night is falling. A form clad in monkish habit, amid the greatest silence, approaches the cross with slow, solemn steps and lights the oil lamps. After the dark figure disappears the bells of the church begin to ring, announcing that the interludes are going to start. Microphones placed at strategic points and skilfully hidden carry the voices to the loud-speakers, which project them into the plaza.

Now that night has fallen completely, one has the feeling that the atrium is illuminated only by the indecisive light of the lamps. In reality, Ruelas is lighting the appropriate spots by means of masked reflectors, in the glow of which Cervantes' personages begin filing past: men and women, governors of fortresses, corregidors, friars, jongleurs, musicians, magicians, street vendors, professional bullies. . . . But before beginning the first interlude, a slender figure, dressed in sixteenth century style, with a sharp little imperial on his sharp face, crosses the courtyard and enters the church.

[1]Ascribed often to Cervantes, but his authorship remains unproven.

Who is he? whispers the audience. The information runs from mouth to mouth. It is Don Miguel de Cervantes Saavedra.

And so that the spectacle should lack nothing, later Don Quixote himself, riding Rosinante, enters the atrium followed by Sancho Panza, whose weight a resigned donkey is enduring.

The student also tells me that curious and unexpected problems arose during the performance of the *entremeses* on this stage, where the only scenery consists of the atrium, the façade of the church, and the houses around the *plazuela*. Now, the performance lasted four hours, and the persons living in those houses at the time had need to go in or out. How to arrange matters so as not to break the spell of the sixteenth-century atmosphere? Whenever the inmate of a house returned home or left it, they would put him in a monk's robe and there went the man through the crowd of players without disturbing the performance. One night a doctor needed to enter one of the houses to see a patient. Ruelas did not hesitate. He covered the physician with a long black cape and put a lighted lantern in his hand. And so the silent personage never imagined by Cervantes came on scene and gave the *entremés* a gratuitous and fortuitous charm.

Today these annual productions sponsored by the State of Guanajuato and by the School of Dramatic Arts of the University are one of the greatest attractions of this fine colonial city, which may well come to be, some day, a species of American Oberammergau.

I communicate this hope to the student, who replies:

*"Pero, señor, ya lo es* (Why, sir, it already is). And much more authentic than the German one!"


Morning of a new day. We are sitting on a bench in the little square in front of the hotel, trying to study a programme for the next few hours. A boy approaches us, offering his services as a guide. He begins by pointing to a tree close to the bandstand:

"Well, here's a nice tree. I don't know who planted it, but I assure you it is very historic."

I give the youngster a copper and send him off. "Find out the name of the hero who planted the tree and then come back."

We see an old Ford for hire parked at the kerb, we get in and ask the driver: "What interesting places are there to see in Guanajuato?"

"The mummies, of course."

"Then let's go to the mummies."

The car moves off through the crooked streets. We climb a hill in the outskirts of the town and stop in front of the cemetery. My wife refuses to get out, alleging that she detests morbid spectacles. "No dead ones for me," she says. "I stay in the car."

Patience. I go alone. I enter the Guanajuato cemetery, which in many ways resembles the one in Cruz Alta. The caretaker comes to meet me.

"*Las momias?*" he asks, looking at me obliquely.

"The mummies."

"Follow me, then."

I obey. We make our way among melancholy angels of marble and stone, touched by the gold of the morning. A little bird with yellow breast is gaily singing, comfortably perched on an archangel's head. The sky is a luminous, porcelain blue. The dry air has the lightness and transparency of crystal. A lizard wriggles between smooth graves. I read fragments of the epitaphs on the old tombstones as I go.

The caretaker stops, bends over and, seizing an iron ring, lifts the round cover of a trapdoor. Now I see that the mummies are to be found in a catacomb beneath the cemetery. The man already has more than half his body inside the earth. He raises his gallow's-bird face to me and mutters: "This way."

I follow. We descend by a narrow spiral stairway of stone. Another nightmare. May it all be for the love of anthropology and archæology!

We are now in a little vestibule of ancient, sinister aspect, in one corner of which are heaped centuries-old skulls of a dirty ivory colour. I can feel all those empty orbits fixed on me. I receive the horrid, decayed-toothed smiles as a greeting of welcome.

"There," grumbles the caretaker, indicating the entrance to the gallery.

Against the doorjamb a solemn inscription exhorts the visitor to humility, for some day he will be reduced to the thing he is now going to see.

"I'll introduce you to the mummies," says the caretaker, as if we were going into a social gathering. It is odd, but the first impression I have is of one of those American parties where the "receiving line" stands next to the door, a line formed by the owners of the house and the guests of honour. The guest enters and goes down the line shaking hands, one by one.

The mummies are in a sort of corridor with vaulted ceiling at least three yards wide by some fifteen or more in length. They are nearly all standing, propped against the walls, and are more horrid than I imagined. The pure and simple skeleton is a classic form, it no longer frightens anyone. It has passed into the commonplace of the horripilant. But the mummies! To begin the horror, they have retained their skin, stiffened over the fleshless bone structures in a colour between ash-grey and light brown which recalls, disturbingly, the *tortilla*. On some of these corpses I find tufts of hair left on the smooth craniums—a detail of the grotesque which does not invite laughter; it freezes. In many faces it is still possible for the observer to reconstruct vaguely the physiognomy possessed by the cadaver in life. Yonder is a mummy which has a stocking left on one leg. I see in the background a gentleman in frock coat, lace shirt and silk cravat—a thing which leaves me intrigued, for I expected to find centenary and millenary mummies here, and that gentleman, if I am not mistaken, is dressed in the fashion of the last half of the past century. I have no reason to conceal the fact that I don't feel well. The initial horror is turning into nausea. Why don't I leave this crypt in search of fresh air? On the other hand, it would be hypocrisy to deny that this macabre, silent party attracts me in a way. Courage, then. I walk hither and thither with a scientific air. The caretaker has not stopped talking since we came in here. What is he saying now? He points to a mummy in an attitude of agony, clenched hands raised to the height of its face. "This one was buried alive," he explains. He shows another cadaver. "See the mark on his neck? Well, this young fellow hanged himself." He leads me to where the very well-preserved remains of two babies are, and murmurs, "Little angels." They look like dolls in their minute coffins.

The postures of these corpses are the most grotesque of all. They are nearly all bent over, hands crossed on their chests, mouths twisted and open. In some, all the teeth remain. A woman holds something that looks like a doll in her left hand. "She died of a caesarian operation," says the caretaker. "See the mark of the incision on the belly? What she's holding is the foetus."

The queerest thing is that the impression I am in a social gathering persists, for I see mummies with their heads turned to one side as if they were chatting with their neighbours. There, in the back, presiding over the funereal cocktail party, is the oldest of the mummies in its coffin of worm-eaten wood, wrapped in a shroud which is gradually disintegrating into dust. Now I perceive that death has restored these figures to their most remote ancestry, giving them the appearance of simians.

"How many centuries old are these corpses?" I ask.

"Centuries?" the caretaker repeats in amazement. "Why, they are corpses brought from our own cemetery. Some of them are less than ten years old!"

Holy Heaven, fresh mummies! Little by little I comprehend the queer situation. As the soil and air of Guanajuato are very dry, after some years the corpses here become mineralized.

"Why do they bring them here?"

"*Bueno*. This happens when their relatives don't pay the grave fees."

He tells me that one day a young man came into the crypt, and on coming across one of the mummies he exclaimed, "My uncle!" With tears in his eyes he went to the cemetery office and, by paying the rent of a bit of ground, got his relative to cease being a tourist attraction and return to the peace of a Christian tomb.

I conclude that it's time to leave the party. The caretaker, though, wants to show me something more. He pulls me over close to a female mummy and says: "This was a rich old woman of Guanajuato. Her nephews strangled her to steal her jewels."

"What happened to them?"

"That was a long time ago. I don't know and don't care. The main thing is the old girl is here with us."

I ask who the mummy in the frock coat is.

"He's a famous doctor of Guanajuato. He did some miraculous cures and was highly thought of. Lived back around 1860 or '70."

He introduces me to other "persons": a prostitute, a friar, a bandit—

"I think we can go up," I suggest.

"*Usted manda, señor*"—"You're the boss, sir."

We are climbing the stairway when he asks me: "Do you live in Guanajuato?"

"Don't worry. You won't get my mummy."

I make a solemn vow to myself: to die and be buried in damp soil which will devour my flesh, reduce me to a clean, honest skeleton, and which with the aid of time will transform me finally into dust. Amen!

I reach the surface of the ground, I absorb with pleasure the free air, the free sky. I am Lazarus and have just returned from among the dead. There is no doubt of it: it is good to be alive. I tip the man who has guided me through the kingdom of the dead, go out of the cemetery and get into the car.

"Well?" my wife inquires. "Very amusing?"

"Driver, to the hotel!"

The automobile moves off toward the city.

"What about the mummies? Tell me."

"Later. . . ."

I cannot forget the crypt, the monstrous smoked herrings in human shape. I feel I can see them now with much greater sharpness than when I was in the catacomb.

"Are you feeling sick?"

"Who? I? On the contrary," I lie. "I'm fine."

"Word of honour? You're green. I think those mummies. . . ."

"Tsk! They're extremely interesting. You don't know what you missed."


At noon we take our seats at a table in the hotel restaurant. In the *tortillas* they bring us I can see the grey-brown dried skin of the mummies. I try to eat something, but cannot. I refuse the soup. The meat makes me gulp uneasily. I look about and begin imagining what the future mummy of each of the guests here will be like. The game amuses me. The nausea continues. It is as if my stomach were a crypt where a hundred mineralized corpses are lined up.

My wife, who has lunched normally, smiles and asks: "Why don't you confess that the excursion to the cemetery has spoiled your appetite?"

I heave a sigh and surrender. I confess everything.

And in the bus that afternoon, en route to Querétaro, after a long hour of silence and reflection, I murmur to my companion: "The solution is the crematory oven. You are hereby authorized. . . ."


We see little or nothing of Querétaro, which we reach at dusk, tired and rather depressed. We go straight to the hotel and retire about ten o'clock, after a quick turn through the central streets.

Querétaro, which means "dance patio" in Náhuatl, is situated at the foot of the hill called Sangremal. It is an old city of a little more than 50,000 population. Founded by the Otomí Indians long before the discovery of America, it became a part of the Aztec empire in the fifteenth century, and was conquered by the Spaniards in 1531.

Very early next day we go out to pay a hasty visit to the spot where the Emperor Maximilian was shot.

We are a little worried about the train, which is to pass here this morning at ten. Will it stop at the local station? Will our bags be in the compartment?


The Hill of the Bells is on the outskirts of the city and is a grey-brown, sad green. We enter the Expiatory Chapel which the Austrian government some years ago had constructed on the top of the hill, on the site of the execution. The caretaker shows us the three small columns in front of the altar.

"Those stones mark the exact spot where Maximilian and his generals Miramón and Mejía stood before the firing squad. The emperor was in the middle, but he ended by giving the place of honour to Miramón."

The walls of the simple little chapel are covered with pictures, photographs: portraits of Maximilian and Carlotta, engravings reproducing the scene of the execution; facsimiles of documents relating to the drama of that ephemeral empire. I stop before the portrait of Maximilian on his death-bed, his face tranquil as if he were only sleeping.

The caretaker comes over to me and murmurs: "Maximilian gave each member of the firing squad a gold coin, so they would aim at his chest, leaving his head untouched. As you see, the soldiers fulfilled the contract."

My wife is praying at the foot of the altar. I begin to hear the wind outside and to think it must have been blowing that way on the tragic day.

"Do you know something?" the caretaker continues. "It was eighty-eight years ago today, exactly today, that they killed Maximilian."

To my memory comes José Vasconcelos's voice: "That useless shooting is one of the stains on our history." Well, as I did not arrive in time to save the lives of the emperor and his generals, the only thing to do is leave.

We emerge from the chapel into the clear light of the tranquil morning. The wind was a pure invention of my imagination. My companion and I descend the hill side by side, in silence. I recall the end of a sonnet by the Mexican poet Rafael López.

"Pobre Max. Sólo quedan de la ciega aventura
una canción burlesca, cinco balas de plomo
que motean de humo la mañana estival,

que llevan de la mano la murete y la locura;
y objetos empolvados en el museo, como
viejas decoraciones de una pieza teatral."

The sense of which is: "Poor Max. Of the blind adventure only a burlesque song remains, and five lead bullets mottling the summer morning with smoke, carrying death and madness in their wake; and dusty objects in the museum, like old scenery from some play."

Yes, in the end nearly everything ends as a stage set, literary theme, museum piece. But I cannot help thinking of the living, sentient man, of his flesh, of his nerves, of the agony of that moment facing death; of the days preceding the execution, of his disappointment, of his abandonment; of the drama of Carlotta knocking futilely on door after door, already half mad, begging the Pope, Napoleon III and other European rulers to save her husband.

Five lead bullets. The phrase pursues me the rest of the day. Five lead bullets. The automobile repeats it, bumping through the streets of Querétaro. Later the train wheels chant it like a refrain.

Because the train did stop in Querétaro. The porter and the conductor waved frenziedly at us from the platform: "Come on, get aboard! We stopped here just for you!" And hardly had we set foot in the Pullman when the train resumed its way. All this lasted only a few seconds. We found our bags in the compartment. We counted. Not one was missing. We breathed in relief.

And now here I am at the car window, looking out at the suburbs of Querétaro which we are leaving behind. This train is cleaner, faster and more comfortable than the other in which we came from Ciudad Juárez. The trip will be less long, almost entirely in the State of Nuevo León. This is the real route of tourism.

Five lead bullets. I try to drive the obsessive phrase out of my mind. I don't want those cruel words to be my last souvenir of

Mexico. I think of brighter and gayer persons, things and moments. Friendly images pass through my mind. Juanito desperately whipping away at my shoes and casting half-tender, half-distrustful glances at *La Gringa*. José and Alberto guiding us through the sacred meanderings of Cholula. A segment of a street in Puebla. The façade of Santa María Tonantzintla. A rutilant cock by Chucho Reyes. The Jardines del Pedregal. The head of Siqueiros. The *mariachis* of El Tenampa. Burros in Taxco.

How many years will I need to digest Mexico? How many lifetimes must I have lived to comprehend it? But one consolation is left and it suffices me. I need no more than a minute to love it.

# Epilogue

My great-aunt Adelina liked novels with prologues and epilogues. And the epilogues of the stories she used to read were always happy. "And they got married, had innumerable children and were very happy for long years."

We are back in Washington. We have already picked up the gentle family routine again. Our house has suddenly become Mexicanized: *sarapes* on the floor, on the walls and on the backs of chairs; Toluca baskets in the corners; Master Timoteo's *caballitos* on the mantelpiece; vases, jugs and dishes from Oaxaca and Guadalajara on sideboards and shelves. . . .

Our record-player, so addicted to the music of Bach, Mozart and Vivaldi, for days has been playing only *huapangos*, *rancheras* and Mexican waltzes.

And to prove that delightful miracles still happen in this atomic era, I add that the colour photographs we took in Mexico turned out magnificently.

At the desk Mary, my inpeccable secretary, reminds me of coming engagements: a lecture on Machado de Assis at Harvard University; another on "The Art of the Novel" at Yale University. A trip to Cincinnati. A round table in Puerto Rico.

It is good to be back. I have to confess to myself that I was already missing this orderliness, this cleanliness, this comfort.

But alas! Time passes, the yearning for Mexico begins to assail me so frequently that I wind up in a confusion of sentiments.

I knew the epilogue of this book couldn't be happy! I am probably condemned to oscillate the rest of my life between those two loves, without knowing exactly which I want more, the magical world or the logical. Only one hope of salvation is left to me. It is that, between the American thesis and the Mexican antithesis, Brazil may some day come to be the desired synthesis.

Y, *quién sabe?*

# Bibliography

AZTEC CIVILIZATION

G. C. Vaillant, *The Aztecs of Mexico*. Penguin Books, London, 1955.

HISTORY OF THE CONQUEST

Bernal Díaz del Castillo, *Historia verdadera de la Conquista de la Nueva España*. Espasa-Calpe Argentina, S.A., Buenos Aires, 1955.
[In English: *The Bernal Díaz Chronicles; the True Story of the Conquest of Mexico*. Translated and edited by Albert Idell. Doubleday, Garden City, N. Y., 1956. 414 pages. Maps.
*The Discovery and Conquest of Mexico, 1517-1521*. Edited from the only exact copy of the original manuscript (and published in Mexico) by Genaro García. Translated with an introduction and notes by A. P. Maudsley. Introduction to the American edition by Irving A. Leonard. New York, Farrar, Straus and Cudahy, 1956, xxxi, 478 pp. Illus., maps.
*The Discovery and Conquest of Mexico, 1517-1521*. Illustrated by Miguel Covarrubias; with a new Introduction by Harry Block. Mexico, printed by R. Loera y Chávez for . . . The Limited Editions Club, 1942. xxii, 263 pp. Coloured illus., coloured maps.]
Fernando Benítez, *La ruta de Cortés*. Fondo de Cultura Económica, Mexico, 1956.

William H. Prescott, *The Conquest of Mexico*. The Modern Library, New York, 1948.
Ramón Iglesia, *Cronistas e historiadores de la Conquista de México* (*El ciclo de Hernán Cortés*). El Colegio de México, México, 1948.

### COLONIAL PERIOD

Francisco J. Clavijero, S.J., *Historia antigua de México*, 2 vols. Editorial Delfín, México, 1944.

### HISTORY OF MEXICO

José Vasconcelos, *Breve historia de México*. Ediciones Cultura Hispánica, Madrid, 1952.
Silvio Zavala, *Aproximaciones a la historia de México*. Colección "México y lo Mexicano." Porrúa y Obregón, S.A., México, no date).
Justo Sierra, *Evolución política del pueblo mexicano*. La Casa de España en México, México, (no date).

### MEXICAN LIFE, CHARACTER AND PROBLEMS

Octavio Paz, *El laberinto de la soledad*. Cuadernos de América, México, 1949.
Paul Westheim, *La calavera*. Colección "México y lo Mexicano." Antigua Librería Robredo, México, 1953.
Mario Picón Salas, *Gusto de México*. Colección "México y lo Mexicano." Porrúa y Obregón, S.A., México, 1952.
Ramón Xirau, *Tres poetas de la soledad*. Colección "México y lo Mexicano." Porrúa y Obregón, S.A., México, 1955.
Jorge Carrión, *Mito y magia del mexicano. Ibidem*, 1952.
Samuel Ramos, *Perfil del hombre y la cultura en México*. Colección Austral. Espasa-Calpe Argentina, S.A., Buenos Aires, 1951.
Frank Tannenbaum, *Mexico, the Struggle for Peace and Bread*. Alfred A. Knopf, New York, 1950.
Leopoldo Zea, *La filosofía como compromiso y otros ensayos*. Collección Tezontle. Fondo de Cultura Económica, México, 1952.
José Moreno Villa, *Cornucopia de México*. Colección "Mexico y lo Mexicano." Porrúa y Obregón, S.A., México, 1952.
Daniel Cosío Villegas, *Extremos de América*. Colección Tezontle. Fondo de Cultura Económica, México, 1949.

MEXICAN ART

José Moreno Villa, *Lo mexicano en las artes plásticas*. El Colegio de México, México, 1948.

Patricia F. Ross, *Made in Mexico*. Alfred A. Knopf, New York, 1952.

Rafael Garza Livas, *"Arte de la Revolución."* In *Artes de México*, Nos. 5 and 6. Frente Nacional de Artes Plásticas, México, 1955.

Antonio Rodríguez, *Eje del desarrollo artístico de México en el siglo XX. Ibidem.*

Siqueiros. Monograph published by the Instituto Nacional de Bellas Artes, México, 1951.

I. Groth-Kimball and F. Feuchtwanger, *The Art of Ancient Mexico*. Thames and Hudson, London, 1954.


OTHER SOURCES

F. S. C. Northrop, *The Meeting of East and West*. Alfred A. Knopf, New York, 1946.

Hubert Herring, *A History of Latin America. Ibidem*, 1955.

Aldous Huxley, *Beyond the Mexique Bay*. Chatto & Windus, London, 1950.

Graham Greene, *The Lawless Roads*. William Heinemann, London, 1950.

D. H. Lawrence, *The Plumed Serpent*. Vintage Books, New York, 1955.

*Le Mexique, Amérique Centrale, Antilles*. Editions Odé, Paris, 1955.

Antonio Castro Leal, *La poesía mexicana moderna*. Colección "Letras Mexicanas." Fondo de Cultura Económica, México, 1953.

Helmuth Terra, *Humboldt*. Alfred A. Knopf, New York, 1954.

# Index

331

tecture and sculpture of, 87–90; arts and crafts of, 84–87; calendar of, 32, see also Calendar Stone; children of, 76–77; as chocolate-makers, 81; cleanliness of, 30–31; clothing of, 83–84; cosmogony of, 11–12, 75 ff.; dance among, 92–93; descent, modern pride in, 276; economic and social organization of, 76, 80–83; Empire of, in 1519, 27–32; faces of, 6–7; flesh eating by, 73; food crops of, 81; furniture of, 86; gods of, 96–97, 249–50; hairless dogs as food of, 28; immortality concept among, 292, 293, 294; marriage among, 77–79; as metal workers, 91; of Mexico City region, 75–76; mirrors of, 85; musical instruments of, 92; Order of Aztec Eagle, 84, 216; pottery of, 85; punishments among, 77, 79–80; religion of, 73–74, 79–80, 96–97; slavery among, 79, 80, 83, 84; Tenochtitlán of, see Tenochtitlán; weaving and basketry of, 86; wheel unknown to, 27, 46, 75, 85; world of, 75–97; writing of, 93–94

Aztecs of Mexico, The (Vaillant), 83

Bach, J. S., 250
Baracoa, 99
Barajas, José, 314
Baroque art, 121–22
'Barricade' (Rivera), 234
Baskets, Toluca market, 253, 325
Benavides, Don Antonio de (El Tapado), 144
Benitez, Fernando, 274
Bergson, 177
Birds, Mexico, 167, 318
'Black Christ of the Candles' (Reyes), 247–48
'Black Legend,' 181–82

Bocanegra (hack poet), 191
Bolivar Amphitheatre, murals at, 230
Bonampak frescoes, 228
Bookshops, Mexico City, 59
Borde (Borda), Joseph de la, 255, 259
Borges de Medeiros, Dr., 201
Borromini, 140
Boutroux, 177
Braque, 232
Brazil, recollections of, 6, 13, 16, 37, 46, 49, 51, 53, 57, 59, 68, 69, 119, 127, 145, 150, 153, 162, 172, 174, 196, 202, 204, 210, 257–58, 260, 282, 285, 314, 318
Brueghel, 60, 61
Buarque de Holanda, Professor Aurélio, and Marina his wife, 63–69, 257 ff., 285
Bullfights, 287–89
Bustamente, Don Anastasio, 184, 189

Cabrera, Don Luis, 210
Calendar Stone of the Aztecs, 32, 35, 159, 234, 297; 'Suns' of, 94
California, loss of, 191, 197
Calles, Gen. Plutarco, 194, 199, 211–20, 234, 301
Calvaras ('Skulls'), by Posada, 229
Calvanism, 192
Camacho, Manuel Ávila, 221
Cambronne, le mot de, 188
Campesinos, (rural populace), 195–96, 203, 204, 207, 217, 229
Cantinflas (comic actor), 70, 277, 281–82
Capilla Real, see Cholula
Capone, Al, 243
Cárdenas, Lázaro, 218–22, 302
Caribs, 179
Carlos IV of Spain, 72
Carlos V of Spain, 102, 104, 114, 131, 156; Cortés writes to, 105–

332

# Mexico

This book was first published in the Portuguese language as *Mexico, História duma Viagem* by Editôra Globo, Brazil, in 1957. This American edition was first published in October, 1960. It was composed, printed and bound by The Haddon Craftsmen, Inc. of Scranton, Pennsylvania, and designed by Wladislaw Finne.

## Erico Verissimo

Erico Verissimo was born in Cruz Alta, Rio Grande do Sul, Brazil. He lived for a long time in the United States where he has lectured extensively and was from 1953 to 1956 Director of the Department of Cultural Affairs at the Pan-American Union in Washington. His novels have been translated into many languages, and probably the best known in this country are *The Rest Is Silence* and *Time and the Wind*.